A Stranger in Jerusalem

A Stranger in Jerusalem

Seeing Jesus as a Jew

Trevan G. Hatch

WIPF & STOCK · Eugene, Oregon

A STRANGER IN JERUSALEM
Seeing Jesus as a Jew

Copyright © 2019 Trevan G. Hatch. All rights reserved. Except for brief quotations in critical publications or reviews, no part of this book may be reproduced in any manner without prior written permission from the publisher. Write: Permissions, Wipf and Stock Publishers, 199 W. 8th Ave., Suite 3, Eugene, OR 97401.

Wipf & Stock
An Imprint of Wipf and Stock Publishers
199 W. 8th Ave., Suite 3
Eugene, OR 97401

www.wipfandstock.com

PAPERBACK ISBN: 978-1-5326-4670-6
HARDCOVER ISBN: 978-1-5326-4671-3
EBOOK ISBN: 978-1-5326-4672-0

Manufactured in the U.S.A.   JUNE 13, 2019

To all of my Jewish mentors and friends

Contents

Acknowledgments | ix

	Introduction	1
	Joshua, Not Jesus	
Chapter One	From Bethlehem to Baptism	22
	Childhood and Family in Ancient Judea and Galilee	
Chapter Two	Establishing Authority	52
	Jesus as Moses and Elisha	
Chapter Three	Mighty in Deed	73
	Jesus as a Jewish Prophet and Miracle Worker	
Chapter Four	The Kings of the Jews	97
	"Messiahs" in the First Century	
Chapter Five	"Who Do Men Say That I Am?"	114
	Jesus as a Messianic Candidate	
Chapter Six	His Friend Judas	134
	Why Didn't He Betray His Messiah?	
Chapter Seven	Jesus' Enemies?	154
	Why Didn't the Pharisees Reject Their Friend Jesus?	
Chapter Eight	Christ Killers?	185
	Why Didn't "the Jews" Reject and Kill Jesus?	
Chapter Nine	I Know You Are, but What Am I?	202
	The Greco-Roman Art of Name-Calling	
Chapter Ten	Why the Conflict and Hostile Rhetoric?	215
Chapter Eleven	Judaism and Jesus	245
	Concluding Thoughts and Considerations	

Bibliography | 263
Index of Subjects | 279
Index of Ancient Texts | 281

Acknowledgments

I want to thank the following for reading large portions of the manuscript and for offering suggestions to improve content, grammar, and formatting: Joshua Brumbach, Leonard Greenspoon, Peter Haas, Paula Hicken, Bradley Kramer, Loren Marks, Joshua Matson, Daniel McClellan, Mary Vogwell, Kim Sandoval, and Thomas Wayment. I am also grateful for my research assistants at Brigham Young University (Summer Glover, Tyler Harris, Jacob Stoeltzing, and Haley Wilson) for assisting me with the many tedious tasks of combing the manuscript for various reasons. Finally, I thank Daniel Lanning, Matthew Wimer, Stephanie Hough, and the rest of the staff at Wipf and Stock Publishers for publishing this book.

Introduction
Joshua, Not Jesus

THIS BOOK ATTEMPTS TO put Jesus in his proper context. And what context is that? Well, Jesus was a Jew, his friends were Jews, his first followers were Jews, he studied the Hebrew Scriptures (either orally or from texts), he worshiped in the synagogue, and he occasionally traveled to Jerusalem to observe the Israelite festivals. As we will explore throughout this book, Jesus does not seem to have rejected Judaism or acted as a radical outsider in relation to his Jewish peers, but rather he functioned *within* a Jewish framework. If this is the case—if Jesus was not a "stranger" to Judaism and his Jewish peers—then why is the title of this book *A Stranger in Jerusalem*? Because the title is an allusion to Jesus in the Gospel of Luke. On the very day in which the tomb is found empty, two followers of Jesus leave Jerusalem to walk seven miles to Emmaus. As they were talking about what had happened to their teacher and prophet (Luke 24:19), the resurrected Jesus approaches them and inquires about the topic of their discussion. The men do not recognize Jesus and ask, "[Are you a] stranger in Jerusalem?" (Luke 24:18). Jesus walks with them all the way to Emmaus but they still do not recognize him. Only until Jesus enters their home and eats with them do they realize that Jesus is with them. At that moment they arise and return to Jerusalem (Luke 24:28–33).

As with these two men, most of us fail to recognize Jesus. He is a strange traveler in some ways. In addition, we too are strangers in Jerusalem. How so? Because most of us are outsiders to Judaism. We either rarely if ever read the New Testament or we read it at a superficial level. We have heard the basic stories in Sunday school and have been fed a healthy serving of juvenile and simplistic interpretations with a side dish of horribly flawed interpretations. Most of us have no comprehension of the Hebrew Bible (also called the "Old Testament"), no exposure to Jewish law, no understanding of Jewish sensibilities, no ability to read the Scriptures in Hebrew and Greek, and no learning in the social and political contexts of Jesus' world. Many church-attending folks do not even know what questions to ask let alone what the answers to those questions are. Consequently, we fail to recognize the first-century Jewish Jesus. Many people think they have a solid grasp of the Old and New Testaments, but it is my experience that nearly all of my students think they know more than they really do. By the end of the semester they admit that they were "blown away" by how much they did not know and that what they thought they knew turned out to be wrong.

Allow me to provide an example. Several years ago I taught a class on Judaism, Christianity, and Islam at a large southern University. Most of the students were Protestant Christians. The day we started the section on the origins of Christianity, I asked the class, "What was Jesus' name?" The purpose of this question was to shake them from the zombie-like state they had been trained to sit comfortably in during a learning session—either in college or Sunday school. They stared at me with utter confusion. I rephrased the question: "What did Jesus' mother call him? What did his friends call him? What did his Jewish peers call him?" A few students caught on, but most were still lost. When I told them that his name was Joshua (the Hebrew *Yehoshua*), they were a bit surprised. An atheist student raised her hand and commented, "It's disturbing that perhaps most Christians don't even know his name."

This example is a bit overstated because "Jesus" is a Greek name that is based on the Hebrew "Joshua," even though few people called him "Jesus" during his lifetime. But the point stands. In my experience, most people in my religious community (as well as my Christian students outside of my religious community) do not even know the meanings of "Christ," "Messiah," or "Son of Man." Is it not peculiar that only a miniscule percentage of Jesus' followers today know that "Jesus Christ"—the very name he is called most often by modern Christians—refers to the man named "Joshua the messiah" or "Joshua the anointed one"? Even among those who would hurry to Google "Jesus Christ," only a small handful could briefly explain what "anointed one" refers to—how Jews at the time of Jesus would have understood that term. As I ask my students, "How can we claim to know him if we do not know the most basic of terms that define his identity according to Christianity?" At this point, I have my students' attention.

This in-class exercise is not a ploy to foster guilt or feelings of ignorance, nor is it an attempt to point blame for lack of knowledge. It is simply to illustrate the point that Jesus is, indeed, a stranger to us. This is understandable because most of my students' exposure to the Gospels is from a highly devotional perspective—essentially a basic reading from the King James Version of the Bible followed by a simple application to daily living.

Ultimately, the sustenance—the meat—has been stripped away in the spirit of "keeping it simple." But the Scriptures are not simple. They were written in a foreign time, at a foreign place, in a foreign language. They are beautifully complex. They are in many ways literary masterpieces. This volume will help readers understand and contextualize Jesus' Jewishness and the nature of the Gospels, which will serve as a foundation to more in-depth exploration. Like the two men on the road to Emmaus, we will go back to "Jerusalem" together. In other words, we acknowledge that we have failed on some level to recognize Jesus, so we will seek to go into his world and try to understand him and the Gospels on their own *Jewish* terms.

The Intended Audience, Tone, and Approach

This book was written with students, clergy, Bible enthusiasts, and other high-interest-but-nonspecialist readers in mind. I am not addressing a highly trained group of scholars at the Society of Biblical Literature, although some of this information will be of interest to them. I have tried to be as scholarly as possible in terms of content and cited sources without alienating or boring the nonspecialist. My tone is one that is appropriate for a university classroom setting. While writing this book I imagined myself in front of an undergraduate class or a beginning graduate class. I imagined myself talking to eager, smart individuals who might not be familiar with some, or even a majority, of the content.

Whenever I teach Bible courses (at my large faith-based university), I do not spend time in class discussing the usual spiritual or devotional messages. In fact, I loathe contrived spirituality and watered-down, feel-good religion. After all, should not spiritual application come to each person at different times and for different reasons? My students certainly do not need me to make those connections (typically low-hanging fruit that inspires no thought) for them and act as their spiritual adviser. But at first, some of my students become confused; indeed, a few are even a little upset that we are not talking in hushed tones about their "personal Lord and Savior Jesus Christ." They have grown up with this approach to learning about Jesus. Anticipating these expectations, I ask them at the beginning of the semester, "How can we talk in class about your personal relationship with Jesus when (1) your personal relationship and spiritual journey is different than the other fifty-nine students in the class, (2) you have likely never read the Gospels from beginning to end, and (3) the context of the Bible is totally foreign to you? If we launch into clichéd devotional discussions about Jesus when you have no foundation by which to interpret the Gospels, then the outcomes will be less powerful." I take the same approach in this book.

We will zoom out away from the typical devotional trees that most Christians have been staring at for their entire lives, and we will explore the contextual forest. The teachings and deeds of Jesus will come alive only after we step back and take a thousand-foot view of his world. A ten-thousand-foot view is too general, and an eye-level view is too nuanced.

Using the ballpark analogy (I apologize to those of you who hate sports analogies), this book takes the reader into the ballpark of the world of Jesus. I want readers to hear the music, see the scoreboard, watch the players from afar, and smell the nachos. Most Christians have spent their entire lives either outside the ballpark hearing faint sounds of the game and observing a few peripheral elements of the experience, or inside the ballpark examining individual blades of grass in centerfield without ever having explored the vast array of elements within their immediate surroundings. Many Christians have a very superficial knowledge base. They do not even know what teams are playing or which team is on defense, let alone who the first base coach is (i.e., a ten-thousand-foot view). Numerous other Christians have an extremely esoteric knowledge base—they know which company manufactured the stadium lights and where the janitor closet is located (eye-level view) but they do not know how the game is played. Detailed information is good but only after one has spent time ingesting and digesting the full range of data within the ballpark. This book attempts to take a middle approach where we survey the ballpark, explain the rules of the game, and occasionally focus on the niceties of the atmosphere. Our approach is neither basic (too boring) nor ultra-technical (too scholarly).

Throughout this book, I introduce several important questions, some of which I will answer briefly and others of which I will spend a great deal of space attempting to answer. As a doctoral-trained social scientist who also has master – and doctoral-level training in the Bible and early Judaism, I tend to focus on relationships, interactions, sociopolitical contexts, and implications. The overarching questions I address in the book are (1) how can early Judaism illuminate our understanding of the Jesus traditions, (2) how did Jesus relate to his Jewish world and vice versa, (3) why did the Gospel writers portray Jesus and his Jewish peers the way they did, and (4) how would Jews in the first and second centuries have interpreted the Jesus traditions upon hearing or reading them? These are not *hard* research questions but, rather, broad questions to keep in mind while progressing through the chapters. For example, we cannot possibly know how "Jews" in the first and second centuries interpreted the Jesus traditions because we have very little data. This question, rather, is meant to remind us that Jews in antiquity would have engaged with the Jesus traditions much differently than twenty-first-century, western, church-attending Christians.

My primary interest is not about *what* happened but *why* and *how* it happened. We are also not primarily concerned in this book with the historical Jesus; rather, we will explore the Jesus traditions within their Jewish context. For me, the Jesus traditions *are* Jewish traditions. This book is an attempt to explain what this means, why it matters, and how it illuminates our understanding of the Jewish world of Jesus, the Gospels, earliest Christianity, and Jesus himself.

Since we are attempting to explore the Jesus traditions within their Jewish context, we will encounter many unfamiliar place-names, ancient book titles, people, and various other terms. I have tried to include brief explanations where these terms arise. If you need a bit more information about a particular Jewish text or historical figure, a quick Google search might suffice. Before proceeding to chapter 1, it may be helpful for us to become somewhat acquainted with the five main bodies of literature most relevant to Jesus' Jewish context: (1) the writings of Josephus, (2) the writings of the rabbis, (3) the Dead Sea Scrolls, (4) the Apocrypha and Pseudepigrapha, and, of course, (5) the New Testament Gospels.

The Writings of Josephus

The writings of Josephus undoubtedly form the most important corpus of literature for understanding the background of early Judaism, including earliest Christianity. Josephus was a Jewish historian (37–100 CE) who was the only contemporary first-century Jewish author—other than the authors of the New Testament—to mention John the Baptist, Jesus, James the brother of Jesus, various Jewish high priests, Herod the Great, Pharisees, and Sadducees. He was also the only first-century author to provide details about the temple complex, Jewish riots against Rome, the Jewish-Roman War, and the geographical landscape of Judea and Galilee. Josephus wrote four major works. The first is the highly detailed, seven-volume work, *The Jewish War* (66–70 CE), which he wrote in the late 70s. Josephus himself fought in this war as a general of a Galilean military band. His next work is an astounding twenty volumes titled *Antiquities of the Jews*, which he completed in the early 90s CE. *Antiquities* covers the creation of the world through the entire history of ancient Israel (according to the Hebrew Bible) and ends with the outbreak of the Jewish-Roman War in 66 CE. His third work is an autobiography: *Life*—the earliest surviving autobiography from the ancient world—which was also completed in the early 90s. His fourth and final work, *Against Apion*, is a two-volume refutation of anti-Jewish accusations and criticisms from several of Josephus's contemporary authors. Without Josephus we would know very little about the Jewish world of the first century.[1]

The Writings of the Rabbis (Rabbinic Literature)

We have available to us one of the most impressive bodies of ancient religious literature ever composed in terms of its breadth and depth. The literature of the rabbis is a massive collection dating from the second century CE to about the tenth century CE. The portion most applicable for understanding Jewish antiquity is dated from the second century CE through the sixth century CE.

The earliest level of rabbinic literature is contained in the Mishnah and Tosefta, which were composed in the second century CE. The word *mishnah* in Hebrew means "repeated study" or "study by repetition." The word *tosefta* means "supplement" or "addition." Before the second century CE, the sages transmitted oral laws based on the biblical laws contained in the Pentateuch (i.e., Genesis through Deuteronomy). Oral law seemed necessary because some of the written laws in the Pentateuch were vague and required explanation, yet no explanation was given in the Hebrew Scriptures. Thus, some Jews believed, like the Pharisees, that God must have given Moses additional explanatory information that was never written down. Other Jews, like the Sadducees, believed that the *only* laws binding upon the Jewish people were the written laws contained in the Hebrew Scriptures. By the second century CE, the unwritten legal traditions had become so numerous that they were too cumbersome to keep organized. The rabbis themselves acknowledged that the body of oral law had become so massive that the Sabbath laws alone "[were] like mountains hanging by a string."[2] The rabbis finally codified the oral laws, and they did so by organizing them by topic.

The Mishnah and Tosefta are the products of that endeavor. These works consist of sixty-three tractates organized into six major topics or "orders." Examples of the many topics contained within the six orders are prayers, tithes, agriculture, Sabbath behavior, festivals, marriage, temple rituals, dietary laws, and purity laws. To give an idea of just how extensive the oral laws had become, Jacob Neusner's English translations of the Mishnah and Tosefta combine to over three thousand pages, which is ten

---

1. For an accessible treatment of Josephus in relation to the New Testament, see Mason, *Josephus and the New Testament*.

2. Mishnah Hagigah 1:8. See translation in Neusner's *Mishnah*, 330.

times bigger than the New Testament! The Mishnah has remained the most authoritative legal code for Jews since its composition in the second century CE. Many ideas, debates, and rabbis mentioned in the Mishnah and Tosefta can confidently be dated to the generation of Jesus or earlier, making them useful for understanding Jewish laws and customs at or near the time of Jesus. In this volume we will refer to these texts often and will see numerous examples of the kind of information contained within them.

The other major work of rabbinic literature is the Talmud. The word *talmud* in Hebrew means "learning." The final written product of the Mishnah and Tosefta fostered even more discussion and expansion of oral law by later rabbis. The sages debated every nuance of the laws contained in both the Hebrew Scriptures and the Mishnah. The Talmud is a written representation of these debates. In a typical section of the Talmud, the rabbis quote a passage from the Mishnah and then expound on it and debate it. These debates often included opinions of several rabbis with a verdict given at the end of the debate. Some debates were short, and some carry on for numerous pages.

There are actually two different sets of the Talmud: the Jerusalem Talmud and the Babylonian Talmud. The Jerusalem Talmud was likely produced in the late fourth or early fifth century by a group of rabbis in the Galilee, close to where Jesus taught and lived. The Babylonian Talmud was written sometime in the sixth century by rabbinic sages in Babylon. The Jerusalem Talmud and the Babylonian Talmud are each at least double the size of the Mishnah and Tosefta combined, which means we have about fifteen thousand pages of writings from the rabbis dating to the sixth century or earlier!

The Talmud is useful for understanding the Jewish world of Jesus. While these texts were written hundreds of years after Jesus died, they preserve many ideas and sensibilities from the time of Jesus. In fact, numerous rabbis in rabbinic literature perform miracles or posit teachings that are strikingly similar to Jesus' miracles and teachings. Nevertheless, we must be careful when using the Talmud and not draw hard conclusions about Jewish life in the first century. For example, if many rabbis interpreted certain laws in a particular way in the Talmud, that does not necessarily indicate that sages at the time of Jesus had the same interpretations. Moreover, if the Talmud provides biographical information about a sage who lived during the lifetime of Jesus, we should not assume that those details are historically accurate. However, while the Talmud is much more relevant to centuries long after Jesus, it does get us closer to the Jewish world in which Jesus lived. At worst, the Talmud invites us into the ballpark—it helps us shed our twenty-first-century western blinders and moves us significantly closer to the Jewish context of the New Testament. With the Talmud we might not be able to see who is up to bat, but at least we can see who is playing the game and feel the soles of our shoes stick to the soda-covered ground (and if you are wondering who spilled the soda, just assume it was the Sadducees and chief priests).[3]

The Dead Sea Scrolls

In the 1940s, a Bedouin shepherd happened upon a cave along the shores of the Dead Sea that contained two-thousand-year-old scrolls. Scholars then swooped in and discovered another ten caves containing scrolls. In the 1950s, a compound, now called Qumran, was excavated near the caves where scholars believe the writers of these scrolls lived. Nearly 900 manuscripts (most in fragments) were resurrected and translated. Among these texts were copies of every book of the Hebrew Scriptures except for Esther. The most copied books were Genesis, Exodus, Deuteronomy, Isaiah, and Psalms. Before the discovery of the Dead Sea Scrolls, the earliest Hebrew manuscripts of the Old Testament dated to about one thousand years after Jesus' lifetime. These scrolls date to at least the time of Jesus and perhaps as many as two hundred years prior. Also among the scrolls were manuals (establishing proper conduct) for the community at Qumran, hymns, a thirty-foot-long temple scroll (detailing matters of temple worship), and biblical commentaries.[4]

These texts are significant for understanding the Jewish context of Jesus' world. They preserve interpretations not only of biblical books but also of Jewish law, as well as discussions of purity. While the Jewish customs posited in these texts are not always representative of most other Jews at that time, they do give us a set of data points predating Jesus that we can compare to the material in Josephus's writings, the Gospels, and rabbinic literature. Thus, we now have a range of Jewish writings from the second century BCE to the sixth century CE that, when surveyed together, provide rich material by which we can better contextualize Jesus as a Jew.

---

3. For a detailed but accessible introduction to these rabbinic texts, see Strack and Stemberger, *Introduction to the Talmud and Midrash*, 108–232.

4. A helpful resource for learning more about Qumran and the Dead Sea Scrolls is Schiffman, *Reclaiming the Dead Sea Scrolls*.

The Apocrypha and Pseudepigrapha

In addition to these major corpuses are numerous standalone Jewish texts dating from the third century BCE to the second century CE. They are often called "apocryphal texts" and "pseudepigraphal texts." Some of these books are historical in nature, such as 1 and 2 Maccabees, while many others are fictional works purported to be written by prominent biblical figures. In fact, the word *pseudepigrapha* means "false writing" or "false inscription," denoting that the texts were not actually written by the suggested authors. Examples of pseudepigraphal books are the Testament of Adam, 1 Enoch, the Testament of Job, and the Testament of Moses. These texts, while fictional in nature, contain useful material for understanding what, for instance, Jews at or near the time of Jesus thought about the corrupt priestly establishment or how they articulated their reverence for certain biblical figures like Joshua, David, and Elijah.

The New Testament Gospels

The Gospels are obviously the most important Jewish texts relating directly to Jesus. But what exactly are the Gospels? I have undoubtedly just confused some of you by describing the Gospels as "Jewish texts." Many academics, including both Jewish studies and New Testament studies' students and professors, consider the Gospels to be "Christian texts." And yes, they are Christian texts in the sense that their authors were followers of Jesus, but the Gospels were written largely by Jews or for Jews (or both), and the central figure in these narratives, namely Jesus, was a Jew par excellence. It seems strange that first-century texts written by Jews that provide a significant amount of information about Judaism at the time of Jesus have been divorced from their Jewish context by medieval and modern Christians. Further, most Jewish-studies graduate programs do not offer courses on the Gospels, but they do offer courses on Josephus, the Dead Sea Scrolls, and rabbinic literature. In any case, most, if not all, Christian youth are introduced to these Gospels as the most authoritative texts for Christian living. Many of these young people read from these same texts for the next sixty years without ever fully considering what they are (in terms of genre), who wrote them, when they were written, or why they were written. These questions are crucial to situating the Gospels within their first-century Jewish setting and for understanding their value for contextualizing Jesus as a Jew. Entire books have been written about each of these questions, but I'll try to briefly answer them here.

When Were the Gospels Written?

This is a very difficult yet interesting question to explore, and numerous scholars have attempted to answer it. There are some clues within the texts and within early Christian tradition that help us narrow the range of dates for when the Gospels were written. Perhaps we can start with the latest possible date and then work backward. According to the sources we have, the Gospel of Matthew was first quoted by the early Christian writer Ignatius in about 110 CE. The Gospel of Mark was mentioned by Papias in the 120s CE. The Gospel of Luke was mentioned by the early Christian writer Justin in about 160 CE. Even earlier writings alluded to Luke in the 90s CE (1 Clement 13:2; 48:4) and in the 150s CE (2 Clement 13:4). Several writers mentioned the Gospel of John in the mid-second century CE (150s–170s CE), but the earliest manuscript containing material from John (18:31–33, 37–38) is dated to the 120s CE. Thus, it seems that all four Gospels were in circulation in the first half of the second century and most likely in the first decade of the second century. The latest Gospel written of these four could not have been composed after about the 110s CE.

That seems straightforward enough, but what about the earliest possible dates? This is much trickier. We start with the Gospel of Mark. Could Mark have been written within a decade or two of Jesus' death—sometime in the 40s or 50s? It is unlikely because the text presupposes that the author knows about the Jewish-Roman War (66–70 CE) and the temple's destruction in 70 CE. For example, in Mark 13, Jesus, in reference to the temple, says "Not one stone will be left here upon another; all will be thrown down" (v. 2). The next few verses mention "wars and rumors of wars" (v. 7). Jesus then mentions the "desolating sacrilege," language that is borrowed from the book of Daniel (9:27) in reference to the Greeks desecrating the temple in 165 BCE.

A large majority of scholars (whether Christian, Jew, or agnostic) have dated the Gospel of Mark to at least the late 60s or early 70s because of the author's knowledge of these events. Although these statements could have been prophecies of Jesus given in about 30 CE, thus allowing the text to be dated perhaps as early as the 40s, this is not likely because the author would have been foolish to include unfulfilled prophecies of Jesus ten or twenty years after Jesus' death. We cannot imagine the author of Mark risking making Jesus look like a false prophet, especially given the instruction for discerning a false prophet in Deuteronomy 18: "If a prophet speaks in the name of the Lord but the thing does not take place or prove true, it is a word that the Lord has not spoken. The prophet has spoken it presumptuously" (v. 22). If Mark was written in the 40s or 50s, and potential converts (or critics) read about these prophecies of wars and a desolated temple, what would they have concluded? Probably that Jesus was another false prophet. It would have been devastating to the Jesus movement if Christians were running around in the 40s and 50s publicly repeating Jesus' prophecies that the temple would be destroyed. Jews throughout Judea and Galilee would not only instantly see the Jesus movement as illegitimate and a threat but would also conclude that this movement was founded by a person who was clearly an illegitimate prophet.

The reason these prophecies are included in the text is precisely because they had occurred. The reader or hearer of this Jesus tradition would say, "Yes, the temple was indeed destroyed, and, therefore, Jesus was a true prophet." Jesus may very well have prophesied of the temple's destruction, but the fact that the author of Mark included it in his text in such a pronounced manner indicates that the event had already occurred. This is why most scholars have concluded that the Gospel of Mark was written in the late 60s during the Jewish-Roman War, when people began to realize that the temple could easily be destroyed. It is also plausible that the text was written in the 70s after the temple's destruction, thus making the prophecies that much more powerful to potential converts.

After working through the Gospel of Mark, dating Matthew and Luke is straightforward. Based on detailed textual analyses, it seems that both the authors of Matthew and Luke borrowed from Mark. They quoted verbatim large sections and precise terminology from Mark; thus, we can rule out a scenario where Matthew and Luke were not familiar with the Gospel of Mark but drew from a pool of similar traditions. No, they actually had the Gospel of Mark in front of them when writing their Gospels, so they must have been written after the Gospel of Mark. Even if they had not borrowed from Mark, both authors knew about the destruction of the temple (Matt 24:2; Luke 19:44, 21:6). Moreover, in the case of Matthew, the author uses the phrase "to this day" (Matt 27:8, 28:15), which implies that a significant amount of time has passed. In fact, it is likely that this phrase (also found throughout the Hebrew Scriptures) indicates that at least a generation had passed since Jesus' ministry and the events written about occurred.

The Gospel of John can also be dated after 70 CE, although the author of John did not borrow from the Synoptic Gospels (*synoptic* meaning "view together" because these three Gospels are so similar that they can be read together), so it cannot be dated in relation to them. It would seem, however, that the author of John also knew about the destruction of the temple (John 2:13–22, 11:48).

Thus it seems that all four Gospels were written at some point between the early 70s and about 110 CE, which means that they represent the third stage of the Jesus traditions:

- Stage I: Roughly 28–30 CE—Jesus' direct sayings and deeds
- Stage II: Roughly 30–70 CE—oral traditions about Jesus, all likely containing both elements of historical truth and embellishments
- Stage III: Roughly 70–100 CE—the written version of the oral traditions combined with the theological and political motives of the Gospels' writers[5]

Who Wrote the Gospels?

This question is also interesting but difficult to answer. Since Mark is probably the earliest Gospel written, we start there. First, the text does not ascribe authorship to a particular individual. The Gospel of Mark was originally anonymous. We can rule out the author being among the original disciples because his text does not assume a firsthand witness of Jesus' ministry. Early Christian tradition, specifically according to Papias in the 120s CE, attributed this gospel to Mark, who apparently was a companion of Peter. There are, however, some problems with this tradition. For example, the author of Mark is not friendly to Peter in his Gospel (as we will see in chapter 10). Would not Mark be more reverential to Peter if he were his companion?

Even if we cannot say exactly who wrote the Gospel of Mark, we might be able to say more about his identity. "Mark" is a Roman name, but this does not necessarily mean that the author was a gentile. Textual evidence suggests that Mark was a Jew, since he seems to know a lot about Judaism and explains nuances of Jewish life to his audience. Scholars usually conclude that the author of Mark was writing to gentiles. While the author of Mark does assume that his readers view the Hebrew Scriptures as the authoritative word of God (Mark 7:8) and that they know what it meant for Jesus to be the messiah (Mark 8:29), he also feels it necessary to explain about the Sadducees and Pharisees (Mark 12:18, 7:2–5), as well as Jewish rituals (Mark 7:3–4; 14:2; 15:42). Further, while he does not feel it necessary to define Latin words for his readers, he does define Aramaic words (see Mark 3:7; 5:9, 15, 41; 7:11, 34; 10:46; 12:15; 14:36; 15:16, 22, 34, 39). This suggests that while his audience is gentile, he might be either a gentile

---

5. This comes from Meier, *Marginal Jew*, 1:167.

convert to Judaism or a Hellenistic Jew (*Hellenistic* meaning relation to Greek language and culture).

The Gospel of Matthew was also originally anonymous. Early Christian tradition from the second century (also associated with Papias) attributed this text to Matthew, one of the original apostles of Jesus. However, it is most likely not written by Matthew. First, the text itself does not presuppose that the author was a firsthand witness of Jesus' deeds and sermons. If the author was a firsthand witness, we would expect him to mention it explicitly, or at least hint at it, especially since doing so would increase credibility and establish superiority over the other Gospels. Second, if the author was a firsthand witness of Jesus' ministry, why did he rely so heavily on the Gospel of Mark when composing his own Gospel? Third, if the author was indeed Matthew the apostle, why did he not relate his own call to discipleship (Matt 9:9–13; cf. Mark 2:13–17) but instead copied the Gospel of Mark when relating his own experience? In terms of identity, we will see throughout this book that the Gospel of Matthew seems to be written to a Jewish audience. The author is highly reliant on the Hebrew Scriptures and assumes that his readers are familiar with Judaism.

As with Matthew and Mark, the author of the Gospel of Luke is also anonymous and does not seem to have been an eyewitness to Jesus' ministry. Early Christian tradition (from the mid-second century) attributes the Gospel of Luke to one of Paul's companions, Luke the physician (Col 4:14). The author of Luke is also the author of the book of Acts (note that both books contain the same terminology and style of Greek). In Acts, the author sometimes writes in the first person as one who was with Paul on occasion (Acts 16:10–17; 20:5–15; 21:1–18). Some scholars have suggested that the "we sections" in Acts are not evidence of eyewitness experience but instead are a literary device. One also calls into question whether the author of Luke was really that familiar with Paul since the timeline of Paul's journeys in Acts is significantly different from Paul's timeline in Paul's own letters. Thus, we have no good reason to claim that the author of Luke was or was not a companion of Paul. We are unclear on whether the author of Luke was a Jew who was educated in the classical literature or a gentile who was educated in the Hebrew Scriptures; he was very knowledgeable of both. If the author of Luke really was a companion of Paul and the person who is identified in Colossians, then he was apparently a gentile (Col 4:11–14). Regardless, his intended audience seems to be Jews and gentiles. He seems to be the most educated of all the Gospels' authors; his Greek is the most sophisticated, and his vocabulary is the richest.

Determining the author of John is a similar struggle. The text itself does not claim who wrote it. In the latter half of the second century (over one hundred years after Jesus' death), Irenaeus attributed this Gospel to an individual named John. He seems to have gathered such information from an aged Christian named Polycarp. Even if the author is John, can we say that he was John the apostle, the son of Zebedee, and not some other elder named John? Internal evidence gives us no reason to either reject or accept such a claim. We just do not know. Some scholars have questioned whether the author was an eyewitness because the Gospel seems to be written by someone who did not witness Jesus' deeds and sayings firsthand. For example, in John 20 (the Last Supper), the author is writing in the third person about the disciple whom Jesus loved, and it was "this disciple" who testified of these events and wrote them. The author then writes, "And we know that his testimony is true," indicating that the author of the Gospel of John was not present but seems to have received information that was written by someone who was present (John 20:20–24). Due to the content, the author seems to have been a Jew whose intended audience was perhaps both Jews and gentiles.

What Are the Gospels?

Many Christian readers assume that the Gospels are simply histories of Jesus' ministry. We know this because Christians have been preoccupied for centuries with combining the four Gospels to create a reliable timeline for Jesus' ministry. In our post-Enlightenment world, we want certainty. We want the Gospels to be historically reliable in every detail, save a few minor discrepancies. But the Gospels are *very* different in *many* aspects, and it is important to understand this from the start, which is why I spend the first session of the semester with my students discussing the following before introducing them to any new substantive material (and which is why we are dealing with this question—what are the Gospels?—here in the introduction).

For example, the Gospel of Mark lacks any information about Jesus' birth, the Sermon on the Mount, Mary and Martha (Jesus' closest friends in the other Gospels), the raising of Lazarus, Jesus' charge to love one's enemies, and Jesus' resurrection and post-resurrection appearance. Only in the Gospel of Matthew do we read about the visit of the Magi, the star in Bethlehem, the escape to Egypt, the denunciation of Pharisees, Judas's suicide, and the mass resurrection of Jews after Jesus' resurrection. Matthew's and Luke's genealogies differ significantly (Matt 1:1–17; Luke 3:23–38); they do not even agree on the name of Jesus' grandfather: Joseph's father is Jacob in Matthew but Heli in Luke. Only in Luke do we find material about the birth of John the Baptist, Gabriel's appearance to Mary, Jesus as a child in Jerusalem, the good Samaritan, the prodigal son, Jesus' appearance on the road to Emmaus, and Jesus' ascension to heaven. The author of Luke seems to go out of his way to omit certain details that are present in Mark and Matthew and often polishes casual expressions found in them. He changes episodes in Mark where Jesus seems to lack control. He omits places where Jesus displays common human emotions. He completely omits violent or harsh acts associated with Jesus, like the cursing of the fig tree and the temple tantrum (i.e., overturning the money changers' tables). He also deletes or changes episodes where Jesus' disciples look foolish.

The Gospel of John is much different than the Synoptic Gospels. It contains no parables, no exorcisms, and no baptism of Jesus (in fact, Jesus does not know John the Baptist in this Gospel). Jesus is much more outspoken and is always in control. Jesus' ministry occurs primarily in Judea in the Gospel of John, whereas his ministry occurs primarily in Galilee in the Synoptic Gospels. Jesus' ministry in John covers at least two years and probably more, whereas his ministry covers only one year in the Synoptics. Jesus cleanses the temple at the beginning of his ministry in John, but at the end of his ministry in the Synoptics. Jesus dies the day before Passover in John, but on Passover in the Synoptics.

Another key issue that illustrates that the authors of the Gospels were not completely unified in their understanding of Jesus is his divinity—specifically when he became divine. The earliest Christian traditions, those that seem to predate the letters of Paul (which predate the writing of the Gospels), maintain that Jesus became God at his resurrection. For instance, a pre-Pauline tradition embedded within Paul's letter to the Romans posits that Jesus "was descended from David according to the flesh and was declared to be the Son of God with power according to the spirit of holiness *by resurrection* from the dead" (Rom 1:3–4; emphasis added). In other words, he came into the world and descended from David as would any human (i.e., "according to the flesh") and was not declared the "Son of God" until his resurrection. A later text, the book of Acts, maintains this understanding. Paul was reported to have taught that when God "raised [Jesus] from the dead," he declared, "You are my Son; *today* I have begotten you" (Acts 13:30–33; emphasis added). Jesus became the Son of God *today*, the day he was resurrected.

Several decades later, when the Gospels were being composed, it seems that the understanding of when Jesus became divine had evolved from his resurrection back to his baptism, when at that moment God declared Jesus his "son" (Luke 3:22; Mark 1:11; Matt 3:17). This seems to be the case with the author of Mark, who does not care about Jesus' birth; he jumps straight to Jesus' baptism as he opens his Gospel, and it is that moment when Jesus becomes divine.

In contrast, Matthew and Luke, both postdating Mark, have Jesus attaining divine status at his birth:

> She will bear a son, and you are to name him Jesus, for he will save his people from their sins. All this took place to fulfil what had been spoken by the Lord through the prophet: 'Look, the virgin shall conceive and bear a son, and they shall name him Emmanuel,' which means, *'God is with us.'"* (Matt 1:21–26; emphasis added)

> Then an angel of the Lord stood before them, and the glory of the Lord shone around them, and they were terrified. But the angel said to them, 'Do not be afraid; for see—I am bringing you good news of great joy for all the people: to you is born *this day* in the city of David a Savior, who is the Messiah, *the Lord*. (Luke 2:9–11; emphasis added)

We see this pattern continue in the Gospel of John, which pushes Jesus' divine status back even further to before Jesus' birth:

> In the beginning was the Word, and the Word was with God, and the Word was God. He was in the beginning with God. All things came into being through him, and without him not one thing came into being. What has come into being in him was life, and the life was the light of all people. (John 1:1–4)

We will explore much of this information in more detail throughout the book, but for now, consider what we would be missing if three Gospels (75 percent) survived and only one Gospel, Matthew or Luke, for example, did not survive. Our understanding of Jesus would be dramatically reduced.[6]

We can now see how these Gospels differ in some significant aspects, but we still have not answered the question: *What are the Gospels?* We know that the Gospels are not detailed histories or biographies in terms of how we think of *history* or *biography* today. The authors did not claim to have written such texts. It seems, rather, that they were writing texts for the specific purpose of persuading people to the Christian cause. One of the most

---

6. For more information on these two questions—who wrote the Gospels, and when were they written—see the following sources (all of these sources will contain additional bibliographies for further exploration): Green et al., *Dictionary of Jesus and the Gospels*, 368–83, 495–510, 514–41; Aune, *Blackwell Companion to the New Testament*, 272–372; Powell, *Introducing the New Testament*, 81–214.

prominent New Testament scholars of the previous generation, E. P. Sanders, explained the issue as follows:

> There is no *biography* in our sense of the word: no development, seldom a concrete setting (such as, "this was an important issue just then, because . . ."), just short accounts stitched together with an introductory word or phrase . . . The synoptic gospels lack most of the things that we now expect in the story of someone's life. Looks, personality, character—we know very little . . . So much romantic imagination has been lavished on the gospels for so many centuries that the modern reader does not at once see how stark they are. We automatically add novelistic details, many of which have reached people who have never entered a church or read the Bible . . . The individual scenes are brief and to the point. This presumably means that they have been *shaped* precisely in order to make their point, other matter being pruned away. The consequence is that we cannot write a biography of Jesus . . . We have the general outline of his life, plus brief stories, sayings and parables, but we cannot write "the life of Jesus" in the modern sense, describing his education, tracing his development, analyzing the influence of his parents, showing his response to specific events—and so on.[7]

In the now classic work *What Are the Gospels?*, author Richard Burridge (scholar at King's College London and priest in the Church of England) posits that the style of the Gospels fits the Greco-Roman biography genre. While some scholars have begun to challenge Burridge's theory, it remains a solid, broad starting point for understanding what the Gospels are or what they were intended to be.

Burridge showed that the Gospels contain the key characteristics of *ancient biography*—or *bios*, meaning "life." The focus of *bios* was the public life of the central figure, not his or her personal life. Works of *bios* were blatantly subjective and typically stylized the main character in a stereotype that most people would understand: a politician, a philosopher, a miracle worker, or a prophet. *Bios* was not concerned about the central figure's motives and psychological development. Perhaps most important is that the major purpose of *bios* was to emphasize a specific point about the main character and persuade people to view that person in a particular way.[8] Therefore, details about mundane aspects of life were not expected to be included in these texts.

---

7. Sanders, *Historical Figure of Jesus*, 74–75, emphasis added.
8. Burridge, *What Are the Gospels?*, 105–307.

Consistent with this form of biography, every story or parable in the Gospels was strategically placed to support an overarching argument about Jesus. The author of John illustrates this perfectly: "Now Jesus did many other signs in the presence of his disciples, *which are not written in this book*. But these are *written so that you* may come to believe that Jesus is the Messiah, the Son of God, and that through believing you may have life in his name" (John 20:30–31; emphasis added). Notice that the author of John acknowledges that his purpose is not simply to present a bunch of stories about Jesus for the sake of preserving them but to include material that will foster belief in Jesus as the Messiah.

As readers of the New Testament, we must identify the primary purpose, or the few primary purposes, of each individual Gospel so that we understand why they were written. As we proceed through this book, we will develop a deeper understanding of the major purposes of each Gospel; however, here are the (very) basics so that we at least have a general reference point from the start.

The author of Mark seems to be particularly interested in reconciling for his readers how one can believe in Jesus even though Jesus was killed. We will discuss this in more detail later, but the fact that Jesus was killed would have been a serious stumbling block to potential followers of Jesus; thus, the author of Mark attempts to explain why it should not be such a problem that Jesus was crucified. The primary purpose of the Gospels of Matthew and John is to demonstrate that Jesus has authority and is the messiah. The authors accomplish this by comparing Jesus to biblical figures like Moses, Joshua, Joseph, Elisha, and David. In addition to illustrating Jesus' authority, like in Matthew and John, a major purpose of the Gospel of Luke seems to argue that Jesus is innocent. Yes, he was tried and executed as a criminal, but he should not have been, according to the author of Luke. For example, in Luke, a centurion at the cross does not declare Jesus the Son of God as he does in Mark and Matthew (Mark 15:39; Matt 27:54), but he calls him *righteous*—in other words, not guilty and not deserving of death (Luke 23:47). Only in Luke does one of the thieves on the cross declare Jesus' innocence: "We indeed have been condemned justly, for we are getting what we deserve for our deeds, but this man has done nothing wrong" (Luke 23:41). Only in Luke does Pilate explicitly say three times that Jesus is innocent. Pilate questions whether Jesus is innocent in Mark and Matthew, but in Luke he says, "I find no basis for an accusation against this man" (23:4), "I have examined him in your presence and have not found this man guilty of any of your charges" (23:14), and "What evil has he done? I have found in him no ground for the sentence of death" (23:22).

In addition to these overarching purposes of the Gospels, especially telling is how much of the Gospels cover only the last three weeks or so of Jesus' life. The climax of Jesus' ministry before he leaves for Jerusalem for the last time is his meeting with his apostles at Caesarea Philippi and his transfiguration. In Mark, these events occur in chapters 8 and 9, only halfway through the Gospel. Thus, about 50 percent of Mark deals with the last two weeks of Jesus' life. About 40 percent of Matthew and 60 percent of Luke cover the last few weeks of Jesus' life (beginning in Matt 16 and Luke 9). In John, Jesus is at Caesarea Philippi in chapter 6 and leaves for Jerusalem in chapter 10, meaning that about 50 to 70 percent of John is focused on the final weeks of Jesus' life. This illustrates further that the Gospels are not fully articulated modern-style biographies of Jesus' life but are CliffsNotes versions with a focus on his authority, messiahship, and death. The authors wanted to highlight his ultimate fate and what this means for Christianity today ("today" meaning 70–100 CE when the Gospels were written). And that is the point!

I like to use the following analogy with my students to help them better understand what the Gospels are. Let us pretend for a moment that when Jesus started his ministry he chose twelve individuals from twelve different regions of the world—what is now Polynesia, India, Japan, the Americas, West Africa, and Russia, among other places. These individuals were transported to Galilee and spent a few years with Jesus. After Jesus' death, they were all transported back to their home regions. They began transmitting stories about Jesus orally, and these oral stories circulated for the next four or five decades. After the original twelve had died, members of each community began writing down the Jesus-traditions. This resulted in twelve different Gospels. Decades later, perhaps a full two generations after Jesus' death, followers of Jesus in one location started gathering copies of all the extant Gospels. They found that four Gospels had survived. When they compared these four, they found that they were very similar in some places, but also very different in other places. Even the similar stories differed; where one Gospel used the word "sled," the others contained "canoe," "chariot," or "horse." These four Gospels contained numerous elements that were only relevant to their specific cultures and their specific regions of the world. This is not a perfect analogy but it suffices. This is essentially what we have in the Gospels but on a much more localized scale. The Gospels date to forty to seventy years after Jesus' death. They were written by authors who did not witness Jesus' ministry firsthand but obtained information orally. Although this treatment of the Gospels is basic, it gives us a reference point as we work through this volume.

Introduction to the Chapters

The first five chapters of this book deal primarily with traditions about Jesus the man, as opposed to his teachings (I will be examining the Jewish teachings of Jesus in a later volume). In chapter 1, we survey various aspects of childhood and family life in first-century Galilee. In the second half of chapter 1, we look at the notions of washing and purity, which will help us contextualize the immersion activities of John the Baptist and the baptism of Jesus. In chapters 2 and 3, we explore Jesus as a first-century Jewish prophet and miracle worker. How did these two societal roles function in the first century? Because Moses and Elisha were two of the great prophets and miracle workers in the Hebrew Scriptures, some of the authors of the Gospels compared Jesus to them. Chapters 4 and 5 are about messiahs and messianic activity in early Judaism. These two chapters will attempt to help the reader understand the early Jewish expectations of a "messiah." We will also situate Jesus within this messianic context.

The last five chapters (6–10) explore the relationship between Jesus and his Jewish peers. Our overarching theme for these chapters is to challenge the common Christian tropes that "Jews killed Jesus" and "Jesus rejected the Jews and Judaism." In chapter 6, we first examine how Jews were treated by Christians through the centuries, specifically in relation to the accusation that Jews killed Jesus. We then take a fascinating look at and reinterpret the relationship between Jesus and Judas. In chapter 7, we explore the relationship between Jesus and the Pharisees. This relationship is complex, and some readers will be surprised by our conclusions. In chapter 8, we examine the relationship between Jesus and the Jewish masses. Did they reject Jesus? Chapter 9 deals with the "art of name-calling" in the first-century Mediterranean world. Much of the vitriolic nastiness in the Gospels toward Pharisees and certain other groups will come into focus and be explained. In chapter 10, we take a step back and examine why the authors of the Gospels felt the need to use name-calling tactics against their opponents. What had happened in the first century after Jesus' death to warrant a war of words between various groups and factions?

While some of Jesus' sayings are explored in this book, the primary focus is on traditions about Jesus the man and his relationship and interactions with his Jewish peers. A subsequent volume will deal primarily with the teachings of Jesus within their Jewish context.

A Few Other Housekeeping Items

A large majority of the scriptural quotations in this book come from the New Revised Standard Version of the Bible (NRSV). In the rare cases that I use other translations, I will alert the reader. Although my own religious community uses the King James Version (KJV), I prefer the much clearer, cleaner, and more accurate NRSV used in most academic settings. For more about this version as well as the history of English translations of the Bible, see Bruce Metzger's *The Bible in Translation* and Bruce Metzger and Bart Ehrman's *The Text of the New Testament: Its Transmission, Corruption, and Restoration*.

At the end of each chapter I include a "takeaways" section. I am not as partial to the traditional "conclusions" section because I personally like the last section of each chapter to include more than just a summary or argument conclusion. I want my students and readers to become comfortable with not always having clean, tight answers to their questions and become accustomed to considering a range of possible interpretations and what the implications are for those interpretations.

Throughout the book, certain issues will be discussed that I anticipate will spark even more questions—broader questions about the historicity of the Jesus traditions or the nature of Scripture, for example. In some instances I will attempt to address such questions at that point in the book, as I would do in a classroom setting. In other instances I will wait until the end of the semester, so to speak; I will attempt to tie up several loose ends and discuss some elephants in the room in the book's conclusion. In these cases, I will alert the reader by raising a question and then pointing the reader to the conclusion.

Chapter One

From Bethlehem to Baptism
Childhood and Family in Ancient Judea and Galilee

MOST SCHOLARS AND POPULAR authors who write on Jesus and the New Testament take one of three approaches: (1) they spend a majority of the time analyzing the literary and textual nuances of the Gospels in order to better understand how the texts were created and redacted; (2) they analyze the deeds and sayings of Jesus using scholarly methods of historical criticism in order to determine what the Jesus of history actually said and did; and (3) they discuss how the teachings of Jesus can help people in their spiritual and faith journeys (i.e., "devotional literature"). I too am interested in these approaches to Jesus studies; however, as a social scientist I tend to be most interested in the social and cultural contexts of Jesus' life and of the Gospels. Regarding Jesus' childhood and upbringing, for example, what were the general living conditions for a boy in the Greco-Roman world in the first century CE, and specifically for a Jewish boy living in Galilee? How did Jewish boys relate to their parents? How were they educated? What types of struggles and challenges did they face?

In most cultures, boys generally like to play, explore, throw rocks, and catch bugs. While the primary sources (see Introduction) are not focused on these sorts of daily-life activities, they do provide some insights that help illuminate the lifestyle of Galilean families. In this chapter we examine several aspects of childhood and young adulthood in first-century Galilee. We also explore ideas of washing and purity in order to better contextualize the immersion activities of John the Baptist and the baptism of Jesus. The material in this chapter will help foster both a better contextualization of the social setting of first-century Judea and Galilee and a greater appreciation for what the boy Jesus would have experienced during his childhood and early adult years before his ministry.

Villages and Houses

The region of Galilee during Jesus' lifetime contained hundreds of villages. According to the first-century Jewish historian Josephus, 204 villages peppered the Galilean landscape.[1] Only a small number of these settlements, perhaps just Sepphoris and Tiberias, were larger than about twenty acres. Sepphoris, the administrative capital of Galilee, may have been as large as 150 acres.[2] Based on several archaeological surveys, a large majority of the villages were between only two and a half acres and ten acres in size. For example, Capernaum, Cana, and Nazareth were probably only five to ten acres in size, the latter containing fifty houses maximum. Accounting for living quarters, estimated persons per household, space for livestock, space for a threshing floor, and crop land, the population was about one hundred inhabitants per acre. This means that most people in first-century Judea and Galilee lived in villages ranging from a few hundred to one thousand inhabitants. Unlike the few larger cities that contained border walls, marketplaces, aqueducts, theaters, stadiums, hippodromes, paved roads, and even sewer systems, these smaller villages contained only a few modest commercial buildings, presses for oil and wine, a small water cistern, narrow and unpaved roads, and a cemetery.[3] As a child, Jesus may have seen the contrast in lifestyles between the villages and cities, since Sepphoris was only about three and a half miles from Nazareth.

Extensive research on Palestinian houses in antiquity by Israeli archaeologist and professor at the Hebrew University of Jerusalem Yizhar Hirschfeld has revealed that most peasant dwellings in villages were on average 2,500–3,000 square feet, including both a courtyard and space for animals. These stone structures were flat-roofed and had one to two rooms. Ceilings were quite low at about five and a half feet high. People typically accessed the upper level by ladders. Most walls were typically plastered and the floors were dirt surfaces. Some extended families built houses that shared a central, open-air courtyard. In the hot months, people usually slept on bedrolls in the courtyard or on the roof. Families experienced little

---

1. Josephus, *Life* 45.235, trans. Mason.
2. Crossan and Reed, *Excavating Jesus*, 81.
3. For a summary of the archaeological surveys and an additional bibliography, see Fiensy, "Galilean Village," 177–207.

privacy in this style of dwelling. Depending on the region and landscape, many houses were built on top of small caves, which were used to store food and keep animals in at night.[4]

The narratives concerning the birth of Jesus and the elements present in the Gospels allow us to examine this event in relation to our focus on housing and peasant life. In what type of house was Jesus born? What was the social setting of his birth? Where were Joseph's and Mary's families during Jesus' birth? Partial answers to these questions are offered in the Gospels, early Christian tradition, and archaeology. Later Christian interpretation places Jesus' birth in a wooden stable somewhere away from an "inn." Most depictions of the episode in cinema and art suggest that Mary and Joseph arrived in Bethlehem at night when Mary was nine months pregnant. She was ready to deliver, but inhospitable Jews (as many Christians portray them) would not give up their rooms, and so Jesus was born in a stable surrounded by animals. The Gospels, however, mention none of this. First, it is unlikely that Joseph and Mary traveled alone all the way from Galilee to Bethlehem in just the nick of time for Mary to deliver Jesus. Travelers, especially the young and vulnerable like Joseph and Mary, journeyed in caravans for protection against bandits and other dangers. Moreover, we would expect Joseph and Mary to arrive in Bethlehem well before the arrival of Jesus. This fits with Luke's account, which states that Mary was already in Bethlehem for some time: "*while they were there,* the time came for her to deliver her child" (Luke 2:6; emphasis added). Most likely, Joseph and Mary lodged with family while in Bethlehem—at least based on material in Luke, which claims that everyone participated in the legal registration in "their own towns" (Luke 2:3). Thus, Mary and Joseph would have certainly had family connections in the region.

And as far as Jesus being born in a stable, the Gospel of Matthew states that the magi (wise men) came to a house (*oikos*) to visit the baby Jesus (2:11). Even if the magi arrived several days, weeks, or even months after Jesus' birth, the fact that a house was available to Mary in Bethlehem suggests that Jesus was probably born in similar circumstances, surrounded by friends and family. But what about Luke's language that Jesus was "laid in a manger, because there was no room for them in the inn" (2:7)? The word "inn," or *kataluma* in Greek, as Luke uses it, does not suggest what we think of as an inn, hostel, or motel. Luke does mention such a place later in his Gospel (10:34), when he described the place the good Samaritan took the injured man. However, there he uses a different word, *pandocheion*. In addition to being translated as "inn," the word *kataluma* means "guest room"

---

4. Hirschfeld, *Palestinian Dwelling*; Dark, "Jesus' Nazareth House," 24–36.

or "house." Note that the author of Luke uses this same word for the guest room where the Last Supper was held (22:11). Thus, we might conclude that all the rooms (*kataluma*), or the main living quarter in the upper level of the house (*kataluma*), were occupied by family members. The host, therefore, would have prepared a more secluded place to provide Joseph and Mary some privacy. Where was this private place? Luke mentions that Jesus was laid in a manger, or feeding trough. The most likely location, then, is on the main floor where the animals were kept, as was the case throughout the ancient Near East. The other guests would have slept on the upper level.[5]

Early Christian tradition suggests that Jesus was born in a cave. As mentioned, houses were sometimes built over a cave or cavity in the rocks, which might serve as a cellar for food or shelter for animals. This especially fits the landscape in Bethlehem, as it is a rocky region replete with caves. Further, the cave tradition was so entrenched by the fourth century that Roman emperor Constantine's mother, Helena, identified a cave in Bethlehem as the place of Jesus' birth. Constantine later built a shrine over the cave, which is now the site of the Church of the Nativity.[6]

Throughout much of Christian history, interpretation of the New Testament was heavily shaped with an anti-Jewish bias. Christians approached the Gospels through an anti-Jewish lens. This continues to some extent today in our discussions relating to the birth of Jesus, even though we do not intend to be anti-Semitic. The story is more powerful and dramatic when its elements are taken to the extreme. If Mary, for example, is just hours away from delivering Jesus, but has no place to stay, and the heartless local Jews in Bethlehem will not make room for her, then the story is more dramatic. This interpretation follows the notion that intense opposition to Jesus was present from the beginning and that he was born in the most humble of circumstances, away from family and among animals. The alternate and perhaps more realistic conclusion presented here paints a different picture—one where we envision the type of house and setting in which Jesus was born. This interpretation is perhaps just as impactful. Joseph, Mary, and Jesus were not turned away and rejected but were accepted, cared for, loved, and surrounded by a close-knit Jewish family.

Family Structure

The age of first marriage and its impact on the culture is of particular interest to this approach. When Mary gave birth to Jesus she was probably in

---

5. Carlson, "Accommodations of Joseph and Mary," 326–42; Bailey, "Manger and the Inn."

6. Brown, *Birth of the Messiah*, 399–401.

her teens. In our contemporary world, marrying before the age of twenty is unusual and discouraged. In the first century, however, sixteen or seventeen was a typical age for women to marry. The minimum age for marriage per Roman law was twelve for females and fourteen for males. This seems to be the custom among Jewish families as well. It was not uncommon for most Jewish women to marry between the ages of twelve and eighteen, although some married older. Most men married later, between the ages of fourteen and twenty-four. Although marrying at an early age was ideal for most women, perhaps due to life expectancy, there is little evidence to support the misconception that a woman who was single in her twenties was ostracized and viewed as undesirable.[7] According to Roman census records in Egypt, 20 percent of women were married by age fourteen and 40 percent were married by age sixteen.[8] Thus, by age seventeen, Mary would have already been of marriageable age for two or three years.

Several Jewish texts in antiquity stress the importance of marrying young, especially for males. The Mishnah (see Introduction) designates ages five to seventeen for males to study and age eighteen for them to marry.[9] The Talmud (see Introduction) states, "Our Rabbis taught: Concerning a man who . . . guides his sons and daughters in the right path and arranges for them to be married near the period of their puberty, Scripture says, 'You shall know that your tent is safe' (Job 5:24)."[10] During another discussion on this issue, one rabbi opined that "he who is twenty years of age and is not married spends all his days in . . . sinful thoughts [i.e., sexual thoughts]." His associate reminded the group that previous rabbis had stated, "As soon as one attains twenty and has not married, He [God] exclaims, 'Blasted be his bones!'" Another rabbi, perhaps with the typical male competitive ego, commented, "The reason that I am superior to my colleagues is that I married at sixteen, and had I married at fourteen, I would have said to Satan, 'an arrow in your eye.'"[11]

The divine mandate of marriage was well understood by Jews at the time of Jesus. The rabbis referred often to the commandments in Genesis to marry. For them it was clear that the purpose of marriage was at least twofold. The first was for companionship, as "it is not good that the man should be alone . . . Therefore a man leaves his father and his mother and clings to

---

7. van der Horst, *Ancient Jewish Epitaphs*, 103–4; Ilan, *Jewish Women*, 65–69; Jeffers, *Greco-Roman World of the New Testament*, 238.
8. Bagnall and Frier, *Demography of Roman Egypt*, 113.
9. Mishnah Avot 5:21.
10. Babylonian Talmud Yebamot 62b, in Slotki, *Yebamoth*.
11. Babylonian Talmud Kiddushin 29b–30a, in Freedman, *Kiddushin*.

his wife, and they become one flesh" (Gen 2:18, 24). A few ancient Jewish texts posited the belief among the rabbis that God looks so favorably upon marriage that he himself is a matchmaker for his people. In one rabbinic story, a Roman woman asked Rabbi Yose ben Halputa what God has been doing since he finished creating the earth. The rabbi answered that God spends all his time making matches. The woman, thinking that matchmaking was easy, said, "You know I have quite a number of slave boys and slave girls, and in a brief moment I can match them up too." The rabbi replied that it is not so easy. In fact, he argued, matching men and women was harder for God than splitting the Red Sea. That night the woman matched up all her slave boys and slave girls: "In the morning they came to her. One had a broken head, the other a blind eye, a third a broken hand, a fourth a broken foot, a fifth said, 'I don't want this one,' and a sixth said, 'I don't want that man.'" The woman sent the rabbi the message, "Your Torah [scriptures] is indeed praiseworthy."[12] Yes, finding an intimate companion was just as difficult in antiquity as it is today, with the added pressure that most of the Jewish population viewed marriage as a divine commandment.

The second major purpose for marriage, perhaps more important than the first, was to reproduce. The rabbis pointed to the commandment to "be fruitful and multiply, and fill the earth" (Gen 1:28) as an injunction to bear children; however, they also observed another passage that elevated the importance of procreation: "Therefore a man leaves his father and his mother and clings to his wife, and they become one flesh" (Gen 2:24). The phrase "They become one flesh," referred to having children, according to some early rabbis. The "one flesh" was the body and soul of a child, which as a single entity was a product of two separate people, the father and the mother, coming together.[13] Consider the following from the Talmud that illustrates the sacred nature of creating one flesh by two people:

> Our Rabbis taught: There are three partners in [the creation of a human], the Holy One, his father, and his mother. His father supplies the semen of the white substance out of which are formed the child's bones, sinews, nails, the brain in his head and the white in his eye; his mother supplies the semen of the red substance out of which is formed his skin, flesh, hair, blood and the black of his eye; and the Holy One gives him the spirit and the breath, beauty of features, eyesight, the power of hearing and the ability to speak and to walk, understanding and discernment.[14]

12. Neusner, *Judaism and Scripture*, 227–28.
13. Lewittes, *Jewish Marriage*, 9.
14. Babylonian Talmud Niddah 31a, in Slotki, *Niddah*.

Several ancient rabbis, based on Genesis 9:6–7, posited that failing to procreate was akin to murder: "R. Eliezer stated, He who does not engage in propagation of the race is as though he sheds blood; for it is said, Whoso sheddeth man's blood by man shall his blood be shed, and this is immediately followed by the text, And you, be fruitful and multiply."[15]

Many factors impacted the size and structure of the family in Greco-Roman Palestine. As many as 5 to 10 percent of women died in childbirth.[16] Infants and children died at high rates as well. Some demographic studies found that women in the Greco-Roman world averaged five or six children during their reproductive years, but many children died young, and more died before reaching adulthood.[17] Census records in Egypt during the Roman period show that nearly half of the population were under age twenty. Only 12 percent of females and 14 percent of males lived past age fifty.[18] According to a study of 227 Jewish burial remains in the Shephelah (the Judean foothills west of Jerusalem and the central Judean highlands) dating to the early Roman period, the average lifespan was twenty-four years.[19] Archaeological data from ancient tombs reveals a similar conclusion—nearly 50 percent of the 197 people buried in the Meiron tomb in Upper Galilee died before the age of eighteen. Of those, 70 percent died before the age of five. For women in this particular study, life expectancy was in the low twenties, and for men, around thirty. Most adults were malnourished and had iron deficiencies. Their molar teeth were worn or missing, which suggests that grain was their primary diet. They probably ate very little meat. Their skeletal remains revealed numerous fractured bones, inflamed joints, arthritic hips and shoulders, crooked backs, and instances of osteoporosis.[20] It is likely that most people experienced chronic pain. The remains of over sixty people in a first-century tomb in Jerusalem reveal the same harsh reality.[21] According to one assessment, a typical individual living at the time of Jesus had a 76 percent chance of having a living father at age ten, a 49 percent chance of having a living father at age twenty, and only a 25 percent chance of having a living father at age thirty.[22] Given these percentages, Jesus' father Joseph was probably deceased by the time Jesus had reached adulthood.

15. Babylonian Talmud Yebamot 63b, in Slotki, *Yebamoth*.
16. Ilan, *Jewish Women*, 118–19.
17. Tropper, "Children and Childhood," 299–343.
18. Bagnall and Frier, *Demography of Roman Egypt*, 75, 91.
19. Nagar and Torgee, "Biological Characteristics," 164–71.
20. Smith et al., "Skeletal Remains," 110–18.
21. Reed, *HarperCollins Visual Guide*, 10, 69.
22. Saller, *Patriarchy, Property and Death*, 49.

What does all this mean for our understanding of the pre-ministry life of Jesus? By age fourteen, or even younger, many of Jesus' peers would have died, had parents who had died, or would have already been married and moved out of their parents' home. As a child, Jesus would have witnessed rampant death, several marriages of his peers, widowhood, many childless parents, and numerous parentless children. This reality would have shaped his worldview in relation to his later ministry and his message of compassion and love for humanity, especially children.

Childhood

One of the obvious subjects that has garnered scholarly attention is agrarian life and the economy in ancient Roman Palestine. It seems that the majority of village folk worked, and often struggled, to produce more than the necessary subsistence level. Families generally produced their own crops, made their own clothes, and built and maintained their own shelters. The average village household could not produce a large surplus of resources to export. Between the needs of their own household, the needs of other households in the village, and taxes (about 20 to 35 percent annually[23]), resources were depleted. Several factors contributed to this problem, including droughts, crop diseases, bandits, and military disturbances. A season that produced a surplus would have been a tremendous boon for any household or village because it could be sold for profits or used to reduce debts.[24]

This economic reality heavily impacted children, particularly their roles in the family and their development to adulthood. This type of a subsistence-level economic lifestyle required children to work and learn a trade at significantly younger ages than children in today's society. Each able-bodied individual in the household necessarily needed to help with the production of goods and crops. Children in wealthy families, however, lived a more luxurious lifestyle and enjoyed a work-free childhood. For example, children living in aristocratic families in Jerusalem or other big cities were well-educated in Greek ("Hellenistic") customs and subsequently entered into lucrative careers, like tax farming, lending, or administrative posts in the government. Wealthy families also owned land and were closer in proximity to the power structures, and therefore had access to more resources.

In contrast, children in poorer villages were required to learn a trade and start contributing to the production of goods and services early in life, as the family's survival depended on it. To clarify, we must not assume that

---

23. Oakman, *Jesus*.
24. Tropper, "Economics of Jewish Childhood," 192–94.

agricultural families in rural Galilee, for example, were utterly destitute. One scholar, Roland Deines at the University of Nottingham, has recently challenged the long-held scholarly myth of the impoverished masses. While it is true that many families in ancient Palestine had to, by necessity, work hard and live frugally from year to year, it seems that most families had sufficient resources for their needs after paying taxes to the government and giving offerings to support the temple.[25] According to the rabbis in the Tosefta (see Introduction)—the contents of which date to as early as the late first century CE—a father was obligated to teach his sons a trade:

> What is a commandment pertaining to the father concerning the son? To circumcise him, to redeem him [if he is kidnapped], and to teach him Torah, and *to teach him a trade*, and to marry him off to a girl . . . Rabbi Judah says, "Whoever does not teach his son a trade teaches him to be a mugger."[26]

This backdrop helps place Jesus' childhood in context. His family had enough resources to survive, but Jesus would have learned how to work as a young child and would have been trained at an early age in the skill of his father. The King James Bible and other English translations suggest that Joseph and Jesus were "carpenters" (Mark 6:3; Matt 13:55). Our modern conception of carpenters is that they create and repair wooden structures, including all of their necessary smaller parts. Movies and art often depict Joseph and Jesus cutting wood beams and making furniture. The Greek word *tektōn*, however, denotes a much broader definition. A *tektōn* was a builder—one who was trained in constructing doorframes, doors, latches, beams for the roofs of houses, boxes, cabinets, plows, yokes, and boats. Many commentators have suggested that because *tektōn* refers to general builders, or craftsmen, they would have also worked with stone. In Hebrew, the word for carpenter also referred to an artisan and builder who worked with many materials, perhaps including stone. This would especially be true considering the rocky, mountainous Galilean environment in which Jesus was raised.

The reference to Jesus as a *tektōn* (Mark 6:3), or the son of a tektōn (Matt 13:55), may have been used by the authors as a literary device for their intended audiences. Indeed, the author of Matthew seems to make a point of drawing readers' attention to the word tektōn, as it is the central theme in a chiasm:

---

25. Deines, "God or Mammon," 327–86.

26. Tosefta Kiddushin 1:11, emphasis added. Translation in Neusner, *Tosefta*. Slight modifications to the translation made for understanding and emphasis.

A. Jesus comes to his *patris*, or hometown. (13:54a)
   B. The people were astounded. (13:54b)
      C. "Where did this man get this?" (13:54c)
         D. Jesus' association with tektōn. (13:55)
      C. "Where then did this man get all this?" (13:56)
   B. The people were offended. (13:57a)
A. Prophets are not accepted in their *patris*. (13:57b)[27]

The Hebrew equivalent of tektōn is *chârâsh*, which can mean artisan but also one who creates, designs, plows, and plants seed (metaphorically used by later rabbis as "sexual intercourse"), possibly pointing to God as both creator of the world and creator of human life.[28]

Another possible connection with this meaning is the mantle that fell upon Jesus at the beginning of his ministry. Near the end of Elijah's ministry, Elijah approached Elisha who was plowing with his *twelve* oxen. The Hebrew word for "plowing" is the verbal form of *chârâsh*. Elijah passed by and cast the mantle upon Elisha (1 Kgs 19:19). The elements of this episode in Mark and Matthew, presenting Jesus as a *chârâsh* (or *tektōn* in Greek) who had already chosen *twelve* disciples, may be highlighting the mantle that had fallen upon him. This interpretation is not a stretch, as the Gospels continually link Jesus with Elisha, as discussed in the next chapter.

Note also that "twelve oxen" are associated with Solomon's Temple—the molten sea was located on the backs of the twelve oxen (2 Chr 4:2–4). The authors of Mark and Matthew seem to have borrowed concepts from the Hebrew Bible in order to link Jesus with the temple, the most important institution for the Jewish people and their relationship with God. Those closest in proximity to God were the architects of the temple. In the Hebrew Bible, the Hebrew and Greek words for craftsman (*chârâsh* and *tektōn*) often directly related to those who served in various capacities in constructing the tabernacle and temple (Exod 35:35, 38:23; 2 Kgs 22:6; 1 Chr 22:15, 29:5; 2 Chr 24:12, 34:11; Ezra 3:7).

For example, the lesser-known but key figure in Exodus, Bezalel (meaning "in the shadow of God") of the tribe of Judah, was called by God to be the chief architect and craftsman (*tektōn*) of the tabernacle. In his role, Bezalel was "filled with the spirit of God, in wisdom, and in understanding, and in knowledge" (Exod 31:1–5, 35:31). God provided an assistant for Bezalel named Aholiab (meaning "Father's tabernacle"), who was given

---

27. Adapted from Davies and Allison, *Critical and Exegetical Commentary*, 451.
28. Jastrow, *Dictionary of the Targumim*, 507.

understanding and wisdom in relation to his role as a *tektōn* to construct the tabernacle furniture and the ark of the covenant (Exod 31:6–11, 35:35, 38:23). Not only was the connection made in the Hebrew Bible between *tektōn* and the tabernacle/temple, but later Jewish commentators associated *craftsman* with *scholar*, probably based on Bezalel and Aholiab being blessed with increased wisdom and knowledge. Note that later Jewish sages associated both the Hebrew and Aramaic words for craftsman (*chârâsh and naggar*, respectively) with recognized scholars, particularly those of God's word.[29]

Regarding socioeconomic status, Jesus and Joseph, as trained builders in Lower Galilee, would not have been "rich" by our modern standards, but Jesus' family would have had sufficient resources to meet their needs. Thus, our often-sensational claims that Jesus was born and raised in the "most humble of circumstances" and that he was the "poorest of the poor" are not entirely accurate. Throughout his life, Jesus, at least according to the Gospels, had connections with all classes of society, ranging from the impoverished to the wealthy. Yes, his status as a prophet figure who worked miracles was questioned by some because he was a builder's son who came from Nazareth (Matt 13:55); however, this suspicion was not raised because of Jesus' economic status but rather because of his circumstances. After all, how could such a gifted miracle worker and prophet be so ordinary—raised in Nazareth as a peasant Jew by a peasant mother and a rural builder? The concern among some seemed to be not that Jesus was from the lowest of classes but that he was too familiar—a common tradesman. Nevertheless, Jesus seemed to have been praised and respected as a teacher by many influential people, at least according to the authors of the Gospels (see, for example, Luke 20:39; John 3:1–2). It seems unlikely that he would have garnered positive attention from so many people if his family was from the lowest socioeconomic class. Jesus' childhood had prepared him to be educated (relative to other small-town tradesmen), socially savvy, and economically competent.

Another issue worth considering here is the education of Jewish children, especially boys, in ancient Palestine. Very little literary or archaeological evidence exists of a systematic and extensive primary and secondary education system in first-century Palestine. Greek and Roman children, at least those from wealthy families, received formal education in classrooms like those among modern societies. Lower-class children received no such formal training, but they learned a trade. Estimates on the percentage of

---

29. Jastrow, *Dictionary of the Targumim*, 507; Vermès, *Jesus the Jew*, 21–22.

children who attended school range from about 5 to 15 percent.[30] Consequently, very few people in the Greco-Roman world were literate. The percentage of literate peasant children in Galilee may have been on the lower end of this scale. From the dearth of primary source material available, it seems that the home was the primary educational institution for most Jewish children. Thus, the level and rigor of the child's education was contingent upon the parents' knowledge base.[31]

But what can be said of religious education? How would Jesus have learned about the stories of the Hebrew Bible and accompanying Jewish law? According to the Gospels, Jesus was highly competent in debating and teaching by age twelve:

> Now every year his parents went to Jerusalem for the festival of the Passover. And when he was twelve years old, they went up as usual for the festival. When the festival was ended and they started to return, the boy Jesus stayed behind in Jerusalem, but his parents did not know it. Assuming that he was in the group of travelers, they went a day's journey. Then they started to look for him among their relatives and friends. When they did not find him, they returned to Jerusalem to search for him. After three days they found him in the temple, sitting among the teachers, listening to them and asking them questions. And all who heard him were amazed at his understanding and his answers. (Luke 2:41–47)

Note the similarities with the experience of another well-known first-century Jew—the historian Josephus: "While still a boy, really, about fourteen years old, I used to be praised by everyone because [I was] book-loving: the chief priests and principal men of the city would often meet to understand the legal matters more precisely with my assistance." A few years later, at age sixteen, Josephus began learning from a tutor, a desert dweller named Banus, who taught Josephus for three years about various groups of Jewish philosophers (i.e., Pharisees, Sadducees, and Essenes) and how they differed in their interpretations of Jewish law.[32]

How did youths like Jesus and Josephus acquire their knowledge in the early years of adolescence? According to Jewish law, most young Jews received religious training at home. For example, Jewish parents would have been aware of the injunction given to Abraham to "charge his children

---

30. Aasgaard, *"My Beloved Brothers and Sisters,"* 45–49; Rawson, *Children and Childhood*, 146–209.

31. Tropper, "Economics of Jewish Childhood," 218.

32. Josephus, *Life* 1.2.9–12, trans. Mason.

and his household after him to keep the way of the Lord" (Gen 18:19). A few passages in Deuteronomy explicitly command parents to teach their children the laws: "Recite them to your children and talk about them when you are at home and when you are away, when you lie down and when you rise" (Deut 6:7, 11:19). Later Jews, including Jewish philosopher Philo, understood from these verses that the obligation to transmit knowledge of commandments and virtuous actions to the next generation fell upon the father.[33]

In addition to basic home-centered religious learning, many Jewish children would have received training at the local synagogue. Young Jewish males may have attended learning sessions outside of gatherings for prayers and readings of the Torah, although this is unclear. It seems that, at minimum, Jesus would have been present to hear the readings, expositions, lectures, and discussions on Scripture when he attended the synagogue with his parents. A passage in Deuteronomy mandates that children gather with their parents in public to learn: "Assemble the people—men, women, and children, as well as the aliens residing in your towns—so that they may hear and learn to fear the Lord your God and to observe diligently all the words of this law" (Deut 31:12). Jesus must have been attentive to this aspect of his education because his knowledge far exceeded his years as a youth, according to the Gospel of Luke; the teachers at the temple were impressed with his knowledge when he was twelve years old (Luke 2:41–47).

Physical Characteristics of Jewish Men

As we imagine Jesus growing into adulthood, we might wonder what he looked like and how others might have viewed him. How tall was Jesus? Obviously we cannot know for certain, but the Gospels and archaeological data provide a few kernels of information that may get us close. In the age of Jesus, adults were much shorter than are adults today. Even Goliath the ancient Philistine was shorter than most professional basketball players. Many English translations of the Bible, including the King James Version, claim that Goliath was "six cubits and a span," or about nine and a half feet tall (1 Sam 17:4)—seven inches taller than the tallest person in recorded history![34] Most of our English Bibles, however, were translated from manuscripts that postdate Jesus by almost one thousand years. The Greek translation of the Hebrew Bible (i.e., the Septuagint) and the Qumran Bible (the

---

33. Philo, *Spec. Laws*, 2:29, 236.

34. Robert P. Wadlow was 8 feet 11 inches when he died in 1940. See a short bio on the Alton Museum website.

Dead Sea Scrolls), both of which predate Jesus, claim that Goliath was four cubits and a span, or about six and a half feet tall. At this height, Goliath was extraordinary. An examination of the remains of fifty-one individuals in ancient Israel, dating to the thirteenth century BCE, revealed that the average height of an adult male was five and a half feet.[35] Similar studies concluded that in the first century CE the average height of adult males worldwide, including in the Mediterranean region, was five and a half feet.[36] Moreover, archaeologists have confirmed from the skeletal remains of 197 people in a tomb in Upper Galilee at Meiron (first century BCE to the fourth century CE) that the average adult male was five feet five inches and the average adult female was four feet ten inches.[37]

If Jesus was of average height, then he would have been around five feet five inches. The only early Christian text that mentions Jesus' size, the Acts of John, describes Jesus as being of "small stature."[38] If this tradition is true, then Jesus would have been smaller than five feet five inches, perhaps five feet two inches or five feet three inches. The Acts of John, however, postdates Jesus by about 150 years and, therefore, must be read with caution. Note, however, that when the Roman soldiers came to Gethsemane, they needed Judas to point Jesus out. In other words, Jesus was similar to his disciples in stature and physical features; he did not have a reputation for being extraordinary in height or appearance. He was just average. If Jesus really was short (or of average height) and lacking a dominant presence, then his ministry is even more impressive. Social science research has shown that people are drawn to leaders who are young, vibrant, majestic, strong, attractive, and charismatic. For example, a group of researchers accurately predicted 70 percent of US congressional elections in 2004 based solely on certain desirable physical traits of the candidates.[39] Similar studies were conducted on samples in Australia, Bulgaria, and Finland. Researchers of those studies found that the more attractive candidates, based on certain measurable variables, received more votes due to their appearance or were more likely to get elected.[40]

The author of 1 Samuel 9 demonstrates this human propensity when he proudly described King Saul, Israel's first king, as being "handsome" and

---

35. Robbins, "Tomb and Teeth."
36. Koepke and Baten, "Biological Standard of Living," 61–95.
37. Smith et al., "Skeletal Remains," 110–18.
38. Acts of John, verses 89, 90, in James, *Apocryphal New Testament*.
39. Todorov et al., "Inferences of Competence," 1623–26.
40. Berggren et al., "Looks of a Winner," 8–15; Sussman et al., "Competence Ratings in US," 771–75; King and Leigh, "Beautiful Politicians," 579–93.

taller than any man in Israel (1 Sam 9:2). King Saul's appearance matched his position in the people's eyes. Absalom, a charismatic leader who attempted to wrest the kingdom away from his father, King David, was described in a similar manner: "Now in all Israel there was no one to be praised so much for his beauty as Absalom; from the sole of his foot to the crown of his head there was no blemish in him" (2 Sam 14:25). In this context, a passage in 1 Samuel 16 is salient. When God told Samuel to find a leader from Israel to replace the tall and beautiful Saul, Samuel set his eyes on Jesse's eldest son, Eliab. Upon seeing Eliab's physical appearance, Samuel believed he would be the next king. "But the Lord said to Samuel, 'Do not look on his appearance or on the height of his stature, because I have rejected him; for the Lord does not see as mortals see; they look on the outward appearance, but the Lord looks on the heart'" (1 Sam 16:7). The fact that Jesus was able to influence many people and garner much attention without being visually attractive or possessing a commanding presence speaks volumes about the power of his message and his ability to garner attention via his healings and miraculous works.

Regarding facial features, based on texts and various ancient depictions, an average Jewish male probably had short hair and a short beard. Long hair and long beards were unlikely styles for men because of lice, heat, and maintenance difficulties.[41] Moreover, social norms discouraged long hair on a man; Paul wrote that "nature" (*physis*), meaning the social custom of the time, "teach[es] you, that, if a man have long hair, it is a shame unto him" (1 Cor 11:14). During Jesus' day and in subsequent centuries, beards were common among the intelligentsia. Wise men, teachers, and philosophers were depicted on busts as having beards.[42] The rabbis also associated beards with wisdom and maturity. Voluntary baldness and smooth-shaven faces were shunned in Israelite and later Jewish culture, as it was associated with youth (or immaturity), pagan practice, and divine disfavor (Deut 14:1; Isa 3:24, 15:2; Jer 47:5; Lev 19:27). But the rabbis loathed long, unkempt beards.[43] If Jesus followed the Greco-Roman and Jewish custom of the time, he probably had shorter hair and a short, clean beard. The contemporary popular image of the European-looking Jesus with pale skin, a mustache and beard, and long, flowing well-manicured brown hair is unrealistic for a first-century Jew from Galilee. The image of Jesus we have today was developed in the Middle Ages by European artists.

---

41. Combs and other products from the first century discovered at Qumran and Masada had "an inordinate number of lice and lice eggs on them." Reed, *HarperCollins Visual Guide*, 69.

42. Hezser, *Rabbinic Body Language*, 51–53.

43. Hezser, *Rabbinic Body Language*, 53–63.

Jewish Immersion Rituals, or "Baptism"

Ritual immersion is another aspect of first-century Jewish life in which Jesus and his Galilean contemporaries engaged. For most Christians, the topic of Jewish immersion immediately evokes the first-century Jewish figure, John the Baptist. All four Gospels mention John's baptizing activities. The word "baptism" comes from the Greek verb *baptō*, or the intensive form *baptizō*, both suggesting an immersion, a flood, or a complete drenching. This primarily applies to water, although the word is also used in relation to the Holy Spirit and fire in the Gospel of Matthew (Matt 3:11). We gather from Josephus that John was known as "John the Immerser."[44]

Later Christian tradition places this activity at a location somewhere in the Jordan River between the Sea of Galilee and the Dead Sea in the Jordan Valley. It seems more likely that John ministered in the Galilee, just north of the Sea of Galilee, in the Jordan River. According to John's Gospel, John the Baptist ministered in "Bethany across the Jordan" (John 1:28). Some early Christians, like Origen (third century), identified this "Bethany" with Bethabara, a location on the east bank of modern Jordan near the Dead Sea. However, it may be that this "Bethany" refers to the region of Bashan in the Galilee, just north of the Sea of Galilee and east of the Jordan River that flows into the Sea of Galilee. The Aramaic Targums refer to this region as *batani*, the same word as Bethany in the Gospels. Bashan, or "Batanea," in Josephus also refers to this region in the Galilee. In the Septuagint (the Greek translation of the Hebrew Bible), Bashan was also known as being "beyond the Jordan."[45]

This northern location of John's immersion activities fits better with details in the New Testament. First, two of John's disciples, Andrew and Peter, lived in the region of Bashan and joined Jesus the day after his baptism (John 1:35–44), suggesting that Jesus was not baptized sixty miles south of the Sea of Galilee near the Dead Sea, but closer to home. Jesus was in this precise area—at the southern side of Bashan in the Plain of Bethsaida near the Jordan River—in Luke when Herod Antipas thought he was John the Baptist risen from the dead (Luke 9:1–10). Moreover, John was popular throughout the Galilee region, which is why Herod Antipas had him killed. When Jesus learned that John was dead, he was concerned that the crowds in the Galilee region "were like sheep without a shepherd" (Mark 6:34). These details favor a location of John's baptizing activities, and especially the location of Jesus' immersion, just north of the Sea of Galilee in the Jordan

---

44. Josephus, *Ant.* 18.116–19.

45. For more on this argument on a northern location of John's baptizing activities, see Riesner, "Bethany Beyond," 1:703–5; Rainey and Notley, *Sacred Bridge*, 350–51.

River. Further, according to later rabbis of the second century, the Jordan River north of Lake Galilee was preferable for ritual immersion. The lower Jordan River waters (between the Sea of Galilee and the Dead Sea) were unfit because they included mixed waters of questionable purity.[46]

The author of Mark indicates that people from the whole region sought out John for baptism (1:5). According to the various Gospels, John's following include not only pedestrian Jews but also Jews with political influence, including tax collectors (Luke 3:12), Pharisees, and Sadducees (Matt 3:7). Josephus explained that John was popular with the crowds because he inspired them with his sermons. Josephus also wrote that many Jews attributed the destruction of Herod Antipas's army to divine punishment for killing John.[47] When the crowds gather, John addresses them in Luke and Matthew as follows:

> You brood of vipers! Who warned you to flee from the wrath to come? Bear fruit worthy of repentance. Do not presume to say to yourselves, "We have Abraham as our ancestor"; for I tell you, God is able from these stones to raise up children to Abraham. Even now the axe is lying at the root of the trees; every tree therefore that does not bear good fruit is cut down and thrown into the fire. (Matt 3:7–10; Luke 3:7–9)

John's "viper sermon" is intriguing. The typical assumption is that John is criticizing his audience. However, in Luke, John the Baptist addresses the *entire crowd* "that came out to be baptized by him" (3:7). It seems strange that John would verbally attack the very people who sought him out for immersion. In an attempt to explain John's seemingly strange use of language, one well-known evangelical scholar, Craig Evans (Houston Baptist University), turned to Josephus, who claimed that John was popular with the multitudes and a threat to Herod Antipas, and therefore, "It is likely, then, that John's harsh criticism was originally uttered against Israel's rulers, rather than against the people themselves."[48] Another scholar similarly argued that John the Baptist did not believe that some, including the Pharisees and Sadducees, were genuine in their motives to be immersed, so he criticized them.[49] However, based on a closer reading of the text, John's sermon does not appear to have been a "harsh criticism" but a planned speech relating to repentance and judgment, specifically intended for an audience eager to accept his baptism. Note that John's sermon is a chiasm, which features a

---

46. Mishnah Parah 8:10.
47. Josephus, *Ant.* 18.116–19.
48. Evans, "Reconstructing Jesus' Teaching," 398–99.
49. Turner, *Matthew*, 112–13.

central, salient theme—in this case, a teachable, repentant crowd (i.e., all those who "came out to be baptized by him"):

    A. Herod the tetrarch of Galilee. (Matt 3:1–2)
        B. John preached in all the region. (Matt 3:3–6)
            C. Impending judgment by fire. (Matt 3:7–9)
                D. Repentant crowd seeks John's counsel. (Matt 3:10–14)
            C. Impending judgment by fire. (Matt 3:15–17)
        B. John preached to the people. (Matt 3:18)
    A. Herod the ruler. (Matt 3:19–20)

John's speech seems to be, at least according to the author of Matthew, "instruction on readiness" rather than a harsh rebuke[50]—a "homily delivered to anyone and everyone who would come to John's baptismal site."[51] Moreover, John's usage of the word *viper* in relation to repentance and imminent judgment parallels symbolic passages in Isaiah and Jeremiah (Isa 11:8, 30:6, 59:1–5; Jer 46:22). John may have used this powerful imagery to motivate those present to participate in the purity immersion *after* having repented, not as an act of repentance itself. In other words, simply existing as a literal descendant of Abraham would not save one from being "hewn down and cast into the fire" (Luke 3:8–9). The Dead Sea Sect at Qumran similarly condemned the practice of immersion without repentance: "None of the perverse men is to enter purifying waters used by the Men of Holiness and so contact their purity. Indeed, it is impossible to be purified without first repenting of evil."[52] We might compare John's approach to an American evangelical pastor who calls his entire congregation "sinners," as all need repentance. John's symbolic rhetoric was a call for repentance intended for those who sought baptism, not a harsh rebuke to critics.

Thus, if crowds came to John specifically for baptism, it would not have been to join some new movement but to engage in a ritual for purity following repentance. This is confirmed by Josephus:

> John . . . was a good man and had exhorted the Jews to lead righteous lives, to practice justice towards their fellows and piety towards God, and so doing to join in baptism. In his view this was a necessary preliminary if baptism was to be acceptable to God. They must not employ it to gain pardon for whatever sins

---

50. Green, *Gospel of Luke*, 173–74.
51. Pickup, "Matthew's and Mark's Pharisees," 444.
52. 1QS 5:13–14. See translation in Tov, *Dead Sea Scrolls*.

they committed, but as a consecration of the body implying that the soul was already thoroughly cleansed by right behavior.[53]

Today, most Christians perform onetime immersions as an initiation into a new group—an outward performance of a new birth and inclusion into the body of Christ's followers. This type of initiation immersion, called *proselyte* baptism, was not customary among Jews in Jesus' day. There is no clear evidence that Jews in the early first century required gentiles to submit to a once-and-for-all convert baptism. No such practice is mentioned in the Hebrew Bible, the Dead Sea Scrolls, the writings of Philo, the writings of Josephus, or early rabbinic literature.[54] As for John's immersion, it seems that most scholars conclude that he conferred baptism on individuals only once. Note, however, that neither the Gospels nor Josephus makes this claim in relation to John. Jews who came to John, including Jesus, were not seeking to join a new Jewish movement by undergoing a onetime immersion. For early first-century Jews, immersion was performed periodically, and seemed to be connected to both purity and repentance.

The Hebrew Bible codified injunctions for a priest to immerse himself in water after becoming ritually impure (Lev 13–17; Num 19). Later prophets used water-cleansing imagery in association with repentance and the renewal of Israel (Isa 1:16; Ps 51:2, 7; Ezek 36:25–27). In subsequent centuries, after Jews wrested the temple and governing control of Judea and Galilee away from the Greeks in the second century BCE, immersion rituals expanded to include not just priests but perhaps a large segment of the population.[55] This phenomenon is clearly revealed in the archaeological record. In the few generations preceding Jesus, the use of full-body tubs (called *mikva'ot*) exploded all over Judea and Galilee. These have been discovered at archaeological sites at the temple, in the ruins of synagogues, in big cities and small towns, and in both wealthy and poor homes.[56] In addition, we know from Josephus and the Dead Sea Scrolls that several other figures also preformed baptisms in the wilderness. These desert washers included Josephus's teacher, Banus, who "washed frequently for purification."[57] Another wilderness group, the Essenes, also immersed themselves frequently because of purity.[58] The priestly sect at Qumran near the Dead Sea practiced

---

53. Josephus, *Ant.* 117–18, trans. Feldman, 81–83.

54. Lawrence, *Washing in Water*; Webb, *John the Baptizer and Prophet*, 122–30.

55. Deines, *Jüdische Steingefässe und pharisäische Frömmigkeit*, 16.

56. Deines, "Religious Practices," 93–96; Magen and Tsfania, *Stone Vessel Industry*; Lawrence, *Washing in Water*.

57. Josephus, *Life* 1.2.11–12, trans. Mason.

58. Josephus, *Ant.* 18.18–22; Josephus, *War* 2.119–61.

similar rituals.[59] The activities of John the Baptist were not new or revolutionary but fit within a first-century Jewish setting.

One possible rationale for this expansion of immersion rituals in the first and second centuries BCE is that God's Spirit is poured out upon his people if they are pure (Ezek 36:25–27). The way to purity is through the cleansing of the soul by repentance that culminates in a purity immersion. A few notable first-century Jews outside of the New Testament—namely, Rabbi Akiva and Josephus—also associated immersion with repentance.[60] Ideally, for many first-century Jews the process of repentance included both the inward change of heart and the outward manifestation of immersion. When Jews approached John to be immersed, they did so as an act of repentance (see Acts 19:3–4). John's message of repentance fits with the expanded phenomenon of immersion during this period. John's concern, however, as revealed in his "viper sermon" (Matt 3:7–10; Luke 3:7–9) was that too many people were relying on immersion rituals without having "a broken and a contrite heart" (Ps 51:17; see also Ps 34:18 and Isa 57:15). Some had missed the point, as is often the case with any group who performs a ritual frequently.

Similar to John, the Dead Sea Sect at Qumran condemned a reliance on immersion without a repentant heart. Consider the following instruction for all members of the community regarding repentance (notice the similarity to John's overall focus on repentance):

> Anyone who refuses to enter [the society of God], preferring to continue in his willful heart, shall not [be initiated] . . . inasmuch as his soul has rejected the disciplines foundational to knowledge: the laws of righteousness. He lacks the strength to repent . . . Surely, he plows in the muck of wickedness, so defiling stains would mar his repentance. Yet he cannot be justified by what his willful heart declares lawful, preferring to gaze on darkness rather than the ways of light . . . Ceremonies of atonement cannot restore his innocence, neither cultic waters his purity. *He cannot be sanctified by baptism in oceans and rivers, nor purified by mere ritual bathing* . . . Through an upright and humble attitude his sin may be covered, and by humbling himself before all God's laws his flesh can be made clean. *Only thus can he really receive the purifying waters and be purged by the cleansing flow.*[61]

---

59. Many scholars have argued that the Qumran community was Essene. Other scholars have disagreed. For a discussion on this issue and the Qumran community in general, see Schiffman, *Reclaiming the Dead Sea Scrolls* and *Qumran and Jerusalem*.

60. Mishnah Yoma 8.9; Josephus, *Ant.* 18.5.2.

61. 1QS 3:1–9. This translation is from the following, with minor bracketed

To be sure, the immersion ritual does not seem to be tied exclusively to the act of repentance, or even primarily to the act of repentance, but more so to purity, which at times requires repentance prior to the purity immersion. In other words, a penitent state must be achieved before performing the purity ritual immersion, per the aforementioned quotes from the Dead Sea Scrolls and Josephus.

The Baptism(s) of Jesus

We now turn to Jesus' immersion. As a Jew, Jesus would have performed this baptism ritual frequently, not just once by the hand of John the Baptist. He would have immersed himself in the *mikva'ot* on occasions related to both purity and repentance. He would have immersed himself before entering the temple complex. First-century Jewish philosopher, Philo of Alexandria, confirms that this practice was performed not only by priests but by the populace.[62] Other references reveal that nonpriestly Jews immersed themselves for various purity reasons, as well as before eating and praying.[63] The Gospel of John assumes a common practice of immersion in the Last Supper episode (John 13:10).

Most Christians today, especially those who are unfamiliar with early Jewish practices, see Jesus as being baptized for reasons familiar to later Christians: that Jesus was baptized to fulfill a commandment and to set an example. Note, however, that repentance immersion, as viewed by modern Christianity, was not a commandment for Jews. Such a commandment is found nowhere in the Hebrew Bible; for Jesus, "fulfill[ing] all righteousness" (Matt 3:15) would not have come to pass simply by following a specific commandment of immersion. The commandment for converts to be baptized in the name of the Father, Son, and Holy Spirit was a post-resurrection injunction that Jesus gave to his followers, at least according to the author of Matthew (Matt 28:19). In that case, Jesus seemed to expand early immersion practices from an exclusively Israelite ritual to a far-reaching repentance and initiation ritual to all believers in him. In other words, according to the author of Matthew, Jesus seemed to appropriate the Jewish custom of frequent immersion and adapt it as a one-time initiation ritual for his post-resurrection movement.

---

revisions and added emphasis in italics: Wise et al., *Dead Sea Scrolls*, 119.

62. See *Quod Deus Immutabilis Sit* ("On the Unchangeableness of God"), 7–8; and *De Specialibus Legibus* ("The Special Laws"), in Philo, *Works of Philo*, trans. Yonge, 1.269.

63. Webb, *John the Baptizer*, 110–11.

For Jesus himself, however, immersion was different; it was not a one-time initiation ritual. Jesus was a Jew. His purpose in being immersed was not to follow a specific baptism commandment or to "set an example" for future gentile sinners. According to the Gospels, Jesus did not minister to gentiles; thus, it would seem strange for him to start his Jewish ministry by "setting an example" of baptism for future gentiles. Any exemplary action of Jesus for future followers may be incidental, but it does not seem to have been his purpose. His primary objective as a Jew, given the context of the time period, would have been to maintain ritual purity and to participate in collective repentance, or rather in *corporate repentance*. Corporate repentance is foreign to us today, but it was salient in ancient Israel. It is the collective process of repentance; everyone periodically engages in repentance immersions, not necessarily for personal sins, but for the sins of Israel. Our modern world is individualistic. Christians often talk about God in terms of a personal, individual relationship. In ancient Israel, however, the prophets emphasized God's relationship with the entire house of Israel. While the prophets did not completely abandon repentance for individuals,[64] their greater emphasis was on the entire nation. The Hebrew Bible is replete with imagery portraying the marriage relationship between God and Israel.[65] The prophets warned that wickedness would bring judgment, not only upon guilty individuals, but upon *all of Israel*. For example, a passage in Deuteronomy explains that if Israel observes God's commandments, all will receive rain for their fields and livestock. If, however, they worship other gods, the God of Israel will close up the heavens (Deut 11:13–21). Every member of Israel would be impacted by divine reward or punishment, not just the individual righteous persons or the individual wicked persons. While lamenting Israel's rejection of repentance, the prophet Amos warned that God would do the same "to you, O Israel" that he did to Sodom and Gomorrah; therefore, "prepare to meet your God, O Israel!" (Amos 4:6–13). In Jeremiah, God called Israel to repentance: "Have you seen what she did, that faithless one, Israel, how she went up on every high hill and under every green tree, and played the whore there?" (7:6–24).[66]

Jesus was baptized, according to the author of Matthew, in order to "fulfill all righteousness" (Matt 3:15), meaning that he sought to participate

---

64. See 1 Kgs 21:27–29; 2 Sam 3:39, 24:10; Hag 1:12, 14; Hos 2–4; Isa 1:9; Job 42:6; Zech 8:6–12.

65. Jer 2:2, 2:32, 3:6–14, 3:20, 31:32; Isa 50:1, 54:5–8; Hos 1:2, 2:2, 2:7, 2:14–20, 3:1–3, 9:1; Joel 1:8; Ezek 16:8–14, 32–34, 43, 59–62.

66. For more references to corporate, or national, repentance, see Num 21:7; 2 Chr 15:8–15, 30:6–9; 1 Kgs 23:1–7; Judg 10:15–16; Jer 18:7–8; 1 Sam 7:3–4; Ezra 10:1, 10–12.

with all of his fellow Jews in corporate repentance so all of Israel would be spared divine judgment. Note that repentance is the *most frequent commandment and most emphasized theme* in the Hebrew Bible. "Fulfilling righteousness" is directly associated with repentance. Note also that executing righteousness in the land of Israel was a characteristic of the messiah in earlier Israelite texts. Jeremiah, for example, included this detail in his sections on the healing and restoration (i.e., repentance) of Israel (Jer 23:5–6, 33:15–16).

Another important issue worth considering is, if Jesus performed frequent immersion rituals, why then did the authors of the Gospels only highlight the immersion at the beginning of his ministry? It seems that this particular immersion was not *the* baptism of Jesus, but *a* baptism of Jesus. Why then did the authors of Mark, Matthew, and Luke place such emphasis on a ritual that numerous Jews performed on numerous occasions? How would this account of Jesus' immersion, such a common ritual, resonate with the target Jewish audiences of the Gospels? The answer, I propose, is that the Gospel writers focused on this particular immersion at the beginning of his ministry in order highlight his authority. They attempted to establish Jesus' authority by (1) connecting him to John the Baptist (because John was highly respected in the early first century per the Gospels and Josephus), (2) connecting him to the prophet Elisha, (3) connecting him to Moses, (4) connecting him to Joshua, and (5) highlighting the heavenly voice at the event. All of these connections in the story were meant to demonstrate unmistakably to a Jewish audience that Jesus had divinely approved authority. We will expound on all of these connections in the following pages and in the next chapter.

How would first – and second-century Jews have interpreted or contextualized the immersion story of Jesus? Obviously, we will not attempt to specifically answer these questions and identify exactly how "Jews" would have interpreted the Jesus-baptism story; we cannot possibly fulfill such a task. Nevertheless, these questions are meant to sensitize us to the sorts of issues that were important for Jews at the time of Jesus, based on their own sacred writings and a host of early Jewish texts. These are important questions to entertain, considering that the large majority of Jesus' first-generation followers were Jews.

The Opening of Heaven

Only two verses in each of the Synoptic Gospels relate details about Jesus' immersion; however, these few verses are pregnant with imagery pointing back to earlier Israelite writings. The first detail in the account is that the heavens open while Jesus is standing in the water (Matt 3:16; Mark 1:10; Luke 3:21). In Jewish Scripture, the "opening of heaven" is associated with the coming of the messiah and the end times (Ezek 1:1; Ps 102:26; Isa 64:1; Hag 2:6). Not only does this account point to Jesus as the messiah for the early Christians, but it may also point to Jesus as *Yahweh* ("Jehovah" in our modern rendition of the title), the God of Israel himself. All four Gospels link John the Baptist to Isaiah 40:3: "The voice of one crying in the wilderness: Prepare the way of the Lord" (Matt 3:3; Mark 1:2–3; Luke 3:4; John 1:23). Jesus subsequently arrives on the scene to be baptized. Thus, if John the Baptist is viewed by the authors of the Gospels as the "one" in Isaiah 40:3, then the subsequent verses would have pointed to Jesus as Yahweh:

> O Jerusalem, herald of good tidings, lift it up, do not fear; say to the cities of Judah, "Here is your God!" See, the Lord God comes with might, and his arm rules for him; his reward is with him, and his recompense before him. He will feed his flock like a shepherd; he will gather the lambs in his arms, and carry them in his bosom, and gently lead the mother sheep. (Isa 40:9–11)

Jewish scholars, and perhaps even most Christian scholars, would not say that this Isaiah passage is connected with Jesus, but it was so for early Christians. The authors of the Gospels also seem to associate the *opened-heavens* detail with a new exodus, referring to Moses and the birth of Israel. For example, Isaiah wrote about God's mercy upon Israel and used Moses and the exodus as a point of reference:

> Then they remembered the days of old, of Moses his servant. Where is the one who brought them up out of the sea with the shepherds of his flock? Where is the one who put within them his holy spirit, who caused his glorious arm to march at the right hand of Moses, who divided the waters before them to make for himself an everlasting name, who led them through the depths? (Isa 63:11–13)

Notice the similarities with Isaiah 40, which mentions a shepherd leading his flock. After Isaiah comments about Moses's and God's act of saving Israel, he adds, "O that you would tear open the heavens and come down" (64:1). Of the three Gospels that mention the opening of the heavens at Jesus' baptism, only the author of Mark uses the word *tear* (1:10), the same word used in Isaiah. A Jew hearing or reading this account in the first or second centuries would recall Isaiah's prophecy and remember Moses and the birth of Israel. The parallel between Jesus and Moses is clear. Yahweh saved Israel and led its people through the waters into the wilderness for forty years. Jesus came to save Israel, a mission that began with the opening of heaven as he came through the waters and was immediately led by the Spirit into the wilderness for forty days (Matt 4:1–11; Mark 1:12–13; Luke 4:1–13). By using language about the heavens opening while referring to elements in Isaiah 40 and 63, the authors of the Gospels were emphasizing to their Jewish readers that Jesus is both a new Moses and a divine figure who had come to save Israel.

I must also mention here that this baptism account not only positions Jesus as a new Moses but connects Jesus with both Joshua and Elisha. As a new Moses, Jesus is portrayed as a successor to Moses. And who originally succeeded Moses? Joshua. Thus, it is fitting that the angel Gabriel commands Joseph and Mary to name their son *Joshua*—"Jesus" being the Greek form of the Hebrew "Joshua" (Matt 1:21; Luke 1:31). Just as the Jordan River is parted for Joshua at the beginning of his ministry (Josh 3:16–17), so too are the heavens parted while another Joshua (i.e., "Jesus") stands in the Jordan River at the beginning of his ministry. Note that the author of the book of Joshua explicitly draws a connection between Joshua and Moses: "This day I will begin to exalt you in the sight of all Israel, so that they may know that I will be with you as I was with Moses" (Josh 3:7). The authors of the Gospels seem to be making the same Moses connection with their own Joshua. We also notice that just as God *speaks to* Joshua and exalts him "this day" at the Jordan River, God *speaks to* another Joshua and exalts him "today" at the Jordan River: "You are my Son" (Mark 1:11), which is a direct quote from Psalm 2: "You are my son, *today* I have begotten you (v. 7).

The Jordan River is also parted for Elisha at the beginning of his ministry (2 Kgs 2:13–14). We will explore in the next chapter the depth of the Jesus-Elisha parallel (and also the Jesus-Moses parallel); however, we should stress just how deliberate the authors of the Gospels were in their Joshua-Elisha-Jesus comparisons. Each of these figures are successors of a great prophet. Each of these figures are situated within a succession narrative that occurs at the Jordan River. Joshua succeeded Moses at the Jordan River, Elisha succeeded Elijah at the Jordan River, and Jesus succeeded John the Baptist at the Jordan River. The connection between Joshua, Elisha, and Jesus is even stronger considering that their names are all based on the Hebrew root letters (*yod, shin, ayin*) meaning "he redeems." These three scenes of initiation are about authority, which is why the authors of the Gospels strategically composed Jesus' baptism story to help make the case to their

Jewish audience that Jesus has authority, just as did Moses, Joshua, Elijah, and Elisha.[67]

The Spirit Descending

The next detail in the account of Jesus' immersion is the presence of God's Spirit (Matt 3:16; Mark 1:10; Luke 3:22; John 1:32). After the heavens open, God's Spirit descends upon Jesus and then leads him to the wilderness for forty days. Again we refer back to Isaiah, where God's Spirit descends upon Israel after they "came up out of the sea" and are saved from Egypt (63:11). The authors of both Mark and Matthew employ this same language—after "[Jesus] came up out of the water," the Spirit descends upon him (Matt 3:16; Mark 1:10). Like Isaiah, other ancient Jewish commentators posited that God's Spirit descended upon Israel while they crossed the water.[68] A Jewish text predating the birth of Jesus by a few generations, Testament of Judah, presents the expectation of a man from the seed of Jacob who will walk with the sons of men in "gentleness and humility." This man will have no sin, and the "heavens will be opened upon him to pour out the Spirit."[69] The Spirit descending upon Jesus while he is *in* the water would have been familiar imagery to Jews.

The Gospels not only link Jesus with Moses and a new Exodus, signaling the birth of a new era, but they also seem to associate Jesus with the Creation as presented in Genesis. When God created the Earth, his Spirit descends and hovers over the waters (Gen 1:2). God then says, "Let there be light" (Gen 1:3). The Spirit resting upon Jesus when he comes out of the water signals a new creation. The parallel with light is also clear. God brings light into the world immediately after his Spirit descends upon the waters at creation; God provides the world with light again just after the Spirit descends upon Jesus. It is Jesus himself who is the "light of the world," according to the author of John (John 8:12, 9:5, 12:36).

All four Gospels mention a dove in relation to the Spirit: the "Spirit descending like a dove" (Matt 3:16; Mark 1:10; Luke 3:22; John 1:32). Similarly, other ancient Jewish texts compared the Spirit descending—literally, "swooping down" or "hovering" (Hebrew *rachaph*)—to a dove. One Jewish text in reference to the creation story in Genesis states, "And the spirit of

---

67. For a more detailed discussion of the three succession narratives of Joshua, Elisha, and Jesus, see Havrelock, *River Jordan*, 135–74.

68. For example, see Exodus Mekilta 14:13.

69. Testament of Judah 24:2, see translation in Charlesworth's *Old Testament Pseudepigrapha*, 1:801.

God hovered over the face of the waters like a dove which hovers over her young without touching them."[70] An Aramaic targum, a translation with some interpolations of the Hebrew Bible, compared the voice of the Spirit to the voice of a turtledove.[71] Rabbi Yossi, an ancient sage, also compared the *echo* of God's voice to the cooing of a dove.[72] It is to this "echo" that we now turn our attention.

The Voice from Heaven

All three Synoptic Gospels state that a "voice came from heaven" after the Spirit descended upon Jesus (Matt 3:17; Mark 1:11; Luke 3:22). How would a Jew in antiquity have interpreted this detail? Several Jewish texts suggest that the voice from heaven is only heard occasionally and is a mere echo of God's voice. The term for this "echo," or distant divine message, is *bat qol*, literally "daughter of a voice." In the Tosefta (see Introduction)—an early Jewish text dated to a few centuries after Jesus but which supposedly preserves traditions and sayings from earlier generations—rabbis explained why God's Spirit and prophecy withdrew from Israel and were substituted by a heavenly echo:

> When the latter prophets died, that is, Haggai, Zechariah, and Malachi, then the Holy Spirit came to an end in Israel. But even so, they made them hear [Heavenly messages] through an echo. Sages gathered together in the upper room of the house of Guria in Jericho, and a heavenly echo came forth and said to them, "There is a man among you who is worthy to receive the Holy Spirit, but this generation is unworthy of such an honor." They all set their eyes upon Hillel the Elder.[73]

The Hebrew Bible preserves many instances when God communicated with prophets through the Bat Qol, the least authoritative form of divine communication among the prophets of old. The later rabbis maintained that after the last prophets died, God's Spirit and prophecy were withdrawn. Some Jews at the time of Jesus eagerly anticipated the return of God's Spirit upon Israel. Through meaningful, widespread repentance, as well as the arrival of a prophet or messianic figure, God's Spirit and prophecy would return.

---

70. Babylonian Talmud Hagigah 15a, trans in Abrahams, *Hagigah*. See also Genesis Rabbah 2:4.

71. Alexander, *Targum of Canticles*, 2:12.

72. Babylonian Talmud Berakot 3a.

73. Tosefta Sotah 13.3, trans in Neusner, *Tosefta*, 1:885; for similar accounts, see Babylonian Talmud Sanhedrin 11a; Jerusalem Talmud Sotah 24b.

In the meantime, communication between God and man was confined to the Bat Qol. Notice in the account above that the heavenly voice proclaimed Hillel the Elder—a contemporary of Jesus and probably the most well-known postbiblical sage in Jewish history—as being worthy to receive the Holy Spirit. Also note the similarities between the accounts of Jesus' baptism and the declaration of Hillel the Elder's worthiness. Both accounts contain the Holy Spirit and the Bat Qol, and both accounts proclaim divine favor upon the central individual in the story: Jesus and Hillel.[74]

We conclude from numerous examples in ancient Jewish literature that the purpose of the Bat Qol was to bestow divine approval upon an individual or upon a legal position under debate among the rabbis. For example, two rabbinic schools, the school of Hillel and the school of Shammai, debate for three years about which school best established Jewish law. The Bat Qol proclaimed that both schools taught the "words of the Living God" but that *halakha* (Jewish law) must follow the rulings of the school of Hillel.[75] Elsewhere in early Jewish literature, the Bat Qol spoke in favor of Rabbi Eliezer, whose associates debated him on every issue. The heavenly voice said, "What have you with Rabbi Eliezer, who the law is like him in every place?"[76] When the beloved, first-century rabbi Akiva was tortured with iron combs and executed by the Romans for openly teaching the Torah, the Bat Qol proclaimed, "Happy are you Rabbi Akiva, for you are destined for life in the World to Come."[77] Rabbi Hanina ben Doza, a first-century teacher who lived about ten miles north of Jesus' hometown of Nazareth, was famous for his ability to heal people. Rabbi Yehudah said about Rabbi Hanina, "Every day the *Bat Qol* goes forth and is heard declaring: 'The whole world draws its sustenance because of the merit of Hanina my son.'"[78] Similar to the case of Hanina, the Bat Qol referred to Jesus as "my Son," both at his baptism and his transfiguration (Matt 3:17, 17:5; Mark 1:11, 9:7; Luke 3:22, 9:35). Notice that the author of Luke refers to the heavenly proclamation as coming not from God, but from the voice: "when *the voice* had spoken" (Luke 9:35–36; emphasis added). Obviously the message was generally understood to have come from God, but the Gospels' description is consistent with ancient Jewish descriptions of the Bat Qol.[79]

---

74. For similar accounts, see Babylonian Talmud Sanhedrin 11a; Babylonian Talmud Sotah 48b; Jerusalem Talmud Sotah 13:2.

75. Babylonian Talmud Erubin 13b, trans. in Slotki, *Erubin*.

76. Babylonian Talmud Baba Mesia 59b, trans. in Freedman, *Baba Mezia*.

77. Babylonian Talmud Berakot 61b, trans in *William Davidson Talmud*.

78. Babylonian Talmud Taanit 24b, trans. in Rabbinowitz, *Taanith*.

79. It must be noted that many of the sources about the *bat qol* are posited in the Talmud, which postdates Jesus by at least four hundred years; however, earlier texts also discuss the *bat qol*, including Josephus, a first-century author.

At Jesus' immersion, the heavenly echo proclaimed, "You are my Son, the Beloved: with you I am well pleased" (Matt 3:17; Mark 1:11; Luke 3:22). Jews educated in the Torah would have recalled a couple of parallel passages in the Hebrew Bible. As briefly mentioned above, the first comes from Psalm 2, where the Lord says to his anointed, "You are my son; today I have begotten you" (2:7). We know that Jesus' first-generation Jewish followers connected this verse to Jesus because Paul, according to Acts, states as much: "And we bring you the good news that what God promised to our ancestors he has fulfilled for us, their children, by raising Jesus; as also it is written in the second psalm, 'You are my Son; today I have begotten you'" (Acts 13:32–33). Regarding the second phrase—"in whom I am well pleased"—Jews would have recalled Isaiah 42, where God states, "Here is my servant, whom I uphold, my chosen, *in whom my soul delights*; I have put my *spirit upon him*" (42:1; emphasis added). The authors of the Gospels likely utilized, or emphasized, these messianic passages to impress upon their Jewish readers that Jesus had authority and was the fulfillment of Hebrew prophecy.

Takeaways

To sum up, Jesus' childhood and young adulthood would likely have been typical of other Jewish males. Jesus likely lived in a conventional Galilean home with a few bedrooms, a courtyard, and a place on the main floor to store food and keep animals. He would have seen rampant death as a child, both among his peers and their parents. Many of his peers would have married early. Jesus would have learned to work and produce at an early age. As he grew he would have learned a trade from his father. Jesus would have also received an education from his parents and at the synagogue. As a child and young adult, Jesus learned the Torah like a Jew, prayed like a Jew, ate like a Jew, worked like a Jew, and performed frequent immersion like a Jew. A consideration of the social circumstances of Jesus' life help modern interpreters understand Jesus within a realistic, human, Jewish experience, as opposed to seeing him as a stoic, wooden, bland, boring, earthly representation of God portrayed in countless movies. I encourage my students to set aside this mental image of the heavenly Christ and to consider the human Jesus as a means to appreciate his actions and teachings.

Regarding Jesus' baptism narratives, John the Baptist's activities as a repentance immerser were not fringe or new but can be situated within a normative Jewish context. Jesus' association with John the Baptist and the accounts of his immersion endeavor to leave little room for misunderstanding, according to the Gospels, that the Holy Spirit did return to Israel and fell upon its new Moses and savior, Jesus of Nazareth. The authors of the Gospels related the baptism episode in a way that would point to Jesus' authority, as evidenced in the appearance of both John the Baptist and the Bat Qol, as well as the connection to Moses, Joshua, and Elisha. Jews in antiquity who heard or read about John the Baptist and the accounts of Jesus' immersion would have been positioned to recognize the connections with their prophets and sacred texts.

It is clear, based on the material in this first chapter, that the authors of the original traditions about Jesus, and the authors of the Gospels themselves, were painstakingly deliberate in how they framed various segments of Jesus' life and ministry. Their goal was not merely to preserve information about Jesus, but to posit in unmistakable terms to their largely Jewish audience that he is the messiah and Israel's savior.

Chapter Two

Establishing Authority
Jesus as Moses and Elisha

IN THIS CHAPTER AND the subsequent three chapters (chapters 3–5) we will explore Jesus' major roles, how the Gospels present them, and how Jesus seemed to fit within a first-century Jewish context in relation to these roles. For our purposes of understanding Jesus within his Jewish context, we are not asking who he *really* was; that is a matter of either faith or historical Jesus scholarship (i.e., what Jesus really said and did). Rather, we are asking, what did Jesus' opponents, peers, and followers—including the authors of the Gospels and their early Jewish readers—view him as?

Jesus studies scholars have posited numerous ideas on who Jesus was historically: a prophet, a messianic candidate, a miracle worker, a teacher, a peasant, a revolutionary, or a zealot.[1] Pieter Craffert (Chair of the Department of New Testament at the University of South Africa in Pretoria), argues that any one of these categories alone does not do justice to Jesus because of the multifaceted nature of his ministry. Jesus cannot be understood within *only* the context of "prophets" or "messiahs" or "revolutionaries" or "sages." Consequently, Craffert labeled Jesus as a "Galilean shamanic figure" because shamans encompass multiple and disparate roles and functions. Craffert analyzed the shaman model cross-culturally, meaning he identified commonalities of similar figures at various times and in various places throughout history. These data allow social scientists to develop a model

---

1. For further discussions and examples, see Aslan, *Zealot*; Evans, *Fabricating Jesus*; Chilton, *Rabbi Jesus*; Ehrman, *Jesus*; Crossan, *Jesus*; Crossan, *Historical Jesus*; Meier, *Marginal Jew*.

with which they can analyze Jesus (or any other "holy man" figure)[2]—a model that can provide insights into certain characteristics and functions of these types of figures. The "shamanic complex" model used by Craffert is defined as a set of "beliefs and practices revolving around a religious practitioner that makes use of alternate states of consciousness."[3] In other words, these religious specialists often experience states of consciousness outside the normal functions of life that allow them to connect with the spiritual realm. Consequently, these figures act as divine mediators (e.g., prophets), visionaries, interpreters of dreams, healers, and controllers of spirits (e.g., exorcists). Shamanic figures are not private mystics who live life in seclusion; both their deeds and their superior spiritual knowledge benefit their communities. A shaman is—simultaneously—the community's healer, mystic, social worker, priest, seer, prophet, sage, historian, and teacher. Shamans are also known to control the weather and natural elements. Shamans often function within "small-scale societies, [and] their activities increase when the society comes into stress, for instance, starvation, poor hunting, bad weather, and other crises."[4]

Perhaps, then, the *shamanic complex model* provides one of the best frameworks to analyze Jesus because he acted in many different roles within his community. I do not intend to suggest that this entire chapter, as well as the next few chapters on Jesus' roles, will deal in-depth with the *shamanic complex model*. I only introduce this model to illustrate that Jesus must be studied within more than one cultural context because, like other shamans throughout history, Jesus fulfilled *many roles* within a small-scale society. When Jesus asked some of his followers, "Who do people say that I am?" and "Who do you say I am?" the answers varied: John the Baptist, Elijah, an ancient prophet, or the messiah (Luke 9:19–21, Mark 8:28–30, Matt 16:13–20). Several opinions about Jesus' primary identity circulated after his lifetime (and perhaps during his lifetime), and we will try to analyze these various identities.

In this chapter specifically, we will examine the comparisons of Jesus to Moses and Elisha in both the Hebrew Scriptures and in Jewish lore in order to highlight Jesus' roles as prophet and miracle worker. What do these comparisons tell us about how the Gospel writers viewed Jesus? Moreover, how might first – and second-century Jews have interpreted these traditions if they had encountered them? Moses and Elisha feature prominently in the Gospels and Acts. Most readers would agree that Moses is most prominent;

   2. Craffert, *Life of a Galilean Shaman*, 135–209.
   3. Craffert, "Shamanism," 151.
   4. Craffert, "Shamanism," 152–53.

he appeared to Jesus on the Mount of Transfiguration and is mentioned fifty-seven times in the Gospels and Acts. In contrast, the Elisha connection is foreign to most casual readers, particularly because he is mentioned only once (Luke 4:27). The prominence of these two prophets in the Gospels extends far past explicit references. They are embedded into the story of Jesus through typology and allusions.

Moses Types in Jewish Tradition

Moses is, without question, the most prominent or revered biblical figure for early Jews. Numerous texts engage the Moses stories and offer various interpretations.[5] This is no surprise since Moses was credited with freeing the ancestors of the Jews from bondage and with giving them their law. Further, by the first century CE, the following prophecy in Deuteronomy was ringing loudly in their ears: "The Lord our God will raise up for you a prophet like me [i.e., Moses] from among your own people" (Deut 18:15, 18). When the Jewish freedom fighters took back the temple from the Greeks in 164 BCE and subsequently established an independent Jewish state, they anticipated the coming of "a prophet," probably referring to Deuteronomy 18:15.[6] Similarly, the Dead Sea sect at Qumran also awaited the coming of a prophet like Moses.[7]

Moses was such a revered figure for early Jews that they spoke of him in mythical and exalted terms. The first-century Jewish philosopher Philo of Alexandria maintained that Moses was the greatest figure in the history of humankind—that in accordance with divine providence, he "was both a king and a lawgiver, and a high priest and a prophet, and because in each office he displayed the most eminent wisdom and virtue."[8] Josephus similarly described Moses as one who "surpassed in understanding all men that ever lived" and as the greatest "prophet" who ever lived, "insomuch that in all his utterances one seemed to hear the speech of God Himself."[9] A second-century BCE Jewish dramatist from Alexandria, Ezekiel the Tragedian, wrote the following about Moses:

> I [Moses] had a vision of a great throne on the top of Mount Sinai and it reached till the folds of heaven. A noble man was

---

5. Allison, *New Moses*, 1–136.
6. 1 Macc 4:46, 14:41.
7. See 4Q175, 1:1–8, in Wise et al., *Dead Sea Scrolls*, 259.
8. *On the Life of Moses II*, 2–3, in Philo, *Works of Philo*, trans. Yonge, 491.
9. Josephus, *Ant.* 4.8.49, trans. Thackeray and Marcus.

sitting on it, with a crown and a large scepter in his left hand. He beckoned to me with his right hand, so I approached and stood before the throne. He gave me the scepter and instructed me to sit on the great throne. Then he gave me a royal crown and got up from the throne. I beheld the whole earth all around and saw beneath the earth and above the heavens. A multitude of stars fell before my knees and I counted them all.[10]

This text preserves an early Jewish tradition that Moses acquired a certain level of divine qualities. Later, in the first century CE, another text perpetuated this tradition. The Testament of Moses, probably dating to some time during the lifetime of Jesus or shortly after, describes Moses as "the divine prophet for the whole earth, the perfect teacher in the world."[11] Renowned Jewish scholar Daniel Boyarin at the University of California, Berkeley, asked, "If Moses could be God in one version of a Jewish religious imagination, then why not Jesus in another?"[12]

Jews in antiquity compared several prominent figures to Moses. Dale Allison, scholar at Princeton Theological Seminary, identified at least nine such individuals in the Hebrew Bible.[13] Later, the rabbis compared Moses to their three most preeminent sages, Hillel the Elder, Yohanan ben Zakkai, and Rabbi Akiva. For instance, according to Deuteronomy 34:7, Moses lived 120 years. Likewise, according to the rabbis, each of these three figures lived 120 years, comprising three periods of 40 years. Note that two of them were contemporaries of Jesus. A rabbinic text based on Deuteronomy, Sifre Deuteronomy, provides the following explanation:

> [Moses] was one of the four who died at the age of one hundred and twenty: Moses, Hillel the Elder, Yohanan ben Zakkai, and Rabbi Akiva. Moses was in Egypt for forty years, in Midian for forty years, and led Israel for forty years. Hillel the Elder went up from Babylonia (to the Land of Israel) at the age of forty, attended upon the sages for forty years, and led Israel for forty years. Rabbi Yohanan ben Zakkai was in business for forty years, attended upon the sages for forty years, and led Israel for forty

---

10. Jacobson, *Exagoge of Ezekiel*, 55. Ezekiel's writings are preserved in the works of Christian historian Eusebius (d. 340 CE).

11. Testament of Moses 11:16. See translation in Priest, "Testament of Moses," 919–34, esp. 934.

12. Boyarin, *Jewish Gospels*, 72.

13. Joshua, Gideon, Samuel, David, Elijah, Josiah, Ezekiel, Jeremiah, and Ezra. Allison, *New Moses*, 23–65.

years. Rabbi Akiva was a shepherd for forty years, learned (Torah) for forty years, and led Israel for forty years.[14]

A few other rabbinic texts discuss Hillel the Elder in relation to Moses. For example, in the Babylonian Talmud (see Introduction), a group of rabbis met at a home in Jericho. While in their meeting, the voice from heaven (Bat Qol) declared that one among them was worthy to have the presence of God rest upon him "as it did on Moses." Then all the sages "set their eyes on Hillel the Elder."[15] Another rabbinic passage explains that Hillel had eighty students (two sets of forty), the best of whom were "worthy to have the Divine Spirit resting upon them, *as it did upon Moses* our Master."[16]

Jesus as Moses

The authors of the New Testament, a largely Jewish corpus of texts, show a similar affinity for Moses, particularly in relation to Jesus. They too speak about a prophet like Moses who is to come. Early in the Gospel of John, Philip told Nathanael that he had found that person, referring to Jesus, "about whom Moses in the law and also the prophets wrote" (John 1:45). Later in John, the crowd which Jesus miraculously fed said, "This is indeed the prophet who is to come into the world" (John 6:14, cf. John 7:40; Acts 3:22). In Matthew, when Jesus entered the east gate of the temple complex and people asked, "Who is this?" the crowd with Jesus said, "This is *the prophet*" (Matt 21:10–11, emphasis added). The Gospels' authors latched onto the Moses traditions to illustrate that Jesus was not only a prophet and miracle worker but also a lawgiver and a figure who possessed unusual divine insight and qualities. Although Moses-Jesus comparisons are present in all four Gospels, Matthew is the most Moses-centric. The following are several examples of Moses-Jesus parallels.

The Gospel of John claims that John the Baptist did not know Jesus prior to his baptism (1:31–33). The author of Luke, however, claims that John and Jesus were relatives and that their mothers had a close relationship (Luke 1:36). The author of Luke wanted to connect John and Jesus by familial relationship, whereas the author of John wanted to dissociate them. Perhaps members of a community of Jesus' believers in the late first century who favored the Gospel of John (including its author) were embarrassed

---

14. Deuteronomy Sifre, 357. This translation is from *William Davidson Talmud*. Text altered slightly for readability.
15. Babylonian Talmud Sanhedrin 11a, in Schachter, *Sanhedrin*.
16. Babylonian Talmud Sukkah 28a, in Slotki, *Sukkah*; emphasis added.

that their messiah and their God sought immersion from John the Baptist. The author of John, therefore, removed any association between Jesus and John the Baptist prior to Jesus' baptism. Note that John's Gospel does not even mention Jesus' baptism. It may be that the author of Luke overstated the familial relationship between John and Jesus in order to connect Jesus to Moses. How so? Jesus' mother, Mary, shares her name with Moses' sister (Exod 15:20–21, 26:59), and John's mother, Elizabeth, shares her name with Moses' sister-in-law, Aaron's wife (Exod 6:23). Thus, just as the offspring of Mary and Elizabeth of the Hebrew Bible were first cousins, so too were the offspring of Mary and Elizabeth of the New Testament. Notice that Luke is the only Gospel that mentions John's mother, Elizabeth, who, according to the author of Luke, is a "descendant of Aaron" (Luke 1:5); he seems to go out of his way to make sure his readers see Elizabeth's connection to the lineage of Aaron. Note further that these are the only two women named Elizabeth in the entire Hebrew Bible and New Testament. In other words, there seems to be a concentrated effort by the author of Luke to force the connection between Jesus and Moses in this case, when none of the other Gospel writers do so.

In both Matthew and Luke, prophecies of Jesus' birth are accompanied by either a dream or an angelic visitation. The author of Matthew details Joseph's dream wherein an angel prophesies of Jesus' birth. He instructs Joseph to name Mary's son "Jesus," or *Joshua* in Hebrew, meaning "Jehovah is salvation." The angel tells Joseph that Jesus would "save" people from their sins (Matt 1:20–21). In Luke, it was not Joseph who has the vision but Mary. The angel Gabriel informs her that she will have a son named Joshua (Luke 1:26–31). As a type of Moses, or a highly anticipated successor of Moses, *Joshua* was the most appropriate name for Mary's son, not only because of its meaning, but because Moses' successor in ancient Israel was also called Joshua!

The Hebrew Bible does not mention similar prophecies of Moses's birth and mission; however, first-century Jewish traditions do contain such elements. For starters, Jesus' father, Joseph, and Moses's father, Amram, are counterparts. The author of Matthew calls Joseph a "just man" (Matt 1:19), and André LaCocque (Professor Emeritus of Hebrew Bible at Chicago Theological Seminary) informs us that early Jewish tradition labels Amram one of the "Seven Just" men in the Hebrew Bible who helped bring the Presence of God (Shekinah) back to the Israel.[17] According to Josephus, Moses's father, Amram, had a dream wherein God stood by him in his sleep. Like Jesus' father, Amram learns that his wife will bear a son who would

---

17. See Numbers Rabbah 13.2. LaCocque, *Jesus the Central Jew*, 185.

save their people.[18] Amram awoke and immediately told his wife, Yochebed, about his dream. As with Luke's Gospel, a later rabbinic tradition contains the presence of the angel Gabriel. He protects Moses from Pharaoh's maidservants who want him dead. Shortly after, Pharaoh's daughter rescues him from the Nile.[19] In several early Jewish texts, Mary becomes a more prominent figure than Moses's actual mother. Moses's sister Mary (or *Miriam* in Hebrew) prophesies that her mother will bear a son who would deliver the Jewish people to salvation.[20] This tradition may not date to the first century, but its central theme of a deliverer who is prophesied to come fits within an early Jewish context, as we will see in a subsequent chapter on "the messiah" at the time of Jesus.

Before continuing, it is worth briefly addressing here the larger context of Jewish miraculous birth stories. The Hebrew Bible and early Jewish literature contain a pattern of deliverers and other important figures who are the result of a miraculous birth. The gestations and births of Jesus and John the Baptist fit neatly into this pattern. Angels announce their births, Joseph is told that Jesus would "save his people" (Matt 1:21), Mary and Elizabeth are comforted by the words "Do not be afraid" (Luke 1:13, 30), and Mary is a virgin while Elizabeth is barren (Luke 1:7, 34). Similarly, the patriarchs Isaac, Jacob, and Joseph all come from barren women: Sarah, Rebekah, and Rachel (Gen 18:11, 25:21, 29:31). Angelic messengers announce the births of Isaac and Jacob (Gen 18:10, 25:23). A first-century Jewish text (2 Enoch) preserves a story about Melchizedek's birth; his mother conceives him "in her old age," "being sterile," and "without having slept with her husband." The angel Gabriel also appears to Melchizedek's father.[21] The book of Judges explains that an angel appears to Samson's mother, who is barren, and announces the birth of her son, who would "begin to deliver Israel." She is commanded not to give Samson strong drink and not to cut his hair with a razor (Judg 13:2–5)—similar injunctions are given to Elizabeth about John the Baptist (Luke 1:15). Hannah is also barren, but God announces the birth of her son, Samuel, and instructs her not to give him strong drink (1 Sam 1:1–20). In a first-century text, The Lives of the Prophets, angelic figures appear to Elijah's father, Sobacha, and announce his birth. The angels say, "Do not be afraid; . . . he will judge Israel."[22] Thus, we see how the birth

18. Josephus, *Ant.*, 2.9.3.
19. Babylonian Talmud Sotah 12b.
20. Babylonian Talmud Megillah 14a and Sotah 13a. See also Exodus Rabbah 1, 22.
21. 2 Enoch 71:1–11; see translation by Anderson, *Old Testament Pseudepigrapha*, 205–7.
22. Lives of the Prophets 21:1–15; see translation by Hare, "Lives of the Prophets," 2:396–98.

ESTABLISHING AUTHORITY   59

narratives of Jesus and John the Baptist, as well as Moses in the Talmud, not only contain many of the same elements but also are firmly entrenched within an early Jewish context.

In addition to prophecy and revelation accompanying the births of Moses and Jesus, both birth traditions contain miraculous displays of light after delivery. For example, a bright star appears in the sky when Jesus is born, according to the author of Matthew (Matt 2:1–7), and, in Luke, an angel appears to shepherds and is accompanied by a bright heavenly throng near Jesus' birthplace (Luke 2:8–14). Similarly, early Jewish tradition maintains that when Moses was born the entire house was filled with light.[23] And when Pharaoh's daughter opened the vessel carrying Moses on the Nile, she saw him enveloped in the glory and presence of God.[24]

In Matthew, the wise men—or *magi* in Greek, referring to "magicians" or "astrologers"—notify Herod of Jesus' birth. Herod becomes paranoid and orders the murder of all children under two years of age (Matt 2:16). This is a mirror of the Moses story in Exodus. Pharaoh too becomes paranoid, not because of Moses's birth but because of the increasing strength and population of the Hebrews. He fears a revolt and therefore commands the drowning of all infant males in the Nile (Exod 1:22). A few early Jewish traditions, however, are strikingly similar to Jesus' birth story. In Josephus's writings, it was not the size and strength of the Hebrew people that worried Pharaoh but Moses' birth. One of Pharaoh's foretellers prophesies that a child would be born among the Hebrews and would subsequently deliver them. This leads to the infant-murder decree.[25] Later rabbinic traditions are even closer to Jesus' birth narrative. Like the Gospel of Matthew, a few rabbinic texts posit that Pharaoh's "astrologers" inform him of Moses's imminent birth, calling him a savior of the Jewish people. And like Herod, Pharaoh becomes paranoid and orders the killing of all male Hebrew babies.[26] In an ancient Jewish commentary on Exodus, Pharaoh's *magicians* are concerned that this Hebrew baby would replace him as king.[27]

As Jesus' birth narrative in Matthew progresses, the Moses parallels continue. Herod tries to kill Jesus, so his parents take him to Egypt (Matt 2:13–14). Pharaoh tries to kill Moses, so he flees from Egypt (Exod 2:15). After Herod dies, an angel instructs Joseph, "Go to the land of Israel, for

---

23. Babylonian Talmud Megillah 14a; Babylonian Talmud Sotah 13a.
24. Babylonian Talmud Sotah 12b.
25. Josephus, *Ant.*, 2.9.2.
26. See Babylonian Talmud Sotah 12b. For other Jewish traditions of Moses's birth, see Kensky, "Moses and Jesus," 43–49.
27. Exodus Rabbah 1, 26.

those who were seeking the child's life are dead" (Matt 2:19–20). Likewise, after Pharaoh dies, God instructs Moses, "Go back to Egypt; for all those who were seeking your life are dead" (Exod 4:19).

As we briefly saw in a prior chapter, Jesus' baptism and wilderness experience parallel the Moses and Exodus narratives. We should note here that earlier Israelite authors—particularly those who wrote Genesis through Joshua—structured the Moses-wilderness story to resemble the lifecycle of a human from conception to birth (and into infancy). There seem to be two birth narratives of Israel in the Hebrew Bible, both of which are strikingly similar to Jesus' ministry, starting with his baptism. The author of Matthew most likely had this in mind when composing his Gospel.

For example, in the first birth story of Israel, Moses is presented as the father of the nation: "Did I *conceive* all this people? Did I *give birth* to them?" (Num 11:12; emphasis added). Just before Israel's birth at the Red Sea (or more accurately, from the Hebrew *yam suf*, "Reed Sea"), God refers to Israel as "my firstborn son" (Exod 4:22). The Lord then "open[s] the womb" in preparation of Israel's conception (Exod 13:2). Israel enters the womb of the Red Sea, where God's spirit (or "life," *nefesh*) comes upon them, just as a fetus receives life in the womb (Isa 63:11). The Israelites are commanded to remember their birthday: "Remember this day on which you came out of Egypt" (Exod 13:3). The wilderness represents infancy when the child is helpless; the Lord instructs Moses, "Carry them in your bosom as a nurse carries a sucking child" (Num 11:12). As a helpless infant, Israel risks dying without parental assistance. Israel's constant cries and murmurings represent that of an infant seeking sustenance. They cry for water and bread, and the Lord gives them both from heaven:

> And the people complained against Moses, saying, "What shall we drink?" He cried out to the Lord; and the Lord showed him a piece of wood; he threw it into the water, and the water became sweet. (Exod 15:24–25)

> The whole congregation of the Israelites complained against Moses and Aaron in the wilderness . . . "You have brought us out into this wilderness to kill this whole assembly with hunger." Then the Lord said to Moses, "I am going to rain bread from heaven for you." (Exod 16:1–4)

The second birth narrative parallels the first up until the womb. As in the first narrative, the seed of Israel is implanted into the womb, which is the Red Sea. In the second birth narrative, the wilderness represents the womb, in which Israel remained for forty years, representing the forty weeks of gestation. They receive sustenance—"water" and "manna"—while growing in the womb. The Lord kept Israel in the wilderness precisely because they were too immature to enter Canaan (Num 32:13). At the end of the gestation period, Israel enters its new world through the waters of the Jordan River, which represents the birth canal (Josh 3). At this point, Israel becomes a people with a land. The twelve stones immediately erected at Gilgal (Josh 4) and the subsequent twelve tribal territories represent the young life of sibling relationships and budding leaders.[28] These two narrative strands are the stories of Israel's birth.

Jesus' experience in the Gospel of Matthew contains all of the major elements in the Moses-wilderness narratives, although not always in direct parallel. Like the Israelites in the second birth narrative, Jesus went to the *Jordan River* for his rebirth and the start of his ministry. The Red Sea and the Jordan River are split; the heavens are split while Jesus stands in the Jordan River. The Lord declares Israel his "firstborn son" on the day of its birth (Exod 4:22); the Lord declares Jesus his "Beloved son" on the day of his baptism (Luke 3:22; Mark 1:11; Matt 3:17). When Israel emerges from "out of the sea," God's Spirit comes upon them (Isa 63:11); when Jesus emerges from "out of the water," God's Spirit comes upon him (Mark 1:10; Matt 3:16). Israel remains in the wilderness for forty years in preparation for its birth, according to the second birth narrative; Jesus remains in the wilderness for forty days in preparation for his ministry.

Israel is "tested" (*peirazó* in the Septuagint, or Greek Old Testament) in the wilderness with *bread* to see "whether they will follow my instruction" (Exod 16:4). The tempter, or "one who tests" (*peirazōn*), confronts Jesus in the wilderness and offers him *bread* (Matt 4:3). Moses ascends a mountain to receive the law for Israel; Jesus ascends a "mountain" and expounds the law to Israel (more on this below). Moses appoints twelve men to be the "heads of the divisions of Israel" (Num 1:5–16). Immediately after their wilderness preparation, Joshua sets up *twelve* stones at Gilgal (Josh 4), representing the twelve tribes. Similarly, after his wilderness preparation, Jesus calls *twelve* apostles, who are chosen to lead the "House of Israel" (Matt 10:1–6). Thus, just as the birth of the Israelite nation resembles the conception and birth of a human being, so too does Jesus' baptism signify a new life and a new time. In the Gospel of Matthew, Jesus represents *both* Moses and the entire nation of Israel at his baptism, which initiated a new chapter in Israel's history—a *second* birth of a nation.

A few additional details on the forty-day wilderness retreat further illustrate the Moses-Jesus connection. Only in Matthew does Jesus fast

---

28. Ilana Pardes's entire book focuses on the theme that the story of Israel is meant to resemble the birth, growth, and development of a typical human being. See Pardes, *Biography of Ancient Israel*.

for "forty days *and forty nights*" (Matt 4:2; emphasis added). In Mark and Luke, he fasts for "forty days" (Luke 4:2, Mark 1:13). This is key because, as Dale Allison (Princeton Theological Seminary) explained, "While 'forty days' appears with some frequency in Scripture, 'forty days and forty nights' does not."[29] *Forty days and forty nights* is associated primarily with Moses and Moses typology in early Jewish texts.[30] Further, the only individuals in the Hebrew Bible who fast for forty days and forty nights are Moses and Elijah (Exod 34:28; 1 Kgs 19:8), the former being typological of the latter.[31] Scholars are fairly confident that the author of Matthew knew about the text of Mark and used it while composing his own text. The fact that Matthew added "and forty nights" to the tradition in Mark signifies that he was specifically pointing his readers to Moses.

We have already mentioned that both the Israelites and Jesus are "tempted" in the wilderness with bread. Most noteworthy, however, are the words of Moses and Jesus during these episodes. When Jesus is tempted to "command these stones to become loaves of bread," his response is, "One does not live by bread alone, but by every word that comes from the mouth of God" (Matt 4:4). These are the precise words of Moses to his people: "He humbled you by letting you hunger, then by feeding you with manna . . . in order to make you understand that one *does not live by bread alone, but by every word that comes from the mouth of the Lord*" (Deut 8:2–3; emphasis added).

As a type of Moses, Jesus miraculously multiplies a few loaves of bread for a starving crowd—a parallel of the Israelites in the wilderness. They "ate and were filled" (Matt 14:20) just as Israel under Moses is told, "You shall eat your fill" (Deut 8:10). The addition in Matthew that Jesus, on two separate occasions, provides bread to four and five thousand men "besides women and children" (Matt 14:21, 15:38) seems to be a direct parallel of Moses bringing thousands of men "besides women and children" out of Egypt with their "baked unleavened cakes of dough" (Exod 12:37). Mark's detail that Jesus organizes the crowd into groups of "hundreds and of fifties" (Mark 6:40, cf. Luke 9:14) reflects Moses's organization of Israel in the wilderness into groups of "thousands, hundreds, fifties, and tens" (Exod 18:21, 25; Deut 1:15).

Jesus' wilderness experience in the presence of Satan also resembles Moses' experience in Jewish lore. The Hebrew Bible does not contain a similar situation with Moses encountering Satan, but early Jewish tradition

---

29. Allison, *New Moses*, 168.
30. Allison, *New Moses*, 166–69.
31. Allison, *New Moses*, 39–45.

does. The Talmud perpetuates the tradition that when Moses descended from Sinai, he encountered Satan, who wanted access to the newly revealed law. In this tradition, Moses bests Satan by tricking him into a fruitless endeavor.[32] Another rabbinic text explains that the altercation ends when Moses commands Satan, "Away, wicked one, from here, you must not speak thus, go, flee before me, I will not surrender my soul to you."[33] Readers of the New Testament will recognize the similarity with the Satan-Jesus encounter in the wilderness, which culminates in Jesus saying, "Away with you, Satan! For it is written, 'Worship the Lord your God, and serve only him'" (Matt 4:10). It is difficult to know if these Moses-Satan traditions date to the first century; however, that similar parallel traditions developed among Jews with Moses and among Christians with Jesus is not surprising.

After Satan tempts Jesus with bread, he takes him "to a very high mountain" where he shows Jesus "all the kingdoms of the world and their splendor" (Matt 4:8). Similarly, Moses walks up "to the top of Pisgah" and is shown "the whole land" (Deut 34:1–4). Following the wilderness section, the Gospel of Matthew continues to walk Jesus in the footsteps of Moses. Just as Moses goes "up on the mountain" to receive the law for Israel (Exod 19:3; Deut 9:9), Jesus goes "up the mountain" to give Israel the second law—the Sermon on the Mount (Matt 5–7). Matthew explains that Jesus comes "down from the mountain" immediately after giving the law (Matt 8:1) as a parallel of Moses "coming down from the mountain" after receiving the law (Exod 32:15, 34:29; Deut 10:5). Moreover, Matthew explains that Jesus delivered the law while he "sat down" (Matt 5:1), just as Moses "sat down"—*yashab* in Hebrew—to receive the law (Deut 9:9). Although the text is usually translated "remained" in this context, several rabbinic commentators interpreted Moses as "sitting" while receiving the law.[34]

Jesus' transfiguration also mirrors Moses's encounter with God on Sinai. When Moses goes up into the "mountain" (Exod 24:12, 15–18), three specifically named associates accompany him: Aaron, Nadab, and Abihu (Exod 24:1). Similarly, three associates—Peter, James, and John—accompany Jesus at the "high mountain" (Matt 17:1; Mark 9:2). A cloud covers Moses, from which the voice of God calls (Exod 24:15–18, 34:5). A cloud also descends and covers Jesus, from which the voice of God proclaims Jesus as his son (Matt 17:5; Mark 9:7). In both stories, the faces of Moses and Jesus shine bright like the sun, which incites fear in their associates (Exod

---

32. Babylonian Talmud Shabbat 89a.

33. Deuteronomy Rabbah, 11:10. See translation in Rabbinowitz, *Midrash Rabbah Deuteronomy*, 7:186.

34. See Babylonian Talmud Megillah 21a; Testament of Moses 12:1–2. See more examples in Allison, *New Moses*, 175–77.

34:29–30, 35; Matt 17:2–6). Not only does this Jesus tradition mirror the Moses story, but Moses appears to Jesus and speaks to him. When Peter sees this, he offers to make Jesus a tabernacle (Greek *skene*), perhaps so that he might stay longer and dwell with Moses for seven days (Matt 17:4; Mark 9:5). Why seven days? Because God commanded the Israelites to dwell in tabernacles once per year for seven days to commemorate the wilderness wandering (Deut 16:13; Lev 23:42–43; Neh 8:14–17). Note that the cloud covers Moses for six days, and "on the seventh day he called to Moses out of the cloud" (Exod 24:16). We will discuss below what these Jesus-Moses parallels mean for understanding the Jewish context of Jesus' life.

Moses	Jesus
Moses' father Amram had a dream wherein God "stood by him in his sleep" and told him that his wife will bear a son who will be a savior of their people (Josephus, *Ant.* 2.9.3).	Joseph had a dream that Jesus would save Israel (Matt 1)
Moses' sister *Mary* prophesied that her "mother will bear a son who will deliver the Jewish people to salvation." *Gabriel* protected baby Moses from danger (early Jewish tradition).	*Gabriel* appeared to *Mary* and prophesied of Jesus' birth (Luke 1)
The offspring of *Mary* (Moses' sister) and *Elizabeth* (Aaron's wife) were cousins (Exod 6:23; 36:59).	The children of *Mary* and *Elizabeth* (Jesus and John) were cousins. There are only two Elizabeths in the entire Bible.
Elizabeth's sons were descendants of Aaron	Elizabeth is a "descendant of Aaron" (Luke 1:5).
In Josephus, one of Pharaoh's foretellers prophesied that a child will be born among the Hebrews and will deliver them. Another tradition: Pharaoh's "*astrologers*" (i.e. *magi*) prophesied of Moses' birth, calling him a savior of the Jewish people.	Wise Men—or "magi" in Greek, referring to "magicians" or "astrologers"—notified Herod of Jesus' birth (Matt 2).
Pharaoh became paranoid and ordered the murder of all Hebrew infants (Exod 1:22; *Ant.* 2.9.2)	Herod became paranoid and ordered the murder of all children under two years of age (Matt 2:16).
Pharaoh tried to kill Moses, so Moses fled from Egypt (Exod 2:15).	Herod tried to kill Jesus, so his parents took him and fled to Egypt (Matt 2:13–14).
After Pharaoh died the Lord told Moses, "Go back to Egypt; for all whose who were seeking your life are dead" (Exod 4:19).	After Herod died an angel told Joseph, "Go to the land of Israel, for those who were seeking the child's life are dead" (Matt 2:19–20).
The only individuals in the Hebrew Bible who fast for *forty days and forty nights* are Moses and Elijah (Exod. 34:28; 1 Kgs 19:8).	Only in Matthew do we get Jesus fasting for "forty days and *forty nights*" (Matt 4:2).

Moses to his people in the wilderness: "He humbled you by letting you hunger, then by feeding you with manna...in order to make you understand that one *does not live by bread alone, but by every word that comes from the mouth of the LORD*" (Deut 8:2–3).	When Jesus was tempted to "command these stones to become loaves of bread," Jesus' response was, "One does not live by bread alone, but by every word that comes from the mouth of God" (Matt 4:4).
Moses encountered Satan in the wilderness and commanded him: "*Away, wicked one*, from here, you must not speak thus, go, flee before me, I will not surrender my soul to you" (early Jewish tradition).	Jesus encountered Satan in the wilderness and said: "*Away with you, Satan*! For it is written, 'Worship the Lord your God, and serve only him'" (Matt 4:10).
Moses went to Mount Nebo "to the top of Pisgah" and was shown "the whole land" (Deut 34:1–4).	After Satan tempted Jesus with bread, he took him "to a very high mountain" where he showed Jesus "all the kingdoms of the world and their splendor" (Matt 4:8).
Moses "went up on the mountain" to receive the law for Israel (Exod 19:3; Deut 9:9).	Jesus "went up the mountain" to give Israel the second law—the Sermon on the Mount (Matt 5–7).
Jesus' and Moses' transfiguration narratives are similar.	See notes under Mount Hermon.

Jesus as Elisha

John the Baptist is portrayed in the Gospels as a type of Elijah, and as such he is destined to act as forerunner to the messiah (Mark 9:9–13; Matt 11:14, 17:10–13; Luke 1:17). Many ancient Jewish texts maintain that Elijah would return as judge[35] and as forerunner to the messiah.[36] Some of these texts date to a century or two after Jesus; however, the Gospels also house this idea (cf. Mark 9:11). The Gospels convey that the relationship between John and Jesus paralleled the relationship between Elijah and Elisha (1 Kgs 19:17–21; 2 Kgs 2). In short:

- Elijah preceded Elisha.
- Elisha's ministry paralleled, in several striking ways, his predecessor's (Elijah's) ministry.
- John preceded Jesus.
- Jesus' ministry paralleled, in several striking ways, his predecessor's (John's) ministry.

35. Mishnah Edduyot 8:7.
36. Targum Pseudo-Jonathan (Deut 30:4); Babylonian Talmud Erubin 43a–b.

- As a new Elijah, John paralleled many aspects of Elijah's ministry.
- As a new Elisha, Jesus paralleled many aspects of Elisha's ministry.

Elijah and Elisha	John and Jesus
Northern prophets (Lower Galilee)	Northern prophets (Lower Galilee)
Elijah preceded Elisha.	John preceded Jesus.
Elisha's ministry paralleled Elijah's ministry.	Jesus' ministry paralleled John's ministry.
As a new Elijah, John paralleled many aspects of Elijah's ministry.	As a new Elisha, Jesus paralleled many aspects of Elisha's ministry.
Many Jews at the time of Jesus held that Elijah was a "descendent of Aaron." This fact, not in the Hebrew Bible, is according to later Jewish tradition. His successor is not understood to be of priestly descent.	The Gospel of Luke posits that John the Baptist was a "descendant of Aaron" (Luke 1:5), and his successor Jesus was a non-priestly miracle worker, and both were northern prophets.

For the Gospel writers, the purpose of comparing Jesus to Elisha is to highlight his roles as prophet and miracle worker. Before further exploring these parallels between Jesus and Elisha, it behooves us to briefly explore a few similarities between Elijah and Elisha, two of the great prophets of Israel who ministered in the Northern Kingdom in the ninth century BCE.

Elijah parts the Jordan River with his mantle and walks through on dry ground (2 Kgs 2:8), after which he is taken to heaven. Elisha then uses Elijah's mantle to part the Jordan River while invoking the "God of Elijah" (2 Kgs 2:8–14). When Elijah ascends to heaven, Elisha calls out, "Father, father! The chariots of Israel and its horsemen!" (2 Kgs 2:12). Likewise, as Elisha lay dying, King Joash of Israel cries out, "My father, my father! The chariots of Israel and its horsemen!" (2 Kgs 13:14). Elijah promises an impoverished widow that if she feeds him before feeding her child, then her oil and meal would not expire (1 Kgs 17:8–16). Similarly, Elisha blesses a poor widow with an abundance of oil. A creditor comes to take her children away as slaves. Elisha instructs her to pour the little oil she has into vessels. The oil continues to pour, and the vessels continue to fill. She has so much oil that she is able to sell it and pay her creditors (2 Kgs 4:1–7). A woman's son becomes ill and dies. Elijah prays and stretches himself upon the child, and the boy's life was restored (1 Kgs 17:17–24). Similarly, Elisha prays over and lays on a woman's son who had died. Soon the boy recovers (2 Kgs 4:18–37).

Elijah	Elisha
Elijah parted the Jordan River with his mantle and walked through on dry ground (2 Kgs 2:8).	Elisha then used Elijah's mantle to part the Jordan River while invoking the "God of Elijah" (2 Kgs 2:8–14).
When Elijah ascended to heaven, Elisha called out "Father, father! The chariots of Israel and its horsemen!" (2 Kgs 2:12)	With Elisha on his deathbed, King Joash of Israel cried out, "My Father, my father! The chariots of Israel and its horsemen!" (2 Kgs 13:14)
Elijah promised an impoverished widow that if she fed him before feeding her child, her oil and meal would not expire (1 Kgs 17:8–16).	Elisha instructed a widow to pour the little oil she had into vessels. The oil continued pouring. She had so much oil that she was able to sell it and pay her creditors (2 Kgs 4:1–7).
A woman's son became ill and died. Elijah ministered to the child; while praying and stretching himself upon him, the child's life was restored (1 Kgs 17:17–24).	A woman's son became ill and died. Elisha ministered to the child. He laid hands on the boy and the child's life was restored (2 Kgs 4:18–37).

Not only did both prophets raise a child from the dead and perform other similar miracles, but they both spent much of their ministry in Samaria and the vicinity of Mount Carmel. The authors of the Gospels, particularly the author of Matthew, seemed to notice these parallels between the two great miracle workers and used this model to highlight Jesus' relationship to John the Baptist.[37] Both are miraculously conceived (Luke 1). The angel Gabriel announces both of their births and declares their names (Luke 1). Both John and Jesus say, "Repent, for the kingdom of heaven is at hand" (Matt 3:2, 4:17). Both say to Pharisees, "You brood of vipers" (Matt 3:7, 12:34). Both teach, "Every tree therefore that does not bear good fruit is cut down and thrown into the fire" (Matt 3:10, 7:10). The people regard both as prophets (Matt 11:9, 14:5; 21:11, 26, 46). Both are rejected by "this generation" (Matt 11:16–19). Herod fears the crowd because they view John as a prophet (Matt 14:5); the Jerusalem authorities fear the crowd because they view Jesus as a prophet (Matt 21:46). Herod is asked to execute John, which he is reluctant to do (Matt 14:6–11); Pilate is asked to execute Jesus, which he is reluctant to do (Matt 27:11–26).

---

37. The following comparative list is adapted from Allison, *New Moses*, 137–39.

John the Baptist	Jesus
Miraculously conceived (Luke 1)	Miraculously conceived (Luke 1)
The angel Gabriel announced his birth and declared his name (Luke 1).	The angel Gabriel announced his birth and declared his name (Luke 1).
He said, "Repent, for the kingdom of heaven is at hand" (Matt 3:2).	He said, "Repent, for the kingdom of heaven is at hand" (Matt 4:17).
He called an audience a "brood of vipers" (Matt 3:7).	He called an audience a "brood of vipers" (Matt 12:34).
He taught: "Every tree therefore that does not bear good fruit is cut down and thrown into the fire" (Matt 3:10).	He taught: "Every tree therefore that does not bear good fruit is cut down and thrown into the fire" (Matt 7:10).
The people regarded him as a prophet (Matt 11:9, 14:5).	The people regarded him as a prophet (Matt 21:11, 26, 46).
He was killed by the authorities (Matt 14:10; Mark 6).	He was killed by the authorities (all four Gospels).

This type of deliberate parallelism is common in Matthew. Since Jesus is a type of Elisha, his relationship to John must necessarily mimic Elisha's relationship to Elijah. Several Jesus traditions perpetuated in the Gospels clearly illustrate that much of Jesus' ministry was viewed through the prism of Elisha's ministry. It is telling that Jesus' most memorable miraculous acts—control over the elements, raising people from the dead, and multiplying food—are all allusions to acts performed by Elisha. A second-century BCE Jewish text, the Wisdom of Ben Sira (or Sirach), demonstrates how some Jews revered Elisha. The following eulogy of Elisha in this text would also be an appropriate description of Jesus:

> Twice as many miracles he wrought, and marvels with every utterance of his mouth. His life long he feared no one, nor was any able to intimidate his will. Nothing was beyond his power; from where he laid buried, his dead body prophesied. In life he performed wonders, and after death, marvelous deeds.[38]

The following are several Jesus-Elisha parallels:

Although not spelled out in the Hebrew Bible, early Jewish tradition maintains a miraculous birth for both Elijah and Elisha, just like John and Jesus. According to a Jewish text, the Lives of the Prophets, dating to the first century CE,[39] multiple angelic figures "of shining white appearance" visit Elijah's father, Sobacha, before Elijah's birth. Sobacha reports this incident in

---

38. Sirach 48:12–14. See this particular translation in Koskenniemi, *Old Testament Miracle-Workers*, 37.

39. Koskenniemi, *Old Testament Miracle-Workers*, 160–61.

Jerusalem, where a prophet says, "Do not be afraid . . . he will judge Israel."[40] This same first-century text posits that Elisha's birth and prophethood are revealed to and proclaimed by the priest in Jerusalem. This proclamation of Elisha's birth was based on a miraculous sign.[41]

The similarities to John and Jesus are apparent. As with Elijah's father, an angel visits John's father, Zechariah, in Jerusalem. The angel states, "*Do not be afraid* . . . he will turn many of the people of *Israel* to the Lord their God. With the spirit and *power of Elijah* he will go before him" (Luke 1:13; emphasis added). Several elements are present in the birth traditions of both Elijah and John: heavenly messengers, Jerusalem, the instruction "Do not be afraid," and the baby being identified as a future leader of Israel. Moreover, just as Elisha's birth is recognized and proclaimed in Jerusalem based on a sign, so is Jesus' birth. The wise men pronounce his birth in Jerusalem (Matt 2:1–6) as does Simeon at the temple (Luke 2:25–32). In short, the first-century Jewish traditions of the births of Elijah and Elisha parallel in key ways the births of John and Jesus, thus giving us some context for how Jews might have interpreted and received the Jesus traditions.

Some early Jews held that Elijah was a "descendent of Aaron." This assertion, not in the Hebrew Bible, appears in Jewish texts at the time of Jesus.[42] His successor, Elisha, is not understood to be of priestly descent. John and Jesus, two "northern" prophets (meaning that they ministered in the region previously known as the Northern Kingdom of Israel), mimic the nature and experience of the two northern kingdom prophets of old, Elijah and Elisha. The Gospel of Luke declares that John the Baptist was a "descendant of Aaron" (Luke 1:5), and his successor, Jesus, was a nonpriestly miracle worker. Just as Elijah and Elisha are associated with the Jordan River, so too are John and Jesus. More specifically, both Elisha and Jesus begin their ministries at the Jordan River. The river is parted for Elisha (2 Kgs 2:8–14), and the heavens are parted for Jesus while standing in the same river.

Both Elisha and Jesus are known for controlling the elements. Elisha parts the waters, and Jesus calms the waters (2 Kgs 2:14; Mark 6:45–52). Elisha causes an ax-head to float on water, and Jesus walks on water (2 Kgs 6:1–7; Matt 14:22–33; Mark 6:45–52; John 6:16–21). Notice that the Gospel writers do not always draw direct, nuanced parallels between Jesus

---

40. Lives of the Prophets 21:1–15, see translation by Hare, "Lives of the Prophets," 2:396.

41. Lives of the Prophets 22:1–17, see translation by Hare, "Lives of the Prophets," 2:397.

42. Hare, "Lives of the Prophets," 396.

and former prophets. In many sections they simply structure Jesus' story to recall for their readers certain stories and themes in the Hebrew Bible.

As explained previously, Elisha raises a woman's son from the dead (2 Kgs 4:18–37). Jesus also raises a woman's son from the dead (Luke 7:11–17). The parallels between these two stories are also apparent in the geography. Elisha performs his miracle at Shunem, and Jesus performs his miracle at Nain. Both villages were located on opposite slopes of Mount Moreh—Shunem on the southern slope (about ten miles in a straight line from Nazareth), and Nain on the northern slope.[43] Many Jewish hearers and readers of this Jesus tradition would have recalled the Elisha miracle, especially if they knew the geography.

Only two individuals in the Hebrew Scriptures and the New Testament heal a leper: Elisha and Jesus (2 Kgs 5:1–19; Luke 17:11–19). The parallels would have been clear to a Jewish reader. Both Elisha and Jesus perform these miracles in Samaria. Both Elisha and Jesus heal foreigners—Elisha heals Naaman of Aram, and Jesus heals a Samaritan. Lepers in both stories are given instructions to follow in order to be healed. Both lepers return to the healers in gratitude. Both stories end when the lepers are instructed to go their way (2 Kgs 5:19; Luke 17:19).

We mentioned previously that Elisha miraculously multiplies oil for a woman who desperately needs it to pay her creditors (2 Kgs 4:1–7). In the same chapter, Elisha converts harmful stew into harmless food (2 Kgs 4:38–41), and then feeds one hundred people with only twenty barley loaves (2 Kgs 4:42–44). Jesus deals with food in similar ways in all four Gospels. He converts water into wine and then increases it (John 2:1–11). He also feeds five thousand with five loaves and two fishes (Matt 14:13–21; Mark 6:30–44; Luke 9:10–17; John 6:1–15; cf. Matt 15:32–39; Mark 8:1–10). Multiple elements in the story parallel Elisha's miracle: the loaves are miraculously multiplied, the crowd eats until they are filled, and a surplus of food is leftover. Further, the author of John supplemented "loaves" with "barley loaves," probably alluding to the barley loaves in the Elisha story.

---

43. Strange, "Nain," 4:1001; Huwiler, "Shunem," 5:1228–29.

Elisha	Jesus
Started his ministry at the Jordan River (2 Kgs 2:8–14) and his predecessor was associated with the Jordan River.	Started his ministry at the Jordan River and his predecessor was associated with the Jordan River.
The Jordan River was parted for Elisha (2 Kgs 2:8–14).	The heavens were parted for Jesus while he stood in the Jordan River.
Elisha controlled the elements; he parted the waters (2 Kgs 2:14) and caused an ax-head to float (2 Kgs 6).	Jesus controlled the elements; he calmed the waters (Mark 6) and walked on water (Matt 14, John 6).
Elisha raised a woman's son from the dead on the southern slope of Mount Moreh at Shunem (2 Kgs 4:8–37).	Jesus raised a woman's son from the dead on the northern slope of Mount Moreh at Nain (Luke 7:11–17).
One person in the Old Testament healed a leper: Elisha. He healed a non-Israelite (Naaman) in Samaria. The leper was given instructions to follow to be healed. He returned to Elisha in gratitude (2 Kgs 5:1–19).	Only one person in the New Testament healed a leper: Jesus. He healed a non-Israelite (a Samaritan) in Samaria. The leper was given instructions to follow to be healed. He returned to Jesus in gratitude (Luke 17:11–19).
Elisha fed 100 people with only 20 *barley loaves*. They were filled and had some left over (2 Kgs 4:42–44).	Jesus fed five thousand with five loaves (Gospel of John has *barley loaves*) and two fishes. They were filled and had some left over.

Takeaways

These Moses-Jesus parallels and Elisha-Jesus parallels are not just "interesting." The parallel data allow us to catch glimpses into the minds of the Gospels' authors. What sources and traditions did they utilize while writing their narratives? What were their motives? What were their beliefs regarding Jesus? What was the nature of their Gospels? How did the Jesus traditions fit within the context of Judaism in the first few centuries BCE and CE? Obviously, the material in this chapter does not sufficiently answer these questions; however, it does get us thinking along these lines. The Gospels are not a matter-of-fact retelling of Jesus' life. They appear to be politically and theologically motivated constructions of a body of traditions about Jesus. Jews in antiquity who heard these traditions would have recognized the themes relevant to Moses and Elisha, as well as the Jewish elements in the story. We suspect this because much of the Gospels were written by Jews or for Jews, or both.

Regarding the parallels between Jesus and these two giants of the Jewish past, the writers of the Gospels were not attempting to make Jesus an equal to Elisha or Moses. For them, Jesus was greater, but they culled stories and ideas from the Hebrew Scriptures and from Jewish lore in order to shape Jesus' story. Many of the Jesus-Elisha parallels, for example, demonstrate that the outcomes of Jesus' miracles were more elaborate than those of Elisha's miracles. The Jordan River was parted for Elisha, but the heavens were parted for Jesus. Elisha caused an ax-head to float on water, but Jesus walked on water. Elisha healed a leper, but Jesus healed ten lepers. Elisha miraculously fed one hundred people with twenty loaves, but Jesus fed thousands with fewer loaves. The authors of the Gospels attempted to link Jesus to Elisha and Moses in order to increase the impact of Jesus' story, and especially to argue for Jesus' authority.

This illustrates another important cultural phenomenon. What we see in the few centuries around the turn of the millennium is a Jewish community that is trying to define, defend, justify, and disseminate its Judean religious heritage. Other Greco-Roman religious heritages at that time were trying to accomplish the same things for their own communities. How would they have attempted to accomplish that? By portraying their religious traditions as not only fully in line with the highest qualities of Greco-Roman religious thinking, but as maybe even older—and so, by Roman standards, *superior*. In order to convince people that their religious heritage met the highest ideal, various Jewish groups portrayed their master as the *oldest and most ideal type*, whether it be Jesus, Hillel, or the Teacher of Righteousness in the Qumran community. There are similarities between their leaders and the earliest and most noble figures (like Moses or Abraham) because they were all addressing themselves in the available vocabulary to essentially the same Greco-Roman Jewish audience. And there also seems to be some one-upmanship going on as well. We can actually see in early Jewish texts arguments to the effect of: "*We* go back to Elijah; well, *we* go back to David; well, *we* go back to Moses; well, *we* go back to Abraham; well, *we* see your Abraham and go back to Adam." An exemplary case is Jesus' genealogy in the Gospels of Matthew and Luke (which we will explore in a later chapter). This is how writers and adherents presented their religious heritage in the public square. Thus, since Jesus was viewed as a prophet and miracle worker by his followers, and since his followers were contending for religious legitimacy, the comparisons of Jesus to Elisha and Moses are expected.

Chapter Three

Mighty in Deed

Jesus as a Jewish Prophet and Miracle Worker

IN THE LAST CHAPTER we learned that the authors of the Gospels highlight two of Jesus' roles—prophet and miracle worker—by drawing conspicuous Moses-Jesus parallels and Elisha-Jesus parallels. Here we continue this discussion by attempting to further situate Jesus within early Jewish contexts and notions of prophets and miracle workers.

Jewish Prophets in the Age of Jesus

Several scattered suggestions throughout the Gospels illustrate Jesus' prophetic status among some segments of the Jewish population. For instance, in the Synoptic Gospels (i.e., Matthew, Mark, Luke) Jesus calls himself a prophet, stating that prophets are rejected by their own people (Mark 6:4; Matt 13:57; Luke 4:24). In Luke, a Pharisee acknowledges that Jesus is considered a prophet (Luke 7:39). Herod's court hears rumors about Jesus, specifically that some view him as a prophet (Mark 6:15; Luke 9:8). When Jesus enters Jerusalem near the end of his ministry, the crowds say, "This is the prophet Jesus from Nazareth in Galilee" (Matt 21:11). The temple priests seek to arrest Jesus but dare not because "the crowds . . . regard him as a prophet" (Matt 21:46). The two men traveling to Emmaus lament Jesus' death because, to them, Jesus was "a prophet mighty in deed and word" (Luke 24:19). In the Gospel of John, the woman of Samaria, the crowd of five thousand, and the blind man in Jerusalem all perceive Jesus to be a prophet (John 4:19, 6:14, 9:17).

These passages, although written decades after Jesus' death, mention Jesus' prophetic status in passing. In other words, these prophet passages grant that Jesus was considered a prophet during his lifetime. Preeminent New Testament scholar N. T. Wright (former Anglican bishop of Durham) explained that the early church was unlikely to have fabricated the notion that Jesus was a prophet if he really was not; such a move was risky because some might then have thought of Jesus as *only* a prophet, or as just another prophet, instead of the messiah or a divine figure.[1] What, however, was a "prophet" to a first-century Jew? What did the Jewish populace expect a "prophet" to do? And where did Jesus fit into the first-century prophetic context? To answer this question, we must briefly review the nature of prophets in the centuries preceding Jesus. Scholars have thoroughly engaged this topic, in relation to both the preexilic period (i.e., before the Babylonian exile in 586 BCE) and the New Testament period. The following is a basic contextualization of the issue sufficient to situate Jesus within the world of first-century Jewish prophets.

The difficulty in understanding the nature of prophets in ancient Israel is that the Hebrew word for prophet, *nabi,* carries a wide range of meanings. *Nabi* in the Hebrew Scriptures means "one called" of God. A prophet's primary role, as reflected in the etymology of the word, was not simply to predict future events. The Greek word for "prophet" and "prophecy," *propheteia,* denotes broadly "one who speaks on behalf of." Thus, one called by God in ancient Israel was a "prophet" whose primary function, ideally, was to speak on behalf of God. Some rabbis of the sixth century CE identified fifty-five prophets in the Hebrew Scriptures, seven of whom were female.[2]

These Israelite prophets vary significantly in their function. Some were associated with divination and consulting spirits of the dead (1 Sam 28). Some were known to receive direct revelations from God (Num 22:8–9; 1 Kgs 22:14), while others were non-revelatory moral guides and repentance preachers. Some prophets were political figures—royal court advisors (like Isaiah) who counseled the king, while others were countryside itinerant preachers who criticized the king. Some prophets were associated with the priesthood (e.g., Samuel), while others were non-priestly miracle workers (e.g., Elisha). Some prophets were war leaders or helped organize war efforts (e.g., Deborah the prophetess). Some were largely religious critics, while others were social and ethical critics. Those who received messages from God did so in different ways: through visions, dreams, divining objects (e.g., the Urim and Thummim), or audible voices (Num 12:6; 1 Sam 3:3–9;

---

1. Wright, *Jesus*, 162.
2. Babylonian Talmud Megillah 14a.

1 Kgs 13:18–22; Isa 1:1; Ezek 3:14). The messages of prophets were also varied: some were predictions of future events, and some were salvation speeches. Perhaps the most common message was a call for repentance. Many prophets delivered oracles of judgment and predicted (or declared) the downfall of certain figures, regimes, or nations due to disobedience to the Mosaic law (1 Sam 3:1–21; 2 Sam 7:1–17; 11–12; 24:1–25; 1 Kgs 17–22; 2 Kgs 9:1–13).[3] During the earliest days of Israelite society, prophets (*nabi*) were distinguished from seers (*ro'eh*), the former serving simply as spokespersons for God and the latter having the ability to predict future events, find lost objects, call up spirits, and interpret dreams.[4] Eventually these two functions merged: "For the one who is now called a prophet was formerly called a seer" (1 Sam 9:9).

As we leave the preexilic period and enter the Second Temple period, we notice a change in the nature of prophets and prophecy. For decades—all the way back to Julius Wellhausen, a German scholar and pioneer of modern biblical scholarship in the late nineteenth century—scholars concluded that prophecy in ancient Israel ceased during Persian rule in the fifth century BCE. The common view was that at the end of the Bible's prophetic books, Israel's communication with the divine went dark.[5] This conclusion is based on a half dozen passages in early Jewish texts. For example, Josephus claimed that "the exact line of succession of the prophets did not continue" after the reign of the Persian ruler Artaxerxes (486–465 BCE).[6] He also claimed that the Urim and Thummim—the divining instrument used by the high priest for receiving revelation for Israel—stopped working a few hundred years before Josephus's own time.[7] Likewise, some second-century CE rabbis maintained that the Urim and Thummim ceased working following the death of the Bible's last prophets.[8] The author of the first book of Maccabees, a late second-century BCE text, awaited a future prophet who would restore revelation through the Urim and Thummim.[9]

In recent years, scholars have reevaluated the evidence. Numerous Jewish texts postdating the Hebrew Scriptures suggest a continued presence

---

3. For more information on prophets in ancient Israel, see Blenkinsopp, *Sage, Priest, Prophet*, 115–65; Grabbe, "Shaman, Preacher, or Spirit Medium," 117–32; Gellar, "Religion of the Bible," 2021–40, esp. 2024–25, 2036–37; Walzer, *In God's Shadow*, 72–108.

4. Horsley, "'Like One of the Prophets of Old,'" 447.

5. Floyd, "Introduction," 5; Henze, "Invoking the Prophets," 120–21; Levinson, "Philo's Personal Experience," 194–95.

6. Josephus, *Ag. Ap.* 1.40, trans. Barclay.

7. Josephus, *Ant.* 3.218, trans. Feldman.

8. Mishnah Sotah 9.12.

9. 1 Macc 4:46.

of the belief in prophetic activity and communication with the divine during the Second Temple period. First Enoch, Daniel, and Revelation are all Jewish texts that illustrate belief in revelatory experiences. The book of Revelation specifically refers to itself as a work of "prophecy" (1:3, 22:7, 10, 18, 19). Moreover, a group of scholars have argued, quite convincingly, that the corpus of the Dead Sea Scrolls demonstrates a robust prophetic activity among the Qumran community in the first centuries BCE and CE.[10] The author of the Wisdom of Ben Sira, or Sirach (second century BCE), is highly concerned with prophets and prophecy and even considers his own functions and activities as "prophecy," according to his understanding of the concept.[11] Josephus mentioned prophetic activity among the priests, Sadducees, Essenes, Pharisees, Samaritans, and Zealots.[12] He also presented himself as a prophet,[13] perhaps a new Jeremiah.[14] He argued that only the prophets were privileged to record Israel's history in ancient times,[15] the very endeavor that he undertook in the first century CE as a historian of the Jewish people. Later, second-century rabbis believed that God's Spirit continued to enable certain people to act prophetically.[16] Thus we see that belief in prophetic activity did not cease after the death of the last biblical prophets in the fifth century BCE, according to several Jewish texts.

There is a difference, however, in how Josephus wrote about prophets of the Hebrew Scriptures versus how he wrote about prophets in the Second Temple period. He specifically called the biblical figures "prophets," even if the Hebrew and Greek biblical texts use no such terms.[17] In contrast, he generally did not use "prophet" as a label or title for prophetic figures after the fifth century BCE, even if they had the ability to foresee and foretell. For Josephus, "prophets" were not only spokespersons for God but also the only individuals whose words could be considered "scripture." Despite describing himself as a prophet in every respect, like great figures of the past, he never specifically called himself a "prophet."[18]

---

10. Parry et al., *Prophetic Voice at Qumran*, 1–188.

11. See Sirach 24:33, 39:1; see also the discussion in Beentjes, "Prophets and Prophecy," 135–50.

12. Josephus, *Ant.* 13.10.7, 17.2.4, 18.4.1; Josephus, *J.W.* 1.2.8, 6.5.2.

13. Josephus, *J.W.* 3.8.9.

14. Feldman, "Prophets and Prophecy in Josephus," 212.

15. Josephus, *Ag. Ap.* 1.37. See Feldman, "Prophets and Prophecy in Josephus," 219–21; Grabbe, "Thus Spake the Prophet Josephus," 240–47.

16. See, for example, Tosefta Pesah 2:15.

17. Feldman, "Prophets and Prophecy in Josephus," 213–14.

18. Feldman, "Prophets and Prophecy in Josephus," 223–25.

In a sense, then, the traditional and authoritative prophetic class did cease after the prophetic books of Haggai, Zechariah, and Malachi; however, belief in prophecy and communication with the divine did not cease. It is within this context that we might interpret the passages previous scholars used to argue that belief in prophets and prophecy ceased in the Second Temple period. Such passages likely refer to a *prophet like Moses* (Deut 18:15), who would restore the practice of producing Scripture and who would resurrect the Urim and Thummim as a living object of divination. For Josephus, and perhaps the later rabbis, postbiblical prophets were of the same kind as ancient prophets in terms of their prophetic ability, but the degree to which they acted prophetically was different; later prophets did not have the same stamp of authority as did the biblical prophets.

Various social scientists have identified a range of prophet classifications among Jews in the Second Temple period. Three or four major categories and several subcategories have emerged, though all of these classifications have been challenged by other scholars.[19] Taking this into account, we might reduce this classification into two major types of prophets, each containing a few subcategories. The first category of prophets in the New Testament period is *literate-group seers*. At the time of Jesus, literate-group seers functioned within upper, literate classes. They possessed gifts of interpreting dreams, hearing and discerning the voice of God, and predicting future events. Since *literate-group seers* were in close proximity to the centers of power, their predictions most often related to the king and court and less to the populace or society as a whole.[20] This type of prophet can be subdivided into two categories (using scholarly terms): *clerical prophets* and *sapiential prophets*.[21] The difference between these two is not in their ability as seers but in their societal role. *Clerical prophets* ministered within priestly circles, and *sapiential prophets* were intellectual leaders of political factions or elite classes. Prophets in these two subcategories performed similar functions.[22]

---

19. Webb, *John the Baptizer and Prophet*, 307–48; Herzog, *Prophet and Teacher*, 101–9; Horsley, *Bandits, Prophets and Messiahs*, 153–87.

20. Horsley, *Bandits, Prophets, and Messiahs*, 153–60.

21. Webb, *John the Baptizer*, 307–48; Herzog, *Prophet and Teacher*, 101–2.

22. Two examples of *literate-group seers* in Josephus are John Hyrcanus (135–104 BCE), who we meet in a later chapter, and Josephus himself. John Hyrcanus, who served as both a king and priest, supposedly foresaw that neither of his sons would be king. He also predicted his son's military victory (Josephus, *J.W.* 1.68–69; Josephus, *Ant.* 13.299–300). Josephus prophesied that Vespasian would become emperor and previously had directly claimed that he received revelations through dreams (*J.W.* 3.351–54; 3.400–402).

The second major category is *popular prophets*. These prophets garnered the support of the peasant class. They largely ministered in the countryside, away from the administrative power structures. Most of these types of prophets mentioned by Josephus came from the Galilee region. They often criticized the ruling class and temple bureaucrats, which helped foster support of the common people. The two subcategories of popular prophets are: *action prophets* and *oracular prophets*.[23] Action prophets were leaders of large movements, many of which anticipated acts of divine deliverance from corrupt domestic and foreign rulers. These groups were similar to, and often the same as, messianic groups who declared their prophet as king. Oracular prophets tended to be popular with the peasant class but did not necessarily lead large movements of hundreds or thousands, although they could have. As the term suggests, these prophets delivered oracles, or pronouncements of judgment, upon the ruling class or the nation as a whole. Both types of popular prophets acted out in symbolic ways, mimicking great prophets of the past like Joshua and Moses. Many of them promised to show signs and miracles to their groups. Josephus mentions several popular prophets who ministered in the first century CE. To him they were a particular annoyance. He called them "deceitful people" who claimed "divine inspiration." They concerned themselves with instigating revolutions and led their groups into the wilderness to show them signs and miracles.[24]

Where did Jesus fit within this prophetic context, at least according to the Gospels? Richard Horsley, Harvard-trained Christian scholar of ancient Judaism, approached this question as follows:

> With regard to Jesus as a prophet . . . the issue for Jesus' contemporaries was . . . clearly not, "Does this man fit the model of our expectations?" Nor is it, "Is prophecy alive again in this man?" Rather, the question is, "Since this fellow is obviously a prophet, what sort of prophet is he?"[25]

It is difficult to determine in which category the *real* Jesus fit. However, if we traveled back in time and asked some of his followers in the late first century, including the authors of the Gospels themselves, they would probably tell us that Jesus transcended our classifications of literate-group seers, action prophets, and oracular prophets. Given what we know about late first-century views of Jesus, he seems to have acted in ways congruous with *all types* of prophets. Although Jesus did not serve the priestly and aristocratic

---

23. Horsley, *Bandits, Prophets, and Messiahs*, 160–87; Herzog, *Prophet and Teacher*, 102–9; Webb, *John the Baptizer and Prophet*, 333–42.

24. Josephus, *J.W.* 13.4, trans. Mason.

25. Horsley, "'Like One of the Prophets of Old,'" 435.

classes specifically, he garnered support and received positive attention from some of them, at least according to the Gospels. As demonstrated in a later chapter on the Pharisees, Jesus was likely well-respected by many Pharisees. Nicodemus, a court official and a Pharisee, approaches Jesus for advice (John 3:1–21). Pharisees save Jesus from Herod Antipas (Luke 13:31). Many Pharisees affiliate themselves with Jesus' movement even after his death (Acts 15:5). According to all four Gospels, Joseph of Arimathea (a Jerusalem court official) follows Jesus (Matt 27:57–60; Mark 15:43–46; Luke 23:50–56; John 19:38–40). A few passages in the Gospels and Acts state that members of the priestly class are followers of Jesus, both during his life and after his death:

> Many, even of the authorities, believed in him (John 12:42);

> The number of the disciples increased greatly in Jerusalem, and a great many of the priests became obedient to the faith (Acts 6:7).

Despite his few associations with the upper class, Jesus seems to fit best within the *popular prophet* classification. He spends much of his time in the countryside with Galilean peasants. Under the *popular prophet* umbrella, Jesus is both an *action prophet* and an *oracular* prophet, as he is described in the Gospel of Luke as "a prophet mighty in deed *and* word" (Luke 24:19; emphasis added). His movement apparently grows large enough to worry leaders, both in Galilee and Judea, and he delivers many oracles of judgment against Jerusalem and its priestly establishment.[26] Recall from the beginning of the previous chapter that some social scientists have used the cross-cultural model of "shamanism" to study Jesus. This model fits well with his multifaceted ministry. He functions in many different roles and is viewed in many different ways by his peers and followers. It is intriguing that Lester Grabbe, an American scholar of the Bible and early Judaism, applied the "shaman" model to Elisha, making the Jesus-Elisha comparison in the previous chapter all the more relevant.[27] Elisha, like Jesus, is a northern prophet who was most known through oral and written traditions for displaying control over the elements, multiplying food for the poor and hungry, healing the afflicted, and raising the dead. As we have seen, the authors of the Gospels utilized the Elisha traditions while shaping Jesus' story for their readers.

---

26. Matt 24–25; Luke 19:42–44, 21:5–37; Mark 11:12–18, 20–25; 12:1–12, 13; 14:56–59; John 2:19.

27. Grabbe, "Shaman, Preacher, or Spirit Medium," 126, 128–29.

One more element in the prophetic context of the first century CE is miracles. In both biblical and postbiblical Jewish literature, prophets are associated primarily with miracles. Eric Eve, scholar at the University of Oxford and specialist in early Jewish miracles,[28] observed the following:

> Roughly 60 percent of the miracles in Josephus's *Antiquities* are associated with prophetic figures (including Moses) and that *[Wisdom of] Ben Sira's* "Praise of Famous Men" tends to associate prophets and miracles . . . From this survey it emerges that prophets (including Moses) form by far the largest category of human miracle-workers in Second Temple literature, and this is attested by a wide variety of writers.[29]

In other words, prophets were known in the age of Jesus to be miracle workers par excellence. And, the other way around, if one performed a miracle, then that person was ipso facto a "prophet." Josephus details many cases when prophet-figures in the first century CE established a following and promised many miracles. Their followers sought signs and wonders in order to discern the true nature of their "prophets." Were they imposters, or were they legitimate, divinely sanctioned prophets? The best way for the Jewish populace to discern whether one was a true prophet was through divination, signs, and miracles as prescribed in Deuteronomy (13:1–2). This may explain why many people, including the Pharisees, approach Jesus for a sign; they want to ascertain whether he really is a prophet as many people claim.

Jewish Miracle Workers in the Age of Jesus

The Gospels' comparisons of Jesus with Moses and Elisha are meant to emphasize Jesus' role as a prophet, the miracle-worker component being the most prominent attribute of prophets in early Jewish literature. It is clear, at least according to the Gospels, that Jesus was viewed as a miracle worker by his followers and perhaps by various other Jews after his death. The Gospels are replete with stories of Jesus controlling the elements and healing the afflicted. For our purposes of contextualizing Jesus within a first-century Jewish setting, we are not concerned about whether Jesus *really* controlled the elements, performed food miracles, or healed people—again, that is the enterprise of historians, or an exercise of faith. Rather, we are concerned about contextualizing these stories within Jewish antiquity. How unique were Jesus' miracle and healing traditions in the Jewish world during the

---

28. See Eve, *Jewish Context*; Eve, *Healer from Nazareth*.
29. Eve, *Jewish Context*, 249, 253.

Greco-Roman era? Did Jesus have miracle-working peers, or was he the only one? In addition, how did miracle workers interact with the populace, and how did the populace perceive miracle workers?

Eric Eve's survey of Second Temple Jewish literature reveals a lack of interest in miracles as a common function of society. The texts most attuned to miracles—Lives of the Prophets and the Testament of Solomon (first century BCE through the second century CE), for example—preserve attitudes about miracle workers in an earlier era but not in their own generation. Outside of Josephus's writings, stories of postbiblical miracles are rare, especially stories purported to have occurred during the author's generation.[30] In other words, it seems that most authors of early Jewish texts generally believed in the existence of miracles as divine actions; however, this function within their own society was minor.[31] To be sure, healers and miracle workers seem to be popular among the masses, not just in Jesus' day but at many other times and places. It seems to be the case, however, as Eric Eve argued, that the authors of the Jewish texts downplayed miracle working in their own generation. Despite the minimal focus on miracles in the first centuries BCE and CE, several categories can be identified in the literature, most prominently healing (including exorcism) and nature miracles (including food miracles).

Healing Miracles

Stories of healing in Second Temple literature are few. Most of them are accounts of healings performed by biblical prophets like Elijah and Elisha. After surveying early Jewish literature for healing stories, Eric Eve observed, "[Healing] references exhibit an awareness that miraculous healings could be associated with powerful prophets like Moses, Elijah, and Elisha, but they do not indicate any great interest in healing, or any great hopes attached to the figure of a healer."[32] In other words, healers in Jesus' day—or those *thought* to be healers—were rare, at least according to the available evidence. Jewish literature does mention, however, a handful of healers that might help us contextualize Jesus' healing activities. Before meeting these figures, it behooves us to step back and explore briefly the ancient Mediterranean conceptions of illness.

Today, we tend to think of sickness in nuanced ways due to both our knowledge of the body and advancements in medical technology. When a

30. Eve, *Jewish Context*, 243–71.
31. Eve, *Jewish Context*, 243–44.
32. Eve, *Jewish Context*, 254.

person experiences pain in the abdomen, for example, that person and his or her medical professionals attempt to identify the specific cause and the affected organs. Such information is necessary for treatment. When we encounter a person who seems a bit "off" (for lack of a better description)—according to our experience and customs—we assume that something is amiss in the brain, that the person might have a mental condition or mental illness. When we conceptualize sickness, we think in terms of germs, viruses, infections, diseases, or defects from birth. In Jesus' day, however, they had little to no conception of disease. They did not understand illness the same way we do. To them, illness was most often the result of divine disfavor on the part of the afflicted or his or her parents. Rabbi Hiyya ben Abba (third century CE) commented that "a sick man does not recover from his sickness until all his sins are forgiven him."[33] Rabbi Ammi similarly taught, "There is no suffering without iniquity."[34] The idea that sin causes illness also found its way into the Gospels. When Jesus' disciples see a blind man in Jerusalem, they ask, "Rabbi, who sinned, this man or his parents that he was born blind?" (John 9:2). Jesus tells another blind man, "See, you have been made well! Do not sin anymore, so that nothing worse happens to you" (John 5:14). Note, however, a counterexample when Jesus teaches in the Gospel of John that "neither this [blind] man nor his parents sinned" (John 9:3).

Imagine if you were sick and your condition was so severe that your community quarantined you. To add insult to injury, as we say, what if your community associated your illness with sin? What more depressing scenario could one imagine? But that was the view in many ancient cultures (and it is actually still the view of some Christians today). We must not overstate it, however—they were not so naive to think that every infected sliver was a curse from God. But for unexplained, highly disruptive illnesses, the default explanation was sin and divine disfavor.[35] This is why we read in early Jewish literature, including the New Testament, that healers were not considered "physicians" in the way we use the term (i.e., experts in biology and medicine) but were perceived as being either prophets of God or magicians influenced by Satan. For example, some think Jesus is a demon-influenced magician after he heals a man (Luke 11:14–20; Mark 3:22; Matt 12:24). Another first-century Jewish healer, whom we will soon meet in our discussion, is asked immediately after a healing if he is a prophet.[36]

33. Babylonian Talmud Nedarim 41a, in Freedman, *Nedarim*.

34. Babylonian Talmud Shabbat 55a, in Freedman, *Shabbat*.

35. For a more in-depth, social scientific discussion of sickness and healing in the world of Jesus, see Pilch, "Sickness and Healing in Luke–Acts," 181–209; Pilch, *Healing in the New Testament*; Theissen and Marz, *Historical Jesus*, 281–315.

36. Babylonian Talmud Berakhot 34b.

Most of Jesus' miracles in the Gospels are healings. We will not dissect all of them here, but we will highlight a few points to demonstrate that Jesus worked within the contemporary Jewish framework of healing, according to the Gospels' portrayal of him. It is difficult to discuss Jewish healing in the New Testament period without mentioning the Galilean miracle worker Rabbi Hanina ben Dosa. What is intriguing about Hanina are the many similarities he shares with Jesus. Both are first-century Jewish healers, and Hanina lived only ten miles from Nazareth, in the town of Arab.[37] According to the traditions, Rabbi Hanina must have ministered in lower Galilee in the middle of the first century, shortly after Jesus, because he is mentioned in association with Rabbi Gamaliel, the teacher of Paul (Acts 22:3).[38] A rabbinic story claims that a voice from heaven called Hanina "my son" and proclaimed that "the whole world is nourished by the good deeds of Hanina."[39] A voice from heaven also calls Jesus "my son" at both his baptism and his transfiguration (Matt 3:17, 17:5; Mark 1:11, 9:7; Luke 3:22, 9:35). Hanina is well-known in rabbinic writings for his ability to heal by means of prayer.[40] Two of his healings are similar to a few of Jesus' healings. The tradition is preserved as follows:

> Once *the son* of Rabbi Gamaliel fell ill. He sent two scholars to Rabbi Hanina ben Dosa to ask him to pray for him. When he saw them he went up to an upper chamber and prayed for him. When he came down he said to them: *Go, the fever has left him* . . . They sat down and made a note of the exact moment. When they came to Rabbi Gamaliel, he said to them . . . "You have not been a moment too soon or too late, but so it happened: at that *very moment the fever left him* and he asked for water to drink." On another occasion it happened that Rabbi Hanina ben Dosa went to study Torah with Rabbi Johanan ben Zakkai. *The son* of Rabbi Johanan ben Zakkai fell ill. He said to him: Hanina my son, pray for him that he may live. *He put his head between his knees and prayed* for him and he lived.[41]

Like Hanina, Jesus heals two people from a distance in a similar manner, including the son of a prominent figure in Galilee (John 4:46–53; Luke 7:1–10; cf. Matt 8:5–13). After Gamaliel's men approached Hanina, he prayed and then said, "Go, the fever has left him," and at that "exact moment . . . the

---

37. Jerusalem Talmud Berakhot 4:1, 7c.
38. Babylonian Talmud Berakhot 34b.
39. Babylonian Talmud Taanit 24b, in Rabbinowitz, *Taanith*.
40. Mishnah Berakhot 5:5.
41. Babylonian Talmud Berakhot 34b, in Simon, *Berakhot*; emphasis added.

fever left him." Jesus, too, says to the official, "Go, your son will live," and at that "hour . . . the fever left him" (John 4:46–53). Note also that Hanina, like Jesus, was compared to Elijah, another northern prophet from the Hebrew Scriptures. Like Elijah, Hanina prayed with his head between his knees (see 1 Kgs 18:42). As we already discussed, Jesus too is associated with a northern prophet who ministered in the vicinity of Nazareth: Elijah's student Elisha.

In another tradition, probably dating to the first century, a poisonous snake bit Rabbi Hanina's heel. The story is repeated in several places in rabbinic literature and is likely embellished in later accounts.[42] In one version, Hanina offered his heel to the serpent; the serpent bit it, then died. Hanina said to his disciples, "See, my sons, it is not the serpent that kills, it is sin that kills."[43] Jesus similarly teaches his disciples: "See, I have given you authority to *tread* upon *serpents* and scorpions . . . and *nothing shall hurt you*" (Luke 10:19; emphasis added). In a separate story, a man approached Rabbi Hanina to inquire about the legitimacy of another healer. The man told Hanina that he knows this other healer is legitimate because people approach him to heal their "ailing eyes." As a firstborn son, this man could heal their eyes with his saliva because, as explained by the rabbis, "it is learned as a tradition that the *saliva of a father's firstborn heals this ailment*."[44] Similarly, one of Jesus' followers ask him about the legitimacy of another healer: "'Master, we saw someone casting out demons in your name, and we tried to stop him, because he does not follow with us.' But Jesus said to him, 'Do not stop him; for whoever is not against you is for you'" (Luke 9:49–50). Could this person have been another well-known healer in the region similar to Hanina and Jesus? What is more intriguing, however, is the Jewish tradition that the saliva of a firstborn son was known to heal ailing eyes. This tradition is directly relevant to a few stories in the Gospels of Mark and John:

> He took the blind man . . . and when he had put saliva on his eyes and laid his hands on him . . . he saw everything clearly. (Mark 8:22–26)

> He spat on the ground and made mud with the saliva and spread the mud on the man's eyes, saying to him, 'Go, wash in the pool

---

42. Mishnah Berakhot 5.1; Tosefta Berakhot 3.20; Babylonian Talmud Berakhot 33a.

43. Babylonian Talmud Berakhot 33a, in Simon, *Berakhot*.

44. Babylonian Talmud Baba Batra 126b; translation from *William Davidson Talmud*; emphasis added. Other places in rabbinic texts preserve traditions of healing saliva and even debates about the propriety of such a practice. See Babylonian Talmud Shabbat 108b. This eye-healing saliva tradition also appears in the Jerusalem Talmud, where it is again assumed that spittle heals blindness (see Jerusalem Talmud Shabbat 14:4, and Sotah 1:4).

of Siloam' (which means Sent). Then he went and washed and came back able to see. (John 9:5–7)

If the saliva tradition was widely known in the first century, and if the stories in Mark and John are historical, then Jesus probably utilized this cultural legend in order to demonstrate to those present, or to the blind man himself, that he was a firstborn son (of the Father). If the story is not historical but an earlier Jewish tradition, then it still follows that the authors of the Gospels would utilize it and fold it into their narratives for the same reason—to speak to their Jewish readers according to the prevailing traditions, customs, and notions.

Several other healing stories have Jesus touching the affected person or defective body part and instantly healing him or her. Jesus touches the eyes of two blind men (Matt 9:27–31), he reaches out and touches a man with leprosy (Matt 8:1–4; Mark 1:40–45; Luke 5:12–14), he lays his hands on a crippled woman (Luke 13:13), and he heals a deaf man by inserting "his fingers into his ears" (Mark 7:31–35). Similar stories are preserved in early Jewish literature of a healer touching and instantly healing the afflicted. For instance, Rabbi Judah the Prince (second century CE) suffered from a toothache for thirteen years. The prophet Elijah appeared to him in the guise of the well-known Rabbi Hiyya. Elijah placed his finger directly on the tooth, and it was healed instantly.[45] Elsewhere, Rabbi Johanan and Rabbi Hiyya ben Abba healed each other by grasping the hand of the other. In separate instances, each lay sick in bed and unable to move. The healer in both cases takes "his hand and raises him."[46] Note the striking similarity to the story of Jesus healing Peter's mother-in-law; while she lay "in bed with a fever," Jesus "took her *by the hand and lifted her up*" (Mark 1:29–31; cf. Matt 8:14–15; Luke 4:38–39).

We should also include exorcisms and demon torments in the healing discussion. Belief in evil spirits was common in Jesus' day, as attested in many ancient Jewish texts; however, accounts of demon-possessed people and their exorcisms are less common.[47] Jewish sources in antiquity provide just enough information for us to situate Jesus within this Jewish exorcistic context. As explained above, illness was often associated with sin; likewise, afflicted people were assumed to have been possessed by evil spirits. The mentally ill were likely all viewed as demon-possessed. Notice the language in Luke when Jesus healed Peter's mother-in-law. Her fever behaves like a demon: "He stood over her and *rebuked the fever, and it left her*"; the

---

45. Jerusalem Talmud Ketubot 12.3.
46. Babylonian Talmud Berakhoth 5b, in Simon, *Berakhot*.
47. Eve, *Jewish Context*, 326–49.

immediate two verses describe other "sick" people with "various kinds" of illnesses, and "*demons* came out of many" (Luke 4:38–41; emphasis added). The author of Luke, in his attempt to explain the tragic case of Judas, concluded that "Satan entered into Judas" (Luke 22:3). We must emphasize here that exorcisms seem to be a crucial aspect of Jesus' ministry, according to at least two Gospels. How do we know? Because when Jesus appoints his twelve apostles in the Gospel of Mark, he gives them authority to do *one* specific thing: "to cast out demons" (Mark 3:15). In Matthew, Jesus only gives them authority over "unclean spirits, to cast them out" (Matt 10:1). The following clause "and to cure every disease and every sickness" is related to unclean spirits, further illustrating that people who had a virus or disease were thought to have been afflicted by an evil spirit.

Josephus introduces us to an exorcist named Eleazar, a contemporary of Jesus, who drew out demons by employing King Solomon's method. Josephus was an eyewitness of one particular exorcism:

> I became acquainted with a certain Eleazar of my own people, who . . . delivered those possessed by demons. The method of healing is as follows: Bringing up to the nose of the demonized person a ring that had under its seal a root from among those prescribed by Solomon, he [Eleazar] would then draw out the demonic [presence] through the nostrils, as the man sniffed. Upon the man's immediately falling down, he adjured the demonic [presence] not to return to him again, making mention of Solomon and likewise reciting the incantations he had composed. Eleazar, wishing to persuade and convince those present that he had this power, first placed a cup or foot-basin filled with water a short distance away and ordered the demonic [presence], which was now outside the person, to knock these over, and so cause the spectators to realize that it had left the person. When this happened, the sagacity and wisdom of Solomon became evident through this.[48]

The similarities between Jesus and Eleazar the exorcist are intriguing. The detail that possessed individuals lose control of their physical functions and "fall down" is present in Mark. Whenever embodied demons encounter Jesus, they "*fell down* before him" (Mark 3:11; emphasis added). Later in the Gospel, when an evil spirit sees Jesus approaching, it sends the afflicted boy into convulsions, "and he *fell on the ground* and rolled about" (Mark 9:20; emphasis added). In addition, both Eleazar and Jesus command the demon to depart and never repossess the body of the demoniac (Mark 9:25).

---

48. Josephus, *Ant.* 8.2.5, trans. Begg and Spilsbury.

The Solomon element in Josephus's account is also important for understanding the demon episodes in the Gospels. Jesus' authority is challenged throughout his ministry, and he is accused of performing miracles by sorcery and magic (Luke 11:14–20; Mark 3:22; Matt 12:24).[49] In Jesus' era, myths circulated widely that King Solomon was skilled in magic and exorcism. Two ancient texts dating to the New Testament period, the Wisdom of Solomon and the Testament of Solomon, discuss Solomon's ability to communicate with spirits and to exorcise demons. This information provides context for Jesus' comment later in his ministry, while discussing evil spirits and seeking signs, that one "greater than Solomon is here" (Luke 11:31; Matt 12:42), meaning that, like Solomon, Jesus not only has the power to cast out demons but can do it better than Solomon.

A few other early Jewish accounts of exorcisms are notable, two of which are found in the Dead Sea Scrolls. In Genesis Apocryphon (second century BCE through the first century CE)—a retelling of the Genesis story through the presuppositions of the Qumran community—we encounter the exorcism of Pharaoh. After Pharaoh took Abraham's wife, he was tormented by an evil spirit. Pharaoh asked Abraham to take his wife away but not before praying for him. Abraham "laid [his] hands upon [Pharaoh] and the plague was removed from him, the evil [spirit] exorcised [from him,] and he was healed."[50] We recall the instances in the Gospels when Jesus lays his hands on a woman and frees her from "a spirit" that ailed her (Luke 13:10–13) and when "all those who had any who were sick with various kinds of diseases brought them to him; and he *laid his hands on each of them* and cured them. Demons came out of many" (Luke 4:40; emphasis added). The other exorcism in the Dead Sea Scrolls is in Apocryphal Daniel (second century BCE through the first century CE). The king of Babylon was smitten by God with an evil disease because of sin. A Jewish exorcist freed him of the evil spirit, and "as for [his] sin, he remitted it."[51] We are reminded that in some sectors of Jewish antiquity, evil spirits are associated with sin and divine disfavor. The Gospels have no parallel where Jesus specifically forgives the sins of demoniacs or tells them to sin no more, but numerous episodes illustrate that Jesus exorcises many demons and tells the afflicted that their sins are forgiven.[52]

49. Welch, "Miracles, *Maleficium*, and *Maiestas*," 349–83.

50. 1Q20 (1QapGen) 20:28–29, translation in Tov, *Dead Sea Scrolls Electronic Library*.

51. 4Q242 (4QPrNab), Fragments 1, 2a, 2b, 3, translation in Tov, *Dead Sea Scrolls Electronic Library*.

52. Matt 8:28–33, 9:32, 12:22, 15:21–28, 17:14–18; Mark 1:32–34, 5:1–20, 7:24–30; Luke 4:35–40, 8:26–39, 9:37–42.

A later rabbinic text presents a story similar to a few in the Gospels. Rabbi Simeon ben Yochai (late first century CE through the early second century CE) learned that a demon had entered into the emperor's daughter. Rabbi Yochai called the demon by name and said, "Ben Temalion leave her," and "as he proclaimed this he left her."[53] Jesus similarly exorcises demons from two children—one from the daughter of a Canaanite woman (Matt 15:21–28; Mark 7:24–30) and another from the son of a man in the crowd (Matt 17:14–20; Mark 9:14–29; Luke 9:37–43). He commands the demon to leave them, and the demoniacs are healed immediately. Even casual readers of the Gospels today recall that demons approach Jesus several times, including Satan, whom Jesus defeats in the wilderness. In Mark 5, for example, a group of demons recognize Jesus as the "Son of the Most High God" and beg him not to cast them "out of the country." Jesus gives them permission to occupy the bodies of swine (Mark 5:1–13). A demonic leader with her 180,000 "destroying angels" similarly recognize Rabbi Hanina ben Dosa as a man of "Heaven." As with Jesus, Hanina ordered the demon from the "region" just before she begged him, "Leave me a little room."[54] Similar stories of Satan appearing to prominent holy men are found elsewhere in rabbinic literature.[55]

We will discuss the overall message and takeaways of these Jewish parallels with Jesus below; however, we should note here that if a person had the reputation of being a healer, his popularity would have spread quickly throughout the region. Another Galilean healer like Rabbi Hanina and Jesus of Nazareth was Rabbi Yose (early second century CE). Due to his ability to heal, his fame and reputation spread so far and wide that a tenth-century sick Jewish man cried out, "Rabbi Yose the Galilean, heal me!"[56] As explained in chapter 1, examinations of numerous skeletal remains reveal that most people in ancient Judea and Galilee were malnourished and iron deficient. Most people died before the age of eighteen, which means that the population, including the child population, was saturated with sickness, disease, lethargy, and chronic pain. Most adults had fractured bones, inflamed joints, arthritis, osteoporosis, and crooked backs—not to mention all the ailments not limited to the skeletal system, like organ malfunctions, skin diseases, and other infections.[57] In addition, certain diseases were especially formidable. Numerous studies have demonstrated that anemia

---

53. Babylonian Talmud Meilah 17b, in Porusch, *Meilah*.
54. Babylonian Talmud Pesahim 112b, in Simon, *Berakhot*.
55. See, for example, Babylonian Talmud Kiddushin 81a.
56. See Silver, *History of Messianic Speculation*, 23.
57. Smith et al., "Skeletal Remains," 110–18.

was widespread throughout the Mediterranean world. Evidence preserved in Roman-era bones reveal that gastrointestinal and respiratory diseases wreaked havoc on the population. These diseases included dysentery, malaria, typhus, typhoid, and tuberculosis. Malaria was particularly nasty, killing twice as many people during the months of August and September than during any other month (according to inscriptions from Roman catacombs). Galilean residents were probably more susceptible to malaria due to both the lake and abundant annual rainfall that resulted in standing pools of water—breeding grounds for mosquitos.[58] Jonathan Reed (scholar of early Christianity at University of La Verne) reminds us of the extremely high death rates due to malaria among early twentieth century settlers in the Galilee.[59] As mentioned above, various ancient sources mentioned several people who suffered from fevers (a symptom of malaria) including Rabbi Gamliel's son, Peter's mother-in-law, and the centurion's son at Capernaum. Josephus confirmed that this area around or near the Sea of Galilee was saturated with pestilence.[60] It is within this context that we can interpret Jesus in relation to his healing activities. If he had the reputation to heal, his fame would have spread quickly throughout the region. No wonder, then, that much of Jesus' ministry—a majority of his miracles in fact—were healings and exorcisms: twenty-eight of thirty-seven (75 percent), depending on how one defines "miracle."

Nature and Food Miracles

Like Elisha, Jesus' second most common type of miracle after healings are nature miracles. Nature miracles were salient for the authors of the Gospels because Jews understood that Yahweh possessed ultimate control over the natural elements. The fight between Elijah and the priests of Baal in 1 Kings is over which god, Yahweh or Baal, has the power to provide rain and end the drought (1 Kgs 17–18, esp. 18:41–45). By emphasizing Jesus' ability to subdue the winds and control the waters, the authors of the Gospels were boldly pointing their readers to Jesus' messiahship and possibly to his divinity (or divine-like qualities).

The two most well-known (nonfood) nature-miracle episodes in the Gospels are Jesus walking on water and calming the storm; however, before discussing these miracles in light of early Judaism, we meet a few

---

58. Several studies are consulted and summarized in Reed, "Mortality, Morbidity, and Economics," 243–49.

59. Reed, "Mortality, Morbidity, and Economics," 246.

60. Josephus, *J.W.* 4.457.

contemporaries of Jesus who were known for performing nature miracles. The first is Honi ha-Me'aggel, or "Honi the Circle Drawer" (late first century BCE) in early rabbinic sources and Josephus.[61] Honi ministered in Galilee in the generation prior to Jesus. Note that many of the holy men similar to Jesus who are mentioned in rabbinic sources resided in the Galilee. Like Jesus, Honi ministered in Elijah and Elisha country, which is why a later rabbinic text claims that no person in the history of Judaism is comparable to Elijah and Honi in inspiring humankind to serve God.[62] In Jewish tradition, Honi is known for praying for rain. The Mishnah, the earliest of rabbinic texts (see Introduction), explain that Honi prayed for rain during a drought. When it did not rain, Honi drew a circle on the ground, stood within it, and prayed, "Lord of the world! Your children have turned to me, for before you . . . I swear by your great name—I'm simply not moving from here until you take pity on your children."[63] Rain immediately began to fall.[64] In later tradition, Honi stopped a dangerous storm through prayer.[65]

Honi's two grandsons, Abba Hilqiah and Hanina ha-Nehba, ministered in Galilee during Jesus' childhood.[66] They too were known for performing nature miracles. In the stories they were both humble men who avoided luxuries and aspirations of popularity. Abba labored hard in the fields during the day and ignored sages passing by, and Hanina hid from people in the lavatory to avoid abundance of praise. Once when sages pled with Abba to pray for rain, he went to the upper room of his home and prayed; clouds then gathered overhead and the rain began to fall. During droughts, rabbis sent little children to Hanina; they "take hold of the hem of his garment" and request a prayer for rain.[67] We find in rabbinic texts several other holy men, many from Galilee, who perform similar nature miracles spanning from the late first century to the late third century CE.[68] The stories of Honi

---

61. Josephus, *Ant.* 14.2.1; Josephus corroborates the primary characteristics of Honi's (called Onias in Josephus) reputation in later rabbinic literature.

62. Bereishit Rabbah (Genesis Rabbah) 13:7, written sometime between the fourth and sixth centuries CE.

63. Mishnah Taanit 3:8; translation in Neusner, *Mishnah*, 312.

64. For a more in-depth treatment of both Honi ha-Me'aggel and his grandson Abba Hilqiah, as well as Hanina ben Dosa discussed previously, see the classic volume by Vermes, *Jesus the Jew*, 69–78.

65. Babylonian Talmud Taanit 23a.

66. It is interesting to note that the "tombs" of Honi and his two grandsons are located in the Galilee, a few miles north of the Sea of Galilee in the town of Hatzor HaGlilit.

67. Babylonian Talmud Taanit 23b, in Rabbinowitz, *Taanit*.

68. Babylonian Talmud Taanit 23b–25b.

and his grandsons are similar to the experiences of Jesus in some ways. Jesus is a Galilean miracle worker who is known for the ability to control the elements. Like these other holy men, Jesus rejects life's luxuries and public praise. People also seek out Jesus for miracles by "touch[ing] even the fringe of his cloak" (Mark 6:56), including the woman in Capernaum who has an issue of blood (Matt 9:20–22; Mark 5:25–34; Luke 8:42–48). As with Hanina ha-Nehba, people send or bring children to Jesus, about whom he says, "Let the little children come to me, and do not stop them; for it is to such as these that the kingdom of heaven belongs" (Matt 19:14).

Jesus' two primary nature miracles as presented in the Gospels position him within the framework of early Jewish miracle workers, not some anti-Jewish fringe miracle worker. One of these miracles is Jesus walking on the water (Matt 14:22–33; Mark 6:45–52; John 6:16–21), and the other is Jesus calming a violent storm on the Sea of Galilee (Matt 8:23–27; Mark 4:35–41; Luke 8:22–25). As the waves beat against the boat, Jesus' apostles fear as the boat fills with water. They awake Jesus and he rebukes the storm. The Gospel of Mark includes the specific words of Jesus' rebuke: "Peace! Be still!" (Mark 4:39). His apostles wonder, "Who then is this that he commands even the winds and the water, and they obey him?" (Luke 8:25). These two stories illustrate for the reader that Jesus is master over the elements, just as God is in the Hebrew Scriptures.[69] Jesus calms the storm; God "stills the sea" (Job 26:12). Jesus walks on water; God "tramples the waves of the sea" (Job 9:8). Jesus "rebukes" the storm; at God's "rebuke the [waters] flee" (Ps 104:6–7). Jesus' disciples awake him to calm the storm; God's people say, "Awake, awake [,] . . . Lord . . . was it not you who dried up the sea, the water of the great deep?" (Isa 51:9–10). Jesus' disciples plead with him in distress to calm the storm; God's people "cry to the Lord in their trouble, and he brought them out from their distress, he made the storm be still, and the waves of the sea were hushed" (Ps 107:28–29).

In addition to positioning Jesus as a divine-like figure, the water-walking episode may have been intended to point readers to Jesus as a second Moses and a second Elisha (as explained in the previous chapter). Through the power of Yahweh, Moses controlled the waters and miraculously crossed the Red Sea. Psalm 106 uses the word *rebuke*, which calls to mind that Jesus "rebukes" the storm: "Yet he saved them for his name's sake, so that he might make known his mighty power. He [God] *rebuked* the Red Sea, and it became dry; he led them through the deep" (Ps 106:8–9; emphasis added). Elisha also controlled the water by parting and crossing the Jordan River and by causing an ax-head to float (2 Kgs 2:8–14, 6:6).

---

69. Exod 14:21; Isa 43:16, 51:15; Job 41:31; Jonah 1–2; Pss 33:7, 77:19.

Why does Jesus sleep during the storm? Because sleeping during troubling times is a sign of confidence in the protective power of God. The book of Leviticus explains that God will "grant peace" so that "you shall lie down, and no one shall make you afraid" (Lev 26:6). The book of Job instructs, "you will have confidence, because there is hope; you will be protected and take your rest in safety" (Job 11:18). Both Psalm 3 and Psalm 4 declare, "I will both lie down and sleep in peace; for you alone, O Lord, make me lie down in safety" (Pss 3:5, 4:8). Proverbs explains, "When you lie down, your sleep will be sweet. Do not be afraid of sudden panic, or of *the storm that strikes* the wicked; for the Lord will be your confidence" (Prov 3:23–24; emphasis added). Many readers may find it odd that Jesus is sleeping during a dangerous storm as water is billowing into the boat. However, in its Jewish context the story makes sense. The detail of Jesus sleeping is not simply a matter-of-fact point in passing; the authors of the Gospels were specifically highlighting Jesus' confidence in divine protection while his spiritually immature followers (according to the Gospels) are afraid of drowning.

Chaotic waters are another element in these nature miracles that situate Jesus within a Jewish worldview. In the Hebrew Scriptures and early Jewish texts, chaotic waters are associated with evil and often house beast-demons or sea monsters. These are not to be taken literally but are symbols of evil in early Jewish literature. For example, in Genesis 1, when God creates the earth, "darkness covers the face of the deep" (Gen 1:2). Darkness, *choshekh* in Hebrew, is a symbol of evil and the underworld in ancient Israel.[70] God subdues this "formless void and darkness" when his "wind" (literally "Spirit") "sweeps over the face of the waters." Then "there is light" that God calls "good." The authors of Daniel and Revelation see beasts come out of the sea (Dan 7:2–3; Rev 13:1, 21:1). Several Israelite authors refer to these evil beasts as Rahab, Leviathan, or a dragon. The author of Isaiah understands that the Lord will "punish Leviathan the fleeing serpent . . . and he will kill the dragon that is in the sea" (Isa 27:1), and that the Lord is known in Israel for cutting "Rahab in pieces" and for "piercing the dragon" (Isa 51:9–10). In rabbinic literature, Rahab is the chief demon of the sea.[71] In the book of Job, Yahweh calms the sea by "striking down Leviathan" (Job 26:12, cf. Job 3:8). The psalmist also gives Jehovah credit for breaking "the heads of the dragons in the waters" and for crushing "the heads of Leviathan" (Ps 74:13–14). The author of the Thanksgiving Hymn in the Dead Sea Scrolls (second century BCE through the first century CE) laments that "Belial," the

---

70. Job 17:13, 22:11; Pss 88:12, 107:10, 14; Isa 5:20, 29:18, 60:2; Joel 2:2; Mic 7:8; Zeph 1:15.

71. Babylonian Talmud Baba Batra 74b; Exodus Rabbah 15.22; Numbers Rabbah 18.22.

devil in early Jewish literature, opposes him, so much so that he compared himself to "a sailor on a ship, when the seas stir up their waves and all their breakers come over me. A staggering wind roars [without] calm to revive the soul . . . The depths roar to my groaning and [my] soul approaches the gates of death."[72] In the Testament of Solomon (first century through the third century CE), King Solomon converses with a demon "who had the form of a horse in front and a fish in back." This seahorse demon refers to himself as "a cruel spirit of the sea" who transforms himself into a wave and "comes in against the ships," hurling "men under the sea" and "lusting after their bodies."[73] The author of 2 Baruch (early second century CE) believed that when the messiah came he would contend with the demon of the sea: "When the Anointed One will begin to be revealed, [the] Behemoth will reveal itself from its place, and Leviathan will come from the sea."[74]

These early Jewish sea-demon notions provide context for Jesus' calming of the storm. This nature miracle makes sense against the backdrop of the association between chaotic waters and demons. For early Christians, Jesus was the messiah; therefore, this story illustrated for them that he triumphed over evil when he conquered the raging storm on the Sea of Galilee. Just as Jesus "rebukes" evil spirits throughout his ministry (Mark 1:25, 9:25; Luke 4:35), he also rebukes the storm. The Hebrew equivalent of the Greek word for "rebuke" (*epitimao*) is *ga'ar*, a term used in rabbinic texts in relation to silencing Satan.[75] Moreover, Jesus' words in Mark, "Peace! Be still!" come from the Greek *pephimoso*, meaning "to muzzle" or "to exorcise" a demon.[76] Thus, Jesus' rebuke of the storm to "be still" demonstrates his control over the elements, even those elements believed to have been the abode of the chief demon. The message of such a Jewish miracle story is not apparent to modern English-speaking readers but would have resonated with Jesus' Jewish peers, especially those educated in the Hebrew Scriptures. A similar miracle story is found in rabbinic literature where Rabbi Gamaliel, the mentor of Paul according to the book of Acts, calms a storm through prayer:

> Rabbi Gamaliel was traveling in a ship when a huge wave arose to drown him . . . Thereupon he arose and exclaimed, "Sovereign

---

72. 1QH-a (Thanksgiving Hymn) 14:22–24; translation in Tov, *Dead Sea Scrolls Electronic Library*.

73. Testament of Solomon 16:1–5; see translation by Duling in *Old Testament Pseudepigrapha*, 1:976.

74. 2 Baruch 29:3–4; see translation by Klijn in *Old Testament Pseudepigrapha*, 1:630.

75. Kee, "Terminology of Mark's Exorcism Stories," 232–46; see also Jastrow, *Dictionary of the Targumim*, 261.

76. Throup, "Mark's Jesus, Divine," 71, 103, 113, 118, 123, 124, 166.

of the Universe! Thou knowest full well that I have not acted for my honor, nor for the honor of my paternal house, but for Thine, so that strife may not multiply in Israel!" At that the raging sea subsided.[77]

Notice that the storm is associated with contention and strife in Israel, and only Gamaliel's righteousness and humility could facilitate such a miracle.

Another type of nature miracle involves the multiplication of food. As illustrated in the last chapter, Jesus' major food miracles resemble in striking ways those of Elisha in the Hebrew Scriptures. The vast body of early Jewish literature contains few similarities to Jesus in terms of other miracle workers multiplying food; however, it does demonstrate a widespread expectation that the messiah will bring an age of plentiful sustenance. Bread, wine, milk, honey, and grain will flow in abundance at the hands of the messiah. For instance, 2 Baruch (early second century CE) explains that when the messiah comes he will "yield fruits ten thousand fold . . . and every branch will produce a thousand clusters, and one cluster will produce a thousand grapes, and one grape will produce a cor of wine . . . [and] manna will come down again from on high."[78] According to the author of the Sibylline Oracles (first or second century CE), the messiah will provide "the most excellent unlimited fruit, grain, wine, and oil and a delightful drink of sweet honey from heaven . . . and there will no longer be war or drought on the earth, no famine or hail damaging to fruits."[79] First Enoch (second century BCE through the first century CE) states that vines will "produce wine for plenitude," every seed will "yield a thousand measures," and every measure of olives will "yield ten measures."[80]

Jesus' experiences of multiplying bread, fish, and wine fit well within the early Jewish frameworks of the messiah providing an abundance of sustenance. Upon hearing the story of Jesus turning water into the best wine (over 120 gallons) in the Gospel of John (John 2:1–10), Jews might have recalled the words of a few Israelite prophets. Joel and Amos explain that in the messianic age "the mountains shall drip sweet wine, and all the hills shall flow with it" (Joel 3:18; Amos 9:13–14). The book of Isaiah maintains that the Lord will provide a "feast of well-matured wines," and then he will "swallow up death forever" (Isa 25:6–8). If Jews in the first few centuries CE

---

77. Babylonian Talmud Baba Mezia 59b, in Daiches, *Baba Mezia*.

78. 2 Baruch 29:3–8; see translation by Klijn in *Old Testament Pseudepigrapha*, 1:630–31.

79. Sibylline Oracles 3:741–50; see translation by Collins in *Old Testament Pseudepigrapha*, 1:378.

80. 1 Enoch 10:19; see translation by Isaac in *Old Testament Pseudepigrapha*, 1:18.

read or heard the stories of Jesus multiplying bread for many thousands,[81] they might have recalled the story of Elisha miraculously feeding one hundred men with twenty barley loaves, with loaves left over after they are filled (2 Kgs 4:42–44). They may have also remembered Moses providing manna from heaven to feed Israel.

The first-century Galilean miracle worker perhaps most similar to Jesus, Hanina ben Dosa, is also known for miraculously multiplying bread. According to the later tradition, Hanina's wife was ashamed because of their poverty. As the Sabbath approached, she lit the oven even though they had no ingredients for bread. The oven miraculously "fills with loaves of bread and the kneading trough full of dough." She quickly fetched a shovel, an act that rabbis later interpreted as, "She actually had gone to fetch the shovel because she was accustomed to miracles [of Hanina]."[82]

Given these parallels between Hanina ben Dosa and Jesus, we should note that we will continue to see in subsequent chapters that some of the Jesus-traditions are strikingly similar to those of other sages. What do we make of these parallels between Jesus and other Jewish holy men? Did Jesus' stories influence the composition of later rabbinic stories, or did these rabbinic stories predate Jesus and then influence the authors of the Gospels? We will explore a range of answers in the last chapter.

Takeaways

We began this chapter by asking how Jesus fit within the Jewish prophetic and miracle-worker context of early Judaism. It seems clear from the data that the prophetic and miracle traditions of Jesus cannot be adequately understood unless interpreted against the backdrop of early Judaism. Hearers or readers of these stories in the first through the fourth centuries CE would have misunderstood or benefited little from these traditions unless they were steeped in the world of Jewish law, texts, traditions, and customs. The prophet and miracle traditions of Jesus were not foreign or fringe stories to Jews but were meant to speak to Jews, which is why so many non-Jewish readers of later centuries had (and still have today) such a difficult time understanding them. Unfortunately, this has led to many flawed interpretations by Christians regarding Jesus' relationship to his Jewish peers. We must also note that although Jews at the time of Jesus believed in prophets and miracle workers and that early Jewish literature contains accounts of other prophets and miracle workers similar to Jesus, we cannot assume that

---

81. Matt 14:13–21, 15:32–39; Mark 6:30–44, 8:1–13; Luke 9:10–17; John 6:1–15.
82. Babylonian Talmud Taanit 24b–25a, in Rabbinowitz, *Taanit*.

such figures were common. The reason why people like Jesus of Nazareth and Rabbi Hanina ben Dosa were praised and eulogized as great Jewish holy men is precisely because they were extraordinary. On the one hand, their deeds fit within an early Jewish framework; they would not necessarily have been viewed by their Jewish peers as eccentric radicals. On the other hand, they were exceptional.

Chapter Four

The Kings of the Jews
"Messiahs" in the First Century

THIS CHAPTER AND THE next advance the discussion about Jesus' functions according to the Jesus traditions preserved in the Gospels. In the previous two chapters we dealt with Jesus as a prophet and miracle worker. In this and the next chapter we seek to situate Jesus within a messianic context.[1] We begin by discussing the messianic context of the first century, and in the next chapter we will situate Jesus within that context.

The terms "messiah" and "Christ" are widely used today, almost exclusively in reference to Jesus, at least among Christians. Modern Christians associate a plethora of notions, implications, and expectations with these titles. The word messiah, or *mashiach* in Hebrew, is synonymous with the word Christ, or *christos* in Greek, both meaning "one who is anointed" (with oil). What, however, were the connotations of these terms in Jesus' day? How did Jews in the first centuries BCE and CE interpret Old Testament passages regarding a messiah, and what did they expect of a future messiah? What did Jesus' followers who viewed him as the messiah expect him to accomplish? Were any figures during the New Testament period, other than Jesus, considered to be the messiah by their followers? We will attempt to answer these questions in this chapter.

---

1. Hatch, "Messianism and Jewish Messiahs."

Origins of the "Messiah" Concept

According to the New Testament, first-century followers of Jesus referred to him as, among other terms, "Messiah," "Son of God," "Son of David," and "Son of Man"; his adjudicators also referred to him, mockingly, as "King of the Jews." For many Christians today, these terms typically refer to a divine being who came in human form to provide salvation to humanity. It is important to understand when and where this notion of "messiah" originated and how the titles "Son of God," "Son of David," "Son of Man," and "King of the Jews" relate, if at all, to it.

Messianism among Jews in the first centuries BCE and CE is rooted in the ideology of kingship of earlier Israelite eras. The primary leaders in ancient Israel, particularly priests and kings, were anointed with oil at coronation.[2] The Hebrew Bible is replete with references to the anointing of Israelite kings, usually by prophets.[3] Israelite kings were frequently called "the Lord's anointed"—or "the Lord's messiah" in Hebrew and "the Lord's christ" in Greek.[4] In early Israelite literature, the root *msh*, meaning in its various forms "to anoint" or "anointed one," did not denote an awaited, future agent of God who would come to deliver Israel from its enemies in the end of days, the messianic era. "Anointed ones" were simply Israel's kings—and, during certain time periods, priests.[5] Even one non-Israelite king, Cyrus of Persia, was called "his anointed" (Isa 45:1) in the only reference to this title in the book of Isaiah.

The Israelite king was not only a "messiah" but a "son of God." Surrounding cultures—those of Canaan, Egypt, Mesopotamia, and Ugarit—influenced Israelite conceptions of kingship. Ancient Near Eastern kings were thought by their constituents to be divine and are specifically referred to as "sons of god."[6] Assyrian and Egyptian kings were thought to have attained divine status at or before birth. King Piye of Egypt (eighth century BCE), for example, stated, "I am he who was fashioned in the womb and created in the divine egg, the seed of the god being in me."[7] In contrast, Hittite and

---

2. Exod 28:41, 30:30, 40:13; Lev 7:35, 16:32; Num 3:3, 35:25. The Old Testament provides only one example of a prophet being anointed—the case of Elijah being commanded to anoint Elisha (1 Kgs 19:15–16; cf. 2 Kgs 9:1–3, 6, 12).

3. 1 Sam 9:9, 16; 10:1; 15:1, 17; 16:1–3, 12–13; 2 Sam 12:7, 22:51, 23:1; 1 Kgs 1:34, 39, 45; 19:15–16; 2 Kgs 9:1–3, 6, 12; 25:4–6.

4. 1 Sam 16:6; 24:6, 10; 26:9, 11, 16, 23; 2 Sam 1:14, 16; 19:21; Pss 2:2; 18:50; 20:6; 28:8; 89:39, 51; 132:10.

5. Fitzmyer, *One Who Is to Come*, 8–25.

6. Collins and Collins, *King and Messiah*, 1–10.

7. Cited in Frankfort, *Kingship and the Gods*, 42.

Canaanite kings were believed to attain godhood at death.[8] Like those from their neighboring nations, early Israelite texts described the king in relation to deity, or even possessing divine qualities. For example, many Near Eastern gods and kings were associated with shepherd imagery: "Good Shepherd" (Egyptian), "Noble Shepherd" (Sumerian), "Shepherd of Mankind" (Hittite), and "Wise Shepherd" (Assyrian).[9] In Israelite literature, just as God was identified as a shepherd of Israel,[10] so too was the king.[11] The god-king rhetoric in Israelite texts seems to be most salient in the book of Psalms. Both Yahweh and King David will rule the sea (Ps 89:9, 25), and the enemies of both Yahweh and David will be scattered (Ps 89:10, 22–23). More explicitly, David is Yahweh's "begotten son" (Ps 2:7) and his "firstborn" (Ps 89:26–27), and he will sit at God's "right hand" (Ps 110:1).

The notion that Israelite kings were both messiahs and sons of God shaped views of *the* messiah for later Jews. But what about Israelites before the exile to Babylon—did they believe that the king was a divine being? Was a "son of God" viewed as an earthly, human figure or a supernatural being? Scholars continue to debate these questions. The primary possible conclusions are (1) Israelite kings were viewed as divine in some sense; (2) Israel's god-king rhetoric was not meant to be literal but was metaphorical court language; or (3) Israel's kings were "adopted" as God's son.[12] It seems that, during the heyday of the monarchy, early Israelites tended to describe the king in terms that suggested divinity in some sense, or at least a very close association with deity. Later authors, it appears, rejected this idea, which is most apparent during the Israelite exile and postexile to Babylonia when the king's role was corrupted and less significant (see Ezek 34).[13] Regardless of whether Israelites viewed their kings as literal or metaphorical sons of God before the exile, exilic Jews interpreted the kingship passages in different ways, leading to a multiplicity of messianic expectations in the age of Jesus. Concerning the association between the messiah and the end times, the late Joseph Fitzmyer, a Catholic priest and professor at Catholic University of America, concluded that the "idea of messiah as an awaited or future

---

8. Lucass, *Concept of the Messiah*, 45–47.

9. See Niehaus, *Ancient Near Eastern Themes*, 39; Cohen, *Death Rituals*, 123; Bryce, *Kingdom of the Hittites*, 20; Sennacherib Prism, column 1, line 3.

10. Gen 49:24; Pss 23:1–4, 28:9, 80:1, 95:7, 100:3; Ezek 34:11–31.

11. 2 Sam 5:2, 7:7–8; 1 Kgs 22:17; Ps 78:70–71; Ezek 34:1–10.

12. For the various arguments, see Collins and Collins, *King and Messiah*, 1–25.

13. Collins and Collins, *King and Messiah*, 10–47; Lucass, *Concept of Messiah*, 66–121.

anointed agent of God in the end time was a late development in Israelite religion."[14]

Another title related to the word *messiah* is "Son of David." Although in ancient Israel the title "anointed one" was generally associated with kings, it was primarily used in relation to the Davidic dynasty of the southern kingdom of Judah. In 2 Samuel 7, God, through the prophet Nathan, covenants with David that his offspring will be God's "son" (2 Sam 7:14) and will establish an everlasting throne and kingdom (2 Sam 7:16). This idealized Davidic dynasty continues through the prophetic books of the Hebrew Bible and intensifies either when the nation is threatened by foreign enemies or when the throne is not held by a Davidic king. For example, Isaiah speaks of a future king who will have authority and bring endless peace to the throne and kingdom of David (Isa 9:6–7). Hosea too prophesies that, although for a time, Israel will be without a king, God will eventually restore the Davidic line to the throne (Hos 3:4–5; cf. Amos 9:11; Isa 55:3; Jer 23:5). And Ezekiel as well predicts that during the exile, after the Davidic king has been dethroned, "David" will again be Israel's "shepherd" (Ezek 34:23–24; 37:22–25).

"Messiah" in the Age of Jesus

After Persia conquered Babylonia, King Cyrus permitted Jews to return to Judea in 538 BCE. However, he did not allow them to reestablish an autonomous state. Jews were therefore kingless, not only during Persian rule (539–332 BCE) but also during Hellenistic (i.e., Greek) domination of the region, which lasted until 142 BCE. It seems that there was a reduced emphasis on a royal "messiah" figure who would restore Israel during most of this 400-year span. Language once associated with Israel's kings in times past (e.g., "anointed one" and "son of God") was transferred to the high priest, the head of the Jewish people.[15]

In the second century BCE, expectations of a king-deliverer flourished for three major reasons. First, oppression from Greek overlords intensified, culminating in the desecration of the temple (164 BCE). Second, when Jewish guerrilla fighters wrested Judea and the temple away from the Greeks, a Jewish dynasty—led by a family called the "Hasmoneans"—controlled the throne (142–163 BCE); although a great victory of the Jews, the Hasmoneans were not descendants of David. Thus, the anticipated Davidic king would not come through the Hasmonean dynasty. Third, the high

---

14. Fitzmyer, *One Who Is to Come*, 8.
15. Lucass, *Concept of Messiah*, 122–43.

priesthood was usurped and corrupted by wealthy non-Aaronide aristocrats, meaning a priestly class who were not descendants of Aaron. Before and during the Hasmoneans, several individuals bought their way into the office of high priest by offering to raise taxes on the Jewish people to stay in the good graces with their Greek overlords. Thus the Jewish populace witnessed attacks on their religion and temple system from all sides, including from within.

The morale of the new autonomous Jewish state worsened and messianic expectations intensified when the Romans, with the help of some Jews, swept in and dethroned the Hasmonean dynasty in 63 BCE. Rome eventually appointed an illegitimate, Jewish-Idumean (or "half-Jew") dictator as local ruler. This man, Herod, with approval from Rome, ruled with an iron fist. According to Josephus, Herod set up a spy network to cleanse the puppet kingdom of Hasmonean loyalists and sympathizers. He executed numerous people whom he suspected of opposing him. Among his victims were his brother-in-law (the high priest!), his mother-in-law, his second wife, three of his sons, and three hundred military leaders.[16]

The populace did not escape corruption and violence even after Herod died. On many occasions, crowds of Jewish citizens protested injustices perpetrated upon them. For example, when Pontius Pilate, the Roman authority of the region (26–36 CE), brought Caesar's effigies into Jerusalem (and possibly into the temple complex) with approval from the priestly class, a multitude nearly rioted and demanded that Pilate remove the effigies.[17] On another occasion, priests permitted Pilate to use funds from the temple treasury to pay for an aqueduct to Jerusalem. When a protest ensued, Pilate dispatched soldiers to disperse the crowds by threatening to kill them.[18] In the face of this oppression and corruption, a more intense messianic fervor spread. In the two centuries before the ministry of Jesus, most Jews greatly anticipated the messiah, who would be a Davidic king and deliverer of Israel. By the time Jesus began his ministry, messianic expectations had reached a fever pitch.

Perhaps the earliest passage that illustrates the shift in messianic expectations during this time period is in the book of Daniel. Here, we encounter a new messianic title, the "Son of Man." This term comes from the Hebrew *ben adam* and the Aramaic *bar enosh*, both meaning a "person" or a "human being." Ezekiel, for example, is addressed as "son of man" nearly one hundred times in the book bearing his name. According to most

---

16. Josephus, *Ant.* 15:50–56, 222–36, 247–51, 365–72; 16:392–94.
17. Josephus, *Ant.* 18:55–57.
18. Josephus, *Ant.* 18:60.

scholars, the book of Daniel was produced in the early second century BCE, concurrent with the Greek persecutions (175–64 BCE).[19] In this book, the author describes Daniel seeing a vision of four great beasts, which are believed to represent Babylonia, Media, Persia, and Greece. Daniel then sees the Ancient of Days on a throne with another figure alongside. Together, they defeat and judge these nations:

> I saw in the night visions, and, behold, one like the Son of man came with the clouds of heaven, and came to the Ancient of days, and they brought him near before him. And there was given him dominion, and glory, and a kingdom, that all people, nations, and languages, should serve him: his dominion is an everlasting dominion, which shall not pass away, and his kingdom that which shall not be destroyed. (Dan 7:13–14)

The figure in this passage is one *like* a "son of man," meaning a divine figure who looks like a human. He will have authority and will be worshiped by all people. Note also the language tying this figure to the Davidic kingship ideal—that he will be a king over an everlasting kingdom. The "clouds of heaven" link this figure to Deity, according to several passages in the Hebrew Bible (see Exod 34:5; Ps 104:3; Isa 19:1). Scholars have debated the precise interpretation of this Son of Man figure in Daniel; however, it seems that he had the appearance of a human and was some kind of divine royal figure destined to defeat Israel's foreign enemies.

Another text, the book of 1 Enoch, which dates to the late first century BCE or early first century CE,[20] also mentions the son of man:

> I saw the One to whom belongs the time before time. And his head was white like wool, and there was with him another individual, *whose face was like that of a human being* . . . This [is the] Son of Man whom you have seen. [He] is the One who would remove the kings and the mighty ones from their comfortable seats and the strong ones from their thrones. (1 Enoch 46:1–4, emphasis added)

> At that hour, that Son of Man was given a name, in the presence of the Lord of the Spirits, the Before-Time; even before the creation of the sun and the moon, before the creation of the stars, he was given a name in the presence of the Lord of the Spirits . . . All those who dwell upon the earth shall fall and worship before him . . . And he has revealed the wisdom of the Lord of the

---

19. Collins, *Daniel*, 1–38; Smith-Christopher, "Daniel," 6:86–94.
20. Collins and Collins, *King and Messiah*, 87.

Spirits to the righteous and holy ones, for he has preserved the portion of the righteous because they have hated and despised this world of oppression (together with) all its ways of life and its habits and it is his good pleasure that they have life ... For they (the wicked kings and landowners) have denied the Lord of the Spirits and his Messiah. (1 Enoch 48:2–10)

Thenceforth nothing that is corruptible shall be found; for that Son of Man has appeared and has seated himself upon the throne of his glory; and all evil shall disappear from before his face. (1 Enoch 69:29)[21]

We learn from these passages that expectations of a divine messianic figure were circulating in the centuries before Jesus' ministry. The heavenly figure in Daniel who looks like a "son of man" was later called "son of man" in the book of 1 Enoch. According to these Jewish authors, this figure was a preexistent being who was closely associated with God, would have dominion over all earthly kingdoms, would be worshiped by all people, would judge the wicked, would overthrow his enemies, would establish an everlasting kingdom, and would be the "messiah."

Alongside these son of man traditions are a number of other messianic traditions in other early Jewish texts. Perhaps the most prominent messianic theme among these texts is the idea that the son of man will descend from the tribe of Judah through David. Genesis 49 and Isaiah 11 serve as the primary sources for this idea: "The sceptre shall not depart from Judah, nor a lawgiver from between his feet, until Shiloh come; and unto him shall the gathering of the people be" (Gen 49:10); "and there shall come forth a rod out of the stem of Jesse, and a Branch shall grow out of his roots" (Isa 11:1). Many Jews during this era interpreted these passages messianically. For example, a Dead Sea Scroll commentary on Genesis discovered in Cave 4 at Qumran held that this future Judahite king would be the "Righteous Messiah, the Branch of David."[22] The Psalms of Solomon, a mid-first-century-BCE text, harks back to 2 Samuel 7, where God promises David that his offspring will be God's son (v. 14) and will establish an everlasting throne (v. 16): "See, Lord, and raise up for them their king, the son of David, to rule over your servant Israel in the time known to you, O God ... And their king shall be the Lord Messiah."[23]

Another emergent messianic theme in early Jewish texts is that the messiah would have worldwide authority and be praised universally by all

21. Isaac, "1 Enoch," in 1:34–36, 49.

22. 4Q252 5:1–4 (Cave 4 at Qumran, manuscript 252, column 5, lines 1 through 4), translation from Wise et al., *Dead Sea Scrolls*, 355.

23. Psalms of Solomon 17:21, 32, in Isaac, "1 Enoch," 2:667.

people. In this role, the messiah will judge the wicked and punish Israel's enemies. Several Qumran texts, for example, assert that "heaven and earth shall listen to His Messiah,"[24] that the rulers of Israel will "sit before him,"[25] and that others "will be handed over to the sword when the Messiah . . . comes."[26] In the Psalms of Solomon, the messiah will "lead the righteous" and "will have gentile nations serving him under his yoke"; he will "expose officials and drive out sinners."[27] The Sibylline Oracles, another first-century-BCE text, declares that "God will send a King . . . who will stop the entire earth from evil war, killing some, imposing oaths of loyalty on others."[28] The expectation of a warrior messiah who would fight Israel's foreign enemies may have been justified based on Isaiah 45: "Thus says the Lord to his *anointed*, to Cyrus, whose right hand I have grasped to *subdue nations before him*" (Isa 45:1; emphasis added). Some Jews, particularly those at Qumran, also expected the messiah to perform miracles. One Dead Sea Scroll text states the following:

> His Messiah . . . will honor the pious upon the throne of His eternal kingdom, setting prisoners free, opening the eyes of the blind, raising up those who are bowed down . . . He shall heal the critically wounded, He shall revive the dead, He shall send good news to the afflicted.[29]

It seems clear from these sources that it was during the first two centuries before Jesus' ministry that the idea of a divine agent of God who would redeem Israel, delivering them from bondage, became more widely accepted, or at least more apparent, among the Jewish population. Whatever earlier Israelites believed about the nature of the future agent of God who would destroy the wicked and redeem Israel, it seems that by the beginning of Jesus' ministry, some Jews had high expectations for the one they called "Messiah," "Son of God," and "Son of Man." These generic terms in earlier centuries were later used as titles for one special individual who would redeem Israel. This divine agent of God would not just be *a* messiah but *the* Messiah; not just *a* son of God but *the* Son of God; not just *a* king but *the* King of kings; not just *a* son of man but *the* Son of Man.

---

24. 4Q521 frags. 2 + 4 ii 1, translation from Wise et al., *Dead Sea Scrolls,* 531.

25. 1QSa 2:14–15, translation from Wise et al., *Dead Sea Scrolls,* 140.

26. CD 19:10–11, translation from Wise et al., *Dead Sea Scrolls,* 59.

27. Psalms of Solomon 17:26–36, in Isaac, "1 Enoch," 2:667–68.

28. Sibylline Oracles 3:652–54, translation from Collins, *Old Testament Pseudepigrapha,* 1:376.

29. 4Q521 frags. 2 + 4 ii 1–12, translation from Wise et al., *Dead Sea Scrolls,* 531.

Before discussing messiah figures during the generation of Jesus, let us recap what we learn from pre-Christian, Jewish texts regarding messianic expectations leading up the ministry of Jesus:

- He would be a preexistent figure with some divine qualities.
- All people would worship him.
- He would be a king.
- He would reestablish the Davidic dynasty.
- His kingdom would be everlasting.
- He would have authority over all nations.
- He would lead Israel.
- He would judge the wicked and overthrow Israel's foreign enemies.
- He would be associated with righteousness.
- He would heal the sick, restore sight to the blind, and raise the dead.

We must be careful not to assume that all Jews expected the messiah to be and do all these things. Some Jews may have expected some of these outcomes while rejecting others. This list is simply a conglomeration of what is apparent in pre-Christian Jewish texts regarding messianic expectations. With that, note one expectation common to most Christians that is missing in these texts: the messiah would be subdued, humiliated, and killed by his enemies. The one text that seems to suggest that the messiah would be killed is 4 Ezra: "For my son the Messiah shall be revealed with those who are with him, and those who remain shall rejoice four hundred years. And after these years *my son the Messiah shall die*, and all who draw human breath."[30] In this ambiguous text, the messiah will not be humiliated and killed by his enemies but will die along with all other humans after four hundred years (one thousand years in the Arabic version of 4 Ezra). Further, this text dates to the late first century CE and may not tell us much about messianic expectations in the two centuries preceding Jesus' ministry.

Some may challenge the conclusion that early Jews did not expect a suffering, defeated messiah by pointing to the "suffering servant" passage in Isaiah 53, which contains perhaps the most contested verses in the Hebrew Bible:

> He was despised and rejected by others; a man of suffering and acquainted with infirmity; and as one from whom others hide their faces he was despised, and we held him of no account.

---

30. 4 Ezra 7:28–30, in Isaac, "1 Enoch," 1:537; emphasis added.

> Surely he has borne our infirmities and carried our diseases; yet we accounted him stricken, struck down by God, and afflicted. But he was wounded for our transgressions, crushed for our iniquities; upon him was the punishment that made us whole, and by his bruises we are healed. All we like sheep have gone astray; we have all turned to our own way, and the Lord has laid on him the iniquity of us all. He was oppressed, and he was afflicted, yet he did not open his mouth; like a lamb that is led to the slaughter, and like a sheep that before its shearers is silent, so he did not open his mouth. (Isa 53:3–7)

Jewish commentators in late antiquity and throughout the Middle Ages disagreed on the nature of the "servant" in Isaiah. Some interpreted it as referring to the messiah; others to Israel. Regardless, it seems that this messianic prophecy was overshadowed by the many other expectations of a victorious messiah in the two centuries leading up to Jesus' ministry. Scholars of messianism have shown through extensive examination of all the messianic passages in pre-Christian Jewish texts that the idea of a suffering messiah was virtually nonexistent.[31] We must note that Daniel 9 refers to an "anointed one" who will be "cut off and shall have nothing" (v. 26), but it is ambiguous whether this passage suggests that this figure will be humiliated and ultimately killed. Could it be that this figure will be defeated for a time and then conquer his foes? We do not know. What we can say is that the few passages in the Hebrew Bible, like this in Daniel 9, are overshadowed a great deal in other early Jewish texts by a victorious messiah.

That messianic expectations did not include a suffering, dying messiah is crucial to understanding the events immediately following Jesus' death. One must remember that not all Jews held a normative set of beliefs about the messiah's divine status—whether he would be divine or mortal—nor did all Jews uniformly expect the messiah to accomplish a specific set of tasks. As we have seen, the various Jewish texts predating Jesus posited a wide variety of messianic expectations and ideas about the divine status of a future messiah. Berkeley scholar Daniel Boyarin, Orthodox Jew and expert in early Jewish literature, noted the disparate messianic beliefs among early Jews:

> There are many variations of traditions about this figure in the Gospels themselves and in other early Jewish texts. Some Jews had been expecting this Redeemer to be a human exalted to the state of divinity, while others were expecting a divinity to come down to earth and take on human form; some believers in Jesus

---

31. Collins and Collins, *King and Messiah*, 1–213; Lucass, *Concept of Messiah* 122–210; Fitzmyer, *One Who Is to Come*, 56–181.

believed the Christ had been born as an ordinary human and then exalted to divine status, while others believed him to have been a divinity who came down to earth. Either way, we end up with a doubled godhead and a human-divine combination as the expected Redeemer.[32]

Early Jewish Messiahs and Messiah-Like Activity

After Herod died in 4 BCE, the regions of Judea and Galilee experienced an increase in messianic personalities. Prior to Herod's death, hope of a conquering messiah seemed to be a somewhat distant hope. In the first century CE, however, the realization of the messiah seemed imminent for much of the populace, especially in response to the Roman authoritarian and militaristic governing style. Josephus detailed approximately a dozen figures in the first century alone—with many more mentioned in passing—who acted in ways that caused portions of the populace to view them as possible messiahs, or "messianic candidates." He explained that many of these figures were declared "king" by their followers and were seen as nuisances by Roman authorities.[33] Only the Roman senate could make someone a king. For example, they made Herod the Great a vassal king of the Judean frontier. Anyone who designated themselves, or whose followers designated them, as kings would have been considered treasonous and subjected to punishment. Consequently, Jerusalem temple bureaucrats and the Roman officials attempted to quash any movement led by a "king" in their land, especially anyone who sought to wrest control of the region away from the Romans and the temple establishment.

One such figure was Judas from Sepphoris, a town in Galilee about five miles from Nazareth. In the wake of Herod's death, Judas gathered a sizable following and besieged several royal armories in 4 BCE. He subsequently targeted other people who had royal aspirations, probably because he himself had his eye on the throne.[34] That same year, Simon of Perea put a diadem on his head and declared himself king. With a group of followers, he proceeded to burn several royal properties, including the palace at Jericho. Roman soldiers eventually intercepted and beheaded him.[35] During the next few years (4–2 BCE), Athrongeus, a shepherd, declared himself king

---

32. Boyarin, *Jewish Gospels*, 34.
33. Josephus, *Ant.* 17.10.8.
34. Josephus, *Ant.* 17.10.5; Josephus, *J.W.* 2.4.1.
35. Josephus, *Ant.* 17.10.6; Josephus, *J.W.* 2.4.2.

and went about killing Roman soldiers and Jewish royalists until Roman authorities captured him.[36] His identification as a shepherd and a king was an overt statement about his messiahship.

A few decades later in the 20s CE, John the Baptist established such a large following that he was imprisoned and eventually beheaded after challenging Herod Antipas. Josephus recorded that Herod Antipas was particularly concerned that John's power and influence with the populace would lead to rebellion. Neither Josephus nor the New Testament indicates that John was viewed as the messiah, but some likely saw him as a messianic candidate due to his ability to garner support from the messianic-minded populace.[37] Approximately ten years after John the Baptist's death, another figure gained a large following among the Samaritans in 35 CE, a people closely related to the Jews both ideologically and geographically. Samaritans awaited a figure like Moses who would restore the ancient temple. This Samaritan prophet promised to show his followers the holy vessels that Moses supposedly buried on Mount Gerizim. Pontius Pilate and his infantry attacked the group, killing some and arresting others.[38] A decade later in 45 CE, Theudas, a prophet who was known for performing miracles, led a group to the Jordan River. He had promised to divide the waters as had Joshua. Before the group arrived at the river, Roman authorities attacked them, beheading Theudas and killing many of his followers.[39] At this same time, Judas from Gamala in Galilee gathered a group and revolted against Rome in order to establish national independence. The group eventually failed (Acts 5:37). Josephus did not explain Judas's fate, but we learn that two of his sons were crucified during Tiberius Alexander's reign (46–48 CE) in consequence of the rebellion. Judas's third son, Menachem, had similar kingly aspirations that he would act on in the future.[40]

A few years later in the 50s CE, an unnamed Egyptian prophet gathered a large group on the Mount of Olives. He claimed that Jerusalem's walls would fall on his command, allowing the multitude to enter the city. Roman authorities rushed to the Mount of Olives and killed or arrested over six hundred people.[41] The prophet escaped and never appeared in Jerusalem again; however, when the apostle Paul made his last trip to Jerusalem a short time later, Roman authorities mistook him for the Egyptian prophet: "You

---

36. Josephus, *Ant.* 17.10.7; Josephus, *J.W.* 2.4.3.
37. Josephus, *Ant.* 18.5.2.
38. Josephus, *Ant.* 18.4.1.
39. Josephus, *Ant.* 20.5.1; Acts 5:36.
40. Josephus, *Ant.* 18.1.1.
41. Josephus, *Ant.* 20.8.6.

are not the Egyptian who recently stirred up a revolt and led the four thousand assassins out into the wilderness?" (Acts 21:38). This prophet seemed to be motivated by the messianic prophecies in Zechariah 14 that speak of a divine warrior figure who would descend from heaven and stand on the Mount of Olives before entering Jerusalem. The goal of this divine figure would be to overthrow the foreign enemies of Israel.

Another figure who challenged the authorities in Jerusalem was Jesus ben Ananias. In 62 CE he went about in the temple complex during the Feast of Tabernacles (i.e., Sukkoth) proclaiming judgment upon Jerusalem. His shouts included direct quotations from Jeremiah 7, precisely the same block of Scripture that Jesus of Nazareth used when he accused priests of turning the temple into a "den of robbers" (Jer 7:11). As they did with Jesus of Nazareth, Roman authorities arrested and whipped Jesus ben Ananias until his flesh gave way, exposing his bones.[42] A few years later in 66 CE, Menachem, son of the aforementioned Judas of Gamala, entered Jerusalem as a "king" wearing royal garb. With an armed group, he managed to kill the high priest and occupy the Roman barracks. He was eventually captured, dragged into a public space, and tortured to death.[43] Within a few years of Menachem's defeat, two other figures from near Galilee—John of Gischala and Simon bar Giora, who were rivals of one another—separately attempted to take control of Jerusalem and reign as king. John was eventually caught and imprisoned for life, and Simon was carried off to Rome where he was executed.[44] The actions of these twelve individuals illustrate the tension between popular messiah-like figures and Roman authorities.[45]

> Messiah-like Figures
> in the First Century
>
> Judas of Sepphoris (4 BCE)
> Simon of Perea (4 BCE)
> Athrongeus the shepherd (4–2 BCE)
> John the Baptist (20s CE)
> **Jesus of Nazareth (30 CE)**
> Samaritan prophet (35 CE)
> Theudas (45 CE)
> Judas of Gamala (40s CE)
> Unnamed Egyptian (50s CE)
> Jesus ben Ananias (62 CE)
> Menachem of Gamala (66 CE)
> John of Gischala (late 60s CE)
> Simon bar Giora (late 60s CE)

---

42. Josephus, *J.W.* 6.5.3.

43. Josephus, *J.W.* 2.17.8–10.

44. Josephus, *J.W.* 2.20.6, 2.21.1, 4.6.1, 4.7.1, 4.9.4–5, 6.9.4, 7.1.2, 7.2.2, 7.5.3–6.

45. For a more detailed treatment of popular prophet and messiah figures in the first century, see Evans, *Ancient Texts*, 431–43; Horsley, *Bandits, Prophets and Messiahs*, 88–187.

A few observations from these twelve cases provide the context for Jesus' ministry and ultimate demise. First, Galilee seemed to be a hotbed for messianic fervor in the first century CE; the majority of these figures come either from Galilee or close by. We learned in the previous chapter that a majority of the miracle workers who shared similar broad characteristics and experiences with Jesus were also from Galilee. Monuments and tombs of prominent rabbis and Jewish holy men in antiquity pepper the landscape in the immediate vicinity of the Sea of Galilee and in Sepphoris, a city located only three miles from Nazareth and the capital of Galilee during Jesus' childhood. These monuments to some of the most prominent figures in rabbinic literature draw modern Jewish worshipers to the Galilee region to this day. To further situate Jesus in his Galilean context, we highlight a few events in the region during the generation immediately preceding Jesus' generation.

As a young boy, Jesus would have learned about the brutality of the Romans and Herodians who severely punished dissenters. For example, before Jesus was born, in 40 BCE, some Jews resisted Herod's appointment as king. Josephus explained that rebels fled to Mount Arbel on the immediate west side of the Sea of Galilee. They hid themselves in caves in the steep cliffs above the Arbel Valley. Josephus related the subsequent details as follows:

> The king, whose men were unable either to climb up from below or creep upon them from above because of the steepness of the hill, had cribs built and lowered these upon them with iron chains as they were suspended by a machine from the summit of the hill. The cribs were filled with armed men holding great grappling hooks, with which they were supposed to draw toward them any of the brigands who opposed them, and kill them by hurling them to the ground. . . . The same method of attack was used the following day, when the men in the baskets fell upon them still more fiercely . . . and threw flaming fire inside, and so the caves, which had much wood in them, were set on fire. Now there was an old man shut up within one of the caves with his seven children and his wife . . . He stood at the entrance and cut down each of his sons as he came out, and afterwards his wife, and after hurling their dead bodies over the precipice, threw himself down upon them, thus submitting to death rather than to slavery."[46]

36 years later, right around the time of Jesus' birth, the Roman general Varus in 4 BCE lined the 20-mile road from Sepphoris to the Sea of Galilee—which

---

46. Josephus, *Ant.* 14.4–5, trans. Marcus and Wikgren.

passed through the Arbel Valley—with 2,000 crucified Jewish rebels. Since Nazareth was only three miles from Sepphoris, it is likely that Jesus heard about this event from his parents and peers as he grew older and was taught about Rome and their role in society.[47] Jesus would have walked through the Arbel Valley while traveling from Nazareth to Galilee. He might have stopped and, while looking around, said, "So this is where that tragedy occurred in those cliffs during my father's childhood, and where Rome crucified those men."

The legacy of Galilee as an incubator for messiahs and rebels became so entrenched that Jews in later centuries associated this place with the coming of the future messiah and with the redemption of Israel. In Jewish lore, the Arbel Valley became the location for the messiah to redeem Israel in the last days. Rabbis in the fourth century CE preserved the following story about two rabbis in the early third century CE:

> It is told of Rabbi Hiyya and Rabbi Simeon that they walked in the valley of Arbel early in the morning and saw the dawn breaking on the horizon. Thereupon Rabbi Hiyya said: So too is Israel's redemption [through King Messiah]; at first it will be only very slightly visible, then it will shine forth more brightly and only afterwards will it break forth in all of its glory.[48]

A later seventh-century tradition explicitly states that the final messianic battle will occur in the Arbel Valley:

> With their own eyes all the children of Israel will see the Lord, like a man of war with a helmet of salvation on his head, dressed in armor. He will do battle against Gog and Magog . . . and [Israel's enemies] will all fall dead in the valley of Arbel."[49]

Some scholars have challenged the view that the Galilee was a special hotbed for messianic and rebel activity in the generation preceding and during Jesus' lifetime; after all, "battles and killings took place all over the country, including Idumea, Jericho, Samaria, and also Galilee," as Morten Jensen (Galilee scholar at MF Norwegian School of Theology) demonstrated.[50] Regardless of how unique Galilee was as a messianic and rebel hub, the region does seem to have a tradition of messiahs in the first centuries BCE and

---

47. See Josephus, *J.W.* 2.5.1–2; *Ant.* 17.10.9–10.

48. From a commentary on the Song of Songs by fourth century rabbis, see translation in Scholem, *Messianic Idea in Judaism*, 10.

49. Book of Zerubbabel, seventh-century Hebrew apocalypse, see translation in Himmelfarb, *Jewish Messiahs in a Christian Empire*, 155.

50. Jensen, "Political History in Galilee," in Fiensy and Strange, *Galilee*, 60.

CE. Jesus would have been raised in this messianic milieu and would have perhaps become sensitized to the anti-Roman and anti-Herodian sentiments throughout the region.

Another observation of these messiah-type figures mentioned in Josephus is the level of volatility between the Jewish populace and the authorities in Jerusalem (both Jewish and Roman). These messiah figures seemed to gain support from sizable segments within the Jewish populace and were met with swift punishment by Roman soldiers. The cases of Jesus of Nazareth and Jesus ben Ananias especially help further illustrate this volatility. During festival seasons, the population of Jerusalem swelled dramatically, which caused the authorities a great deal of angst. On several occasions, the crowds protested in opposition to Roman and Jewish temple authorities. The bureaucrats themselves feared such protests and riots because they would lead to regional unrest and would infuriate Caesar. Josephus provided a few examples of such protests during festivals. In the early first century BCE, a large crowd protested against the high priest at the temple during the Feast of Tabernacles. It seems that they rejected the priest because he was not a descendant of Aaron. After people in the crowd threw objects at the high priest, he called in the soldiers and killed six thousand protesters.[51] Josephus related another protest that occurred in the first century CE during Passover when a Roman soldier raised his robe, exposing his backside—or, according to a second account, "uncovered his genitals and exhibited them"—to the Jewish crowd at the temple. When the crowd erupted in a protest, soldiers killed no fewer than "twenty-thousand" Jewish pilgrims and worshipers.[52]

The festivals were times of volatility. Passover especially invited protests because the festival commemorated Israel's deliverance from a foreign oppressor in Egypt during the Exodus. Many Jews during Passover anticipated a similar deliverance over a foreign oppressor under the messiah. Moses delivered the people the first time; a messiah would deliver the people this time. Thus, if an individual entered Jerusalem during Passover with an entourage and claimed to be the messiah or Son of David, that individual would be in the crosshairs of the soldiers.

Takeaways

In this chapter, we have seen that early Israelite kings were called "messiahs" and "sons of God." Later tradition focused on an everlasting kingdom of David. During the Second Temple period, the kingly traditions expanded

---

51. Josephus, *Ant.* 13.372–73.
52. Josephus, *J.W.* 2.12.1; *Ant.* 20.5.3, trans. Feldman.

further into a body of expectations that included a figure who would be a divine agent of God and savior of Israel. The literature of the two centuries preceding the ministry of Jesus reveal that some Jews expected the messiah to be a preexistent, divine figure, worshiped by all. He would be a king and reestablish the Davidic dynasty. He would have authority over all nations and lead Israel. He would judge the wicked and overthrow Israel's foreign enemies. The messianic expectations at Qumran also included healing the sick, restoring sight to the blind, and raising the dead. The one expectation not found in these sources is that the messiah would be subdued, humiliated, and killed by his enemies. The many first-century messianic figures provide context into the relationship between Roman authorities and messianic movements that sought to establish a kingdom free of Roman influence. These messiahs were viewed as traitors and rebels; most were punished severely, usually with death. In the next chapter, we will discuss how Jesus fit within this first-century Jewish messianic worldview.

Chapter Five

"Who Do Men Say That I Am?"
Jesus as a Messianic Candidate

How did Jesus' experience compare to Jewish messianic expectations in the centuries immediately preceding and succeeding his birth? Did Jesus' "lukewarm" followers see him as the "anointed one"? Did his closest disciples uniformly recognize him as the messiah? If so, did they refer to him as such? These questions are difficult to answer because the primary sources about Jesus were written forty to seventy years after his death. While the Gospels retain some authentic material about the Jesus of history, they also present a "CliffsNotes" version of his ministry—a brief, carefully crafted, idealized presentation of Jesus' deeds and sayings. By the time the Gospels' writers were putting pen to paper, so to speak, they had already established in their minds that Jesus was, indeed, the messiah, and their written accounts were an attempt to demonstrate his messiahship to others. What we do not have are firsthand accounts from Jews who witnessed some of Jesus' ministrations and heard at least a few of his sermons.[1] Nevertheless, the Gospels do provide useful material to help situate Jesus within the tumultuous messianic milieu of the first century CE.

Jesus as a "Messianic Candidate"

During his ministry, the belief that Jesus was the messiah was not cut and dried for his followers. A reason for this ambiguity may be that, according

---

1. The final chapter discusses this issue.

to the Synoptic Gospels, Jesus seems to avoid using the term "messiah" in reference to himself. A rare occasion when Jesus acknowledges outright that he is the messiah to someone outside his close circle is to the Samaritan woman at Jacob's well. The woman claims she is waiting for the messiah. In reply, Jesus says, "I am he" (John 4:26). Later, when another non-apostle, the high priest, asks Jesus in private whether he is the messiah, Jesus acknowledges that he is (Mark 14:61–62). His responses in Matthew and Luke, however, are more ambiguous. In Matthew, Jesus responds, "You have said so" (26:64), in other words, "That is your way of putting it."[2] In Luke, Jesus responds, "If I tell you, you will not believe; and if I question you, you will not answer" (22:67–68).

Jesus also seems apprehensive to embrace the messiah label among his closest disciples. When Nathaniel first meets Jesus, he exclaims, "Rabbi, you are the Son of God! You are the King of Israel!" Jesus responds, "Do you believe because I told you that I saw you under the fig tree? You will see greater things than these" (John 1:49–50). Again, Jesus hesitates to say, "Yes, I'm the Messiah." At Caesarea Philippi, Jesus asks his closest disciples how others perceive him. They answer that some think he is Elijah or a prophet. Jesus then asks his disciples what they think of him, to which Peter answers, "You are the Messiah." Without confirming Peter's answer, Jesus "strictly warns" them (*epitimesas* in Greek, also meaning "rebuke") not to tell anyone (Luke 9:19–21; Mark 8:28–30; Matt 16:13–20). This secrecy regarding Jesus' messiahship is most evident in the Gospel of Mark. New Testament scholars, beginning with William Wrede in 1901, have referred to this command for silence in Mark as the "Messianic Secret."[3] In this gospel, Jesus repeatedly instructs his apostles to keep quiet about his deeds that might cause some to see him as a messianic candidate.[4] It is peculiar that in Mark, Jesus' followers disobey him and reveal his secrets, which leads to Jesus' fame spreading quickly: "Then Jesus ordered them to tell no one; but the more he ordered them, the more zealously they proclaimed it" (Mark 7:36).

Perhaps Jesus refrained from referring to himself directly as the "messiah" in public because of the baggage the word had accumulated over the centuries, as illustrated in the previous chapter. Jesus may have wanted to distance himself from such expectations, as well as with all the associated folklore. Further, he may not have wanted to draw too much attention from the authorities, considering their disdain for messianic movements. On one occasion, after Jesus' popularity reaches a high point, according to the

---

2. Fitzmyer, *One Who Is to Come*, 138.
3. Wrede, *Messianic Secret*.
4. See, for example, Mark 1:43–45, 4:11, 5:43, 7:36, 8:29–30.

author of John, a large crowd attempted to "take him by force *to make him king*"; Jesus immediately flees into the "the mountain by himself" (John 6:15; emphasis added). It seems that Jesus, according to the New Testament, preferred the title "Son of Man," which occurs over eighty times—more than the use of "Messiah," "Son of David," and "Son of God" combined. Even so, many of Jesus' actions during his ministry, according to the Gospels, did point to his messiah status for early Jesus followers.

Jesus as Joseph and David

In order to establish Jesus' messiah status, the Gospels compare him to two major figures in the Hebrew Bible—Joseph the Patriarch and King David. The Jesus-David comparison is explicit—as the Synoptic Gospels refer to Jesus in many instances as the "Son of David"—whereas the Jesus-Joseph comparison is implicit. Some Jews in antiquity awaited two messianic figures. Several early Jewish texts perpetuated traditions of (1) a messiah who would descend from the lineage of Judah through David, and (2) a messiah who would descend from Joseph. The first messiah, the "Son of David" figure, was significantly more salient for Jews; however, the messiah son of Joseph is also mentioned in several early Jewish texts. In a Targum (an Aramaic translation of the Hebrew Bible with additional material and commentary) of Zechariah 12:10, the Josephite messiah is mentioned alongside the house of David:

> And I shall cause to rest upon the house of David and upon the dwellers of Jerusalem a spirit of prophecy and true prayer. And afterwards Messiah bar Ephraim shall go forth to engage in battle with Gog, and Gog will slay him before the gate of Jerusalem. And they will look to me and inquire of me why the nations pierced Messiah bar Ephraim, and they will mourn for him just as a father and mother mourn for an only son and will be in bitterness over him like the bitterness over a firstborn.[5]

In this passage the Josephite messiah, called here "Messiah son of Ephraim" (Ephraim being a son of Joseph), is a defeated, pierced messiah who will be mourned. Another Targum text on Song of Songs explains: "Two deliverers shall there be to deliver you, Messiah bar David and Messiah bar Ephraim."[6]

---

5. Targum Tosefta to Zechariah 12:10. See translation and explanation in Mitchell, "Messiah bar Ephraim," 221–41.

6. Targum Tosefta to Zechariah 12:10 and the Targum to Song of Songs 4:5 and 7:4. See translation and explanation in Mitchell, "Messiah bar Ephraim," 221–41. Both Messiahs are also mentioned alongside one another in the Targum Pseudo-Jonathan to

The Babylonian Talmud (see Introduction) also portrays a slain Josephite messiah alongside the Davidic messiah:

> Our Rabbis taught, The Holy One, blessed be He, will say to the Messiah, the son of David . . . "Ask of me anything, and I will give it to thee." . . . But when he will see that the Messiah the son of Joseph is slain, he will say to Him, "Lord of the Universe, I ask of Thee only the gift of life."[7]

These references to a Josephite messiah are late, dating to a few centuries after Jesus; however, biblical scholar David C. Mitchell has shown that a few texts in the Dead Sea Scrolls not only refer to two messiahs but specifically point to the messiah son of Joseph.[8] Origins of the dual-messiah tradition likely come from Zechariah 9–14. These chapters introduce both a slain figure (9:4–7, 12:10) and a victorious, warrior figure who will fight for Israel (14:1–20). The authors of the Gospels and Acts probably utilized these traditions to emphasize Jesus as perhaps fulfilling both sets of expectations for the Davidic and Josephite messiahs.

Jesus and Joseph

Although the Gospels do not explicitly call Jesus a "son of Joseph" in reference to Joseph the Patriarch, numerous direct and indirect parallels between Jesus and Joseph are conspicuous: both Rachel and Mary, the mothers of Joseph and Jesus, respectively, are associated with Bethlehem; and both travel to Bethlehem while pregnant (Gen 35:16–20; Matt 2:2; Luke 2:4–5).[9] Joseph and Jesus are both conceived under unusual circumstances: Rachel is barren, and Mary is a virgin (Gen 30:22–24; Matt 1:18–23). Before their ministries, Joseph and Jesus are taken into Egypt (Gen 37:28; Matt 2:13). They are both shepherds of their fathers' flocks (Gen 37:2; John 10:11–14). Both are favored, or the most beloved sons, of their fathers: "Now Israel *loved Joseph more* than any other of his children" (Gen 37:3; emphasis added); "This is my Son, *the Beloved*; with him I am well pleased" (Matt 3:17, 17:5; emphasis added). Joseph and Jesus both begin their ministry at age thirty: Joseph "[is] thirty years old" when he "[goes] throughout all the land" and stores up grain for the people "in such abundance—like the sand

---

Exodus 40:9–11.

7. Babylonian Talmud Sukkah 52a, in Slotki, *Sukkah*.

8. See Mitchell, "Fourth Deliverer," 545–53; Mitchell, "Dying and Rising," 181–205.

9. This parallel is not direct, as Rachel was not pregnant with Joseph but with Benjamin when she traveled toward Bethlehem.

of the sea—that he [stops] measuring it" (Gen 41:46–49). Similarly, Jesus, at "about thirty" (Luke 3:23), travels throughout the region providing both literal and figurative bread in abundance. Just as Joseph provides grain for the people amidst a famine, Jesus provides "enough bread in the desert to feed so great a crowd" who are on the verge of "fainting" (Matt 15:32–33; Mark 8:4). Notice also that Joseph's interpretation of *seven* ears of grain in Pharaoh's dream predicts *seven* years of plenty (Gen 41:29). Alluding to the Joseph story, the authors of Matthew and Mark explain that Jesus feeds the crowd with *seven* loaves of bread and has *seven* baskets left over (Mark 8:5–8; Matt 15:37).

Both Joseph and Jesus are, in a way, rejected by those within their own tight-knit circles. Joseph's brothers hate him (Gen 37:4–8), and Jesus' "brothers" reject him (John 7:5). Moreover, just as Joseph's *eleven* brothers desert him, allowing him to be taken by foreigners, Jesus' *eleven* apostles (after Judas departs) "desert him and flee" from Gethsemane, allowing Jesus to be taken and imprisoned by foreigners (Matt 26:56). Joseph and Jesus are both handed over to these foreigners precisely because of "jealousy" (Gen 37:11; Matt 27:18). The two individuals willing to sell off Joseph and Jesus as slaves for "profit" are both named Judah—"Judas" being the Greek form of "Judah" (Gen 37:26–28; Matt 26:14). While the story in Genesis has Joseph being sold for twenty pieces of silver (Gen 37:26–27)—instead of "thirty pieces" like Jesus (Matt 26:15, 27:3, 9)—a text dating to near the time of Jesus, Testament of Gad, changes that number to "thirty pieces,"[10] perhaps reflecting the meager price of a slave as contained in Exodus (Exod 21:32). Joseph and Jesus are stripped of their robes and condemned falsely (Gen 37:23; Matt 27:28; John 19:23). They are both punished with two other criminals (Gen 40:1–3; Luke 23:32–33). One of the prisoners with Joseph, the chief baker, is hung on a tree (Gen 40:19, 22); likewise, Jesus, the ultimate baker, the one who provides "living bread" (John 6:35, 51), is "hung on a tree" (Acts 5:30). After emerging from prison, Joseph is exalted to the right hand of Pharaoh: "You shall be over my house, and all my people shall order themselves as you command" (Gen 41:40). Similarly, after emerging from the tomb, Jesus is exalted to the right hand of God (Acts 2:32–34).

Finally, the author of John places Jesus in Samaria, "near the plot of ground that Jacob had given to his son Joseph" (John 4:5), when he meets the woman at Jacob's well. This location is significant for John's narrative because Jesus first pronounces his messiahship here (John 4:25–26)—it is

---

10. Testament of Gad 2:3–4.

no coincidence that John situates this episode at Jacob's well, near Joseph's plot of ground.[11]

The fact that the Gospels' authors compare Jesus to Joseph the Patriarch is not surprising, not only for the reasons mentioned above, but also given that some Jewish authors near the time of Jesus celebrated Joseph as a prototype for a political statesman and a righteous man.[12] For example, the first-century Jewish philosopher Philo wrote a biography of Joseph, wherein he explained that Joseph was occupied with the "business of a shepherd, which corresponds to political business." Philo further explained that "a shepherd will probably be also a most excellent king," due to his experience in "superintending a flock."[13] Philo elsewhere reiterated his belief that "the business of a shepherd is a preparation for the office of king."[14] We have already seen in the previous chapter that "shepherd" and "king" were terms commonly associated with the messiah in early Jewish literature; thus, Joseph the Patriarch seems to make an easy comparison to Jesus, at least in the view of the authors of the Gospels. Maren Niehoff, scholar at Hebrew University of Jerusalem, explained that first-century historian Josephus saw himself in Joseph's story, and even wrote parts of his autobiography to correspond to Joseph's experiences in Egypt.[15] Given the reverence toward Joseph in several early Jewish texts, it is no wonder that the authors of the Gospels present Jesus as a type of Joseph. The patriarch was a righteous man who was mistreated by his own people and sent to Egypt where he eventually became a supreme ruler. Andries van Aarde (University of Pretoria, South Africa) suggested that the author of Matthew, like other early Jewish authors, used Joseph the Patriarch as an "ideal type," not only in relation to Jesus, but also in relation to Jesus' father Joseph. When Greek-speaking Jews encountered the Joseph and Mary episode in the Gospel of Matthew, they might have recalled the apocryphal romance story of Joseph and his wife Asenath.[16] This text, Joseph and Asenath (100 BCE–100 CE), explains how God's intervention in Joseph's life leads to his holy marriage with a *virgin* wife.[17]

It is difficult to ascertain the nature of these parallels in the Gospel of Matthew—to what extent they are direct, or if the author of Matthew even

---

11. Römer and Ruckel, "Jesus," 77.
12. Niehoff, *Figure of Joseph*, 54–145.
13. Philo, *On Joseph*, 2, in *Works of Philo*, 435.
14. Philo, *On the Life of Moses*, book 1, 60, in *Works of Philo*, 465.
15. Niehoff, *Figure of Joseph*, 101, 109–10.
16. van Aarde, "Jesus as Fatherless Child," 65–83.
17. Burchard, *Joseph and Asenath*, 177–246.

knew about the elements in the Joseph and Asenath story. What we may conclude, however, is that the Gospels of Matthew, Luke, and John do contain striking parallels between Jesus and Joseph, and that other early Jewish authors are similarly interested in utilizing elements in the Joseph story in creative ways while composing their narratives.

Joseph of Egypt	Jesus of Nazareth
Rachel the mother of Joseph was a woman of Bethlehem; she traveled to Bethlehem while pregnant (Gen 35:16–20).	Mary the mother of Jesus was a woman of Bethlehem; she traveled to Bethlehem while pregnant (Matt 2:2; Luke 2:4–5).
Miraculously conceived—Rachel was barren	Miraculously conceived—Mary was a virgin (Matt 1:18–23)
Before his ministry, he was taken to Egypt (Gen 37:28).	Before his ministry, he was taken to Egypt (Matt 2:13).
A shepherd of his father's flock (Gen 37:2)	A shepherd of his father's flock (John 10:11–14)
Most loved by his father: "Now Israel *loved Joseph more* than any other of his children" (Gen 37:2)	Most loved by his father: "This is my Son, the *Beloved*; with him I am well pleased" (Matt 3:17, 17:5)
Began his ministry at age thirty (Gen 41:46)	Began his ministry at age thirty (Luke 3:23)
He "went up throughout all the land" and stored up grain "in such abundance—like the sand of the sea—that he stopped measuring it" (Gen 41:46–49).	He went throughout all the region and provided both literal bread and figurative bread in abundance.
He provided *grain* for the people amidst a famine. Joseph's interpretation of *seven* ears of grain in Pharaoh's dream predicted *seven* years of plenty (Gen 41:29)	He provided "enough *bread* in the desert to feed so great a crowd" when they were starving and "might faint" (Matt 15:32–33; Mark 8:4). Jesus fed the crowd with *seven* loaves of bread and had *seven* baskets left over (Mark 8:5–8; Matt 15:37).
He was rejected by his own. His brothers "hated" him (Gen 37:4–8).	He was rejected by his own. His "brothers" rejected him (John 7:5) and his apostles "deserted him and fled" from Gethsemane (Matt 26:56).
He was handed over to foreigners precisely because of "jealousy" (Gen 37:11).	He was handed over to foreigners precisely because of "jealousy" (Matt 27:18).
The individual willing to sell him off as a slave for "profit" was named *Judah* (Gen 37:26–28).	The individual willing to sell him off as a slave for "profit" was named *Judah*—"Judas" being the Greek form of "Judah" (Matt 26:14).

He was stripped of his robes and condemned falsely (Gen 37:23).	He was stripped of his robes and condemned falsely (Matt 27:28; John 19:23).
He was punished with two other criminals (Gen 40:1–3). One of the prisoners, the chief baker, was hung on a tree (Gen 40:19, 22).	He was punished with two other criminals (Luke 23:32–33). Jesus, the chief baker, the one who provides "living bread" (John 6:35, 51), was hung on a cross.
After escaping from prison, Joseph was exalted to the right hand of Pharaoh: "You shall be over my house, and all my people shall order themselves as you command" (Gen 41:40).	After emerging from the tomb, Jesus was exalted to the right hand of God (Acts 2:32–34).
Joseph was buried in Shechem, in the region of Samaria (Josh 24:32).	Gospel of John places Jesus in Samaria, "near the plot of ground that Jacob had given to his son Joseph" (John 4:5), when he met with the woman at Jacob's well. It is no coincidence that John situates Jesus at Jacob's well, near Joseph's plot of ground, when he first revealed his messiahship.

Jesus and David

In the Gospels, Jesus' connection with David is much more explicit than with Joseph the Patriarch. In Matthew and Luke, for example, the reader is informed from the beginning that Jesus is the messiah, "son of David" (Luke 1:27, 32; Matt 1:1). In the Gospels and Acts, the name David is mentioned forty-five times, all of which are directly or indirectly related to Jesus. Several individuals cry out to Jesus during his ministry, calling him "Son of David" (Luke 18:38–39; Mark 10:47–48; Matt 9:27, 15:22, 20:30–31). Aside from these explicit references, the Gospels' writers also embedded several indirect David-Jesus parallels in their works. Casual readers tend to overlook many of these parallels, but Jews in the first and second centuries who knew their sacred texts would have identified them much more easily.

The David-centric nature of the Gospels bring us to Jesus' genealogies in Matthew and Luke. Perhaps nothing in the Bible is less engaging to the modern reader than genealogical lists of people begetting other people, who then beget more people. Jesus' genealogy, however, reveals salient themes and ideas in the Gospels of Matthew and Luke. We learn much about the purpose of these Gospels right from the beginning in Jesus' genealogies. I use the plural *genealogies* because Matthew's and Luke's differ significantly (Matt 1:1–17; Luke 3:23–38). They do not even agree on the name of Jesus' grandfather, for example. We will discuss the historical reliability of the

Gospels in general in more depth in the final chapter, but here we focus on what the authors of Matthew and Luke were attempting to emphasize. Jesus' genealogy in Matthew focuses on three figures: "Jesus the Messiah, the son of David, the son of Abraham" (1:1). The stated purpose of this genealogy is not simply to present Jesus' lineage but to demonstrate that Jesus is the messiah, the Son of David. To illustrate this, the author of Matthew compartmentalizes the genealogy into three periods, each containing fourteen generations: "So all the generations from Abraham to David are fourteen generations; and from David to the deportation to Babylon, fourteen generations; and from the deportation to Babylon to the Messiah, fourteen generations" (Matt 1:17). In order to maintain a clean, symmetric genealogy of Jesus, with three groups of fourteen generations, the author of Matthew omits five names: Ahaziah, Joash, Amaziah, Jehoiakin, and Zedekiah. But why was the author of Matthew so intent on forcing this structure even to the point of leaving out a handful of names?

The answer is, as we will see, *David*. The author of Matthew was employing an ancient numerological technique called "gematria," from the Greek *geometria*, which is the origin of the word "geometry." This technique assigned a numerical value to each consonant in a word (e.g., A = 1, B = 2, C = 3, etc.). The sum of the consonants was believed to contain a hidden message or connection.[18] An example of gematria can be found in the book of Revelation: "Let anyone with understanding *calculate* the number of the beast, *for it is the number of a person*. Its number is six hundred and sixty-six" (13:18; emphasis added). The person most likely referred to here is Nero Caesar (37–68 CE), as the Hebrew letters in his name total 666. Some ancient manuscripts of Revelation use "616," which also fits with the alternate spelling in Greek of Nero Caesar.[19] Nero persecuted Christians, so it is no surprise that the author of Revelation portrayed him as a "beast rising out of the sea" (Rev 13:1). Similarly, the author of Matthew totaled the values of the letters in the Hebrew spelling of David's name (*dvd*). The value of the Hebrew letter *dalet* is four, and the value of *vav* is six: d + v + d, or 4 + 6 + 4, equals fourteen. The author of Matthew deliberately pointed to the three consonants totaling fourteen in Jesus' genealogy—there are *three* time periods, each containing *fourteen* generations.[20] Appealing to his readers, the author of Matthew used gematria to shine a spotlight on David, one of the greatest figures in Jewish history, through whose lineage the messiah would come. It is not surprising that the author of Matthew, the most

---

18. Derovan et al., "Gematria," 7:424–27.
19. Koester, *Revelation*, 540.
20. Brown, *Birth of the Messiah*, 74–84; Davies, "Jewish Sources," 499–500.

Jewish of all the Gospels' writers, created a genealogy composed of symmetrical parts. The late Raymond Brown, Catholic priest and professor at Union Theological Seminary, identified at least eight other early Jewish ancestral lists that are similar in numerical style to the genealogy in Matthew, although they do not all use the numbers three and fourteen.[21] Note, however, that in the Mishnah tractate Avot ("Fathers"), a rabbinic text dating to a few generations after Matthew (see Introduction), the rabbis list fourteen links in the legal lineage from Moses to Hillel, a contemporary of Jesus.[22] Like the author of Matthew, the rabbis omit several names and manipulate the list in various ways in order to maintain the number fourteen.[23] Louis Finkelstein, Jewish scholar and former chancellor of the Jewish Theological Seminary, explained:

> The number "fourteen" is not accidental. It corresponds to the number of high priests from Aaron to the establishment of Solomon's Temple; the number of high priests from the establishment of the Temple until Jaddua, the last high priest mentioned in Scripture. It is clear that a mystic significance attached to this number, in both the Sadducean and the Pharisaic traditions. Each group maintained that it was no accident that the number of links in the chain of what it considered the authoritative tradition from Moses and Aaron . . . was a multiple of the mystic number "seven."[24]

Rabbi and scholar of early Judaism, Samuel Lachs, suggested that perhaps the author of Matthew was jabbing at the Pharisees/rabbis in Jesus' genealogy. He writes, "You think that the tradition has been transmitted to you from Moses by way of fourteen generations . . . On the contrary, [Jesus] received the tradition from Abraham, and his genealogy has three times fourteen generations going back to the patriarch!"[25] Luke's genealogy does not employ the same symmetrical structure and numerological technique as Matthew, but it does contain a multiple of seven. Instead of listing forty-two figures (3 x 14), Luke's genealogy extends the line back to Adam, containing seventy-seven names.

Also noticeable in Matthew's genealogy is the presence of five women, including Mary, who are all absent in Luke's genealogy. That all five women had questionable extramarital sexual profiles is glaring. The first woman,

---

21. Brown, *Birth of the Messiah*, 80–81.
22. See Mishnah Avot 1:1–12.
23. Johnson, *Purpose of Biblical Genealogies*, 202–6.
24. Finkelstein, *Mabo le-masekhtot Avot*, x–xi.
25. Lachs, *Rabbinic Commentary*, 3.

Tamar, marries Judah's oldest son, Er. Sometime after Er dies, Tamar disguises herself as a prostitute in order to seduce Judah after his wife's death. Her goal is to bear a child through Judah's line. Judah passes by Tamar, sees the "prostitute," and sleeps with her, not knowing who she is (Gen 38). Tamar conceives twins, Perez and Zerah, the former of which is the ancestor of David (Ruth 4:18–22). The second woman mentioned in Jesus' genealogy is Rahab the harlot, who bears Boaz, also an ancestor of David (Ruth 4:21–22). Next is Ruth, the non-Jewish ancestor of David who also appears to engage in sexual sin with Boaz (Ruth 3:1–9). The fourth woman is the "wife of Uriah" (referring to Bathsheba). She commits adultery with David and bears Solomon (2 Sam 11). As for the fifth woman, Mary, rumors had circulated that she conceived Jesus out of wedlock. According to John's Gospel, "Jews" say to Jesus, "We are not illegitimate children" (John 8:41), likely implying that Jesus was. Several Jewish texts maintain that Mary committed adultery with a Roman soldier named Panthera, who fathered Jesus. Some scholars have argued that the "Jesus ben Panthera" in the Talmud is a different Jesus whose mother also happened to be named "Mary."[26] However, the rumor that Mary committed adultery with Panthera is also posited by Origen (185–254 CE), a third-century Christian theologian:

> Let us return, however, to the words put into the mouth of the Jew, where "the mother of Jesus" is described as having been "turned out by the carpenter who was betrothed to her, as she had been convicted of adultery and had a child by a certain soldier named Panthera."[27]

Rumors of Mary's supposed adultery seem to have been swirling around in the Jewish community from the late first century through the sixth century CE. The author of Matthew likely included Tamar, Rahab, Ruth, and Bathsheba in his genealogy in response to accusations that Jesus was the result of Mary's adulterous relationship and, therefore, could not be the messiah. If Israel's great King David, however, could descend from a line of adulterous women, and the Lord allowed this lineage to produce the messiah, then it should not be problematic if Jesus were conceived through an adulterous act. Regardless of whether the author of Matthew himself believed that Mary was guilty of sexual sin, he used the genealogy of Jesus to counter such claims for his readers. Notice that Mary's conception immediately follows Jesus' genealogy (Matt 1:18–25), after he had prepared his readers for

---

26. See "uncensored texts" of Babylonian Talmud Shabbat 104b, Sanhedrin 67a, and Erubin 100b. For an explanation of these texts, see Schäfer, *Jesus in the Talmud*, 1–21.

27. Origen, *Contra Celsum*, 31. See Origen's larger response to this myth in 27–32.

the potentially scandalous story, whereas the author of Luke situated the genealogy after Jesus' baptism.

Another element in Matthew's genealogy is an emphasis on royalty, which places Jesus within a long line of Davidic kings, through Solomon. This emphasis extends past the genealogy into Jesus' birth narrative. Only in Matthew do the magi—we know them as "wise men," but *magi* actually means "magicians" or "astrologers"—bring gold, frankincense, and myrrh to celebrate Jesus' birth (Matt 2:1). The author of Matthew pulled this tradition from the Hebrew Bible. In Isaiah, the future promise to Israel is that the nations of the earth will flee their darkness and "come to your light and kings to the brightness of your dawn." Representatives from these foreign nations will come from the kingdom of Sheba and "bring gold and frankincense, and shall proclaim the praise of the Lord" (Isa 60:2–6). In 1 Kings, the queen of Sheba brings spices and gold to King Solomon (1 Kgs 10:10). Psalm 72 anticipates that the "kings of Sheba [will] bring gifts" and "fall down before" Solomon with their "gold" (vv. 10–11, 15). Note that these passages speak of gentiles bringing gifts to Israel's king, the precise focus of Matthew's birth narrative. Myrrh is not mentioned in these passages; however, Psalm 45 is written to a victorious king whose "robes are all fragrant with myrrh" (v. 8). Since the author of Matthew sees Jesus as a "son of David," it is perhaps expected that royalty from a foreign nation would present gifts to and praise him, the same way they did to another son of David, King Solomon. It is clear that the author of Matthew, in both Jesus' genealogy and his birth narrative, links Jesus inextricably to royalty—to Judahite kings in David's line through Solomon, and to noblemen of the earth who will praise him.

The author of Luke, conversely, deemphasizes royal figures in Jesus' genealogy and birth narrative. Luke's genealogy (Luke 3:23–38) does not present a long line of kings. In addition, Jesus does not descend from David's son Solomon, as in Matthew, but through David's son Nathan. Mark Goodacre, renowned New Testament scholar at Duke University, suggested that the author of Luke attempted to situate Jesus within the prophecy of Isaiah 11:1, which declares that the messiah will come from the "stump" of David's father Jesse, rather than from the branch of the Davidic kings of Judah—a branch that was cut down with the exile to Babylon. In other words, the author of Luke wanted to bypass the kingship lineage of Judah that went awry and instead sought to trace the messiah back to the "stump of Jesse," showing that God would restore Israel through a new branch of David through Jesus.[28]

---

28. Goodacre, "Jesus' Genealogy."

Notice also that the author of Luke does not include magi in his birth narrative. In fact, we can infer from his writing that he may have distrusted magi. The only time he mentions them in his works is in Acts, in which Simon *Magus*, or Simon the *Magician*, is portrayed negatively (Acts 8:9–11). Philo also, for example, disparaged Balaam by calling him a *magos*. Balaam was a non-Israelite figure known for his gift of prophecy and ability to curse (Num 22:5–6)—he was "celebrated for his skill in divination, dwelling in Mesopotamia, who was initiated in every branch of the soothsayer's art."[29] Balaam conspires against Israel in the days of Moses and is defamed by several New Testament authors (2 Pet 2:15–16; Jude 1:11; Rev 2:14). The author of Luke may have replaced Matthew's magi from the East with local shepherds in Jesus' birth narrative (Luke 2:8–20). It seems that the objective of the author of Luke was to portray Jesus not among the kings of the earth but in more humble circumstances. Remember that messianic expectations were accompanied by shepherd imagery in early Jewish texts, as explained in the previous chapter. In Luke, angels appear to the shepherds and say, "To you is born this day in the city of David a Savior, who is the Messiah" (2:11). Although the authors of Luke and Matthew disagree in drastic ways regarding Jesus' genealogy and birth narrative, their shared purpose was to highlight Jesus' connection to David, the shepherd and king.

There are many other David-Jesus parallels in the Gospels outside the genealogy. David, like both Joseph and Jesus, is associated with Bethlehem—it is his birthplace and the location where the prophet Samuel anointed him as king (1 Sam 16:1–3). A later Israelite tradition placed the birth of the messiah at Bethlehem: "But you, O Bethlehem of Ephrathah, who are one of the little clans of Judah, from you shall come forth for me one who is to rule in Israel" (Mic 5:2). "Ephrathah" is another name for Bethlehem, according to Genesis (35:16–19, 48:7).

Although this section is about the David-Jesus parallels, this seems like an ideal place to discuss the star of Bethlehem. The star element as contained in Matthew is part of the Jewish messianic tradition. It is fitting, then, that the author of Matthew included it within the Bethlehem episode. The relationship between the star and the messiah originates in Numbers 24. Here, Balaam, under the influence of the "Spirit of God" (Num 24:2), prophesies that "a star shall come out of Jacob, and a sceptre shall rise out of Israel . . . [who] shall rule" (Num 24:17–19). Again, as mentioned just above, Philo referred to Balaam, who came from Mesopotamia in the *East*, as a "magos," singular for magi.[30] What we have, then, are two first-century Jew-

---

29. Philo, *On the Life of Moses*, book 1, 264 in *Works of Philo*, 484.
30. Philo, *On the Life of Moses*, book 1, 264.

ish authors, Philo and the author of Matthew, who linked the messiah-star passage in Numbers 24 with magi from the East.

Josephus also spoke about a star in the heavens in relation to the messiah. During the Jewish-Roman War, as the temple was burning down, a "false prophet" claimed that the Jews would receive a miraculous sign "of deliverance."[31] One of these signs was a "star" that "stood over the city."[32] Josephus explained that many Jews joined in the fight against the Romans with heightened confidence based on one of their ambiguous prophecies, likely referring to Balaam's prophecy in Numbers 24. We assume this because Josephus wrote the following: "What more than all else incited [these Jews] to the war was an ambiguous oracle, likewise found in their sacred scriptures, to the effect that at that time one from their country would become ruler of the world. This they understood to mean someone of their own race, and many of their wise men went astray in their interpretation of it."[33] Josephus confirmed that many Jews believed in the traditions of stars signaling deliverance by an anointed one who would displace the Romans.

Some Jews believed this messianic "star" was not an actual star but a personage—either an angel or the messiah himself. This is not a surprise since several ancient Jewish authors generally equated stars with angels.[34] Specifically, regarding the star in Numbers 24, the Damascus Document, a Dead Sea Scroll text dating to the second century BCE, interprets the star as being a messianic figure called the "Interpreter of the Law."[35] In the Testament of Levi (second century BCE), the star of Balaam's prophecy is an angelic figure "like a king . . . [who] will shine forth like the sun . . . and there shall be peace in all the earth." When this angel appears, the "heavens will be opened," the "earth shall be glad, the clouds will be filled with joy . . . and the angels of glory of the Lord's presence will be made glad by him."[36] Note the striking similarities with Luke's account. Each of these elements—angels, opened heavens, joy, gladness, glory, heavenly hosts, and peace on earth—are present in Luke. Instead of a star, an angel appears nearby to shepherds. The angel stands in the *glory* of the Lord and brings a message of *great joy*. The heavens are opened and the angel is accompanied by a heavenly host who sings praises to God for bringing *peace* on earth (Luke 2:8–14). Heav-

31. Josephus, *J.W.* 6.5.2, trans. Thackeray.
32. Josephus, *J.W.* 6.5.3, trans. Thackeray.
33. Josephus, *J.W.* 6.5.4, trans. Thackeray.
34. See Judg 5:20; Job 38:7; Dan 8:10; and Rev 9:1, 12:4. For a more detailed discussion, see Allison, *New Moses*, 152–54.
35. See the translation in Wise et al., *Dead Sea Scrolls*, 58.
36. Testament of Levi 18:3. See translation by Kee, "Testaments," 1:794–95.

enly hosts were not foreign to Jews, as the Hebrew Scriptures mention them multiple times (Deut 4:19, 33:2; 1 Kgs 22:19; Jer 8:2, 19:31). Whether early followers of Jesus believed his birth was accompanied by an actual star as in Matthew or by an angel of light surrounded by heavenly hosts as in Luke, either interpretation would have been familiar to first – and second-century Jewish ears. Jews would have recognized such traditions and associated them with the messiah. In fact, in the second century, when the Jews revolted against Rome, a Jewish military leader, Simon bar Koseba (d. 135 CE), was believed by some, including the famous Rabbi Akiva, to be the messiah. Based on the messiah-star prophecy in Numbers 24, Rabbi Akiva nicknamed him "Simon bar Kokhba," or "Simeon son of *the Star*."[37]

We now return to our discussion on specific David-Jesus parallels. Like Joseph the Patriarch and Jesus, David begins his ministry at age thirty (2 Sam 5:4). Also like Joseph and Jesus, David is a shepherd of his father's flock (1 Sam 16:11; Ps 78:70). Jesus is referred to as God's "son." Likewise, David is God's "begotten son" (Ps 2:7). More specifically, Jesus is called God's "beloved" son (Matt 3:17, 17:5; Mark 1:11, 9:7; Luke 3:22). Note that one of the meanings of the Hebrew root of *David* is "beloved."[38] Thus, the word *beloved*, used at Jesus' baptism and transfiguration, may be a rhetorical device pointing to both Jesus' relationship with the Father and his messianic status as the Son of David.

Several parallels between David and Jesus are also embedded in Jesus' activities on the Mount of Olives. Jesus' first act after arriving on the Mount, according to the Synoptic Gospels, is to obtain a donkey, which highlights his messiahship. The author of Matthew even quotes Zechariah 9:9: "Tell the daughter of Zion, Look, your king is coming to you, humble, and mounted on a donkey, and on a colt, the foal of a donkey" (Matt 21:5; cf. John 12:15). The messiah-donkey tradition is also hinted at in Genesis 49:10–11, which declares that the future ruler from the tribe of Judah will bind "his foal to the vine and his donkey's colt to a choice vine." Israel's kings, David and Solomon (i.e., David and a *son of David*), also ride donkeys on the Mount of Olives in relation to their roles as king. When Absalom attempts to overthrow his father, David flees Jerusalem and climbs the Mount of Olives. Before reaching the summit, David weeps over Jerusalem (2 Sam 15:30). Upon reaching the top, David's servants obtain "a couple of donkeys . . . for the king's household to ride" (2 Sam 16:1–2). Jesus' acts on the Mount of Olives mirror David's in reverse order. First, Jesus obtains a donkey on the summit

---

37. For background and the name change of Simon bar Kokhba, see Abramsky and Gibson, "Bar Kokhba," 3:156–64; emphasis added.

38. Brown, *Hebrew and English Lexicon*, 187.

of the Mount of Olives, then, when he comes within view of Jerusalem, he weeps over the city (Luke 19:41).

Solomon rides his donkey down the Kidron Valley, at the base of the Mount of Olives, where he is anointed king over Israel (1 Kgs 1:32–37). During King Solomon's royal procession, his followers shout, "Long live King Solomon" (1 Kgs 1:39). Similarly, Jesus' followers hold a procession for him as he rides a donkey from the Mount of Olives to the east gate of Jerusalem while they shout, "Hosanna! Blessed is the son of David. Blessed is the king who comes in the name of the Lord!" (Matt 21:2–9; Mark 11:1–10; Luke 19:29–44; John 12:12–19). This shout is quoted from Psalm 118:26: "Blessed is the one who comes in the name of the Lord."

Jesus' donkey episode alludes not only to the David and Solomon narratives but also to Absalom's narrative. It seems ideal for the Gospels' writers to have Jesus, their messianic "Son of David," mirror the literal *sons of David*. For instance, Absalom mounts a mule when he attempts to wrest the throne from his father David (2 Sam 18:9), an act that highlights the messianic elements of his story, as perhaps viewed by the authors of the Gospels. As discussed in the previous chapter, the messiah was expected to become king. Absalom, however, failed in his quest to obtain the throne, unlike Solomon. While Absalom rides his mule during a battle against David's army, his long hair becomes tangled in a tree. David's general sees Absalom hanging helplessly and thrusts a spear into his body (2 Sam 18:9–17). Likewise, what could be viewed as his failure to obtain the throne, according to the Gospels, Jesus is hung on a cross and pierced with a spear (John 19:34).[39] The portrayal of Jesus' final entry into Jerusalem is an allusion to Zechariah, who prophesies of both a future slain figure (who would be pierced) and a victorious figure (Zech 12:10, 14:4). It may be that this dualistic portrayal of Jesus is meant to highlight the two sets of messianic expectations, one for the victorious Davidic messiah and the other for the slain Josephite messiah. The Gospels collectively highlight both Jesus' short-term messianic failure and his long-term messianic victory, and they do so by alluding to two sons of David, Absalom and Solomon, a slain figure and a victorious figure, respectively.

Jesus' royal procession into Jerusalem culminates in the mini temple riot when Jesus overturns the money changer's tables. This episode is contained in all three Synoptic Gospels (Matt 21:10–17; Mark 11:15–17; Luke 19:45–46), but the author of Matthew includes a seemingly random detail that, upon closer examination, is yet another attempt to link Jesus with David. After Jesus enters Jerusalem and contends with the temple

---

39. Thompson, "If David Had Not," 55–56.

establishment, "The blind and the lame" come into the temple complex (Matt 21:14). Jesus heals them and then little children exclaim, "Hosanna to the Son of David" (Matt 21:15). The inclusion of both "the blind and lame" and children in this episode seems a bit out of place. Why are children and people with disabilities rushing into the temple complex, or lingering, during a riot? I have become accustomed when I approach a head-scratcher in the Gospels to ask myself, "Did the author of this Gospel have something in mind from the Hebrew Scriptures when he composed this episode?" I find that the answer is often, "yes." Knowing that the Jesus-David connection is salient in the Gospel of Matthew, it would behoove us to investigate the David material in the Hebrew Bible to see if it contains any details that might help us make sense of the association between David and the "blind and lame." Sure enough, we turn to 2 Samuel and bam!

In 2 Samuel 5, David *and his men* enter Jerusalem just after his coronation, which parallels Jesus' experience in Matthew. David is immediately thrust into conflict with the Jebusite leaders. They taunt David, saying that he will not be able to break into the city and conquer it. The city is so well fortified that "even the blind and the lame will turn you back" (2 Sam 5:6). David responded that he will take the city and attack the blind and the lame and that from that day forward, "The blind and the lame shall not come into the house" (2 Sam 5:8). We do not know exactly what to make of this episode, but its author may have had the legal injunctions in Leviticus in mind: "For no one who has a blemish shall draw near, one who is blind or lame . . . shall not come near the curtain or approach the altar . . . that he may not profane my sanctuaries" (Lev 21:18–23). However, in the book of Jeremiah we find a prophecy that at a future time, the "blind and the lame" will be welcomed back "to Zion to the Lord our God"—i.e., the temple (Jer 31:6–8).

Regarding the children who cry out, "Hosanna to the Son of David" (Matt 21:15), we notice that the author of Matthew quotes Psalm 8 (Matt 21:16), which is a "Psalm of David" (Ps 8:1): "Out of the mouth of babes and infants you have founded a bulwark because of your foes, to silence the enemy and the avenger." Thus, it seems that the author of Matthew is making the connection for his reader that Jesus, as the "Son of David," marched into Jerusalem, contended with the sanctuary's leaders, restored into the temple complex the blind and lame who were once turned away when David first marched into and conquered Jerusalem, and fulfilled some kind of "out of the mouth of babes" prophecy associated with David.

Also noteworthy is that in every case (except one) where someone yells out to Jesus and calls him "Son of David" in the Gospel of Matthew, a blind person is present (9:27, 12:22–23, 20:30–31, 21:9–15). In the one exception, Jesus referred to the Pharisees as "blind guides of the blind" just before being called "Son of David" (Matt 15:14–22).

It is difficult to know what exactly the author of Matthew had in mind when he included the "blind and lame" bit in the temple tantrum episode, but it seems that he made a conscious effort, both in this episode and throughout his Gospel, to present Jesus multiple times in relation to David's curious relationship with the blind and lame and the accompanying prophecy in Jeremiah that blind and lame will be welcomed back to the temple.

Jesus' Gethsemane episode in the Gospel of John also pulls elements from the Hebrew Bible in relation to David. When the police arrive to arrest Jesus, they "stepped back and fell to the ground" when Jesus said "I am he" (John 18:6). Remember that "I am" is a name for God in the Hebrew Scriptures. It is what Yahweh calls himself at the burning bush (Exod 3:14). The author of John probably had Psalms 27 and 35 in mind when writing this portion of his Gospel. Psalm 27 states that when David's "adversaries and foes" attack him, they will "stumble and fall" before his face (vv. 1–2). Psalm 35 explains that the Lord will cause David's enemies to be "turned back and confounded" when they contend with him (vv. 1–6).[40] Other parallels to David in Gethsemane are also present. When David learns about Absalom's conspiracy against him, he says to his men, "Get up! Let us flee" (2 Sam 15:14). Similarly, in Gethsemane, Jesus says, "Get up, let us be going. See, my betrayer is at hand" (Matt 26:46; Mark 14:42). In addition, it is notable that the conspirators want *twelve thousand* men to fight David (2 Sam 17:1; emphasis added); when Jesus is confronted by his conspirators, he asks, "Do you think that I cannot appeal to my Father, and he will at once send me more than *twelve legions* of angels?" (Matt 26:53; emphasis added).

David	Jesus
David was born and anointed king in Bethlehem (1 Sam 16:1–3). Israelite tradition placed the birth of the Messiah in Bethlehem (Micah 5:2).	Jesus was born and recognized as the messiah (i.e., king) in Bethlehem.
David became king at age thirty (2 Sam 5:4).	Jesus began his ministry at age thirty (Luke 3:23).
David was a shepherd of his father's flock (1 Sam 16:11; Ps 78:70).	Jesus is called a shepherd of his father's flock (John 10:11–14).
David (meaning *"beloved"*) was called God's "begotten son" (Ps 2:7).	Jesus was called God's "beloved" son (Matt 3:17, 17:5; Mark 1:11, 9:7; Luke 3:22).

40. For a much more extensive examination of David in the New Testament and for David-Jesus parallels, see Zacharias, *Matthew's Presentation*; Miura, *David in Luke*.

David's servants obtained two donkeys atop the Mount of Olives for David to ride (2 Sam 16:1–2).	Jesus' disciples obtained two donkeys atop the Mount of Olives for Jesus to ride (Matt 21:2–9; Mark 11:1–10; Luke 19:29–44).
Solomon, the "son of David," rode his donkey down the Kidron Valley, at the base of the Mount of Olives, where he was anointed king over Israel. During the royal procession, his followers shouted, "Long live King Solomon" (1 Kgs 1:32–39).	Jesus, a "son of David," rode his donkey down the Mount of Olives in a royal messianic procession as his followers shouted, "Hosanna! Blessed is the son of David. Blessed is the king who comes in the name of the Lord!" (Matt 21:2–9; Mark 11:1–10; Luke 19:29–44; John 12:12–19).
Midway up the Mount of Olives, David wept over Jerusalem (2 Sam 15:30).	Midway down the Mount of Olives, Jesus wept over Jerusalem (Luke 19:41).
Psalm 27 states that when David's "adversaries and foes" attack him, they will "stumble and fall" before his face (Ps 27:1–2). Psalm 35 explains that the Lord will cause David's enemies to be "turned back and confounded" when they contend with him (Ps 35:1–6).	When the police arrived to arrest Jesus in Gethsemane, they "stepped back and fell to the ground" when Jesus said "I am he" (John 18:6). "I am" is a name of Jehovah (Exod 3:14).
When David learned about Absalom's conspiracy against him, he said to his men, "Get up! Let us flee" (2 Sam 15:14).	In Gethsemane, Jesus said, "Get up, let us be going. See, my betrayer is at hand" (Matt 26:46; Mark 14:42).
The conspirators wanted *twelve thousand* men to fight David (2 Sam 17:1).	When Jesus was confronted by his conspirators he said, "Do you think that I cannot appeal to my Father, and he will at once send me more than *twelve legions* of angels?" (Matt 26:53).
David's close friend and counselor, Ahithophel, joined the "conspiracy" against David (2 Sam 15:12, 31). Afterward, Ahithophel "hanged himself" (2 Sam 17:23).	Jesus' apostle, Judas, conspired against Jesus. Afterward, Judas hanged himself (Matt 27:3–10).
Psalm 41 put words in David's mouth regarding Ahithophel: "Even my *bosom friend* in whom I trusted, *who ate of my bread*, has lifted the heel against me" (Ps 41:9).	Regarding Judas Jesus said: "The one who *ate my bread* has lifted his *heel against me*" (John 13:18).
Amasa, David's nephew, participated in the conspiracy against David. Amasa's rival Joab, approached Amasa wearing a "soldier's garment," and while greeting him with "my brother," betrayed him with a kiss as he stabbed him with a sword, making Amasa's bowels "pour out on the ground" (2 Sam 20:4–10).	Judas approached Jesus with soldiers, and while greeting him with "my master" ("Rabbi"), betrayed him with a kiss (Mark 14:45). Judas the conspirator, later died as his "bowels gushed out" (Acts 1:18).

Takeaways

The parallels between Jesus and Joseph the Patriarch, and between Jesus and David, highlight Jesus' messiah status in the eyes of the Gospels' authors. At the time of Jesus, a dual messianic tradition involving the lines of both Joseph the Patriarch and King David had developed in some Jewish circles. It seems that the authors of the Gospels wanted to fold those messianic traditions into their narratives to make a strong case that Jesus was, indeed, the anointed one. Jews in the first and second centuries would have made these connections as they encountered the Jesus traditions. What do all these parallels tell us? What do they mean for our understanding of the Gospels? Some interpreters conclude that the Gospels' writers completely fabricated the Jesus story based on events in the Hebrew Bible. Christian fundamentalist scholars, on the other hand, tend to conclude that events in the lives of both Joseph and David in the Hebrew Scriptures and Jesus were divinely shaped to parallel each other, the purpose of which is to show that Jesus is a fulfillment of all things prior. A more moderate and scholarly interpretation is that these parallels are a combination of (1) the Gospels' writers telling the Jesus story through a creative blend of historical events and the adoption of stories from the Hebrew Bible, and (2) Jesus using the Hebrew Bible as a guidebook for his ministry. In other words, Jesus may have performed certain deeds and taught certain ideas precisely to mirror the deeds and teachings of prominent figures of the past. In fact, the precedent had been set during Jesus' generation for Jewish prophets and messiah-figures to pattern their actions after prophets of old. For example, fifteen years after Jesus' death, a prophet miracle worker named Theudas led a group to the Jordan River and promised to part the water as did Joshua.[41] Also in the mid-first century, an unnamed Jewish Egyptian prophet promised to march into Jerusalem and command the walls to fall, as Joshua did to Jericho.[42] Yet another figure in the mid-first century, Hanina Ben Dosa, prayed like Elijah with his head between his knees (cf. 1 Kgs 18:42), and his ministry was compared to Elijah by later rabbis. We will further discuss the implications of the many parallels between Jesus and the Hebrew Bible in the final chapter.

---

41. Josephus, *Ant.* 20.5.1.
42. Josephus, *Ant.* 20.8.6.

Chapter Six

His Friend Judas
Why Didn't He Betray His Messiah?

IN THE FIRST FIVE chapters we examined the many Jewish contexts of Jesus—childhood and family life, immersion ritual, prophets, miracle workers, and messiahs. We also attempted to situate Jesus within these contexts, at least according to how he was understood by the earliest Christians, especially the authors of the Gospels. The primary conclusion from this survey is that Jesus was Jewish. Many Christians pay lip service to the fact that Jesus was Jewish, which to them means that he was Jewish at a distance. Too often, Christians interpret Jesus as coming to make the Mosaic law obsolete, condemn Jewish leaders (as evidenced in his conspicuous display of righteous indignation toward them), and institute a system totally foreign to Jews. However, as we have seen, Jesus' relationship with Judaism is a bit more complex than the Christian world has understood it. It appears that, according to the authors of the Gospels, Jesus loved the Hebrew Scriptures. His life paralleled the many great Israelite prophets and leaders like Joseph, Moses, Joshua, David, and Elisha. Many of Jesus' deeds and sayings were strikingly similar to the rabbis, both his contemporaries and those subsequent.

A question that Christians might ask is, if Jesus was so entrenched within and embracive of Judaism, then why did he condemn Jewish leaders and why was he ultimately rejected and killed by his fellow Jews? In this and the next four chapters (chapters 6–10) we will challenge the assumptions of that very question and illustrate that "the Jews" did not reject and kill Jesus, and that Jesus did not reject and condemn "the Jews." We will explore the relationship between Jesus and his peers. We start in this chapter by looking at

Judas, whose story is perhaps Exhibit A that illustrates the Christian charge that "Jews killed Jesus." Judas serves as a representation of Jews according to later Christians. However, before turning our attention to Judas, it behooves us to grasp the extent of the "Christ killer" accusation hurled at Jews by Christians from late antiquity to the present day. After reviewing this heart-wrenching material, we can then proceed by asking ourselves, "did Jews really kill Jesus?" and "was Christian persecution of Jews warranted?"

Christian Persecution of "Christ-Killing Jews"

The New Testament is one of the most—if not *the* most—foundational texts in the history of western civilization regarding religion and spirituality; however, it is also foundational in the most extensive and tragic bloodbath in recorded history. The very corpus that stresses love, forgiving enemies, and turning the other cheek (i.e., not retaliating) is the same corpus that led to the unjustified slaughter of millions of Jews, including women and children. Perhaps the most common accusation among Christians from late antiquity to the mid-twentieth century was that Jews were "Christ killers." The writings of a few well-known early Christian personalities illustrate this theme. Melito (d. 180), bishop in western Anatolia (modern Turkey), labeled Jews as "Christ killers" and blamed all of Israel for the death of God, as he put it.[1] Prominent early Christian theologian Origen (d. 254) said of the Jews:

> I challenge anyone to prove my statement untrue if I say that the entire Jewish nation was destroyed . . . on account of these sufferings which they inflicted on Jesus . . . For they committed the most impious crime of all, when they conspired against the Savior of mankind."[2]

Archbishop of Constantinople John Chrysostom (c. 347–407) referred to Jews as "Christ-killers,"[3] claiming that the synagogue "is not simply a gathering place for thieves and hucksters, but also of demons; indeed, not only the synagogues, but the souls of the Jews are also the dwelling places of demons."[4] Saint Augustine (d. 430), the well-known early Christian theologian, wrote that Jews not only killed Jesus, but they were happy to do it as they shouted "Crucify him!" To intensify the insult, Augustine used the

---

1. Melito, *On the Pascha*, see explanation and text in Cohen, *Christ Killers*, 56–70.
2. Origen, *Contra Celsum*, 198–99.
3. See English translation in Chrysostom, "Patrologia Graeca 48.843–856" (852).
4. Cohen, *Under Crescent and Cross*, 20.

Jews' own sacred texts purported to be written by David (Psalms 57 and 64) to describe the Jewish people!

> [Jews are] lions that greedily devour human prey; their teeth are spears and arrows, their tongues sharp swords . . . [they are] scheming evildoers, who whet their tongues like swords, who aim bitter words like arrows, shooting from ambush at the blameless; they shoot suddenly and without fear. They hold fast to their evil purpose; they talk of laying snares secretly, thinking, "Who can see us? Who can search out our crimes? We have thought out a cunningly conceived plot". . . but God will shoot his arrow at them; they will be wounded suddenly . . . [and] all who see them will shake with horror (Psalms 57:4, 64:2–8).[5]

Pope Gregory the Great (d. 604) believed Jews were "deviant souls" whose ways were equivalent to vomit. He instituted a Sunday commemoration in late summer, during the time when Jews mourn the loss of their temple (ninth of Av); Christians celebrated the destruction of the temple and defeat of the Jews, and they gleefully repeated legends that Jews became slaves to Rome as part of their divine punishment for killing Jesus.[6]

When the Fatimid Muslims under the leadership of Caliph Al-Hakim burned down Christianity's holiest site, the Church of the Holy Sepulcher in Jerusalem, in 1009, French Christians immediately blamed Jews for convincing Al-Hakim to destroy the church. Rodulfus Glaber, an eleventh-century writer, explained that Christian pilgrimage to Jerusalem had increased significantly during this time, which caused the devil to worry. He, therefore, called on his demonic minions, the Jews, to dampen these activities by conspiring with Al-Hakim to destroy the premier pilgrimage site. Christian and Jewish sources confirm that as a result of these accusations, many French Jews were massacred. One year after Al-Hakim burned the church, King Robert of France commanded Jews to either convert to Christianity or die. These persecutions drove numerous Jews to commit suicide.[7]

The destruction of the Church of the Holy Sepulcher led to other tragedies for Jews in Europe. Muslim-Christian relations worsened over the next several decades and animosity toward Muslims increased. By the 1090s, Christian armies were marching to Jerusalem to take back the Holy Land—what is now called the First Crusade. Despite calls by some Christian leaders throughout western Christendom to leave Jews alone while their "Soldiers of Christ" trekked across Europe, Jews were nevertheless targeted.

5. See Cohen, *Christ Killers*, 75.
6. Abulafia, *Christian Jewish Relations*, 22–25.
7. Jestice, "Great Jewish Conspiracy?," 25–42.

These Christ killers would have to pay a price. Many Jews were murdered, forced to convert, or driven to commit suicide. During the Second Crusade (1145–1149), knights harassed and physically assaulted a revered rabbi in Ramerupt, France. They ripped up the community's Torah scroll and then preceded to inflict five wounds to the head of Rabbi Jacob ben Meir, the grandson of Rashi, perhaps one of the top three most recognized rabbis of all time. The five wounds were revenge for the crucifixion where Jesus was wounded five times: nails to two feet, nails to two hands, and a wound in the side (Catholics called these five wounds the "Stigmata of Christ"). Rabbi Meir called out to a passerby to save him. A Christian man intervened and stopped the beating; but he then warned Rabbi Meir that if he did not convert to Christianity, the attackers would be allowed to return. Such incidents were not isolated; many Jews throughout Europe experienced similar treatment.[8]

Pope Innocent III (d. 1216) stated that Jews deserved to be in perpetual servitude to Christians due to their role in Christ's suffering. He also reinstituted old practices of forcing Jews to wear a certain style of clothing to be identified easily by the Christian population.[9] In the twelfth century, some Christian theologians heightened their criticisms of Jews by claiming that Jews were not only inherently evil, they were less than human. Their evidence? Jews must not be fully human because of how dumb they are; they do not seem to understand the obvious proof of Christianity and the error of Judaism. For example, Peter the Venerable, a Benedictine monk, wrote in 1147:

> I know not whether a Jew is a man because he does not cede to human reason, nor does he acquiesce to the divine authorities which are his own ... Why are you not called a brute animal, why not a beast, why not a beast of burden? Consider the cow or, if you prefer, the ass—no beast is more stupid. . . .The ass hears but does not understand; the Jew hears but does not understand.[10]

Thirteenth-century friar Raymond Martin, in his work *The Muzzle of the Jews*, demonized Jews and their covenant of circumcision when he wrote:

> But do not the Jews, who take the sexual organ of everyone who is circumcised, adult or child, into their most defiled of mouths, mouths with which they blaspheme Christ, and then suck for as long as the blood flows—do they not eat just like the pig who

---

8. Abulafia, *Christian Jewish Relations*, 135–66.
9. Abulafia, *Christian Jewish Relations*, 50–51.
10. See context and translation in Novikoff, "Middle Ages," 72.

soils his snout with abundant filth? Abraham did not do this. Moses did not order it. God did not command it.[11]

The notions of Jews being children of the devil and inherently evil became so commonplace that accusing Jews of atrocious, sickening behavior became easy. Throughout medieval Christian Europe Jews were accused of poisoning Christians. For example, in 1161 in Bohemia (in modern-day Czech Republic), eighty-six Jews were burned to death based on accusations that they had conspired with Jewish physicians to poison the Christian populace.[12] Such accusations were so common that Martin Luther, the most famous of the Reformers who is also known for his intense hatred of Jews,[13] said in a sermon shortly before his death, "[Jews] are our public enemies... If they could kill us all, they would gladly do so, aye, and they often do it, especially those who profess to be physicians. They can give poison to a man of which he will die in an hour, or in ten or twenty years."[14] Queen Elizabeth I of England was compelled to execute her Jewish physician, Rodrigo Lopez, in 1594 after he was found guilty of plotting to poison her, even though she did not believe the accusation.[15]

As Christ killers, Jews were also accused of murdering Christian boys during Easter season as an attempt to reenact Jesus' crucifixion. Perhaps the most well-known case is William of Norwich, England. After young William's dead body was found in March 1144, Jews were blamed. Three years later, several Jews of Würzburg, Germany, were murdered after being accused of killing a Christian.[16] In 1235, Christians in Germany murdered thirty Jews, mostly women and children, in a violent protest after Jews were accused of killing two boys. Rumors circulated that they used the boys' blood for their Passover rituals.[17] In 1255, King Henry III in England imprisoned ninety Jews after hearing rumors that they killed a young Christian boy. He eventually executed eighteen of these Jews when they refused to be tried in an all-Christian court.[18] Accusations of ritual murder spread not only from

---

11. Martin, *Capistrum Iudaeorum*, 2:286–88, see the translation in Cohen, *Christ Killers*, 91–92.

12. Trachtenberg, *Devil and the Jews*, 97.

13. Kaufmann, *Luther's Jews*.

14. Trachtenberg, *Devil and the Jews*, 99.

15. For these and numerous other examples of Jews being accused of attempting to poison Christians, see Trachtenberg, *Devil and the Jews*, 97–108.

16. Abulafia, *Christian Jewish Relations*, 169–70.

17. Abulafia, *Christian Jewish Relations*, 170, 184–85.

18. Abulafia, *Christian Jewish Relations*, 186–87.

England to Germany, but also to France and Spain.[19] It has been argued that "nearly all the accusations [of ritual murder] arose from the clergy, who profited directly from them; the martyred 'saint' and his shrine brought pilgrims and offerings." In the William of Norwich case, for example, one cleric scrambled to obtain the body in order to profit off the incident.[20] As an outgrowth of these rumors, legends developed in various parts of Europe, even until the nineteenth century, that a Jewish bogyman ("*Jüdel*" in Germany, for instance, is a folk representation of the wicked demon Jew), will come snatch kids away if they misbehave.[21] Given these legends, it would not be surprising if the German-born fairy tale of the nineteenth century, Rumpelstiltskin, was meant to represent Jews (i.e., evil extortionists who make immoral bargains that only benefit themselves), especially considering the alleged anti-Semitism of the Grimm brothers.[22]

Rumors of ritual murder were coupled with other accusations that Jews engaged in cannibalism—eating the corpses or hearts of their "little Jesuses."[23] Still other rumors flooded the literature that Jews would steal the communion wafer and desecrate it, recreating the crucifixion of Jesus. Transubstantiation, the idea that the communion wafer and wine literally become the body and blood of Christ, was formally established at the Fourth Lateran Council in 1215. In subsequent years, rumors abounded throughout Western Europe that Jews conspired to obtain the wafer so that they could murder Christ again and again. Jews supposedly would stomp, stab, and burn the wafer. These tales in medieval literature often contained miracles of blood flowing from the wafer and Jews being struck dumb or paralyzed. The first recorded accusation of this host desecration occurred in 1243 in Beelitz, Germany. Christians retaliated based on these rumors and all Jews of the city were burned to death. Many more thousands were killed following similar accusations in, among other places, Germany in 1298, France in the 1330s, and Prague in 1389.[24]

Libels against Jews not only flooded medieval Christian literature but also art. Christian iconography portrayed Jews both suckling from pigs and eating their excrement with Satan standing by. Jews were depicted as horrific goats standing on their hind legs, and they were given horns and a tail

19. Cohen, *Christ Killers*, 94–102.
20. Trachtenberg, *Devil and the Jews*, 124–25.
21. Trachtenberg, *Devil and the Jews*, 125, 243 n. 5.
22. Martin, "Jew in the Thorn Bush," 123–39.
23. Abulafia, *Christian Jewish Relations*, 188; see discussions about cannibalism as an outgrowth of ritual murder rumors in Cohen, *Christ Killers*, 109–17.
24. For the context and many more examples see Cohen, *Christ Killers*, 103–9; Trachtenberg, *Devil and the Jews*, 109–23, 140–55.

as a representation of demons. They were also shown attending Satan while wearing the "Jew badge."[25] Michelangelo's famous statue of the horned Moses—displayed in the Church of San Pietro in Vincoli in Rome—has been attributed to the perpetuation of Saint Jerome's mistranslation of Exodus 34, where he inadvertently changed Moses' "shining skin of his face" when he descended Mount Sinai (Exod 34:35) to the "horns of his face." The more likely interpretation, however, is that Michelangelo's statue was meant to perpetuate the notion of Jewish evil that was common in medieval and early modern Europe.[26]

Centuries of Jewish persecution culminated in the atrocities of the Holocaust. Perhaps when many of us think of Nazi Germany, we tend to associate their hatred for Jews due to race, views that they were deceitful money-grubbers, or perceptions of them as minorities unwilling to fully embrace the local customs. Alongside these attacks in Nazi propaganda were accusations that Jews were Christ killers. Susannah Heschel, prominent Jewish Studies scholar at Dartmouth, has shown that the popular Institute for the Study and Eradication of Jewish Influence on German Church Life attempted to purify Christianity of Judaism—to eradicate all Jewish elements from the German Church and to transform Jesus from a Jew into an Aryan, a white European:

> In the six years of its existence, as the Nazi regime carried out its genocide of the Jews, the Institute redefined Christianity as a Germanic religion whose founder, Jesus, was no Jew but rather had fought valiantly to destroy Judaism, falling as victim to that struggle. Germans were now called upon to be the victors in Jesus' own struggle against the Jews who were said to be seeking Germany's destruction.[27]

This well-funded and pro-Nazi institute composed of Protestant theologians argued that any opposition to National Socialism from within Christian organizations in Germany must necessarily have arisen from Jewish influences, "such as the arguments of Jewish scholars that Jesus was a Jew."[28] They attempted to establish a national German church. They mimicked the structure and culture of the Nazi government, placing swastikas on church altars next to the cross. They argued that when the Assyrians conquered the northern kingdom of Israel in the eighth century BCE, they expatriated the

---

25. See Strickland, *Saracens, Demons, and Jews*, 95–155; Cohen, *Christ Killers*, 204–9; Trachtenberg, *Devil and the Jews*, 27–30, 45, 53.

26. Bertman, "Antisemitic Origin of Michelangelo's Horned Moses," 95–106.

27. Heschel, *Aryan Jesus*, 1.

28. Heschel, *Aryan Jesus*, 2.

Israelites in the region and replaced them with Aryans. Thus, Jesus' ancestors were Aryans, not Jews. They also attempted to eliminate any suggestion that Jesus was the messiah, which is a Jewish notion; instead, Jesus was God, the Son of Man.[29] The Institute attempted to restore the New Testament and Christianity back to its original pristine form by, for instance, eliminating the Old Testament from the Christian Bible and eradicating all Hebrew words (like *Hallelujah* and even *Moses*) from Scripture and the hymnal.[30]

Some theologians, along with Hitler himself, argued that Paul was responsible for Judaizing the teachings of the Aryan Jesus.[31] One Institute theologian, Hugo Pich, suggested that they should eliminate Paul from the German church canon—because if they kept Paul, they would be perpetuating "Jewish Christianity." Another theologian, the bishop of Mecklenburg, argued that such a proposition is unacceptable because by eliminating Paul, a hero of Martin Luther and the German Lutherans, the superior German nation would be conceding that they "had been duped . . . by some stinking Jew for 1,500 years."[32] Some in the Institute argued that the effeminate, gentle Jesus common in late medieval art was really a corruption from Judaism. Consequently, Jesus was changed to a masculine, tough, heroic fighter.[33] The purification of Christianity from Judaism not only included the altering of texts and ideas, but also the purging of Jews who had converted to Christianity. Complaints from pastors and laity grew louder in the 1930s about the practices of missionizing and baptizing Jews. For example, a propaganda piece published in 1933 stated, "Just as a pig remains a pig, even if you put it in a horse's stall, so a Jew still remains a Jew, even if he is baptized."[34] One of the most striking statements to come out of the Institute was from a theologian, Siegfried Leffler, who said:

> As a Christian, I have to follow the laws of my nation, which are often presented in a very cruel way, so that again I am brought into the harshest of conflicts with the Jew. Even if I know "thou shalt not kill" is a commandment of God or "thou shalt love the Jew" because he too is a child of the eternal Father, I am able to know as well that I have to kill him, I have to shoot him, and I can only do that if I am permitted to say: Christ.[35]

29. Heschel, *Aryan Jesus*, 55–63.
30. Heschel, *Aryan Jesus*, 106–65.
31. Heschel, *Aryan Jesus*, 42, 50, 140.
32. Heschel, *Aryan Jesus*, 146.
33. Heschel, *Aryan Jesus*, 52–53.
34. Heschel, *Aryan Jesus*, 54–55.
35. Heschel, *Aryan Jesus*, 10.

Arguments have been posited that the German masses, especially the good Christians, were unaware that Hitler was murdering Jews, and that the churches opposed the Nazi program. This myth started to be exposed in the 1980s. It is now clear that the German churches (and universities) were complicit in the Holocaust.[36] The Institute was filled with pastors, bishops, theologians, and laity who knew what the Nazi government was doing. Those German citizens whom previous generations of scholars thought were the "good Germans" heard gushing praise of Hitler over the pulpit. Christian sermons did not exclusively deal with social problems regarding Jews but theological problems. Jews, as the claim went for centuries, were inherently evil Christ killers. The people who heard these sermons supported a regime that was open about their intentions toward Jews.

The United States was not without anti-Semitism. *The International Jew*, the anti-Semitic booklet of Henry Ford, the great American icon, got him an award from Hitler, and he was praised in *Mein Kampf*.[37] In the late 1930s, public polling revealed that anti-Semitism was at its highest point in American history. A 1938 survey revealed that 77 percent of respondents answered "No" when asked, "Should we allow a larger number of Jewish exiles to come to the United States to live?"[38] These details of American anti-Semitism do not explicitly claim that Jews were hated because they killed Jesus, but it is implied. America is a predominantly Christian country. In a 2002 national survey, nearly 40 percent of Americans agreed that Jews were responsible for killing Jesus. It is likely that this question in the 1930s would have revealed a much higher percentage.[39] Many people will recall that a Christian man shot and killed eleven Jews at a Pittsburgh synagogue on October 27, 2018. His justification? "Jews are the children of Satan," taken from John 8:44.[40]

This section has served as a reminder of the atrocities against Jews from late antiquity to the twentieth century. After encountering this deplorable display of humanity on the part of Christians toward Jews, we are left with a disturbing conclusion. Such behavior would be bad enough even if it were true that "Jews killed Jesus," especially given Jesus' admonition to forgive enemies and turn the other cheek. However, unimaginable Jewish suffering for a crime their ancestors did not commit is unfathomable. In short, the demonization and murder of millions of Jews because "they killed

---

36. Ericksen, *Complicity in the Holocaust*.
37. Rubinstein, "Anti-Semitism in the English-speaking World," 160.
38. Dinnerstein, *Antisemitism in America*, 127.
39. Tobin and Groeneman, *Anti-Semitic Beliefs*, 19–20.
40. Turkewitz and Roose, "Who Is Robert Bowers?"

Jesus" was unwarranted—it was based on horribly flawed interpretations of the New Testament and on poor logic. The remainder of this book seeks to demonstrate this, as well as to contextualize the many New Testament passages that demonize Jews. We also seek to understand Jesus' relationship with his Jewish peers and to answer the question, "why didn't the Jews kill Jesus?" when the New Testament seems to claim otherwise? First, we deal with the Judas story.

Judas the Betrayer?

Because Jesus was humiliated and killed by his enemies, many Jews who thought he might be the messiah abandoned such hope after the crucifixion, including some of Jesus' close followers. For example, the Gospel of Luke describes two "saddened" non-apostle followers who, not knowing they are speaking with the disguised Jesus, reflect that he had been a great "prophet," but they "*had hoped* that he was the one *to redeem Israel*" (Luke 24:13–21; emphasis added). Some of Jesus' apostles even "doubted" after they met the resurrected Jesus in Galilee (Matt 28:16–20). The text is unclear on the nature of their doubt, but it may have concerned Jesus' role as the messiah in relation to their previous messianic expectations. According to Acts, when the resurrected Jesus gathered the apostles together, their first question was, "Lord, is this the time when you will restore the kingdom to Israel?" (1:6). Their entire worldview was centered on when the messiah would come and defeat Israel's enemies and subsequently reign as king. Consequently, Jesus' death scandalized many Jews who thought he was the messiah. Paul identified the crucifixion of Jesus as "a stumbling-block to Jews" (1 Cor 1:23). In fact the Greek word for "stumbling-block" here is *skandalon* (where we get "scandal"). Most Jews simply did not expect the messiah to be killed.

The case of Judas may also illustrate that some (or all?) of Jesus' closest disciples believed him to be the messiah but did not expect him to die, at least not before fulfilling the messianic expectations of achieving freedom from Rome. Judas is most infamous for handing Jesus over to the authorities, but the accounts conflict as to why he did so. According to the author of Matthew, greed compelled Judas to betray Jesus (26:14–16). The Gospels of Luke and John conclude that Judas was possessed by satanic influence (Luke 22:3; John 6:70–71, 13:2, 27). Note that greed and evil influence are standard explanations as to why people commit horrendous acts that are difficult to explain—the perpetrators are either "bought and paid for" (i.e., morally compromised because of greed) or they are possessed by evil spirits or crazy (i.e., a lunatic).

There is, however, another option for interpretation, especially considering Jewish messianic expectations. If Judas believed, like most other Jews, in a conquering messiah, then he would have anticipated Jesus subduing Israel's enemies. He would not have expected Jesus to die. The earliest Gospel, Mark, provides no motivation for why Judas handed Jesus over to the authorities. Mark makes no mention of greed or evil forces on the part of Judas. In fact, in Mark, it was not Judas who asked for money in return for handing over Jesus (as in Matthew) but the chief priests who offered the money to Judas (Mark 14:10–11). Further, Mark does not refer to Judas as a betrayer. Many English translations of the Bible use the word "betray" in reference to Judas, but the Greek *pareden* in its various forms means "to hand over" or "deliver," not "to betray."[41] William Klaussen (scholar at numerous universities—most recently at Cambridge) explained:

> Not one ancient classical Greek text has surfaced in which [this verb] means "betray" or has a connotation of treachery . . . Josephus, the most prolific historian of the first century, uses [this word] 293 times, but not once can one legitimately translate it employing the word "betray." . . . There is no linguistic basis—in classical Greek, in the Greek translation of the Hebrew Bible, in Josephus or patristic sources—for a translation of "betray" to describe what Judas did.[42]

Clearly the author of Luke was not referring to betrayal. During the Last Supper, Jesus mentions that one person in the room would hand him over to the authorities (Mark 14:18), which scandalizes the apostles. According to the author of Matthew, Judas himself wonders whether he would be the one to deliver Jesus (Matt 26:25). The Gospel of John adds that Jesus encourages Judas to "do quickly what you are going to do" (John 13:27). Given Jesus' increased discussion near the end of his ministry about an imminent realization of his divine mission, coupled with the pervasive expectations of a conquering messiah, Judas likely thought that the time had come for the great messianic battle to be waged.[43] Thus, when Jesus tells Judas during the Last Supper to deliver him, Judas is glad to do it. His rationale may have been, "I'll be happy to arrange this meeting between the messiah and our enemies; he'll light them up! It's about time the messiah fulfills his mission and deals with Rome and our corrupt temple bureaucrats."

---

41. See most English translations of Mark 3:19 and 14:10–11.

42. Klassen, *Judas*, 48–49, 57.

43. Other scholars and authors have made similar arguments about Judas. See Paffenroth, *Judas*, 86–92.

The portrait of Judas in Mark, supplemented by a few bits of information in the other Gospels, shows a disciple firmly entrenched within the brotherhood of Jesus' close circle. He is not demonized in this earliest Gospel as he is in later Gospels. When Judas exits the upper room during the Last Supper after being told to deliver Jesus, the other disciples assume he is leaving to buy food for the feast or to give to the poor (John 13:29–30). There is no hint of tension between Jesus and Judas, nor between Judas and the other apostles. On the contrary, based on Greco-Roman mealtime customs,[44] the act of Jesus offering food to Judas during the meal suggests a deep friendship, not a ruptured relationship. This interpretation of Judas makes the most sense in both Mark's portrayal of Judas and of first-century messianic expectations. As mentioned, Jesus' role as messiah was unclear to his disciples. The fact that Jesus asks his closest disciples, "Who do people say that I am?" and "Who do you think I am?" illustrates this lack of clarity (Luke 9:19–21; Mark 8:28–30; Matt 16:13–20). When Jesus claims at Caesarea Philippi that authorities in Jerusalem would kill him, Peter takes him aside and says, "God forbid it, Lord! This must never happen to you" (Matt 16:22). If Judas had a similar expectation of the messiah, he would have been willing to help Jesus overthrow Israel's enemies by arranging their meeting.

The Gospels themselves are conflicted and unclear on Judas's motives. This ambiguity has led many interpreters to conclude that either Jesus commanded Judas to hand him over as part of a divinely-ordained plan, or Judas was greedy and evil and, therefore, betrayed Jesus. Both interpretations, however, seem problematic given the subsequent events. If Judas was demonic, evil, greedy, and easily compromised by money—as the author of Matthew claimed—then why would he so quickly slip into a depressed and repentant state, return the money, and kill himself after Jesus' conviction? Why the immediate remorse? Similarly, why would Jesus command Judas to hand him over in order to accomplish a divinely ordained mission if he knew that such a commandment would not exalt Judas—as Abraham was exalted after following the commandment to sacrifice his son—but rather lead to Judas's disgraced death? Many conservative theologians have argued that Jesus, being all-knowing, called Judas to "the twelve" precisely *because* he was a devil and would "betray" him. According to the author of John, Jesus knew from the beginning that Judas would hand him over to the authorities, yet he chose him anyway: "Jesus answered them, 'Did I not choose you, the twelve? Yet one of you is a devil.' He was speaking of Judas son of

---

44. See Neyrey, "Ceremonies in Luke–Acts," 361–87; Smith "Greco-Roman Meal Customs," 4:651–53.

Simon Iscariot, for he, though one of the twelve, was going to betray him" (John 6:70–71).

A more realistic explanation is that Judas expected Jesus to fulfill the prevailing messianic expectations. When Jesus was convicted and killed, Judas realized he had made a mistake (albeit an honest mistake) and had misunderstood what Jesus as the messiah was supposed to have accomplished. Note that once Jewish authorities handed Jesus over to Pilate, Judas immediately returned the money to the chief priests and proclaimed, "I have sinned by handing over innocent blood" (Matt 27:4). The word "sinned" here may not be an admission of "sin" against God by Judas but may have been placed on Judas's lips by the author of Matthew; however, even if the author of Matthew correctly preserved Judas's exact words, the Greek word *hamartanó* can also mean "to miss the mark" or "to be mistaken." It seems that Judas did not anticipate this outcome of his messiah's defeat. For the author of Mark, Judas simply was the means by which Jesus accomplished his goal, a goal that Judas may have misinterpreted. Jesus knew he would be killed, while Judas expected him to be the victor.

We do not know what ultimately happened to Judas. It may be that he did not even commit suicide, as the author of Matthew claimed. The ancient sources disagree on his fate, and we are left to fill in the gaps through scholarship. The earliest Christian writings, for example, do not even mention Judas's death. In 1 Corinthians, which predates all four Gospels, Paul refers to the night Jesus was "handed over" (*paredoken*), but he does not mention Judas (11:23). A few chapters later, Paul explains that the resurrected Jesus met with "the twelve" (1 Cor 15:5), which includes Judas. Had Judas really betrayed Jesus and then committed suicide, Paul should have stated that Jesus appeared to the *eleven* apostles. Further, the earliest Gospel, Mark, does not mention Judas again after Jesus' arrest. Similarly, the authors of Luke and John say nothing of what happened to Judas after Jesus' crucifixion. Only in the "M" tradition (i.e., material exclusively contained in Matthew) does Judas commit suicide (Matt 27:3–10). According to the book of Acts, Judas died after taking a fall (1:18–19). An early Christian leader, Papias, wrote a few decades after the Gospels of Matthew and Luke were written that a chariot hit and killed Judas.[45] The Gospel of Judas, a second – or third-century text, claims that the apostles persecuted and stoned Judas.[46] That Jesus' followers within two hundred years of his death were unclear, and in fact contradicted each other, regarding Judas's fate is apparent.

---

45. Papias, "Frag. 3," trans. Roberts and Donaldson.
46. Kasser et al., *Gospel of Judas*, 31.

Some scholars have posited that the demonization of Judas in the Gospels was an unfair portrayal, developed decades later by late first-century followers of Jesus.[47] The authors of Matthew, Luke, and John seem to go out of their way to use Judas as a symbol and microcosm for "Jews," or at least for a certain influential segment of the Jewish population. The convenient and anti-Jewish portrayal of Judas in the Gospels seems suspicious, indeed. Here, we discuss four examples.

First, Judas's name means "Jew"; it is the Greek version of "Judah," the progenitor of the southern kingdom of Judah, the later inhabitants of which were called "Jews." Further, Judas Iscariot may have been the only apostle not from Galilee (perhaps from Kerioth in Judea).[48] It seems a bit suspicious that the only apostle capable of "betraying" Jesus is the one named "Jew" from Judea, the home of the corrupt aristocracy.

Second, the Gospels portray Judas as having been influenced by Satan and his demons (Luke 22:3; John 6:70–71, 13:2, 27). Judas was evil to the core, according to the authors of Matthew, Luke, and John. Similarly, these Gospels portray some Jews as being demonic. For example, in John, Jesus supposedly tells "the Jews" (8:31):

> You are from your father the devil, and you choose to do your father's desires. He was a murderer from the beginning and does not stand in the truth, because there is no truth in him. When he lies, he speaks according to his own nature, for he is a liar and the father of lies. (8:44)

The Gospel of Matthew strangely describes Jesus in a few places as a non-Jew, an outsider who enters "their" synagogues (12:9), and describes the Pharisees, the popular leaders of Israel, as "evil" (12:34, 39), "children of hell" (23:15), "dead" inside and full of "filth" (23:27), "descendants of those who murdered the prophets" and destined for hell (23:31, 33). In both the Last Supper and Gethsemane episodes, Matthew paints Judas as the worst kind of betrayer, someone who must be wholly in league with Satan. For instance, Judas calls Jesus "Rabbi" during the Last Supper and again in Gethsemane (Matt 26:25, 49). Such a term is anathema in the Gospel of Matthew. It is in this story that Jesus excoriates Jewish leaders for desiring "to have people call them rabbi. But you are not to be called rabbi, for you have one teacher, and you are all students" (Matt 23:7–8). The author of Matthew is deliberate in his use of titles. Only in two places in this Gospel is Jesus addressed by the negative term (in Matthew's view) of "rabbi"; on

---

47. Maccoby, *Judas Iscariot*; Klassen, *Judas*, 1–204.
48. Zwiep et al., "Judas Iscariot," 14:938.

both occasions, his own disciple, Judas, uses the term![49] Here, the author of Matthew provides evidence for Judas's hostility toward Jesus—Judas calls him the very title that Jesus rejects. In addition, Judas "betrays" Jesus with a kiss of intimate friendship. Again, the author of Matthew was trying to portray Judas as the most evil kind of person, one who displays overt hostility toward a dear friend in order to make a measly profit. Here, Judas dishonors his mentor in the most nefarious way possible, outside of killing him himself. This portrayal of Judas mirrors that of "Jews"; the demonic Judas was a representation of the demonic Jews.

Third, the Gospel of Matthew attributes Judas's "betrayal" to greed (Matt 26:14–16). Only in Matthew does Judas approach the chief priests and ask for payment to hand over Jesus. The Gospel of John also accuses Judas of greed: "[Judas] said this not because he cared about the poor, but because he was a thief; he kept the common purse and used to steal what was put into it" (John 12:6). The other Gospels likewise accuse Jews of being greedy. In Luke, Israel's leaders are charged with being "lovers of money" (Luke 16:14). In Matthew, they are "full of greed and self-indulgence" (Matt 23:25). Jesus criticizes the temple establishment for being extortionists and thieves, making the temple complex a "den of robbers" (Matt 21:13; Mark 11:17; Luke 19:46). Again, the greedy Judas serves as a symbol for "Jews" in general. As we will see in the next chapter on Pharisees, the phenomenon of accusing one's opponents of being motivated by money was common, especially among the competing philosophical schools.

Fourth, the Gospels link Judas with the corrupt temple priests. Whereas Jesus hardly speaks to them during his trial, Judas deals directly with them (Luke 22:3–6; Matt 26:15, 27:3). The Jewish populace despised the corrupt chief priests and may have even cheered on Jesus as he cleansed the temple. Josephus stated, "No one need wonder that there was so much wealth in our temple, for all the Jews throughout the habitable world, and those who worshiped God, even those from Asia and Europe, had been contributing to it for a very long time."[50] Second Maccabees, a Jewish second century BCE text, agrees: "The Treasury in Jerusalem was full of untold sums of money, so that the amount of funds could not be reckoned" (3:6). Rome charged the priests to implement taxation. Josephus reported that Ananias, the high priest, sent servants to confiscate by violence the "tithes that were due to the priests."[51] Qumran texts refer to Jerusalem priests as wicked, robbing the

---

49. Luz et al., *Matthew 21–28*, 360.
50. Josephus, *Ant.* 14.7.110.
51. Josephus, *Ant.* 20.8.181.

poor, acquiring massive wealth, and defiling the temple.[52] Thus, tying Judas to the chief priests by association was a way of illustrating that he was not just a Jew, but a Jew entrenched within the corrupt bureaucracy responsible for Jesus' arrest and death.

Other details contribute to suspicions about Judas's portrayal in the Gospels being historically reliable. For example, the author of Matthew claims that Judas delivered Jesus for a measly thirty pieces of silver (Matt 26:15, 27:3, 9)—worth about 120 days' wages. Today the equivalent of this act would be a lower middle-class laborer who makes $40,000 annually betraying and conspiring against his mentor, teacher, friend, and religious leader for a mere $13,000. Judas sells his messiah for the low price of a slave (Exod 21:32); even the bottle of ointment used to anoint Jesus was worth more than double that of Judas's betrayal price (Mark 14:5; John 12:3).[53] Further, the author of Matthew uses Jeremiah's condemnation of Israel, or "the Jews," as a parallel to Judas's condemnation. The "thirty pieces of silver" is an allusion to both Jeremiah (19:11) and Zechariah (11:12–13). The author of Matthew references "Jeremiah" in this fulfillment of prophecy (Matt 27:9); however, the parallel in this verse is closer to Zechariah, and indeed some ancient manuscripts of Matthew 27 contain the name "Zechariah" instead of "Jeremiah."[54] After Judas delivers Jesus, he returns the money to the temple treasury, but the chief priests reject it (Matt 27:3–10). The word *treasury* in Zechariah 11:13 is translated in other ancient manuscripts as "potter."[55] When the priests reject Judas's silver for the temple treasury, they use the money to buy the *potter's* field for burying foreigners (Matt 27:7–10), also an allusion to Jeremiah (19:1–13, 32:1–15). The author of Matthew refers to this field as "the Field of Blood" (27:8). Based on Jeremiah 19, the traditional site for the potter's field is in the Hinnom Valley; the priests smashed the potter's jug in the Hinnom Valley as a symbol of Israel's destruction. In short, the author of Matthew is using the condemnatory material of Israel in Jeremiah and Zechariah in relation to Judas.

Matthew also links Judas with Judah in the Joseph of Egypt story. All of Joseph's brothers reject him, but *Judah* suggests selling him for twenty pieces of silver in order to make a "profit" (Gen 37:26-27). Similarly, in

---

52. 1QpHab. For a detailed discussion on temple corruption in the age of Jesus, see Evans, *Jesus and His Contemporaries*, 319–66.

53. Thirty pieces of silver was approximately the same as 120 Roman denarii. The women who anointed Jesus used a bottle of ointment worth about 300 denarii. See Betlyon, "Coinage," 1:1076–89, esp. 1086.

54. Omanson, *Textual Guide*, 49.

55. For more detailed treatments of the arrest narratives and their connections to Hebrew Bible prophets, see Luz et al., *Matthew 21–28*, 466–77.

Matthew, Jesus' disciples "deserted him" (26:56), but only *Judas* is willing to sell him for profit. Suspicion of how the Judas story unfolds in Matthew is warranted because the only two people in all of Jewish and Christian Scripture willing to sell their own brother or beloved teacher to slavery or death for a measly profit are both named "Judah." The goal here was not only to tie Jesus to Joseph but to tie the betraying apostle *Judas* to *Judah* in order to blame "Jews" for the death of Jesus.

We have already encountered several David-Jesus typologies. Not mentioned, however, is that the author of Matthew also infuses elements from the King David narrative into the Judas story. Specifically, Judas's actions mirror those of David's counselor, Ahithophel. When David's son Absalom attempts to steal the throne, Ahithophel joins the "conspiracy" against David (2 Sam 15:12, 31). When the conspiracy fails, Ahithophel "hangs himself" and dies (2 Sam 17:23), just like Judas (Matt 27:5). In fact, these are the only two suicide hangings in all of the Hebrew Bible and New Testament. Further, Judas's suicide seems to be directly related to Ahithophel's suicide because these two literary units are the only ones in the Bible and Greek texts to include both the words *aperchomai* ("went away") and *apagcho* ("hang oneself"). The authors of the Gospels apparently had Psalm 41 in mind when presenting the Judas episode. The author of John quotes Psalm 41 (see John 13:18), putting words into David's mouth regarding Ahithophel: "Even my *bosom friend* in whom I trusted, *who ate of my bread, has lifted the heel against me*" (Ps 41:9). Likewise, Jesus says, according to John, "The one who ate my bread has *lifted his heel against me*" (John 13:18).[56] These details present a strong case that the Gospels, particularly Matthew, wrote the Judas portion of the story with the Hebrew Bible open so that Jesus and Judas would mirror King David and Ahithophel.

The only other book in the New Testament that mentions Judas's death is Acts. This passage, however, says nothing about suicide but rather mentions Judas's fall that results in his bowels gushing out (Acts 1:18). Like the author of Matthew, the author of Acts connects Judas's story with King David, through David's nephew Amasa, who also participated in Absalom's conspiracy against David. After Absalom fails in his attempt to obtain the throne, David welcomes Amasa back into his circle, appointing him as a general. Amasa's rival, Joab, another of David's generals, becomes jealous. He approaches Amasa wearing a "soldier's garment," and while greeting him with the words "my brother," betrays him with a kiss on his cheek as he stabs him with a sword, making his bowels "pour out on the ground" (2 Sam

---

56. For more on the connection between the Judas story and Davidic elements in the Hebrew Bible, see Zacharias, *Matthew's Presentation*, 152–70.

20:4–10). The Amasa-Joab episode and the Judas material in the Gospels and Acts contain the same elements: the conspiracy, the betrayal, "soldiers," the friendly verbal greeting, the kiss, the sword, and death as bowels gushed out on the ground.

All of these parallels between Judas and "Jews" and between Judas and David's conspiratorial counselors have caused some scholars to conclude that the Judas story is either wholly fabricated at worst or grossly embellished at best.[57] The rhetoric and details of the Judas material do seem hyperbolic. As we saw previously, Christians accused Jews of the very sins Judas was accused of in the Gospels and Acts—greed, satanic influence, conspiracy, and the murder of Jesus.[58] The Judas case was Exhibit A for the nature of Jews, as Kim Paffenroth has explained:

> The simplest anti-Semitic use that Judas's story could serve is one of simple equation: Judas was bad; all Jews are bad. The equation can run both ways: Judas was evil because he was a Jew; Jews are evil, demonstrated by their similarity to Judas. This has certainly been the most frequent anti-Semitic use of Judas's story through Christian history.[59]

Archbishop of Constantinople, John Chrysostom (c. 347–407), who referred to Jews as "Christ-killers,"[60] equated Jews with Judas when he wrote:

> When God forsakes a place, that place becomes the dwelling of demons. But at any rate the Jews say that they, too, adore God. God forbid that I say that. No Jew adores God! . . . Shall I tell you of their plundering, their covetousness, their abandonment of the poor, their thefts, their cheating in trade? The whole day long will not be enough to give you an account of these things.[61]

The portrayal of Judas's development from the earliest Gospel (Mark) to the later Gospels is clear. In Mark, the picture of Judas is somewhat neutral. William Klassen observed, "Compared with Peter . . . Judas comes out relatively well."[62] By the end of the first century, however, Judas had become a symbol of evil, greedy, conspiratorial Jews. Getting at the historical Judas is

---

57. Maccoby, *Judas Iscariot*, 22–168; Klassen, *Judas*, 1–204.

58. See Cohen, *Christ Killers*; Strickland, *Saracens, Demons, and Jews*; Trachtenberg, *Devil and the Jews*.

59. Paffenroth, *Judas*, 37–38.

60. See English translation in Chrysostom, "Patrologia Graeca 48.843–856" (852).

61. Chrysostom, *Discourses against Judaizing Christians*, 11, 25–26.

62. Klassen, *Judas*, 91.

difficult because the sources leave us with uncertainty regarding Judas's role in Jesus' arrest, his motivation for his actions, and his ultimate fate.

Ambiguity in the sources has led to numerous interpretations by later exegetes.[63] This perhaps alerts us to be cautious with this data. Some of the aforementioned points regarding Judas are stronger evidence than other points. Some points are also more speculative. However, when all points are viewed together, it is difficult to take the story at face value. It is difficult to conclude that Judas was the villainous traitor that some of the Gospels portray him to be. It is also difficult, however, to conclude that the Judas story was fabricated entirely. Perhaps the authors of the Gospels embellished the story for political and theological reasons, though several historical kernels seem to be embedded in their texts. Most likely, one of Jesus' apostles did deliver him to the chief priests. This apostle, named "Jew" (i.e., "Judas") in the story, believed that Jesus was the messiah and, therefore, was willing to arrange the meeting between the messiah and his foes. He did not expect Jesus to die. Later authors struggled to make sense of Judas's actions and attributed to him the worst motives. The revision of Judas's character by the authors of the Gospels may have been an attempt to deflect their embarrassment that one of Jesus' own followers had handed him over to the authorities. This act could have provoked some Jews to proclaim throughout the Roman Empire that the Jesus movement was illegitimate: How great can the Jesus movement be when one of Jesus' own students delivered him to the authorities for the price of a slave? The authors of the Gospels in their various contexts, therefore, may have revised the story to allow the response, "No, Judas was not one of us. Judas, a 'typical' Jew, was the only non-Galilean apostle; he was evil and greedy to the core and had connections to the Jerusalem establishment. He was not really one of us. He was one of you, a quintessential Jew." We will discuss more on the issue of rhetoric and embellishments in the Gospels, particularly in relation to Jews, in later chapters.

Takeaways

What did we learn here and why does it matter? First, Christians have blamed Jews for two millennia for Jesus' death. They called Jews "Christ killers," they accused Jews of murdering Christian kids and youths, and they claimed that Jews were inherently evil children of Satan. This accusation has led to the deaths of millions of Jews. Were these accusations, persecutions,

---

63. Paffenroth, *Judas*, 1–142; Cane, *Place of Judas Iscariot*; Zwiep et al., "Judas Iscariot," 14:938–58.

and murders warranted? Well, according to Christian ethics based on the teachings of Jesus, the answer is, no!

Second, we learned that, regarding the Gospels, things are not so simple—there is usually more to the story. A careful examination of the Judas episodes reveal that the Gospels' conclusion that he was an evil betrayer is fraught with ambiguity and contradiction. Our soft conclusion here is that Judas thought Jesus was the messiah, as did the other apostles. Thus, he did not expect Jesus to die. I call this a "soft conclusion" because we cannot enter the mind of Judas and prove what he did or did not think. We can only go by what the authors of the Gospels related to us. However, if we line up all the data from the four Gospels, and we examine that data critically, we find it extremely difficult to understand what Judas actually did, what his motives were, and what happened to him after Jesus' death. Since the Gospels lack uniformity on these three main issues, we are left to put the puzzle pieces together. It seems that the only sure detail is that Judas handed Jesus over to the authorities, and that is it. All other details are ambiguous. In my assessment, only one conclusion makes sense based on the prevalent messianic expectations among many first-century Jews: Jesus' friend Judas handed him over to the authorities—for reasons we do not fully know—but Judas did not expect Jesus to be killed. After Jesus died, something unfortunate happened to Judas, which, again, is unclear. Was he killed? Did he kill himself? Was he banned and "excommunicated" by the other eleven apostles? We simply do not know. All we have now are several accounts dating to the late first century and the second century wherein early Christians present their understanding of the tragic case of Judas.

Chapter Seven

Jesus' Enemies?
Why Didn't the Pharisees Reject Their Friend Jesus?

IN THIS CHAPTER WE turn our attention to the Pharisees. In doing so, we hope to gain broad insight into how Jesus fit within the Jewish social hierarchy in first-century Galilee and Judea, at least according to the Gospels. Any conclusions we draw must be understood within a broad framework, not a nuanced, highly historical framework. We are not assuming that literally *every* Pharisee fit this description. Pharisees are central figures in the Christian demonization of Jews from late antiquity to the present. The Gospels portray Pharisees as self-righteous, hypocritical, spiritually hollow, overly ritualistic, and even demonic. Some of the Gospels portray Pharisees as the chief opponents of Jesus, the people largely responsible for his death. But is this portrayal fair? In this chapter, we explore the primary characteristics of Pharisees according to both Josephus and the authors of the Gospels to answer this question, as well as to understand better the nature of Jesus' relationship with the Pharisees, who were Israel's leaders at the time of Jesus. Based on evidence and inference, I posit that not only were Jesus and the Pharisees not vicious enemies, but that they had a cordial relationship.

Briefly, Who Are the Pharisees?

Josephus published *Antiquities of the Jews* in 93 CE, roughly twenty years after publishing his account of the Jewish-Roman War (*Jewish War*).[1] Josephus

---

1. For a brief discussion on the dating of Josephus's *Antiquities* and *Life*, see Rajak,

mentions the Pharisees in both of these works, but they are featured only briefly and often incidentally. From what we can gather, Pharisaism as a distinct movement developed about 150 years before the birth of Jesus (second century BCE) amidst the turmoil of Greek persecutions and the corruption of the Jewish priestly establishment. When Jews wrested the temple and the region from the Greeks and took control of their own state in 152 BCE, the Jews had in place two major branches of leadership: priests and kings. But where were the prophets? In times past, Israel was led by *prophets*, priests, and kings. As we learned in chapter 3, the standard conclusion among many Bible commentators is that prophets ceased with Haggai, Zechariah, and Malachi. This is false. Many Jews in the Second Temple period identified several prophets of their time, including John the Baptist and Jesus. It is likely that when Jews began ruling their own state, Pharisees swept in to fill the leadership void that was formerly filled by the great prophets of old, such as Isaiah, Jeremiah, and Ezekiel.

Pharisees likely did not see themselves as equals with these former prophets, but it seems that they did attempt to reestablish that class of social reformers and moral gatekeepers who would hold the kings accountable and ensure that God's laws were observed properly. Pharisees may have sought to fill this role "until a true prophet [shall] arise," as stated in the first book of Maccabees.[2] Evidence for this is found throughout the ancient sources. For instance, note that the early rabbis, intellectual heirs of the Pharisees, traced their leadership lineage through the prophets back to Moses, as opposed to through the priestly lines back to Aaron, like other groups: "Moses received [the law] at Sinai and handed it on to Joshua, Joshua to elders, and elders to prophets. And the prophets handed it on to the [rabbis]," including Gamaliel, the famous Pharisaic leader and teacher of Paul, who was also a Pharisee.[3]

Several scholars have defined the Pharisees as a reformist group, as opposed to an *introversionist*, or separatist, sect—a group that separates itself from the world like the Dead Sea sect at Qumran.[4] Like the former Israelite prophets, Pharisees were not revolutionaries but "moral reformers."[5] They sought to *reform* the Jewish system. They did not seek to react "against the society [but] to shape the society and agitate *in* it and *for* it"[6]—to improve

---

Josephus, 237–38.

2. 1 Macc 14:41. See also 1 Macc 4:46.
3. Mishnah Avot 1:1, 2–18. See translation in Neusner, *Mishnah*, 672.
4. See Saldarini, *Pharisees, Scribes, and Sadducees*, 286; Deines, "Pharisees," 449.
5. Walzer, *In God's Shadow*, 82.
6. Deines, "Pharisees," 449.

the system already in place in earlier centuries, in this case, the temple-state system run by prophets, priests, and kings. Their aim was to preserve the law and national traditions as they came from Moses (not as distorted by Sadducean priests). Like the prophets of old, Pharisees were a repentance group. They preached obedience to God's laws. As reformers, the Pharisees mirrored the prophets of old who consistently counseled and challenged the kings. Harvard-trained political theorist Michael Walzer reminds us that, other than "Moses, whose position is unique in biblical history, the prophet as a political figure *first appears together with the king*."[7] Note that it was not until the Jewish guerrilla fighters, led by a priestly family called "Hasmoneans," took the throne in 152 BCE that Josephus first mentioned Pharisees, as they were immediately thrust into political jousting with the new Hasmonean leaders. One of the first Hasmonean leaders, John Hyrcanus, sought out Pharisees for moral guidance. The populace rejected a subsequent king, Alexander Jannaeus, because the Pharisees disapproved of him. This is precisely why Alexander Jannaeus admonished his successor, Alexandra Salome, to make peace with the Pharisees and heed their counsel. After the Hasmonean dynasty, the Pharisees challenged King Herod on multiple occasions. For example, Josephus mentioned a Pharisee named Samaias, an "upright man" who challenged Herod and the Sanhedrin.[8] All of this is reminiscent of the relationships between prophets and kings in times past: Samuel and King Saul, Nathan and King David, Elijah and King Ahab, Amos and King Amaziah, Isaiah and King Hezekiah, and Jeremiah and King Zedekiah. Israel's prophets developed a legacy of both "stand[ing] against the social power structures" and "serving Israel's kings as trusted counselors."[9] It seems that Pharisees also sought to implement this kind of check and balance of power.

Not only did Pharisaic characteristics resemble those of ancient Israelite prophets, but Josephus described the Pharisees as those who made men think that God favored Pharisaism.[10] Josephus added that the populace viewed Pharisees as prophet-type leaders, as they "were believed to have foreknowledge of things through God's appearances to them."[11] He also

---

7. Walzer, *In God's Shadow*, 75; emphasis added.

8. Josephus, *Ant.* 14.172–74, 15.3, trans. Marcus and Wikgren; Mason, *Flavius Josephus on the Pharisees*, 261–62.

9. Leuchter, *Samuel and Tradition*, 43.

10. Josephus, *Ant.* 17.2.4.

11. Josephus, *Ant.* 17.2.4, trans. Marcus and Wikgren.

provided examples of their prophetic gifts when they prophesied of Herod's future deeds and tribulations.[12]

The Popularity of the Pharisees

One of the salient Pharisaic attributes that emerged in Josephus's writings is their popularity with the Jewish masses, not just in Galilee but also in Judea, the home of the temple establishment and ruling class. Josephus even seemed to claim on one occasion that he was a Pharisee, but a closer examination of his brief autobiographical statement,[13] when coupled with his other statements about Pharisees, reveals that this was not so. Rather, he was a proud descendent of the priestly class. In his groundbreaking work on the Pharisees in Josephus's writings, Steve Mason, presently working at the University of Groningen in the Netherlands, challenged the "consensus" that Josephus was a Pharisee. He posited that Josephus's original statement in Greek, "I began to follow the school of the Pharisees," should actually be read, "I began to engage in public life, following the school of the Pharisees."[14] Josephus acknowledged that to be successful in public life he must behave according to the rulings of the Pharisees, because they had the support of the populace. This interpretation is the most plausible based on other statements he made about Pharisees, including the following:

> [Sadducean] doctrine is received but by a few, *yet by those still of the greatest dignity*. But they are able to do almost nothing of themselves; for when they become magistrates . . . they addict themselves to the notions of the Pharisees because the multitude would not otherwise bear them.[15]

As a member of the priestly clan and a non-Pharisee, Josephus acknowledged that Pharisees' opinions and legal rulings held sway with the masses; therefore, he, as well as the larger Sadducean body, were forced to capitulate to them. This does not mean that Josephus was a Pharisee himself. This passage also claims that Pharisees were popular with the masses. Using modern political language, if the Sadducees did not uphold the rulings of the popular Pharisees, then they would have been a lame-duck ruling body. Obviously we are using modern democratic terminology here, which is a

---

12. Josephus, *Ant.* 14.163–176; 15.1–4.
13. Josephus, *Life* 2.12.
14. Mason, "Was Josephus a Pharisee?," 40–41.
15. Josephus, *Ant.* 18.1.4; emphasis added. Translation in Mason, "Josephus's Pharisees," 30.

bit misplaced because Jews lived within an ancient authoritarian model. Clearly the masses had no power, so why would the priestly ruling class care to follow Pharisees simply because Pharisees were popular with the masses? The answer is apparent in the following paragraph.

Another passage in Josephus that illustrates the popularity of the Pharisees details their contention with the high priest John Hyrcanus (135–104 BCE). The Pharisees, explained Josephus, are "so great [in] their influence with the masses that even when they speak against a king or high priest, they immediately gain credence."[16] Josephus lamented that Pharisees, with the support of the populace, criticized John Hyrcanus, who was his hero. Josephus believed that God had blessed Hyrcanus with the gift of prophesy. He also named his oldest son after Hyrcanus.[17] Later, Josephus essentially blamed the Pharisees for the collapse of the Hasmonean dynasty.[18] Pharisees had incited opposition among the populace toward the Hasmonean king, Alexander Jannaeus (103–76 BCE). While on his deathbed, Jannaeus convinced his successor, Alexandra Salome (his wife), to give the Pharisees a larger role in the polity, which would undoubtedly result in higher approval ratings for her, so to speak, with the Jewish populace.[19]

These passages are significant because when Josephus, in the late first century CE, wrote about the Pharisees' popularity in the late first century BCE during the reign of Herod, his comments were in the present tense. "He gives no narrative reason," observes Mason, "to think that the Pharisees' influence waned appreciably" from the Hasmonean and Herodian periods to his own time.[20] In other words, it is assumed throughout Josephus's writings that the Pharisees were the dominant movement (though not necessarily the ruling class, meaning those who enforced laws and tried criminals) and had strong support from the populace for more than two hundred years prior to the publication of Josephus's last work in the late first century CE.

The Gospels and Acts contain clues that seem to support Josephus's claim that the Pharisees were popular with the masses, and that help to explain Pharisaic popularity. For example, in Luke, while Jesus teaches a crowd (11:1–36), a Pharisee invites Jesus to eat with him as an honored guest, which invitation Jesus accepts (11:37–44). The context of this episode presupposes Pharisaic popularity. That a Pharisee interrupts Jesus' sermon, that he invites Jesus to join him and other Pharisees as a guest (Luke

16. Josephus, *Ant.* 13.10.5, trans. Marcus.
17. Josephus, *Ant.* 13.10.7; *Life* 1.5.
18. Josephus, *Ant.* 13.15.5–13.16.6
19. Josephus, *Ant.* 13.15.5
20. Mason, "Josephus's Pharisees," 30.

11:39–44), that Jesus accepts this request, and that the crowd does not seem troubled by the presence of Pharisees implies that Pharisees were influential and maintained a degree of respect from the people. If Pharisees had been as hypocritical and nefarious as some Gospel passages claim, then we would expect the crowds, or Jesus' closest followers, to have rebelled against the constant presence of Pharisees and even to have challenged them physically, just as they did on many occasions with the chief priests, Roman soldiers, and Pilate, as recounted by all four Gospels and Josephus.[21] Nothing in Josephus and the Gospels even hint that the populace were ever annoyed or disturbed at the presence and leadership of Pharisees.

The Religious Devotion of the Pharisees

On multiple occasions Josephus referred to the religious nature of Pharisaism. For example, Josephus claimed that the high priest, John Hyrcanus, was disciple of the Pharisees. Hyrcanus told several prominent Pharisees, after inviting them to a feast, that he followed Pharisaism because "he wished to be righteous and in everything he did tried to please God," to which Josephus added that "the Pharisees [also] profess." Hyrcanus, recognizing that Pharisees were known to interpret the laws accurately, also admonished them to offer corrective advice if they were to ever observe him offending God by his actions.[22] Elsewhere, Josephus explained that Pharisees had the "reputation of excelling the rest of their nation in the observances of religion" and that Queen Alexandra "being herself intensely religious, listened [to Pharisees] with too great deference."[23] In this passage Josephus used the word *eusébeia* to describe the Pharisees. Throughout his writings it becomes apparent that *eusébeia* is Josephus's "one-word summary of the whole Jewish system of religion, instigated by God, articulated by Moses, administered by the priests, and shared by the whole nation."[24] He also used the word *eusébeia* in relation to Abraham, King David, and King Solomon. Josephus stated that John the Baptist—who, like the Pharisees, was popular with the masses—exhorted the Jews to exercise piety (*eusébeia*) toward God. Josephus distinguished in his writings between piety toward men (*díkaios*) and piety toward God (*eusébeia*).[25]

21. Mark 14:47; Matt 26:51; Luke 22:49–50; John 18:10; Josephus, *Ag. Ap.* 2.17; Josephus, *Ant.* 13.13.5 (cf. Mishnah Sukka 4:9); 18.3.1–2; 20.105; Josephus, *J.W.* 2.12.
22. Josephus, *Ant.* 13.10.5, trans. Marcus.
23. Josephus, *J.W.* 1.110, trans. Thackeray.
24. Mason, *Flavius Josephus on the Pharisees,* 85–86.
25. Mason, *Flavius Josephus on the Pharisees,* 85–86.

Several passages in the Gospels support Josephus's claim that Pharisees were highly devoted to God. The first episode occurs early in Jesus' ministry. In all three Synoptic Gospels Jesus invites a toll collector to eat with him. The toll collector and other individuals of ill-repute accompany Jesus to eat (Matt 9:9; Mark 2:14; Luke 5:27). Pharisees query Jesus' disciples as to why he is eating with toll collectors and sinners. Jesus, overhearing the Pharisees, responds that those who are healthy need no physician and that he seeks out not the righteous but the sinners (Mark 2:17; Luke 5:32; Matt 9:13). According to the author of Luke, the "call" to the sinners is that of "repentance" or "reform" (*metánoia*). Here, the Pharisees' problem with Jesus is not that he entertained toll collectors and sinners *because* they were toll collectors and sinners, but that these individuals, according to Pharisaism, were impure as a *result* of being toll collectors and sinners. In other words, Pharisees were not necessarily concerned with oppressing or shunning vagabonds and miscreants because they were viewed as a hindrance and a threat to a healthy, functioning society—which is how many individuals today react to "druggies" and the homeless, whom they fear will crowd them and beg for money, or do worse—rather, Pharisees were concerned with impurity. Toll collectors, or tax farmers (*telônai*), engaged in bidding wars for the right to collect additional taxes at elevated rates for Rome,[26] probably through the transportation of material goods. It was this dishonest practice that likely caused Pharisees to consider toll collectors to be impure. Another reason for this impurity may be that collectors worked closely with non-Jews and were in direct contact with Roman coins, which contained idolatrous images.[27]

Just as the Pharisees and Jesus debated about who was permitted to join in a meal, so did Peter and Paul. In his letter to Galatians, Paul "opposed" Peter because he, along with Barnabas, refused to eat with gentiles (Gal 2:11–13). Pharisees supported the segregation of people who were considered impure, particularly during religious activities like synagogue worship and mealtime symposia. Justification for this practice is based on Jewish law: "You are to distinguish between the holy and the common, and between the unclean and the clean" (Lev 10:10). In Christian Sunday school classes, the usual interpretation is that Pharisees rejected sinners, and that they challenged Jesus because he associated with sinners. This is usually followed with the injunction, "Do not be like the Pharisees. We must help sinners, not shun them and judge them. Jesus taught us to help them." Notice here, however, that Pharisees did not criticize Jesus for teaching or helping "sinners" in general; their concern was that he was *eating* with

26. Donahue, "Tax Collector," 6:337–38
27. See Marcus, *Mark 1–8*, 225–26.

them, and therefore, becoming vulnerable to impurities during religious mealtime activities. Every accusation from Pharisees toward Jesus about entertaining sinners was in the context of mealtime activities.[28] They would rather have had Jesus wait until after mealtime to go outside and minister to impure sinners. In fact, "sinners" in this context does not merely refer to people who are violating God's laws, as we often define sinners today. James Dunn (emeritus professor of New Testament at the University of Durham) has provided numerous examples all throughout early Jewish literature of almost every Jewish sect calling outsiders, *harmartoloi*, translated as "sinners."[29] Thus, many Jewish groups not only labeled gentiles *sinners* but they also called any "Jews who practiced their Judaism differently" *sinners*.[30] Living in a society that was very tribalistic and concerned with boundary maintenance and impurities, Pharisees were not trying to be mean-spirited to the lowly sinner seeking help.

I once witnessed an intoxicated, homeless man in Orlando, Florida, enter a worship service and walk up and down the aisles talking to people during communion. When a leader in the congregation quietly ushered the disrupter outside, the man started singing (loudly) Brownsville Station's "Smokin' in the Boys Room." If first-century Pharisees had been in attendance, they would have said something like, "This outsider must leave. We can help him in a few minutes, but right now during our sacred religious ritual is neither the time nor the place to minister to him." Another experience illustrates this thinking further. Years ago when I was in Jerusalem, I ordered food in the Jewish Quarter of the Old City from a "nonkosher" food stand. I took my food around the corner and looked for a seat in a small dining complex. A man approached and asked me to eat elsewhere because the tables in that section were reserved for people eating food from a "kosher" stand. At the time, I was not attuned to the policies of that particular location, but I understood and moved to another area out of respect. These experiences illustrate the concerns of the Pharisees regarding purity, mealtime activities, and separation from certain types of individuals at particular times. We will discuss more about mealtime activities later.

Despite the fundamental disagreement between Jesus and the Pharisees on eating with sinners, Jesus seemed to acknowledge that the Pharisees were indeed righteous,[31] meaning that they were right in the eyes of God with respect to their moral purity, that they were in conformity to God's

---

28. See Matt 9:10–13, 11:19; Mark 2:15–17; Luke 5:30–32, 7:34, 15:1–2.
29. Dunn, *Jesus, Paul, and the Law*, 73–77.
30. Dunn, *Jesus, Paul, and the Law*, 75.
31. Gowler, *Host, Guest, Enemy, and Friend*, 199.

law, and that they were "model citizens."[32] It appears that Jesus was not concerned with the Pharisees needing to "repent" or "reform" (*metánoia*) in great measure. Rather, his concern was directed to those "sinners" who fell far shorter of meeting God's expectations for the House of Israel. According to all three Synoptic Gospels regarding this mealtime episode, Jesus appears to acknowledge Pharisaic religious devotion.

In a later episode in the Gospel of Luke, Jesus is approached by "all the tax collectors and sinners" (15:1) and, again, Pharisees question why he eats with them. Jesus answers the Pharisees using three parables. The first parable concerns a person who has one hundred sheep (Luke 15:4–8; Matt 18:12–14). If one sheep in the flock wanders off, asks Jesus, how many would not leave the ninety and nine and search for the one lost? Jesus emphasizes the joy of the one whose sheep is safely returned: "There will be more joy in heaven over one sinner who repents than over ninety-nine righteous people who need no repentance" (Luke 15:7). The second parable appears only in the "L" material (i.e., information unique to the Gospel of Luke), and is similar to the first. A woman who loses one of her ten coins will search the home carefully until she finds it. When she does, she and her neighbors will rejoice. Likewise, as is declared in the conclusion to the first parable, "There is joy in the presence of the angels of God over one sinner who repents" (Luke 15:8–10). The assumption of these two parables is that the Pharisees (those who ask Jesus about sinners) are part of the "ninety-nine righteous people who need no repentance" (Luke 15:7)!

The third parable is also exclusive to the Gospel of Luke (15:11–32). Here, in the parable of the prodigal son, Jesus speaks of a father with two sons. The younger son pleads for his inheritance, and his father grants his request. The younger son soon after leaves home for a distant region, where he eventually squanders his inheritance and becomes destitute. He returns to his father not intending to assume the role of a son but of a hired laborer. Upon his arrival, the father rejoices and gives his son a robe, a ring, and a fatted calf to be slaughtered in celebration. When the older son hears the music and learns that the younger son has returned after squandering his livelihood, he becomes angry. He had remained obedient to the "commands" of his father, yet he had never received "even a young goat" to celebrate his obedience. The father reassures the older son, "You are always with me, and all that is mine is yours;" however, "we had to celebrate and rejoice, because this brother of yours was dead and has come to life; he was lost and has been found" (Luke 15:31–32).

---

32. Arndt and Danker, *Greek-English Lexicon*, 195–96.

These three parables are important for understanding Jesus' view of Pharisees. He attempts to build common ground with the Pharisees whereby they would understand his motivation and rationale for disregarding the purity laws they espouse. He also uses the parables to motivate Pharisees to follow his example and minister to sinners. These three parables imply that Pharisees were not "sinners" and that God approved of their piety. Jesus' vision is that those who are already living the law will shift their focus from an exclusive observance of purity laws to administering to lost sheep who are outside the flock of the covenant people of Israel. In essence, the older brother of the prodigal son *represents the average Pharisee*, or at least those Pharisees who were associated with Jesus.[33] How do we know this? Because the Pharisees ask Jesus about why he ministers to "those sinners." Jesus' response implies that Pharisees and Jesus are on the same team—they represent the ninety-nine sheep and the older brother of the prodigal son. To the Pharisees, Jesus says, "You are always with me, and all that is mine is yours" (Luke 15:31). The struggle for Jesus, however, is to help Pharisees realize their own potential and to join him in seeking out those who were failing to meet God's expectations for covenant Israel.

As the story progresses in the Gospel of Luke, Pharisees approach Jesus and ask him when the kingdom of God would arrive. Jesus answers that the kingdom of God is *within* (*entos*) them (Luke 17:21). In other words the Pharisees, through their righteousness, devotion to God, and ability to persuade the masses, were in a position to join Jesus in bringing the kingdom of God to the people. After Jesus' discussion on the kingdom of God (Luke 17:22–37), he delivers two parables that emphasize characteristics essential for being rewarded in the world to come: (1) the parable of the widow and the unjust judge, which emphasizes faith through continual supplication to God (Luke 18:1–8), and (2) the parable of the Pharisee and the tax collector, which emphasizes humility (Luke 18:9–14). It is this second parable that concerns us here.

The focus of this parable, like many others in Luke, is righteousness. Jesus speaks this parable to individuals who do good deeds and consider themselves to be righteous but who regard sinners with contempt. Jesus undoubtedly included Pharisees in his intended audience for this parable because it was Pharisees who originally approached him. In the parable, a righteous Pharisee who prays, fasts twice a week, and gives a tenth of his income thanks God that he is not like the sinners: "thieves, rogues, adulterers, or even like this tax-collector" (Luke 18:11). The tax collector also prays but does not "even look to heaven, but [beats] his breast" while pleading

---

33. Mason, "Chief Priests, Sadducees, Pharisees and Sanhedrin," 141.

with God to show him mercy because he is a sinner. The parable acknowledges that those whom Jesus addresses, the Pharisees, follow the law and are righteous, but it indicates that they must not become proud because of their devotion. Jesus does not accuse the Pharisees of being vile sinners but of lacking humility (Luke 18:9).

Another episode involving Pharisees implies that the crowd at the temple viewed Pharisees as religiously devoted and considered them friendly to Jesus. On this occasion while Jesus is teaching at the temple, obtrusive Jewish leaders question his authority to teach and perform miracles. According to the author of Matthew, the inquisitors were "chief priests and elders" (21:23). After hearing Jesus' response, the "chief priests and Pharisees" seek to lay hands on Jesus but cannot because "they fear the multitude" (21:46). The "Pharisees" in the Matthean account subsequently send different Pharisees and Herodians to Jesus to "entangle him in his talk" (22:15). They approach Jesus as imposters and say, "Master, we know that you are true and teach the way of God" (22:16). This Matthean account is characteristically confusing and hostile to Pharisees. First, the chief priests and elders approach Jesus to question him. Second, the chief priests and Pharisees (not elders) are offended at Jesus' response and wish to seize him. Finally, Pharisees send different Pharisees with Herodians back to Jesus to pretend they are his friends and to cause him to say something illicit. In the parallel passage in Mark, however, it is the "chief priests, scribes, and elders" (11:27) who approach Jesus at the temple and subsequently send back Pharisees and Herodians to "catch him in his words" (12:13). First, it is unlikely that Pharisees and Herodians would acquiesce to Jerusalem aristocrats and perform their dirty work. Second, the fact that authorities are apprehensive to approach Jesus after the incident at the temple, and, therefore, send Pharisees and Herodians to him as friends, implies that Jesus and the crowd trusted Pharisees and Herodians, at least enough to mingle with them.

The Gospel of Luke elucidates this episode. The author of Luke agrees with the author of Mark that chief priests, scribes, and elders questioned Jesus at the temple, were offended at his response, attempted to lay hands on him (but did not because they feared the people), and then sent back imposters to trap Jesus in his words. However, while the authors of Mark and Matthew have Pharisees and Herodians approaching Jesus in a friendly manner, the author of Luke explains that the authorities sent "spies pretending" to be righteous men (20:20). These spies were most likely men from priestly circles *pretending* to be "righteous" Pharisees and Herodians. The interpretation of this episode in the Gospel of Luke fits precisely with what Josephus wrote about Pharisees—that the populace supported them and that they had a contentious relationship with Sadducees and the Jerusalem temple establishment. That temple bureaucrats would send their minions to Jesus *pretending* to be Pharisees, and that these imposters would address Jesus respectfully as "master," suggests that Jesus and the crowds trusted Pharisees and that the populace viewed them as righteous men.

Theological Positions of the Pharisees

We will not spend much time on the theological positions of the Pharisees, but we do want to highlight a few points. Josephus claimed that the Pharisees' theological positions endeared them to the populace. Pharisees accepted the tenet of human agency and also recognized the hand of God in human affairs.[34] They believed that divine providence (*heimarméne* or *prónoia*) and free will were complementary. Regarding the afterlife, the Pharisees taught that the human soul is incorruptible—that it will be resurrected and that all souls will be judged and receive eternal reward or punishment based on their actions during their mortal lives: "eternal imprisonment is the lot of evil souls, while the good souls receive an easy passage to a new life."[35] In contrast, the Sadducees disagreed with these positions. As Josephus writes:

> Sadducees, the second order, do away with Fate altogether and place God beyond both the committing and the contemplating of evil: they claim that both the honorable and the despicable reside in the choice of human beings, and that it is according to the judgment of each person to embrace either of these. The survival of the soul, the punishments and rewards in Hades—they do away with them.[36]

Josephus asserted that because of these doctrines, the Pharisees were "extremely influential among the townsfolk."[37] Josephus specifically stated on another occasion that the populace not only agreed with the Pharisees on important theological issues but also observed "all prayers and sacred rites of divine worship" according to the direction of the Pharisees. The "inhabitants of the cities" recognized the "excellence of the Pharisees" because they "practiced the highest ideals both in their way of living and in their discourse."[38] The Gospels and Acts support these claims of the theological

---

34. Josephus, *J.W.* 2.8.14; Josephus, *Ant.* 18.12–17.

35. Josephus, *Ant.* 18.1.3. (See also *J.W.*, 2.8.14). See translation in Loeb Classical Library.

36. Josephus, *J.W.* 2.8.14, trans. Mason.

37. Josephus, *Ant.* 18.1.3, trans. Feldman.

38. Josephus, *Ant.* 18.1.3, trans. Feldman.

positions of both Pharisees and Sadducees (Matt 22:23; Mark 12:18; Luke 20:27; Acts 23:6–8).

The Lenient, Good-Natured Pharisees

Although Josephus seemed annoyed by Pharisees and lamented that Pharisees had the support of the masses, he described them as being cordial and merciful. He explained that Pharisees "are mutually affectionate, and cultivate concord in relation to the community." The Sadducees, on the other hand, "have a rather harsh disposition even toward one another: encounters with their peers are as uncouth as those with outsiders."[39] Elsewhere, Josephus explained that Pharisees respected the elderly and that they never "contradict[ed] their proposals."[40] Josephus also admitted that Pharisees generally avoided a lavish lifestyle: "The Pharisees simplify their standard of living, making no concession to luxury."[41] In addition to their affable nature and prudent lifestyle, "the Pharisees are naturally lenient in the matter of punishments."[42] Josephus related an incident when a man named Eleazar was brought before the Jewish ruling body. The Sadducees pursued the punishment of death for Eleazar, whereas the Pharisees favored a more lenient punishment; they argued for whipping because death seemed to be excessive.[43] This incident is congruous with at least two others in Josephus. The first explains briefly that Sadducees were "indeed more heartless than any of the other Jews . . . when they sit in judgement."[44] The second passage details the occasion when Pharisees criticized Herod for executing thieves without granting them a trial, as prescribed by Jewish law. When the Sanhedrin summoned Herod to court, all of the members present feared Herod and refused to speak against him. The only exception was an "honored" man, whom we later discover was a Pharisee.[45]

One relevant issue regarding the social position of the Pharisees is that of the Pharisaic presence in Jerusalem among the ruling class. Josephus highlighted a few occasions when Pharisees were involved in judicial affairs alongside the priestly establishment and the Sanhedrin in Jerusalem. If this was true, how then can we argue that Pharisees were not considered

---

39. Josephus, *J.W.* 2.8.14. See Josephus, "Judean War 2" translation by Mason.
40. Josephus, *Ant.* 18.1.3, trans. Feldman.
41. Josephus, *Ant.* 18.1.3, trans. Feldman.
42. Josephus, *Ant.* 13.10.6, trans. Thackeray.
43. Josephus, *Ant.* 13.10.5–6.
44. Josephus, *Ant.* 20.9.1, trans. Feldman.
45. Josephus, *Ant.* 14.9.3–4, 15.3, trans. Marcus and Wikgren.

members of the ruling class? One answer is that Pharisees, while involved in some of the more high profile or complex criminal cases, were not major figures in the normal affairs of the ruling class in Jerusalem. Evidence from the sources reveals that not only did Pharisees play a limited role in the normal judicial affairs in Jerusalem, they were also at loggerheads with the chief priests and Sadducees regarding the law. Josephus, the Gospel of John, and the Gospel of Matthew all demonstrate that the Pharisees were involved with the chief priests;[46] however, it is likely that this involvement was limited to the "notables among the Pharisees"[47] who, because of their legal expertise and support from the masses, were able to persuade the chief priests on various issues. Josephus especially seemed to have highlighted the limited role of the Pharisees on the political scene and showed them being consulted and included in judicial affairs *only* to ensure political stability. Pharisaic involvement, as Mason has posited, was rare:

> Josephus remarks (*War* 2.411) that "the elite came together in the same place with the chief priests and those who were *eminent among the Pharisees*," to discuss [a] brewing crisis . . . Elsewhere, Josephus almost formulaically pairs the elite with the chief priests as Jerusalem's leaders (*War* 2.243, 301, 316, 336, 422, 428, 648) *without mentioning the Pharisees* . . . So the notice at *War* 2.411, that the standard pair of priestly elite groups met with the leading Pharisees at that crucial point, seeming to stress that they also convened in the *same place*, hints that such a coalition was unusual in more normal times . . . Like *War* 2.411, *Life* 21 makes only passing mention of the "principle men of the Pharisees" alongside the chief priests, in the coalition trying to manage the clamor for war . . . Although Josephus has preferred to speak of hereditary aristocratic-priestly leadership, he has grudgingly acknowledged that the immensely popular lay movement of the Pharisees must always be reckoned with by those in power.[48]

The notion of the Pharisees as political outsiders is also supported in several places in the Gospels and Acts. For instance, although the authors of Matthew and John mention "chief priests and Pharisees" together on occasion, the authors of Mark and Luke do not.[49] In fact, the author of Luke seems to go out of his way to change the accounts in his Gospel that are also present

---

46. Von Wahlde, "Relationships," 506–22.
47. Josephus, *J.W.* 2.409–417. See translation in Josephus, "Judean War 2."
48. Mason, "Josephus's Pharisees," 11–12, 33; emphasis added.
49. See Matt 21:45, 27:62; John 7:45, 11:47, 11:57, 18:3.

in the Gospel of Matthew. In Acts, some of Jesus' closest followers are arrested by the high priest "and all those who were with him, that is, the sect of the Sadducees" (5:17). When they are brought before the council, a Pharisee named Gamaliel, a legal expert and one who had a "reputation among all people," convinces the court to release Jesus' disciples (Acts 5:34–40). Just as in Josephus, the Sadducees and chief priests seek more severe punishments whereas the Pharisees are more lenient. Similarly, when Paul stands before the Jerusalem court, the Sadducees want to charge him for claiming a vision of the resurrected Jesus, and they attempt to physically harm him. On the other hand, the Pharisees in the council "stand up and contend, 'We find nothing wrong with this man. What if a spirit or an angel has spoken to him?'" (Acts 23:9). It seems that if the Pharisees were as ruthless as many Christians have assumed, then the Pharisees would have argued for Paul to be scourged and killed. After all, Paul, a Pharisee, was an outspoken follower of Jesus.

Moreover, all four Gospels agree that Pharisees were not included in Jesus' infamous trial. Had they been present at the trial, it is likely that they would have challenged the guilty verdict of the chief priests and Sadducees, and Jesus may have been released. Earlier in Jesus' ministry, it is a Pharisee, Nicodemus, who challenges the Jerusalem authorities when they attempt to arrest Jesus. He asks, "Our law does not judge people without first giving them a hearing to find out what they are doing, does it?" (John 7:51). As strict observers of the law, Pharisees undoubtedly took seriously the injunction in Exodus to "keep far from a false charge, and do not kill the innocent or those in the right, for I will not acquit the guilty. You shall take no bribe, for a bribe blinds the officials, and subverts the cause of those who are in the right" (Exod 23:7–8). This is precisely what the populace accused the chief priests and Sadducees of doing.

Jesus' Relationship with Pharisees

What can this material tell us about the nature of Jesus' relationship with Pharisees? It seems likely that Jesus was cordial and friendly with the Pharisees, at least according to the information in Josephus and the New Testament. Some scholars have even argued that Jesus was a Pharisee himself.[50] A review of Jesus' main roles and characteristics in the previous chapters and in this chapter reveals that he has much in common with them. Like the Pharisees, he was popular with the masses; like the Pharisees, he was known

---

50. See Heschel, *Abraham Geiger*; Maccoby, *Jesus the Pharisee*; Falk, *Jesus the Pharisee*.

for being religiously devoted and concerned about following Jewish law; like the Pharisees, he was viewed by many as a prophet; like the Pharisees, he believed in divine providence, resurrection, angels, visions, and reward and punishment in the afterlife; like the Pharisees, he was known as a wise teacher of Jewish law; he supported the various purity rituals and washings; he was friendly to the public; he rejected a life of luxury; he was lenient in punishment; and he despised the chief priests and the Sadducean establishment. This set of characteristics defines Pharisaism!

Not only did Jesus and the Pharisees share characteristics and theological beliefs, but it was Pharisees, according to the author of Luke, who warn Jesus that Herod Antipas is trying to kill him (Luke 13:31). It is because of this warning that Jesus leaves the Galilee. Between the time Jesus departs the Galilee and when he arrives in Jerusalem he has several discussions with Pharisees. Most of these are positive encounters wherein Jesus, as explained previously, praises the Pharisees for their devotion to God and even equates them with the older brother in the parable of the prodigal son, whose father (representing God) says, "Son, you are always with me, and all that is mine is yours" (Luke 15:31). Jesus also tells a group of Pharisees that the kingdom of God is within them (Luke 17:21). Later, during Jesus' journey to Jerusalem, he and his disciples pass through Jericho. Upon their arrival, a beggar sees Jesus and shouts, "Jesus, Son of David, have mercy on me!" Some of Jesus' followers rebuke him and demand that he be quiet (Luke 18:35–39). We suspect it was Pharisees in the group who order the man to be silent, because Pharisees act likewise when Jesus subsequently approaches Jerusalem; when Jesus' close followers start shouting about his messiahship, it is Pharisees who call out, "Teacher, order your disciples to stop" (Luke 19:39). They may have feared that such declarations would lead to Jesus' arrest and possibly to his death (which is precisely what happened). Both Jericho and Jerusalem were aristocratic and priestly hubs;[51] thus, loud exclamations of a new king, or a "Son of David," would have been met with swift and fierce action by the authorities. Pharisees knew this and tried to protect Jesus in these Judean centers of government.

It is also Pharisees who Jesus identifies as leaders of Israel whom the people should follow (Matt 23:3). It is a Pharisee, Nicodemus, who approaches Jesus respectfully and seeks counsel (John 3:1–21). It is Pharisees

---

51. Jericho not only contained the former palaces of Herod but also a hippodrome and an amphitheater, according to both Josephus and archaeological excavations (see Netzer, *Architecture of Herod*, 42–80). Jericho was a major city within walking distance of Jerusalem. Many members of the priestly class would have lived in Jericho. The parable of the good Samaritan illustrates that priests and Levites would have frequently traveled the route between Jericho and Jerusalem (see Luke 15:11–32).

who, as followers of Jesus twenty years after his death (Acts 15:5), participate in the Jerusalem Council with the leaders of the Jesus movement. One of these Pharisee followers of Jesus is Paul. Recall that on multiple occasions Paul touts his Pharisaic training to establish commonalities and credibility with the Jewish crowds (Acts 22:3, 26:4–6). How bad could the Pharisees have been if Paul was using his Pharisaic background as a badge of honor? Finally, it is Pharisees who eat with Jesus on multiple occasions.[52] This last point is key for understanding Jesus' relationship with Pharisees. Although Pharisees debate with Jesus and question his practice of eating with people of questionable purity, the fact that Jesus eats with them on several occasions, including as their guest of honor, illustrates that their relationship was more cordial than most modern readers assume.

In the Greco-Roman world, banquets involving hosts, guests, and servants were ceremonies.[53] Jews adopted the structure and ceremonial aspects of the Greco-Roman banquet. In preparation for a banquet, the host would typically extend invitations to several guests, some of whom would be most "honored." Hosts did not invite or dine with those outside their community; the banquet served as a boundary marker. This is precisely why Pharisees are frustrated that Jesus welcomes outsiders (i.e., impure sinners) to the banquet. It was widely understood that the banquet was a place designated for community fellowship and for fostering community identity; it was a place of deep friendship, not of rival interaction.[54] The banquet was also a sacred space for many Jews. Jewish scholar Jacob Neusner demonstrated that of the 341 passages in rabbinic literature on Pharisaism, 229 (67 percent) pertain to table-fellowship.[55] For Pharisees, the banquet was not to be taken lightly. It was a form of worship. The banquet was perhaps an extension of the temple and the synagogue, where purity, prayer, and discussion on Jewish law were the focus. Thus, in this specific time and place, the Pharisees would not welcome to their private dinners outsiders who did not share their values. By inviting Jesus to dine with them, the Pharisees welcome Jesus as their friend. When Jesus then invites sinners and is seen eating with them, Pharisees ask why Jesus is a *friend* to these sinners (Luke 7:34; Matt 11:19). Jesus himself

---

52. Luke 5:27–39, 7:36–50, 11:37–41, 14:1–24 (1–6); Mark 2:13–22, 7:1–23; Matt 9:9–17, 15:1–20.

53. Corley, *Private Women, Public Meals*; Smith, "Table Fellowship," 613–38; Koenig, *New Testament Hospitality*, 15–51; Neyrey, "Ceremonies in Luke," 361–87; Smith, "Historical Jesus at Table," 466–89.

54. Classical authors like Plato and Plutarch wrote on the friendship dynamic at the banquet. See Plato, *Laws* 2.671C–672A; Plutarch, *Table Talk* 612D, 614E–15A, 616C, 616E, 660B. See also Smith, "Table Fellowship," 633–38.

55. Neusner, *From Politics to Piety*, 86.

acknowledges that banquet ceremonies typically involve "friends," "brothers," "relatives," and "rich neighbors." Jesus urges the Pharisees, however, to widen their banquet hospitality to "the poor, the crippled, the lame, and the blind" (Luke 14:12–13).

Upon arrival at a banquet, household attendants would wash the guests' feet, and occasionally the host would greet the guests with a kiss and anoint them with scented oil. These hospitable acts in the Greco-Roman banquet are attested to in both Greek and Jewish sources.[56] The Gospels specifically mention each of these elements: washing guests' feet before the meal, greeting guests with a kiss, and anointing them with scented oil (Luke 7:36–46; Mark 14:3–4; John 13:1–10). Multiple Greek authors, Philo of Alexandria, Qumran texts, and the Gospels all mention that guests would be positioned in order of their status at the table. The host's most honored guests would be positioned next to the host, and the remaining guests would follow in descending order.[57] The participants would recline during the banquet, meaning they did not sit up at the table, but rather leaned lengthwise on couches on their left elbows.[58] Modern readers are somewhat confused by the odd practice during the Last Supper of one of Jesus' disciples leaning "on Jesus' bosom" during the meal (John 13:23, 25 KJV). The Greek word *anakeîmai* means to "recline." Jesus' disciple would have leaned on his left elbow on the right side of Jesus, thus positioning his left shoulder and head near Jesus' chest, or "bosom." The banquet was an intimate, personal experience among like-minded friends, not a place of hostility and conspiracy.

---

56. Plato, *Symposium* 175A (fourth century BCE); Athenaeus, *Deipnosophistae* or "The Dinner" 14.641d (early third century CE); Mishnah Hagigah 2:5 (late second century CE); Tosefta Berakhot 4:8 (late second century CE).

57. Plato, *Symposium* 177D–E; Plutarch, *Table Talk* 616F–617F; Philo, *Contemplative Life (De Vita Contemplativa)*, 67–68; 1QSa 2:11–12 (Qumran Rule of the Congregation); Luke 14:7–11; see also Smith, "Table Fellowship."

58. Plato, *Symposium* 175A; Tob 2:1, 7:9; 1 Esd 4:10; 3 Macc 5:16; John 21:10. An early rabbinic source, dating to the mid – to late second century CE, details the order of the banquet, including washings, reclining, and prayers: "What is the order of the meal? As the guests enter, they are seated on benches or chairs while all the guests assemble. Once all have assembled and the attendants have given them water for their hands, each guest washes one hand. When they have mixed for them the cup of wine, each guest recites the benediction over wine for himself. When the attendants have brought before them appetizers, each one recites the benediction over appetizers for himself. When the guests have arisen from the benches or seats and reclined to the second stage of the meal, the attendants again give them water for their hands . . . When the attendants again mix for the guests the cup, even though each has recited a benediction over the first cup, he recites a benediction over the second also" (Tosefta Berakhot 4.8. Quote is based on translation from Neusner, *Tosefta*, 1:23).

After the meal, participants would engage in philosophical discussions.[59] It was in this "symposium" setting that Jesus and the Pharisees debated legal matters, just as they did in the synagogue and temple complex. The precedent for debating Jewish law during a banquet was established long before Jesus' generation. The Jewish text Wisdom of Ben Sira, or Sirach (second century BCE), counseled participants regarding debate during the banquet:

> Let your conversation be with men of understanding, and let all your discussion be about the law of the Most High. Let righteous men be your dinner companions, and let your glorying be in the fear of the Lord . . . Do not reprove your neighbor at a banquet of wine, and do not despise him in his merrymaking; speak no word of reproach to him, and do not afflict him by making demands of him.[60]

Note the emphasis in this passage on eating with righteous men, debating Jewish law, and refraining from hostile arguments during the banquet. This is the setting in which we can interpret Jesus' banquet interactions with Pharisees (see, for example, Luke 14:1–24).

Explaining Pharisaic Hostility toward Jesus in the Gospels

Given the somewhat rosy portrait of Pharisees above, how do we make sense of the New Testament passages that seem to suggest a hostile relationship between Jesus and the Pharisees, as well as their highly negative portrayal of Pharisees in general? The word *Pharisee* appears 97 times in 38 different episodes or settings in the Gospels and Acts. Those who have received a healthy dose of anti-Pharisaism in Sunday school might naturally impose a negative context onto the Pharisee episodes, even if no such interpretation is warranted in all of them. If we look critically at each setting in which Pharisees appear, we see that some are clearly positive; Nicodemus immediately comes to mind, as well as mealtime episodes where Jesus is invited to dine with Pharisees as an honored guest.

We lack the space to dissect in depth all of these passages here; however, if we eliminate from this discussion the positive encounters between Jesus and Pharisees that we have already discussed, we are left with seventeen of

---

59. Plato, *Symposium* 176E; Plutarch, *Table Talk* 612D–E; Philo, *Contemplative Life (De Vita Contemplativa)*, 57, 64.

60. Sirach 9:15–16, 32:31 (Revised Standard Version).

thirty-eight (44 percent) episodes in which the authors of the Gospels seem to portray Pharisees negatively. About half of these seventeen episodes can be categorized as invective, or name-calling episodes, which we will discuss in chapter 9; but first, we tackle the remaining episodes that Christians typically identify as the best illustrations of negative Pharisaic characteristics. Keep in mind that many of the episodes regarding the Pharisees are unclear and contradictory. For example, it is *often* the case that where the Gospel of Matthew uses "Pharisees" in a particular story, the Gospel of Luke does not. Very few of the thirty-eight episodes are unified across the Gospels on what happened in the story. This ambiguity about Pharisees and Jews in the New Testament proved to be an enemy to Jews living in medieval Christian Europe as we saw in chapter 6.

"Testing" Jesus?

In four of the seventeen negative Pharisees episodes, Pharisees approach Jesus to "test him." Many readers today assume these to be hostile encounters—that the "tests" were designed to push Jesus into blaspheming God or rejecting Jewish law. The problem with this interpretation is that Pharisees were not in the business of trying to get fellow Jews arrested for their stances on Jewish law. Jews everywhere debated the law, and numerous examples in the literature show that rarely did any two sages initially agree on a particular precept. They did not chase each other around like petty children trying get their interlocutor in trouble (or, in this case, arrested).

For example, in one episode, Pharisees approach Jesus and "to test him they ask, 'Is it lawful for a man to divorce his wife for any cause?'" (Matt 19:3–12; Mark 10:2–12). Jesus responds and the story continues with no conflict. This type of debate was customary in Jewish circles. In another episode, Pharisees respectfully approach Jesus "to test him" by asking "Teacher, which commandment in the law is the greatest?" Jesus answers their question, and then he queries them in a similar manner on a different topic, showing that he was willing to engage in debate with them (Matt 22:34–45). In the parallel accounts in Mark and Luke, no Pharisee is mentioned. Further, Jesus tells the "scribe" in Mark, "You are not far from the kingdom of God" (12:34). The "lawyer" in Luke, who may have been a Pharisee, is also respectful to Jesus (10:25–37). In the third episode, Pharisees approach Jesus for a sign "to test him" (Mark 8:11–12). The author of Matthew includes "Pharisees *and Sadducees*," as is often the case in this Gospel (16:1–4; emphasis added). As explained previously, Pharisees and Sadducees were ideological rivals. Based on evidence in Josephus, they worked against each other more than with each other. We certainly would not expect aristocratic snobs from Judea (i.e., Sadducees) to traipse around the Galilee with Pharisees questioning Jewish teachers. It simply defies our understanding of how members of these two sects related to each other. Further, the author of Luke injects ambiguity into this episode when he replaces "Pharisees" with "others" (Luke 11:16).

Jesus' scholastic relationship with the Pharisees would have inevitably led to legal debates between them. The "tests" of the Pharisees were meant to gauge the validity or integrity of Jesus' faith in God. The Greek word for "test," *peirazo*, also means "trial" and is the equivalent of the Hebrew word *nasah*. In Genesis 22:1, God "tempts" or "tests" (*nasah* or *peirazo*) Abraham to ascertain his devotion and loyalty.[61] In these episodes, Pharisees are not testing Jesus with the intent to have him arrested but to judge whether he really is devoted to God and knowledgeable in Jewish law. As mentioned, this type of exchange was customary in early Judaism—the rabbis debated everything. Again, we can see how sloppy interpretations of the New Testament have distorted both the text and the reputation of first-century Jewish leaders. The idea that Jesus and his Jewish peers were constantly bickering is simply not supported robustly in the texts.

Two episodes, however, do refer to Pharisees "testing" Jesus in order to get him arrested. One is in John, in which they test him "so that they might have some charge to bring against him" (John 8:6). The Gospel of John is highly problematic and unreliable when dealing with both "the Jews" generally and the Pharisees specifically. Further, John 8:1–11 does not appear in the earliest Greek manuscripts of the New Testament but was a later Christian addition. We will discuss these two issues shortly. The second episode appears in all three Synoptic Gospels, and to this we now turn our attention.

The Sabbath Synagogue Healing

The synagogue healing episode in Mark 3, Matthew 12, and Luke 6 makes the Pharisees look melodramatic and morally bankrupt. The accounts agree on five major details: (1) Jesus enters a synagogue on the Sabbath, (2) a man with a crippled hand is present, (3) Jesus addresses the Pharisees' concern, (4) Jesus heals the man's crippled hand without touching him, and (5) the Pharisees exit the synagogue after the healing and counsel together regarding Jesus.

---

61. For those who do not know Hebrew or Greek, a helpful resource for conducting basic word studies is Renn, *Expository Dictionary*; this particular discussion of Greek and Hebrew words for "testing" is on page 965.

The problems with this episode are many. First, according to the author of Matthew, when Jesus enters the synagogue and notices a crippled man, the Pharisees immediately interrogate him on whether it is "lawful to heal on the Sabbath," the purpose of which is to "accuse" Jesus (12:10). After Jesus answers their question and subsequently heals the man, the Pharisees exit the synagogue and begin plotting his death. According to the authors of Mark and Luke, Jesus is the one who incites the debate, not the Pharisees. The author of Mark adds that Jesus looks upon them with "anger" and is grieved at their "hardness of heart" just prior to healing the man (3:5), and that the Pharisees immediately exited the synagogue and "conspired against him, how to destroy him" (3:6). Some scholars have argued that readers must not understand the word "destroy" in this instance as referring to physical death. The late Phillip Sigal (professor at University of Pittsburgh), for example, argued that the Pharisees did not seek to end Jesus' life but rather "to renounce him," "to place him under a ban," or "to excommunicate him."[62] However, the Greek word *apollumi* in its various forms is rendered as "to destroy," "to kill," "to ruin," or "to lose."[63] In each of the approximately ninety cases where the verb *apollumi* (or some form of it) is used in the New Testament, not one indicates excommunication, defeat, or the renouncement of an individual. Moreover, the Hebrew equivalent of *apollumi*—*abad*—does not refer to excommunication or the defeat of an opponent in an academic debate but rather to the utter destruction of a person, idol, or nation. In fact, several uses of the word *abad* in the Hebrew Bible and *apollumi* in the Greek Old Testament (i.e., "Septuagint") refer to "execution" upon the violation of a certain law.[64]

Are Jesus' teachings and healing in the synagogue controversial, so much so that Pharisees would have sought to kill him? According to all three Synoptic Gospels, Jesus heals the man by speech alone. No physical contact occurs. Jesus and the Pharisees were undoubtedly aware that any individual—according to Jewish law—who performed "work" on the Sabbath would be punished by death (see Exod 31:14–15, 35:1–3; Num 15:31–33). However, no Jewish group during the Second Temple and rabbinic periods, or any period for that matter, interpreted the law in such a way that would justify killing a man for talking on the Sabbath. In other words, they did not consider talking to be "work." The only Sabbath prohibition against speaking is found in the Damascus Document at Qumran, which indicates that

---

62. Sigal, *Halakah of Jesus*, 141–42.

63. Renn, *Expository Dictionary*, 725.

64. Renn, *Expository Dictionary*, 275. See, for example, Lev 23:30; Deut 7:10, 20, 24; 12:2, 3; Josh 7:7; and 2 Kgs 10:19, 19:18.

"no man shall speak any vain or idle word on the Sabbath day," such as "work or labor to be done on the morrow."[65] If a member of the Qumran community violated the Sabbath by working, he was not sentenced to death (as required by the law in Exodus) but imprisoned.[66] This source states that "no man who strays so as to profane the Sabbath and the feasts shall be put to death; it shall fall to men to keep him in custody." The Temple Scroll at Qumran posits that an individual is sentenced to death only for committing crimes against his own people, not for violating the Sabbath.[67] If Josephus is correct that Pharisees were lenient in punishment compared to the other main Jewish groups and that the populace preferred the laws and punishments of the Pharisees because of their leniency,[68] then it is unlikely they would have lobbied for Jesus' death for such a minor infraction.

Even if, for the sake of argument, Jesus had placed his hands on the man to heal him, the Pharisees would not have called for the draconian penalty of death. No evidence exists in the Hebrew Scriptures that healing by touch on the Sabbath is "work." Similarly, no passages in the Mishnah (see Introduction) prohibit healing or assisting a sick person on the Sabbath.[69] It is possible, however, that some believed healing by touch on the Sabbath was a violation. Consider, for example, a Lukan passage, independent from the other Gospels, that depicts Jesus healing in the synagogue on the Sabbath (Luke 13:10–17). After Jesus heals a woman by laying his hands on her, the leader of the synagogue says to the crowd, "There are six days on which work ought to be done; come on those days and be cured, and not on the Sabbath day" (Luke 13:14). Jesus answers the critic by comparing a sick person to an animal: "Does not each of you on the Sabbath untie his ox or his donkey from the manger, and lead it away to give it water? And ought not this woman . . . be set free from this bondage on the Sabbath day?" (Luke 13:15–16). Jesus' critics are ashamed after hearing his response, and the crowd rejoices over Jesus' teachings (Luke 13:17). Jesus' critics do not storm out of the synagogue and begin plotting his death. It is nearly impossible to conclude that Pharisees, or any Jews, would kill someone because of a legal dispute. In a few places in the book of Acts where Jesus' followers were killed (Acts 6 and 12), the issue seems to be more serious than a legal dispute. It may be that Jesus' closest followers were viewed with suspicion

---

65. Damascus Document 10.16–19, see translation in Vermes, *Complete Dead Sea Scrolls*, 139.

66. Damascus Document 12.4–6, in Vermes, *Complete Dead Sea Scrolls*, 141.

67. See Yadin, *Temple Scroll*, 204–8, esp. 206.

68. Josephus, *Ant.* 13.10.6.

69. For a list of the 39 Sabbath prohibitions, see Mishnah Shabbat 7:2; see also Mishnah Besah 5:2.

among the ruling class because they supported a messianic candidate who directly challenged the Jerusalem aristocracy. This certainly seems to be the case with Stephen who was heard saying that "Jesus of Nazareth will destroy this place and will change the customs that Moses handed on to us" (Acts 6:14).

Further, the text in Luke casts additional doubt on the traditional interpretation of this synagogue-healing episode. The translations in most English versions of the Bible inaccurately convey the meaning in Luke 6:11. For example, the New Revised Standard Version (NRSV) renders the passage, "But they were filled with fury and discussed with one another what they might to do Jesus." The Greek word *anoia*, translated here as "fury," also translated as "rage" in the New American Standard Bible (NASB) and "madness" in the King James Version (KJV), does not mean to be "angry" or "furious," but rather to be "perplexed," "confused," or "bewildered." Mark Powell (Trinity Lutheran Seminary) explained that "[*anoia*] implies uncertainty."[70] Steve Mason (University of Groningen) translated this word as "incomprehension,"[71] and David Flusser (the late scholar at Hebrew University of Jerusalem) pointed out that *anoia* "is never elsewhere translated 'anger, fury, wrath.'"[72] Thus, the story in Luke is much different; when Jesus heals the man, the Pharisees were "confused" or "bewildered" because of Jesus' actions in relation to his queries. Therefore, they "discussed with one another" what they should do in the case of Jesus, meaning they counseled together about how they should understand Jesus' legal stance on this matter.

Another problem with this episode is that the author of Matthew has Jesus entering "their synagogue" (12:9). In fact, six of the nine passages that mention a synagogue in Matthew use the definite article "their," suggesting that Jesus is an outsider who preaches to *them* in *their* synagogues. Perhaps the best example is in Matthew 13, where Jesus enters "his hometown" and preaches in "their synagogue" (v. 54). Moreover, seven of the nine passages are characteristically negative toward the Pharisees, or Jews in general—quite typical in the Gospel of Matthew. A review of these nine passages[73] shows that the author of Matthew either designates the Pharisees as leaders of the synagogues or identifies the Jesus-believers as outsiders to the Jewish community—hardly an accurate representation of early first-century,

---

70. Powell, "Religious Leaders in Luke," 99.
71. Mason, "Chief Priests, Sadducees, Pharisees and Sanhedrin," 135.
72. Flusser and Notley, *Jesus*, 64.
73. Matt 4:23, 6:2, 6:5, 9:35, 10:17–18, 12:9–14, 13:53–58, 23:1–7, 23:34.

synagogue-attending, Jesus-believing Jews.[74] The portrayal of Jesus being an outsider to the Jewish community is a position that cannot be historically accurate given all the data. Jewish studies scholar Nina Collins (University of Leeds) further details the problem with this early Jesus–Pharisee encounter:

> The discussion . . . on the previous scene of Jesus and his men in the Galilean fields [plucking corn to eat] has shown that this story is almost certainly midrashic [meaning nonhistorical additions to a text in order to elucidate its meaning], so that the event itself is non-historical and probably never took place and means that the midrashic Pharisees in the Galilean fields cannot turn into historical Pharisees in the following event. In any case, even if the historical Jesus met historical Pharisees in the Galilean fields, the possibility that the same Pharisees were also present at the cure of the man with a withered hand is difficult to accept. It would mean, for example, that after their meeting with Jesus in the Galilean fields, the Pharisees correctly anticipated that Jesus was going to a local synagogue, and then rushed on ahead and waited patiently in the synagogue until Jesus arrived, expecting him to cure a man with a withered hand who happened to be there. Even more unlikely is the assumption that Jesus would leave his starving disciples in the Galilean fields in order to visit a nearby synagogue, rather than to procure help for his men.[75]

Simply put, the story seems to represent late first-century polemics against Jews by Jewish Christians who wanted to portray their own group as morally superior to Pharisaic Jews.

The Johannine Passages

The remaining negative, non-name-calling passages about the Pharisees in the New Testament are unique to the Gospel of John (which is why we call them "Johannine"). The historical reliability of this Gospel is hotly debated because it differs so starkly from the Synoptic Gospels. The Synoptic Gospels are structured similarly and contain many of the same stories and traditions, whereas the Gospel of John contains numerous episodes not included in the other Gospels. Jesus' ministry occurs primarily in Judea in the Gospel of John, whereas his ministry occurs primarily in Galilee in the Synoptic

---

74. Runesson, *Origins of the Synagogue*, 356; Cohen, "Were Pharisees and Rabbis the Leaders"; Horsley, "Synagogues," 61–64; and Horsley, *Galilee*, 233–35.

75. Collins, *Jesus, the Sabbath and the Jewish Debate*, 149–50.

Gospels. Jesus' ministry covers at least two years and probably more in John, whereas his ministry covers one year in the Synoptics. Jesus cleanses the temple at the beginning of his ministry in John but he cleanses the temple at the end of his ministry in the Synoptics. Parables and exorcisms are prominent in the Synoptics, whereas the Gospel of John contains neither. These are just a few examples of the numerous differences between the Gospel of John and the Synoptic Gospels.

The portrayal of the Pharisees in the Gospel of John is confusing in light of the writings of Josephus and the Synoptics. The Pharisees seem to be conflated, or even confused with, Judean leaders (i.e., Sadducees or chief priests) in John. The author of Matthew tends to do this as well, but the authors of Mark and Luke do not. For example, "Pharisees and Sadducees" appear together only in Matthew,[76] and "chief priests and Pharisees" appear together only in Matthew and John.[77] This is expected since the Gospels of Matthew and John are the most anti-Pharisee. In the first of these Johannine passages under consideration, "chief priests and Pharisees" send temple police to arrest Jesus (John 7:32). After hearing Jesus teach, they return to the chief priests and Pharisees without arresting Jesus because "never has anyone spoken like this" (7:46). The Pharisees respond, "Surely you have not been deceived too, have you? Has any one of the authorities or of the Pharisees believed in him? But this crowd, which does not know the law—they are accursed" (7:47–49).

This passage is problematic for several reasons. First, we have already determined, based on Josephus and the Synoptic Gospels, that the Pharisees did not have high representation in the Jerusalem aristocracy. Some prominent Pharisees were part of the Sanhedrin, but they tended to be the most lenient and liberal in their rulings of punishment. They were backed by the populace, and together, the Pharisees and the people were able to check any overreach of the Jerusalem authorities. In no other ancient text do Pharisees conspire *with* chief priests and have jurisdiction over the temple police. Second, this episode claims that the temple police believed Jesus' words and were reprimanded by the Pharisees for doing so. The implication is that if it were not for the Pharisees, the temple police might have become followers of Jesus! Third, the Pharisees claim that never did any "authorities or Pharisees" believe in Jesus (John 7:48); however, the Synoptic Gospels and Acts provide significant evidence, especially in Luke and Acts, that many Pharisees did follow Jesus, whereas some within the temple establishment assist in Jesus' arrest and death. In fact, the narrator in the Gospel of John later

---

76. Matt 3:7, 16:1, 16:6, 16:11–12.
77. Matt 21:45, 27:62; John 7:32, 7:45, 11:47, 11:57, 18:3.

claims that many authorities did believe in Jesus (John 12:42). Here in this passage, however, the roles are reversed. It is the Pharisees who seek to arrest Jesus and who stifle Jesus' influence with the temple establishment. This episode (John 7:32–53) diverges so drastically from what we learned above that it seems to be an inaccurate representation of first-century Pharisees—it contradicts too much other material to accept it as is. We will discuss in chapter 9 why the author of John slandered the Pharisees in his Gospel.

The next verses in the Gospel of John (8:1–11) continue to portray the Pharisees in a peculiar and confusing way. This episode, one of the most well-known and emotionally charged depictions in all of the Gospels, details how Pharisees bring a woman to Jesus and attempt to stone her for adultery. Jesus confounds them with his famous line, "Let anyone among you who is without sin be the first to throw a stone at her" (John 8:7). As with the last episode, this one is highly problematic. First, this episode does not appear in any of the oldest manuscripts. Its Greek style and vocabulary are noticeably different from the rest of the Gospel of John, suggesting a later addition by a different author. This story first appears in a fifth-century manuscript.[78] Most English translations alert the reader of this fact through bracketing and a note. Despite this, many Christian commentators today claim that although the episode is a later addition, the details of the story fit a first-century setting. This, however, is false. The story counters critical conclusions based on a combination of the writings of Josephus and the Synoptic Gospels for the same reasons presented in dealing with the previous episode (John 7:32–53). If Pharisees really did send temple police after popular teachers and if they ganged up on sinners in the public square with the threat of stoning, then their support from the masses would have been nonexistent. Again, the evidence seems overwhelming that the Pharisees garnered support of the populace in the first-centuries BCE and CE for several reasons, including their leniency in punishment.

The narrative continues in the Gospel of John in the next verses (8:12–59). In this section, the author of John appears sloppy in his redaction. The Pharisees ask Jesus a question (8:13), and Jesus gives a long answer (8:14–21). The story then switches from using the term "Pharisees" to "the Jews" in the middle of the episode (8:22), suggesting that the author was inconsistent regarding the identity of Jesus' accusers. For the author of John, it did not matter whether Jesus' antagonists were the Pharisees or "the Jews" as long as he was successful in making his broader theological point. What is more intriguing is that Jesus then turns his attention from his antagonists

---

78. Codex Bazae (D). For an in-depth treatment of this episode, see Peterson, "ΟΥΔΕ ΕΓΩ ΣΕ [ΚΑΤΑ]ΚΡΙΝΩ," 191–221; Omanson, *Textual Guide,* 183–84.

to Jews who "believed in him" (8:31). Within a few verses, Jesus apparently forgets who he is addressing because he accuses these very Jews who believe in him for seeking opportunities to kill him (8:37). He also tells them, "You are from your father the devil, and you choose to do your father's desires" (8:44). By the end of the episode, these same Jews who believe in Jesus "picked up stones to throw at him" (8:59).

The author's lack of precision regarding Jesus' interlocutors and his irrational portrayal of Jesus speaking to Jews may illustrate that the Johannine community was responding to contemporary squabbles and conflicts with other Jews in the late first century and then reading them back into the Jesus story. Another possibility is that a later scribe added material to this chapter, making it confusing. We suspect this not only because of its erratic nature, but also because similar insertions are found elsewhere in the Gospel of John. For example, in John 11 the author reminds the reader that Mary anoints Jesus (v. 2), but the reader does not encounter the actual episode until the next chapter. Such a literary phenomenon makes little sense. The original author is not expected to step outside his own story and prematurely introduce the reader to a key event that shows up later in the story. It makes better sense that a later scribe tampered with the text. Another example of potential text tampering is in John 14. Here, Jesus closes his discourse and says, "Rise, let us be on our way" (John 14:31), only to have his discourse resume for another two chapters. Again, it seems that a later scribe might have inserted this material. Regardless of whether John chapter 8 was written by a single author or altered by later scribes, the story makes little sense and must be read with caution regarding its portrayal of Jews.

In John 11 the narrator explains that, again, "the chief priests and the Pharisees" call a "meeting of the council" and decide to arrest Jesus (11:47–57). The crime? He raised Lazarus from the dead. The authorities worry that this miracle might attract many more Jews to Jesus. In the next chapter (John 12), Pharisees lament that the "world has gone after" Jesus (12:19). Even many "of the authorities believed in him," but they did not confess such belief "for fear that they would be put out of the synagogue" at the hands of the Pharisees (12:42). The final episode in this group of Johannine passages about Pharisees explains that "a detachment of soldiers together with police from the chief priests and the Pharisees" arrested Jesus "across the Kidron valley" (18:1–3). Again, these episodes are confusing regarding the Pharisees for the reasons previously specified. They have Pharisees convincing—or threatening—Jerusalem authorities not to follow Jesus! Such a claim is in direct opposition to what we understand about the Pharisees from Josephus and the other Gospels.

Further, the Pharisees did not have authority to expel priests from the synagogue. Although the author of Matthew seems to indicate that the Pharisees did control the synagogues (12:9), evidence suggests that this was not the case. Philo, for example, recorded that priests and elders read and explicated the Torah readings in the synagogue, not the Pharisees. He explained that when the Jews sit in the synagogue on the Sabbath, "some priest who is present, or some one of the elders, reads the sacred laws to them, and interprets each of them separately."[79] An inscription from a first-century Jerusalem synagogue, discovered in 1913, states that three generations of priests oversaw the affairs of the synagogue: "Theodotus, son of Vettenus, priest and ruler of the synagogue, son of a ruler of the synagogue, grandson of a ruler of the synagogue, built the synagogue for reading of the law and the teaching of the commandments, and also the guest chamber and the upper rooms and the ritual pools of water for accommodating those needing them from abroad."[80] That the three most important sources for information about the Pharisees—the New Testament, Josephus, and the Mishnah—are virtually silent on the issue of Pharisaic control of the synagogue is strong evidence. Of the approximately eighty references to the synagogue in the New Testament and the writings of Josephus,[81] a large majority do not even mention the presence of Pharisees, and only three references seem to imply that they controlled the synagogue—two from Matthew (12:9–14, 23:34) and one from John (12:42–43). Moreover, one prominent scholar of early Judaism, Jacob Neusner, has shown that rabbinic passages about the Pharisees "supply no rules about synagogue life, all the more so about reading the Torah and preaching in synagogues."[82] If the Pharisees were leaders of the synagogue, then one would expect to find evidence of this in the sources.

All of these details about the Pharisees in the Gospel of John tend to contradict both Josephus and the Synoptic Gospels. Josephus demonstrates that Pharisees did not control these multiple institutions. They did not work in tandem with, or even supervise, Sadducees and chief priests. The Pharisees were not leaders of the synagogue, the Sanhedrin, or the temple police. To conclude otherwise obliterates any credibility of Josephus, the author of Mark, and the author of Luke. If the Pharisees really were the supreme leaders in Jerusalem in every facet as the author of John seems to suggest, then it is odd that the Pharisees disappear from the story in the Passion narratives

---

79. Philo, Hypothetica 7:13, in *Works of Philo*, 744.

80. Runesson et al., *Ancient Synagogue*, 52–54.

81. Runesson et al., *Ancient Synagogue*, 52–54. There are approximately sixty references to the synagogue in the New Testament and approximately twenty references to the synagogue in Josephus.

82. Neusner, *Rabbinic Traditions*, 289–90.

in all three Synoptic Gospels. From what we know about the Pharisees in Josephus, the Synoptic Gospels, and Acts, if Pharisees were allowed to participate in Jesus' arrest and trial, he probably would not have been killed.

Takeaways

In today's passive-aggressive western culture, readers assume that the Jesus–Pharisee interactions were hostile and negative. This could not be further from the truth. The Gospels contain several episodes where Pharisees debated Jesus. Their debates and criticisms of each other must be understood within a dialectical, that is, "academic" context. In addition to the mealtime debates, the author of Luke explains that on one occasion, Pharisees were sitting near Jesus talking with him; in the midst of this discussion a paralytic was brought to Jesus and he was healed. When Jesus forgave the man's sins, a debate ensued between Jesus and the Pharisees about the propriety of Jesus' actions. After Jesus argued his position, all who were present, including Pharisees "glorified God and were filled with awe" (Luke 5:17–26). Early Jewish literature is saturated with similar debates among the rabbis. Many of them espoused opposing views but nowhere do they attempt to murder each other. Jesus' criticisms of the Pharisees were not on the same level as his criticisms of the corrupt priestly establishment, whom the Pharisees also criticized.

The close association between the Pharisees and the early Jesus movement is the root of later hostility in the late first-century Gospels of Matthew and John. In today's dictionaries, "Pharisee" has become a standard description of a hypocritical person with nefarious motives. Such defamation, however, is offensive to Jews, because many Jews today consider themselves to be Pharisaic, or "rabbinic" Jews. Rabbinic Judaism developed in the age of Jesus. The rabbis, after the destruction of the temple in 70 CE, were the spiritual and ideological heirs of the Pharisees. The Pharisees were leaders of Israel during Greek and Roman rule and helped prepare an entire nation to survive the destruction of their temple. When the temple—the very core of Judaism—was destroyed in 70 CE, Judaism largely survived because of the Pharisees and later rabbis. Based on the literature of the rabbis, as well as Josephus, we must acknowledge that Israel's Pharisaic leaders in the age of Jesus were highly moral and ethical people.

During the early rabbinic era, Christians defined themselves in relation to Judaism, and as a result, they demonized Jews unfairly and blamed them for the death of Jesus. In the view of most Christians, Jews not only killed a revered teacher, but they killed God himself—under the leadership of the Pharisees. This interpretation is weak and irresponsible.

Pope Francis seems partial to the argument laid out in this chapter. On May 9, 2019 a scholarly conference exclusively on the Pharisees was held in Rome. In his keynote address, Pope Francis said:

> Among Christians and in secular society, in different languages the word "Pharisee" often means "a self-righteous or hypocritical person". For many Jews, however, the Pharisees are the founders of rabbinic Judaism and hence their own spiritual forebears. The history of interpretation has fostered a negative image of the Pharisees, often without a concrete basis in the Gospel accounts. Often, over the course of time, that image has been attributed by Christians to Jews in general. In our world, sadly, such negative stereotypes have become quite common. One of the most ancient and most damaging stereotypes is that of a "Pharisee," especially when used to cast Jews in a negative light . . .
>
> Your Conference's examination of interdisciplinary research into literary and historical questions regarding the Pharisees will contribute to a more accurate view of this religious group, while also helping to combat antisemitism . . .
>
> Love of neighbor represents a significant indicator for recognizing affinities between Jesus and his Pharisee interlocutors. It certainly constitutes an important basis for any dialogue, especially among Jews and Christians, even today. Indeed, to love our neighbors better, we need to know them, and in order to know who they are we often have to find ways to overcome ancient prejudices. For this reason, your Conference...will make it possible to present them more appropriately in teaching and preaching. I am certain that these studies, and the new avenues they will open, will positively contribute to the relationship between Jews and Christians, in view of an ever more profound and fraternal dialogue. May your Conference find a broad echo within and outside the Catholic Church, and may your work receive abundant blessings from the Most High."[83]

---

83. Pope Francis, "Address of His Holiness Pope Francis to the Pontifical Biblical Institute."

Chapter Eight

Christ Killers?
Why Didn't "the Jews" Reject and Kill Jesus?

As we saw in chapter 6, throughout the Middle Ages (and even today) Christians accused Jews of killing Jesus. These accusations tended to be vague and implicated all Jews. We have already made the case that Israel's most influential group, the Pharisees, was largely cordial to Jesus and would not have pursued the death penalty for him. In fact, the Pharisees were not even present at Jesus' arrest and trial according to all three Synoptic Gospels. But what about the Jewish masses—the peasants in the countryside? Did they reject Jesus? Did they support his arrest and crucifixion?

Jesus and the Jewish Populace

To begin, most Jews in the Roman Empire would have never encountered Jesus because he spent most of his time in its remote frontier—Galilee and Judea. Scholars have estimated the Jewish population in the entire empire at six to eight million people, with roughly two million Jews living in Palestine.[1] Regarding Jesus' home region, if Josephus is accurate that the Galilee contained about two hundred villages,[2] and if archaeological estimates are correct that a large majority of villages were between three and ten acres in size (a few were much larger)—with about 100–150 residents per acre—

---

1. McKnight, "Jewish Missionary Activity," 11; Baron, "Population," 866–903; Reinhardt, "Population Size of Jerusalem," 237–65.
2. Josephus, *Life* 45:235.

then the population of Galilee, assuming an average of ten acres per village, was roughly 300,000 people.[3] If even 10 percent of the Jewish population in Judea and about 30 percent of the population in Galilee heard about Jesus, then we are dealing with about 280,000 people. If, say, 20 percent of this subset went out of their way to travel several miles to Capernaum to hear Jesus teach or witness a healing, then the number decreases to 55,000–60,000 people who saw Jesus teach or perform a miracle. While this quick exercise lacks scientific rigor and is somewhat speculative, it allows us to emphasize a broader point about the Jewish population in relation to Jesus: it is unlikely that hundreds of thousands of Jews encountered Jesus up close. It may have been only tens of thousands. Thirty-thousand Jews, for example, represents *less than one half of 1 percent* (0.5–0.38 percent) of the Jewish population in the Roman Empire. What percentage would have had to "reject" Jesus and call for his death for later Christians to be justified in blaming Jews wholesale for Jesus' death and also for demonizing and murdering millions of them? One percent? Three percent? How about five percent? How could Christians accuse "the Jews" of being evil Christ killers when perhaps less than one half of one percent of their ancestors even interacted with Jesus?

In addition, if Jesus really was viewed as a prophet, a sage, a healer, a miracle worker, a messiah, or a combination of these, then it is unlikely that even 0.5 percent of the Jewish population wanted Jesus dead; his fame and reputation would have spread rapidly. If people even considered that Jesus might possibly possess the ability to heal, for example, they would have flocked to him. Also, if Jesus was associated with Pharisaism and was frequently debating the law with Pharisees and eating at their homes as an honored guest, then Jewish peasants in the region would have recognized him as an authorized teacher of the law, especially considering the popularity of the Pharisees. Moreover, that Herod Antipas targeted Jesus, as he did John the Baptist, suggests that Jesus had gained a sizable following in the Galilee region, which was under the stewardship of Herod Antipas. Herod killed John the Baptist not only because John criticized him but because he feared John's tremendous influence with the people in the region: "[Herod] feared the crowd, because they regarded him as a prophet" (Matt 14:5; cf. Mark 6:20). Josephus confirms this:

> For Herod had put him to death, though he was a good man and had exhorted the Jews to lead righteous lives, to practice justice towards their fellows and piety towards God [this is the same description Josephus provides about Pharisees!] . . . When

---

3. For a summary of the archaeological population surveys and an additional bibliography, see Fiensy and Strange, *Galilee*, 1:180–94.

others too joined the crowds about him, because they were aroused to the highest degree by his sermons, Herod became alarmed. Eloquence that had so great an effect on mankind might lead to some form of sedition, for it looked as if they would be guided by John in everything that they did. Herod decided therefore that it would be much better to strike first and be rid of him before his work led to an uprising.[4]

Perhaps Jesus' association with John the Baptist increased his popularity in the Galilee. We suspect this because Herod himself recognized the relationship between Jesus and John and also became aware of Jesus' popularity (Luke 9:7–8; Matt 14:1; Mark 6:14). Further, that Jesus was targeted by Jerusalem authorities, including Pilate, also shows that he had established a significant following among the Jewish masses (Luke 23:14). Pilate and the Jerusalem police would not have worried about some crackpot lunatic teacher from Galilee who headed a puny band of unimpressive fishermen. However, if Jesus was a popular teacher in the immediate regions of Galilee and Judea who appealed messianically to a few tens of thousands of Jews, the authorities would have acted quickly to quell the movement. Scholars of the historical Jesus vigorously debate these issues, but we mention them to allow us to pause and reconsider the common Christian trope that "Jews rejected Jesus." There is clearly more to the story.

It is telling that although much of the Gospels criticize and defame Jewish leaders, they are favorable toward the Jewish masses. The evidence for the popularity of Jesus in the Gospels is overwhelming. A quick tally exercise while reading through the Gospels reveals over 350 references to, or indications of, Jesus' popularity with the people. Approximately once in every ten verses (out of roughly 3,700 verses), Jews approach Jesus respectfully with a question, petition Jesus for a healing, or gather in a crowd to hear Jesus teach. This far outweighs the few perceived negative interactions between Jesus and Jews in the Gospels. As we have demonstrated in the messiah chapters (chs. 4 and 5), Jesus' perceived messianic activity would have set the local Roman rulers and the Jewish temple establishment on high alert. But what exactly did Jesus do to position himself as a dangerous opponent of Rome and the Jewish establishment in Jerusalem?

Collision with Authorities in Jerusalem

Jesus' activities during the last week of his life provide context into why he was targeted and ultimately arrested by the authorities in Jerusalem. Many

4. Josephus, *Ant.* 18.5.2, trans. Feldman.

of Jesus' actions were saturated with messianic symbolism. It is likely that the authors of the Gospels amplified or embellished the messianic connections to some of Jesus' actions decades after his death to make the case for his messianic status. However, if the Gospel accounts of Jesus' actions in the few days preceding his arrest contain even a kernel of historical accuracy, then Jesus would have indeed set himself on a collision course with Jerusalem authorities.

According to the Gospel of John, after Jesus had been in Jerusalem for some time, he is notified that Mary's brother, Lazarus, is ill. Lazarus lived on the eastern slope of the Mount of Olives in Bethany. Jesus does not immediately go to Lazarus but remains where he is for two days (John 11:6). By the time Jesus arrives in Bethany, Lazarus had already been buried, and his remains had lain in the tomb for four days (John 11:17). Jesus subsequently goes to the tomb and raises Lazarus (John 11:19–44).

These details are crucial for understanding Jesus' deliberate actions in relation to the Mount of Olives. The southern portion of the Mount of Olives was replete with tombs,[5] and Jewish tradition identified this place with the final judgment and resurrection, an act the messiah would perform after his coming (Joel 3; Zech 14). It seems Jesus deliberately waited to raise Lazarus until he had been in the tomb for longer than three days. Some later Jews, and possibly some at the time of this event, maintained that the soul remained near the body for three days after the moment of death.[6] Thus, the corpse was not technically dead until the fourth day. Jesus waited until after the third day to raise Lazarus in order to demonstrate unmistakably that he is the author of resurrection, this act serving as a symbol or a foreshadowing of resurrection. In the other two cases where Jesus raises individuals from the dead, Jesus arrives just moments after their deaths (Luke 7:12–15; Luke 8:40–42, 49–55; Mark 5:22–23, 35–42; Matt 9:18–25). Thus, the Lazarus episode, according to the Gospel of John, is an unprecedented, singular, and salient performance in the ministry of Jesus that occurred only on the Mount of Olives. Such an act on this *messianic mountain* would have raised suspicion among the local authorities—anything that hinted at messianic activity worried the Jerusalem establishment and local Roman rulers because they feared that Rome would replace them with new leadership if riots or rebellions occurred. In fact, the Gospel of John explicitly states that the raising of Lazarus is what motivated the chief priests to kill Jesus: "The chief priests and the Pharisees called a meeting of the council, and said, 'What are we to do? This man is performing many signs. If we let him go

---

5. Kloner and Boaz, *Necropolis of Jerusalem*, 197–230, 241–315.
6. Mishnah Yebam 16.3; Babylonian Talmud Shabbat 151b.

on like this, everyone will believe in him, and the Romans will come and destroy both our holy place and our nation.'... So from that day on they planned to put him to death" (John 11:47–53).

The Lazarus episode is not contained in the other Gospels. Jesus' first act after entering into the vicinity of Jerusalem in the final week of his ministry is ordering two of his disciples to procure a donkey from the village of Bethphage located on the summit of the Mount of Olives. We have already been introduced in a previous chapter to Jesus' royal procession from the Mount of Olives to the east gate of Jerusalem while riding a donkey (Matt 21:2–9; Mark 11:1–10; Luke 19:29–44; John 12:12–19). Such an act was conspicuously messianic. It was a deliberate act, based partly on David's experience and Solomon's royal coronation. Anyone entering Jerusalem riding on a donkey during the Passover season while his followers hailed him as a king from the line of David would have signed his own death certificate, as it were. The author of Luke adds that when Jesus' followers began shouting, thus drawing attention to Jesus as a royal messianic figure, some Pharisees who were present pleaded with Jesus to "order [his] disciples to stop" (Luke 19:39). Jesus responded, "I tell you, if these were silent, the stones would shout out" (v. 40). Given the context, the Pharisees seemed to be concerned for Jesus because he was in the vicinity of Jerusalem and the Jewish and Roman authorities were on high alert, as the city's population swelled during Passover. Josephus and the Gospels–Acts preserve accounts where Jewish and Roman authorities arrested or killed several popular prophets and messianic figures for similar acts and pronouncements against Jerusalem and Israel (see chapter 4).

Descriptions of Jesus' messianic procession were also based on passages in Ezekiel and Zechariah, which prophesy that a messianic figure will descend from heaven to the summit of the Mount of Olives and then enter Jerusalem through the east gate (Ezek 43:1–5; Zech 14). Jesus did enter Jerusalem by the east gate and subsequently cleansed the temple as prescribed in Zechariah: "There shall no longer be *traders* in the house of the Lord of hosts on that day" (14:21; emphasis added). A few elements in this verse are crucial for understanding Jesus' *temple tantrum*, so to speak. An expectation that *traders* would no longer be active in the temple illustrates why Jesus targets those "who were selling and buying in the temple" (Matt 21:12; Mark 11:15; cf. Luke 19:45). The other important element in this verse is the phrase *Lord of hosts* (Zech 14:21)—a reference throughout the Hebrew Bible to a warrior deity who leads both human and heavenly armies.[7] This fits the cleansing tradition in the Gospels; Jesus is portrayed

---

7. The term hosts, or *sabaot* in Hebrew, occurs 486 times in the Hebrew Bible, 284

as a warrior—a combative, strong figure who overturns the traders' tables in the Gospels of Matthew, Mark, and John (Matt 21:12; Mark 11:15; John 2:15) and who uses a weapon to drive out the traders in the Gospel of John (John 2:15). Note also that Passover was a time of cleansing the temple of idols, male temple prostitutes, and other corruptions. This occurred during the reforms of Hezekiah and Josiah, who sought to rid Jerusalem, including the Mount of Olives, of the altars of foreign gods (2 Chr 29:3–19, 30:1–14; 2 Kgs 23:4–14, 21–24). Jesus too entered the east gate from the Mount of Olives and cleansed the temple just prior to Passover. Jesus' activities mirror the three-part structure in Zechariah 14 that refers to the future divine messianic figure: (1) he arrives on the Mount of Olives, (2) he pronounces judgment on Israel, and (3) he enters Jerusalem and cleanses the temple. Thus, Zechariah 14 serves as a guide of sorts to Jesus' messianic activity on the Mount of Olives.

Three-part Structure in Zechariah 14	Jesus
1. Jehovah arrives on the Mount of Olives (Zech 14:4)	1. Jesus arrives on the Mount of Olives
2. Judgment is pronounced upon Israel (Zech 14:6–20)	2. Jesus pronounces judgment upon Israel during his procession
3. The temple is cleansed: "And there shall no longer be traders in the house of the LORD of hosts on that day" (Zech 14:21)	3. Jesus cleanses the temple after his procession into the city

According to the Synoptic Gospels, when Jesus rioted in the temple complex, he said, "Is it not written, 'My house shall be called a house of prayer for all the nations? But you have made it a den of robbers'" (Mark 11:17). Jesus quotes Isaiah, "My house shall be called a house of prayer for all peoples" (Isa 56:7), and quotes Jeremiah 7: "den of robbers" (Jer 7:11). Josephus mentioned another Jesus and messiah-type figure, Jesus ben Ananias (62 CE), who also challenged the chief priests with a sermon based on Jeremiah 7. He was arrested and whipped until his bones were exposed, but he was later released despite calls for the death penalty from chief priests.[8] Jesus' condemnation of "scribes" who "devour widows houses" (Mark 12:38–40) fits the criticism of the priestly class in other Jewish literature. His comment regarding the poor widow (i.e., the widow's mite) was most likely a lament and an implicit criticism of the temple establishment (Mark 12:41–44). The priests at the temple must help the poor financially, not demand that

---

of which are in relation to Yahweh. See Mullen, "Hosts, Hosts of Heaven" and Seow, "Hosts, Lord of," in *Anchor Bible Dictionary*, 3:301–4, 304–7.

8. Josephus, *J.W.* 6.5.3.

they pay tribute to the temple establishment. Rabbi Akiva (one of the most prominent rabbis in the early second century CE) also abhorred the idea of making a profit in the temple, especially off the poor.[9] The Testament of Moses (dated to during the lifetime of Jesus sometime in 7–29 CE) similarly criticized the priestly class: "Destructive and godless men who represent themselves as being righteous . . . consume the goods of the poor, saying their acts are according to justice."[10]

While at the temple complex, Jesus pronounced judgment upon Jerusalem and dared to prophesy in the presence of temple priests of the temple's destruction (Mark 11:15–18, 12:1–12, 14:56–59; John 2:19). His parable of the vineyard was a direct criticism of the priests:

> A man planted a vineyard, put a fence around it, dug a pit for the wine press, and built a watch-tower; then he leased it to tenants and went to another country. When the season came, he sent a slave to the tenants to collect from them his share of the produce of the vineyard. But they *seized him, and beat him*, and sent him away empty-handed. And again he sent another slave to them; this one they *beat over the head and insulted*. Then he sent another, and that *one they killed*. And so it was with many others; some they beat, and *others they killed*. He had still one other, a beloved son. Finally he sent him to them, saying, "They will respect my son." But those tenants said to one another, "This is the heir; come, *let us kill him*, and the inheritance will be ours." So they seized him, *killed him*, and threw him out of the vineyard. (Mark 12:1–8; emphasis added)

This parable is even more combative when understood in the context of Isaiah's parable of the vineyard in Isaiah 5, which warned Israel of impending judgment. Jesus' temple riot was an act of rebellion that instantly set Jesus on a collision course with the temple establishment and the Roman authorities who viewed him, like other messianic figures of the first century, as a rabble-rousing, messianic aspirant who needed to be silenced and punished.

Later that night Jesus returns to the Mount of Olives to retire at Bethany (Matt 21:17; Mark 11:11). The chronology in Mark differs from Luke. In Luke's account, Jesus enters Jerusalem and cleanses the temple on the same day, whereas the author of Mark has Jesus cleansing the temple the next day. Further, the Gospel of Mark contains the cursing of the fig tree, which is not found in Luke. The day after the messianic procession, when Jesus and some of his followers are walking back to Jerusalem, Jesus spots a fig tree on

---

9. Mishnah Sheqalim 4:3.
10. Testament of Moses 7:1–7, in Priest, "Testament of Moses," 1:920, 930.

the Mount of Olives with no fruit. The author of Mark explains to the reader that it was not the season for fruit. Despite this, Jesus curses the tree so that it would never produce fruit again (Mark 11:12–14). Jesus then cleanses the temple and departs from the city. The next morning they pass the fig tree again and notice that it had withered (Mark 11:20–25).

The emphasis of the story seems to be judgment. A fig tree in earlier Israelite texts was a symbol of Judah and Israel (Mic 7:1–6; Jer 8:13).[11] Thus Jesus' cursing of the fig tree on the Mount of Olives near Bethphage, meaning "house of unripe figs," was a pronouncement of judgment upon Jerusalem and Israel. The cleansing of the temple is sandwiched between the two fig tree sections (Mark 11:12–14, 20–25).[12] Jesus' focus on the divine judgment of Jerusalem is a continuation of the previous day when he wept and pronounced judgment upon the city. Note also that when Jesus' disciples brought his attention to the withered tree, Jesus, pointing to "this mountain," meaning the Mount of Olives, said, "Truly I tell you, if you say to this mountain, 'Be taken up and thrown into the sea,' and if you do not doubt in your heart, but believe that what you say will come to pass, it will be done for you" (Mark 11:23). With this statement Jesus may have meant to recall Zechariah 14:4, which prophesies that the Mount of Olives will experience topographical upheaval when the messiah arrives to fight Israel's enemies.[13]

According to the author of Mark, after Jesus spends the third day in Jerusalem (the end of the second day in Matthew) contending verbally with the Temple authorities, he leaves the city and while sitting "on the Mount of Olives opposite the temple" (Mark 13:3) gives the commonly named *Olivet Discourse* to some of his disciples. The discourse includes prophecies of the Temple's destruction, wars, famines, persecution, desolation, the coming of the Son of Man, and parables of judgment (Matt 24–25; Mark 13; Luke 21:5–37). We will not attempt to examine the eschatological and theological nuances of the discourse here. For our purpose, note that the entire discourse on judgment harks back to Joel 3, which employs similar language and contains similar judgments on the wicked. For example, both Joel and Jesus mention wars and a darkened sun and moon (Joel 2:10, 31, 3:15; Mark

---

11. Telford, *Barren Temple*, 132–56, 176–204; Kinman, *Jesus' Entry into Jerusalem*, 124–32.

12. The account in Matthew agrees in part with both Luke and Mark. Like Luke, Matthew positions Jesus' procession into Jerusalem and the cleansing of the temple on the same day. Like Mark, Matthew contains the cursing of the fig tree but only after Jesus cleanses the temple, whereas Mark has Jesus cursing the tree before the cleansing of the temple.

13. Beale and Carson, *Commentary on the New Testament*, 71.

13:24–25; Matt 24:29).[14] Joel prophesies that the wicked will be judged in the Valley of Jehoshaphat (i.e., the Kidron Valley; Joel 3:12). As Jesus was sitting on the Mount of Olives "opposite the temple" (Mark 13:3) discoursing with Joel 3 in mind, he would have been looking out over the Valley of Jehoshaphat. Jesus' main emphasis in the discourse of the coming of the Son of Man who will judge the wicked fits not only with Joel 3 that locates the final judgment in the Valley of Jehoshaphat, but also with Zechariah 14 that locates the final judgment on the Mount of Olives just after the messiah comes in glory[15]—on the "clouds" of heaven in Mark and Matthew (Mark 13:26; Matt 24:30). Jesus, then, according to the Gospels, is deliberate in his choice to deliver this discourse on the Mount of Olives while overlooking the Valley of Jehoshaphat and Jerusalem.

According to the various Gospels, Jesus' activities during the few days leading up to his arrest demonstrate that he satisfied several expectations of a messiah prescribed by Jewish texts in the two centuries prior to his ministry, which would have undoubtedly set him on a collision course with the authorities. Jesus' followers held a messianic parade for him as he entered Jerusalem, he pronounced judgment upon Israel on multiple occasions, he rioted in the temple complex and overturned the money changers' tables, and he accused the priests of corruption. Like many of his contemporary messianic figures, Jesus was arrested, mocked, and punished for being a messiah, or "king of the Jews" (Mark 15:26). As for who was primarily responsible for Jesus' death, it would have been the Roman authorities and the small band of unpopular and corrupt Roman-sympathizing chief priests in Jerusalem. In fact, one of the earliest Roman sources to mention Jesus does not deny that the Romans were responsible for killing him. Tacitus, writer and member of the senate, wrote in 116 CE, "Christus . . . suffered the extreme penalty during the reign of Tiberius at the hands of one of our procurators, Pontius Pilate."[16]

"Jews" and the Trial of Jesus

But what about Jesus' trial? Did not the Jewish masses call for Jesus' crucifixion? A massive amount of scholarship has examined the trial of Jesus and the responsibly of "the Jews" in the trial. We will not delve into all the

---

14. Jesus also quoted from other prophets concerning the darkened sun and moon (see Isa 13:10, 34:4; Ezek 32:7).

15. Ham, "Reading Zechariah," 2:85–97.

16. Tacitus, *Annals* 15.44.3. For a translation and interpretation of this source, see Theissen and Merz, *Historical Jesus*, 81–83.

nuanced details of Jesus' trial here, but we touch on a few broader issues to highlight the problems with blaming Jews for the death of Jesus solely based on the Gospels.

All four Gospels contain the "Crucify him!" episode. Despite the variations between the accounts, all the Gospels agree that (1) a prisoner pardon occurred during Passover, (2) a man named "Barabbas" was placed alongside Jesus, and (3) the crowd called for Barabbas's release and for Jesus' crucifixion (Mark 15:6–15; Matt 27:15–26; Luke 23:17–25; John 18:39–19:15). Using this story as evidence of broad Jewish guilt for killing Jesus is unwarranted given the story's many problems.

First, there is little or no evidence that a Jewish custom of a Passover prisoner release ever occurred. No early Jewish text outside the canonical Gospels mentions such a custom. Josephus's writings, which provide a plethora of nuanced details on the Judean politics of the first century, contain no Passover prisoner pardon by the Roman prefect.[17] The Greeks did have a tradition of releasing a prisoner at a March festival that survived until the first century.[18] Some have suggested that the author of Mark appropriated this tradition from the Greeks and transferred it to Jews in his narrative. He wrote to a gentile audience, so this story would have resonated with them. This interpretation does not seem overly speculative since the author of Mark seems to have utilized elements from pagan tradition and woven them into his retelling of Jesus' ministry.[19] As the earliest Gospel written, Mark cemented this folkloristic tradition into the Jesus story, and all the later Gospels incorporated it into their narratives.

Second, perhaps some scholars have overstated the position that the author of Mark invented this story. Maybe it did occur just as all four Gospels claim. However, the "Barabbas" element in the episode also generates suspicion that every detail in this episode is historical. The Gospels' authors explain that the prisoner in the story is named "Barabbas." But some early manuscripts of Matthew claim that his first name is "Jesus"[20]:

> At that time they had a notorious prisoner, called *Jesus Barabbas*. So after they had gathered, Pilate said to them, "Whom do you want me to release for you, *Jesus Barabbas* or Jesus who is called the Messiah?" (Matt 27:16–17; emphasis added)

---

17. Aus, *Caught in the Act*, 138; Merritt, "Jesus Barabbas," 57–68.
18. Merritt, "Jesus Barabbas," 59–63.
19. See MacDonald, *Mythologizing Jesus*.
20. Omanson, *Textual Guide*, 49; Crook, *Parallel Gospels*, 283–85 note a.

The reason why "Jesus" as Barabbas's first name is not found in several modern English translations is because later Christians omitted "Jesus" in these verses to avoid having a criminal share a name with Jesus of Nazareth. Origen (a third-century theologian) opined that the early manuscripts were mistaken in identifying Barabbas's first name as Jesus, saying, "In the whole range of the scriptures we know that no one who is a sinner is called Jesus."[21] The name "Barabbas" is Aramaic for, among other possibilities, (1) "Son of the Father" (*Bar Abba*), and (2) "Son of a teacher" (*Bar Rabba[n]*).[22] In this episode, *Bar* could refer to a literal "son," or it could be used as a generic term, a synecdoche, for "one who is." Thus, Barabbas's name was "Jesus, son of the father" or "Jesus who is a teacher." We must note that "Barabbas" is not a name (a proper patronymic) but a title or nickname.[23] The phenomenon of using nicknames was common in early Judaism. The New Testament itself gives us Simon who is called Peter (John 1:42), John who is called "the Baptist" (Luke 7:20, 28, 33), James and John who are called "Sons of Thunder" (Mark 3:17), Simon who is called "the Zealot" (Acts 1:13), and Joseph who is "called Barsabbas" (Acts 1:23). Further, the author of Matthew attests that both Jesuses had nicknames: "They had a notorious prisoner *called* Barabbas . . . 'Whom do you want me to release for you, Jesus Barabbas or Jesus *who is called* the Messiah?'" (Matt 27:16–17, emphasis added). This nickname of Jesus Barabbas sets the prisoner up in great irony against Jesus of Nazareth who also had other informal titles, some of them being "teacher" and a "son of the Father" (as he referred to God as his "Abba," or father). The fact that these two prisoners had the same name and similar nicknames suggests either an embellishment to the original story to create dramatic irony or an actual historical conspiracy on the part of Pilate or the chief priests (or both).

One argument is that the chief priests rigged the pardon by handpicking Jesus Barabbas to stand aside Jesus; therefore, if the crowd yelled, "We want Jesus" or "Release our teacher Jesus," the priests could say, "Pilate, they want you to release Jesus Barabbas" even if the crowd wanted Jesus of Nazareth to be released. They probably figured the crowd would call for Jesus' release because just a few days prior they sought to arrest Jesus in the temple complex but could not because of the pro-Jesus crowd (Matt 21:46; Mark 12:12; Luke 20:19). Thus, the chief priests would have had to cleverly manipulate the process to prevent Jesus' release.[24] Another theory is that Pilate

---

21. Omanson, *Textual Guide*, 49.
22. See Wilkins, "Barabbas," 1:607; Maccoby, "Jesus and Barabbas," 55–60.
23. Davies, "Who Is Called Bar Abbas?," 260–62.
24. Collins, *Mark*, 720.

was not the puppet in this story as the Gospels portray him to be—releasing whomever the Jewish council demanded. Pilate himself may have decided to set Barabbas up against Jesus. He may have wanted to agitate and embarrass Jesus' followers who, a few days prior, held a provocative parade for their messiah and shouted out his messianic identity while he rode on a donkey. On this occasion, however, it was Pilate who acted as provocateur by creating space for Jesus' followers to again shout out on his behalf. Pilate could then humiliate Jesus and his followers by releasing "Jesus Barabbas" regardless of which "Jesus" the crowd wanted to be released. Although speculative, this interpretation of Pilate harassing Jews and humiliating messianic candidates is congruous with what we know about Pilate from Josephus.[25] He was ruthless and had no patience for messianic shenanigans.

Still another argument is that Jesus Barabbas in this story is actually Jesus of Nazareth himself. This position is obviously problematic based on a literal reading of the Barabbas story; however, Stevan Davies (professor of religious studies at Misericordia University, a small Catholic university in Pennsylvania) and the late Hyam Maccoby (scholar at the University of Leeds) reached the same conclusion.[26] The crowd really did call for the release of the only prisoner placed before them, Jesus of Nazareth. Maccoby explains:

> The pre-Marcan story, in the time when relations between the early Christian Church and the Jewish people were relatively friendly, was that the crowd shouted for the release of [the only prisoner before them], Jesus Barabbas, i.e., "Jesus the Teacher," while the "high priests" shouted "Crucify him!" . . . Later when the hatred grew between Christians and Jews, the story was altered. Now [in the late first century] it is the Jewish crowd who shout for the death of Jesus. It is another Jesus whose release they want, Jesus Barabbas, who is a different person from Jesus of Nazareth. The duplication of designations becomes a duplication of persons. And now the story achieves a certain drama, for a choice has entered the picture—a choice between two Jesuses.[27]

---

25. Josephus, *Ant.* 18.3.1–2, 18.4.1.

26. Davies, "Who Is Called Bar Abbas?," 260–62; Maccoby, "Jesus and Barabbas," 55–60.

27. Maccoby, "Jesus and Barabbas," 59–60.

According to Maccoby, as the church became more anti-Jew, or anti-Pharisee, it altered the traditions to shift blame for the death of Jesus away from the Romans and toward the Jewish leaders.[28]

Numerous other scholars have also suggested that the Barabbas figure is fictional;[29] however, Helen Bond (professor of New Testament at the University of Edinburgh) rejects all of the proposed theories. But even she acknowledges that the story is strange and ambiguous, and she offers several suggestions herself on what might have happened:

> There is little scholarly agreement over Barabbas . . . In view of these difficulties, most scholars find themselves somewhere between the two extremes and accept some degree of historicity. Perhaps there was some confusion over which "Jesus" was to be brought to trial, and the prefect needed to seek clarification. Or perhaps Pilate granted a one-off amnesty to a prisoner, and the evangelists, removed from a Palestinian context, simply assumed that it was an annual event. Alternately, Barabbas may have been arrested after some kind of disturbance and then released at about the same time Jesus was sentenced. Christians may have reflected on the apparent injustice of Jesus' execution and Barabbas' release, with the two events becoming conflated in Christian consciousness . . . Barabbas might well have been an historical person, but the precise details surrounding him are elusive.[30]

Regardless of whether the Barabbas story is historical or fictional—and if historical, then regardless of which of the three aforementioned positions is more accurate—it seems clear enough that the Barabbas element in the story is fraught with confusion and is highly suspect.

In quick review, our first two problems with this episode are the historical reliability of the Passover pardon and the ambiguity surrounding the figure of Barabbas. The third problem is the nature of the crowd. Would they have been at this event yelling to crucify Jesus, either a relatively unknown individual or a well-known healer whom the crowds thought to be a prophet? It seems that if Jesus were unknown, then why would the hundreds of thousands of Jews who traveled to Jerusalem care to attend this event on the morning of Passover (following a late night with their families) to rally for a criminal they did not know? If Jesus were a well-known healer, then why would a large crowd of peasant Jews from the countryside gather

---

28. Maccoby, *Revolution in Judea*, 159–68.
29. Bond, "Barabbas Remembered," 59–61.
30. Bond, "Barabbas Remembered," 61–62.

and call for his crucifixion? Either scenario makes no sense. Thus, it seems that a large Jewish crowd was not present at this event. If the crowd was present, then why were not the priests intimidated by them like they were a few days prior in the temple complex? The author of Mark mentions that the chief priests "stirred up the crowds" (Mark 15:11), which might imply that they planted people in the crowd after instructing them to ask for Barabbas's release—and if Barabbas was really a fictional character and, therefore, not present, then the priests would have instructed the crowd to called for Jesus' crucifixion. That the priests manipulated and sabotaged Jesus' pardon by planting agitators makes sense given Mark's earlier claim that the Judean court had already sought false witnesses against Jesus (Mark 14:56–57). Manipulating the entire crowd would not have been difficult if Jesus' disciples were not present; and the reason for their absence is that they all deserted Jesus and fled about twelve hours before (i.e., the prior evening at Gethsemane). The absence of Jesus' followers during is arrest, trial, and crucifixion is most likely the case given that Rome often killed and arrested the followers of messianic claimants as we learned in chapter 4.

Even if we grant that a large Jewish crowd was present, and that a Pharisaic, nonpriestly segment of the crowd called for Jesus' crucifixion (which, again, makes no sense), it is unlikely that they would have yelled out *in unison*, "His blood be on us and on our children!" (Matt 27:25). Such a detail smacks of a literary creation. Why? Because this detail is absent in every Gospel except Matthew. Further, only in Matthew does the entire crowd place the blame upon their own heads and the heads of their children (Matt 27:22, 25). In addition, only in Matthew does Pilate's wife dream about Jesus' innocence (Matt 27:19), and only in Matthew does Pilate demonstrate his own innocence regarding Jesus' death by symbolically washing his hands (Matt 27:24). After seeing how the author of Matthew unfairly blames Judas for the arrest of Jesus and repeatedly slanders Pharisees (Matt 12 and 23), it is no surprise that these key details are found only in his Gospel! Moreover, Pharisaic Jews and the later rabbis were ardent followers of the Mosaic Law—a law that rejects the precept of the sins of the parents falling to subsequent generations:

> Parents shall not be put to death for their children, nor shall children be put to death for their parents; only for their own crimes may persons be put to death. (Deut 24:16)

> A child shall not suffer for the iniquity of a parent, nor a parent suffer for the iniquity of a child; the righteousness of the

righteous shall be his own, and the wickedness of the wicked shall be his own. (Ezek 18:20)[31]

Thus, it is highly unlikely—indeed, even absurd—that Jews would yell, "His blood be on us and on our children!" If we had only the Gospel of Matthew available to us, we would likely have only two directions for interpretation. One is that this episode is historical and that the entire crowd did call for Jesus' crucifixion and did place the consequences of this verdict upon the heads of their children. If so, then this crowd was almost certainly comprised of a small priestly crowd with very few Pharisee-following peasant Jews in attendance. Another interpretation is that this episode is not historical and was created by later Christians and then embellished by the author of Matthew. Either option leads us to the same conclusion: the Jewish masses were not present at this Passover pardon; therefore, this episode cannot be used as evidence that "the Jews" killed Jesus. If we disregard Matthew, and leave room for the possibility that many Pharisee-following Jews were in attendance, we still cannot conclude that they would have clamored for Jesus' death and placed the consequences of their decision upon their children.

The fourth problem with the "Crucify him!" episode, which we have mentioned briefly in the previous paragraphs, is that Pilate is portrayed as a politically naive nice guy who cannot understand why these irrational Jews want Jesus to be killed. As mentioned, Pilate was a ruthless leader who threatened Jews on many occasions and punished other messianic candidates (see chapter 4). He had to be ruthless to ensure peace in the rebellious Judean frontier of the Roman Empire. According to Philo, Pilate had a reputation of being "stubborn" and "vindictive"; he was described as having a "furious temper" and had "executed [numerous people] without trial."[32] There is zero chance that Pilate would have dared to release a popular figure during Passover who some thought should be their king. Pilate's authority would have been threatened. Also, if Jesus did enter Jerusalem in a parade riding a donkey just before rioting in the temple complex over the presence of traders, Pilate would not have said, "I . . . have found no fault in this man" (Luke 23:14; John 18:38) or "What evil has he done?" (Matt 27:23; Mark 15:14). Playing nice with Jews and releasing a messianic wannabe (in his view) during Passover, a festival specifically centered on remembrance of political emancipation from foreign rulers, would have risked rioting and demonstrations against Rome. If Pilate failed to keep Jews in line, then Caesar would have punished him or removed him from power. Why would the Gospels want to place the blame for Jesus' death on Jews (or at least in-

31. The rabbis repeat these verses in, for example, Babylonian Talmud Shabbat 55a.
32. Philo, *On the Embassy to Gaius,* 300–303, trans. Colson.

fluential Jews) while going out of their way to free the Romans of any guilt, especially since we have shown repeatedly in all the previous chapters that the Gospels were either written by Jews or for Jews (or both)? We will tackle this important question in chapters 9 and 10.

Takeaways

We have seen that most Jews in the Roman Empire would not have known about Jesus. We have also seen that Jesus would have gained enough followers in the Galilee to worry Herod Antipas and the Jerusalem authorities. We illustrated that favorability among the masses toward Jesus was significantly stronger than hostility toward Jesus. Indeed, we are hard-pressed to find even one instance in the Gospels of Jesus being threatened, accosted, or verbally assaulted by a Jewish peasant during his ministry. There is little or no evidence in the Gospels that the Pharisees or the masses were influential or even present at Jesus' trial. The only episode that seems to place blame on the Jews for Jesus' death is the "Crucify him" episode. But this story is highly problematic and is most likely either a later Christian embellishment or a historical conspiracy on the part of Pilate or the chief priests, or both. In short, it is simply too irresponsible to claim that "the Jews" rejected Jesus, and even more irresponsible to blame them for Jesus' death based on the Gospels.

Not only did many Jews follow Jesus as a teacher, a messianic candidate, or a healer, but numerous Jews believed in Jesus after his death. Perhaps it behooves us to mention here that Oskar Skarsaune and Reidar Hvalvik and company—professors at the MF Norwegian School of Theology in Oslo, along with an international team of fourteen other scholars—demonstrated in their volume *Jewish Believers in Jesus: The Early Centuries* that numerous Jews, including the authors of the Gospels and their communities, as well as Paul and many other Pharisees (Acts 15:5), believed in Jesus in the early centuries of the common era. It is noteworthy that even after Jesus died, his followers continued to live Jewish law while believing in Jesus! Peter and John prayed at the temple (Acts 3), Peter ate only kosher food (Acts 10), Paul and Barnabas attended the synagogue on the Jewish Sabbath (Acts 13), Timothy was circumcised (Acts 16), Paul took the Nazarite vow as prescribed in Numbers 16 to convince potential followers of Jesus that he still observed Jewish law (Acts 18), Paul traveled to Jerusalem to attend the Jewish fall festivals (Acts 18), Paul observed Passover and the Feast of Weeks (Acts 20), and Paul sacrificed animals at the temple on the Day of Atonement (Acts 21). Further, when Paul entered Jerusalem from his third missionary journey, he heard that "*many thousands* of believers [in Jesus] there are among the Jews, and they are all *zealous for the law*" (Acts 21:20; emphasis added)! In the late first century and in subsequent centuries, there were numerous Jewish Jesus believers throughout Galilee and Judea and in Rome, Asia Minor, and Syria. Jewish Jesus believers are also mentioned in Greek Christian literature, in Latin Christian literature, in Syriac Christian literature, in Christian-Jewish dialogues and liturgical texts as much as five hundred years after Jesus' death, and in rabbinic literature (second through fifth centuries).[33]

The painful implication of this chapter and the previous two chapters is that Christians from the second century through the twentieth century (and still today) were not justified in their persecution of Jews. Instead of blaming "the Jews" for killing Jesus, Christians should have (based on their own logic) blamed the Romans and a very small, corrupt, Roman-sympathizing Jewish priestly class. And, if Christians were in the business of blaming an entire group for Jesus' death and subsequently slandering and killing this group's descendants, then they should have done so to the Romans. Why? Because Roman authorities killed Jesus, and, therefore, according to their logic, Christians should have labeled *all* Romans and later Italians as "Christ killers" and then slandered and murdered them. It is most ironic that the very group whom Christians would have blamed (the Romans) is the very group whom Christians themselves became! The very location of the headquarters of the largest Christian movement is in Rome! Also appalling is that Jews did not reject Jesus any more than later Christians rejected Jesus by completely disregarding his central message of loving one's enemies and turning the other cheek. Obviously no group in totality should be blamed and persecuted for Jesus' death, but you can see just how ironic and tragic this rationale is.

---

33. Skarsaune and Hvalvik, *Jewish Believers in Jesus*, 55–782.

Chapter Nine

I Know You Are, but What Am I?
The Greco-Roman Art of Name Calling

I ONCE PRESENTED THE information in the previous two chapters to a group of committed Christians (non-scholars) to show that Jews did not reject and kill Jesus and that Jesus and Pharisees were most likely cordial associates (and that Jesus may have been a Pharisaic Jew). I laid out the argument as I did in the previous chapters, which seemed to intrigue the audience; however, most in the room rejected my conclusion because the Gospels are replete with statements that clearly demonstrate hostility between Pharisees and Jesus and describe Pharisees as hypocrites and vipers. These are, indeed, the elephants in the room regarding Pharisees. One can talk all day long about the episodes where Pharisees appear to be delightful friends of Jesus, but one cannot escape the several passages where Pharisees are called hypocrites, vipers, lovers of money, adulterous sign-seekers, and whitewashed tombs that house rotting corpses. How can we contextualize much of the material in the previous two chapters, especially the anti-Pharisee passages in chapter 7?

The Greco-Roman Art of Name-Calling

In review, 38 episodes in the Gospels involve Pharisees. More than half of these are either positive or neutral portrayals (see chapter 7). About seventeen episodes seem to portray Pharisees negatively; however, many of these cannot be accurate representations of Pharisees, or of Pharisaism. The remaining episodes we have yet to explore are the "name-calling" episodes, what we might term "polemic" or "invective" episodes, meaning they are meant to be abusive and highly caustic attacks. Some of these passages are problematic for the same reasons the aforementioned episodes (in chapter 7) are problematic. There is another key factor at play, however, that very few New Testament teachers discuss (whether at prep Bible schools, in higher education courses, or in Sunday school). This factor is competition rhetoric.

A few prominent psychologists have demonstrated that we are hardwired to view other people or groups as either enemies or friends. We constantly size up people or groups and label them as either allies or rivals. We do this in every aspect of life—both as individuals and as members of various groups. We witness this every day among sports rivals, in the workplace, among family members (especially in-laws), in politics, and in religious communities. We tend to be ethnocentric, tribalistic, and nationalistic. In other words, we feel our group is the best, and we tend to judge all external groups and individuals by our own "correct" standards. Our country, our race, our political party, our religion, our school, our neighborhood, and our family are superior. Psychiatrists would call *ethnocentrism* or *nationalism* "a pathological contamination of the mental process" because when we identify strongly with a particular group, we tend to lose the ability to be neutral, objective, or open-minded. We adhere more stubbornly to our tribe when we feel threatened or humiliated by outsiders, and we identify them as *targets of externalization*.[1]

Psychologists have also demonstrated that we tend to reserve our most intense hostility for those who are like us—insiders, former insiders, and outsiders who are in close proximity to our group ideologically or geographically. Vamik Volkan, an expert in political psychology and a four-time Nobel Peace Prize nominee, explained this phenomenon:

> It is interesting to contemplate the subtle fact that the enemy *often resembles us in obvious ways*, while what we perceive to be his offense constitutes only a narrow area of disagreement. Freud (1917) spoke of "the narcissism of minor differences" in reference to the way small differences among people [who are] otherwise alike make for hostility and alienation. He was curious as to why people living in contiguous lands so often came into conflict—why the Portuguese and Spanish were at odds, or the English and the Scots, or the Northern and Southern Germans, when each pair of opponents had so much in common. It seems that we often seek out as enemies (targets) those like

---

1. Volkan, "Need to Have Enemies and Allies," 221, 241–43.

ourselves or our neighbors—in other words, *familiar people* . . . We focus obsessively, when stressed, on our differences in order to *cling to the illusion that the enemy is quite unlike us.* This process strengthens our sense of self and our sense of solidarity with "our side."[2]

The late Jonathan Z. Smith (University of Chicago), preeminent scholar of religion, similarly articulated that kindred groups tend to see one another as most threatening. And the polemic against the opposing group is often an attempt to strengthen the identity of one's own group:

> While the "other" may be perceived as being either LIKE-US or NOT-LIKE-US, he is, in fact, most problematic when he is TOO-MUCH-LIKE-US . . . This is not a matter of the "far," but, preeminently of the "near." The problem is not alterity, but similarity—at times, even identity. A "theory of the other" is but another way of phrasing a "theory of the self."[3]

This process of creating enemies often involves the use of polemic and invective, what we are referring to as "name-calling." If our *targets of externalization* appear to be a threat to our purposes, we gossip about them, we undercut them, we discredit them, and we focus on perceived negative traits. This psychological phenomenon of creating enemies of familiar groups and then lobbing verbal attacks at them is highly relevant for our examination of polemical statements in the Gospels about Jews in general and Pharisees in particular.

New Testament polemic is perhaps best understood within the context of the contemporary Hellenistic (i.e., Greek) art of rhetoric.[4] The Greco-Roman world had a canonized set of works on navigating rhetorical disputes. The most salient of these works among the Greek philosophical schools was Aristotle's *Rhetoric.*[5] Aristotle lived in the fourth century BCE. One of his students was Alexander the Great, who conquered the region of Judea and Galilee in the 330s BCE. Aristotle detailed the best way to expose and defeat one's philosophical opponents through rhetoric. The aim was to destroy their social and political personas. Since the people generally had difficulty discerning the differences between two competing philosophical schools, it was necessary for the members of those schools to highlight the differences.

---

2. Volkan, "Need to Have Enemies and Allies," 243–44; emphasis added.

3. Smith, "What a Difference a Difference Makes," 47.

4. Many thanks to my RA, Jacob Stoeltzing, for helping flesh out this material on Greco-Roman polemic and invective.

5. Rapp, "Aristotle's Rhetoric."

This was important because these schools sought to (1) recruit students, and (2) turn the favor of the populace toward their ideology. They accomplished this using loaded and provocative words about their opponents. They saved the most sharply worded and insulting statements for groups that posed threats to their identity and self-esteem,[6] as Freud and Volkan later observed.

Aristotle instructed his students to highlight their own virtues and, at the same time, highlight their opponents' vices. Even more effective is to draw direct comparisons. One must also focus, in his argument, on virtues that people generally espouse. Aristotle mentioned justice, courage, temperance, magnanimity, liberality, gentleness, prudence, and wisdom (notice the similarity with Paul's list of virtues in Gal 5:22–23).[7] The goal is to convince one's hearers that these virtues reside in one's own group and that the corresponding vices plague the other group: we are just, they are unjust; we are gentle, they are harsh; we help the poor, they covet money; we are courageous, they are cowards. Aristotle also taught that one skilled in rhetorical disputes can easily turn opponents' virtues into vices. For example, if your opponent is perceived as impressive, you might label him "arrogant." If your opponent is perceived as courageous, you might label him hotheaded or "rash." If your opponent is clearly pious, you might accuse him of zealotry or hypocrisy.[8] Finally, if your opponent performs a good deed that cannot be denied, you might argue that his or her intentions and motives were compromised; whereas, if a member of your own group accidently stumbles into a good deed, you would argue that the generous deed was both intentional and common for this person.[9]

The Roman author Cicero later developed ideas from Aristotle's *Rhetoric* in his *De Oratore* (first century BCE) and offered similar advice in Rome. He suggested that most people are less rational and more emotional. Thus, arguments must appeal to emotion. Since "feelings are won over by a man's merit," the focus must be on emotion and not on actual achievements, which can easily be exaggerated or diminished. One skilled in rhetoric must convince his hearers that he himself displays "tokens of good-nature, kindness, calmness, loyalty and a disposition that is pleasing and not grasping or covetous." Accordingly, "the very opposites of these qualities must be ascribed to our opponents."[10] A survey of several disputes between various philosophical schools in the Greco-Roman world reveals the following com-

---

6. Freyne, "Vilifying the Other," 118.
7. Aristotle, *Rhetoric*, bk. 1, ch. 9, 1366b, p. 1354.
8. Aristotle, *Rhetoric*, 1367a–1367b, p. 1356.
9. Aristotle, *Rhetoric*, 1367b, p. 1357.
10. Cicero, *De Oratore* 2.43.182–183, trans. Sutton and Rackham, 327–29.

monly used pejoratives to describe philosophical and religious opponents: "ignorant," "boastful," "evil-spirited," "impious," "liars and deceivers," "flatterers," "charlatans," "demagogues," "buffoons," "prostitutes," "magicians," "they [who] criticize others without examining themselves," "they [who] make a great show out of virtue yet never practice it," "they [who] have the outward appearance of virtue but are themselves corrupt," and "they [who] are only after pleasure and wealth."[11]

Theaters and literature spread unfettered stereotypes and invective across the Hellenistic world. Such disputes and language were so commonplace in the first and second centuries CE that Roman satirists like Lucian of Samosata (d. ca. 180) ridiculed philosophers for their inconsistency and hypocrisy.[12] Lucian wrote that lying was "a common practice even among men who profess philosophy." He was surprised that philosophers "thought that they could write untruths and not get caught."[13] He accused them of "hoodwinking" their audiences with deceptive rhetoric.[14] He charged them with picking their opponents "to pieces in talk and insulting [them] in every way" so that they cannot "escape their meddling tongues."[15] Lucian elsewhere explained that philosophers "divided themselves into schools" and then, as prescribed by Aristotle and Cicero, "cloaked themselves in the high-sounding name of virtue."[16] In order to convince the masses of their intellectual and moral superiority over their philosophical opponents, "they amass *biting phrases* and school themselves in *novel terms of abuse*, and then they censure and reproach their fellow-men; and whoever of them is the most noisy and impudent and reckless in *calling names* is held to be the champion."[17] Josephus similarly accused the various philosophers of spreading untruths: "For the most part they refute each other in their books, and do not hesitate to say the most contradictory things on the same topics."[18]

We can place New Testament polemical passages within the conventional literary standards of the time. We see the same pejoratives used in similar contexts in both the New Testament and other Greco-Roman texts. Most of the philosophical groups unethically (according to our standards) slandered and defamed their opponents. Early Judaism was a

11. Johnson, "New Testament's Anti-Jewish Slander," 430–33.
12. Johnson, "New Testament's Anti-Jewish Slander," 432.
13. Lucian, *True Story* 1.4, trans. Harmon, 251–52.
14. Lucian, *Carousal* 28–30, trans. Harmon, 441–43.
15. Lucian, *Icaromenippus* 21, trans. Harmon, 303.
16. Lucian, *Icaromenippus* 29–30.
17. Lucian, *Icaromenippus* 29–30; emphasis added.
18. Josephus, *Ag. Ap.* 1.15, trans. Barclay.

philosophy—Josephus called Pharisaism and Sadduceeism, for example, "philosophies."[19] The authors of the Gospels did to Pharisees what every other group did to their opponents; they followed precisely the model posited by Aristotle and Cicero. In light of this phenomenon, we would expect the authors of the Gospels to use the most inflammatory and hyperbolic language against their opponents; in fact, we would be suspicious and even surprised if they did not utilize their contemporary rhetorical conventions. We must remember that defamation of Jews, and of Pharisees specifically, in the New Testament is competition rhetoric and does not necessarily represent a realistic portrayal.

Some of the most common verbal accusations among the various philosophical schools in Greco-Roman literature were hypocrisy, the love of money, and murder. The Gospels are no exception. They also use these pejoratives and do so following the formula in Aristotle's *Rhetoric*. The Gospel of Matthew contains perhaps the best illustrations. The entire chapter of Matthew 23 is a diatribe against Pharisees. As prescribed by Aristotle, the author of Matthew uses offensive and slanderous language to describe Pharisees, turns their virtues into vices, and draws readers' attention to their motives. For instance, he acknowledges that Pharisees are respected authorities and even encourages his readers to "do whatever they teach you and follow it" (Matt 23:2). However, to spin this virtue, he cautions them, "But do not do as they do, for they do not practice what they teach" (Matt 23:3). Perhaps without realizing it, the author of Matthew validates the entire Pharisaic system by encouraging people to follow it. He also contradicts himself by claiming that Pharisees are hypocrites (Matt 23:13–15, 23–29).

Today we usually describe hypocrisy as preaching one ideal and purposely doing the opposite; however, as prominent New Testament scholar at Trinity Lutheran Seminary Mark Allan Powell explains, "The popular notion of a hypocrite as someone who says one thing and does another has no support in Matthew's Gospel even though, ironically, it probably derives from mistranslations and misrepresentations of this Matthean text (23:2–3)."[20] The Greek word for "hypocrite," *hypokritēs*, denotes an "outward show," a "pretender," or a "play-actor," specifically one under disguise (e.g., wearing a costume and mask in a play).[21] By calling Pharisees "hypocrites," the author of Matthew is conceding that Pharisees do, indeed, practice what they preach even though he said the opposite in verse 3. Remember that Josephus, an opponent of Pharisees, explained that the populace perceived

---

19. Josephus, *Ant.* 18.1.2., trans. Barclay.
20. Powell, "Do and Keep What Moses Says," 423.
21. Arndt et al., *Greek-English Lexicon*, 845.

that Pharisees were pious in word and deed: they had the "reputation of excelling the rest of their nation in the observances of religion,"[22] and they "practiced the highest ideals *both in their way of living and in their discourse.*"[23] Thus, in order to spin this virtue into a vice, the author of Matthew claims that even though Pharisees live piously and practice what they teach, they are simply pretending—their motives are compromised; they "do all their deeds to be seen by others; for they make their phylacteries broad and their fringes long" (Matt 23:5). When they fast, they "disfigure their faces so as to show others that they are fasting" (Matt 6:16). In other words, they look and play the part of righteous leaders, but they are morally bankrupt according to the author of Matthew: they "are like whitewashed tombs, which on the outside look beautiful, but inside they are full of the bones of the dead and of all kinds of filth . . . [and] are full of hypocrisy and lawlessness" (Matt 23:27–28).

We pause here for a quick moment and remember that while reading the Gospels and Josephus regarding the Pharisees, we must develop an eye for identifying those bits of information that they *accidentally* reveal. Polemical attacks tend to be poorly constructed. The primary purpose is to criticize, not to represent accurately. Thus, authors preoccupied with slandering often provide information that discredits the very arguments they are trying to make. Amid his obsession with demonizing Pharisees, the author of Matthew accidently concedes that they practice what they preach.

This accusation of hypocrisy and its accompanying rhetoric was so common in the Greco-Roman world that we can easily find similar examples. For instance, just as the author of Matthew claimed that Pharisees' hypocrisy involved the deceptive outward appearance of piety while hiding a rotting moral core, Lucian in the early second century CE wrote a strikingly similar accusation of philosophers. He claimed that "their practice directly opposed their preaching;"[24] they pretend (hypocritically) to be pious and virtuous while "marching along deep in haughty meditation," and while "elevating their eyebrows, wrinkling up their foreheads, and letting their beards grow long, they go about hiding loathsome habits under a false garb, *like actors in tragedy*; for if you take away . . . their gold-embroidered robes, nothing is left but a comical little creature hired for the show."[25] Again, these common accusations among philosophical opponents are sensational and

---

22. Josephus, *J.W.* 1.110, trans. Thackeray; emphasis added.
23. Josephus, *Ant.* 18.1.3, trans. Feldman; emphasis added.
24. Lucian, *Menippus*, 5, trans. Harmon, 83.
25. Lucian, *Icaromenippus*, 29; Lucian, *Timon*, trans. Harmon, 317, 387; emphasis added.

hyperbolic on purpose. They were not simply written by vindictive authors in a state of bitterness but were carefully crafted to help shift or maintain popular support for a particular ideology.

Just as Lucian labeled his opponents as "actors," so did the author of Matthew. We must note that the primary translation of *hypocrite (hypokrites)* as *theater-actor* is not insignificant in a Roman context. When an author labeled his opponent a "hypocrite," he was not just accusing him of acting or pretending to be wise or righteous—his attack was much more vicious. He was not just tossing his opponent into the mud but was violently casting him into the sewer, as it were. How so? While play-actors were held in high esteem by the Greeks, they were regarded as shameful and immoral in Roman society. Catharine Edwards, historian at the University of London, explains:

> Acting was incompatible with *honestas*, "honour," and *dignitas*, "social standing," the qualities which were supposed to mark out those of senatorial and equestrian status above all. Moralists characterized the theater as a storehouse of obscenity, a place where lust, laughter and political subversion were incited in almost equal measure. Actors were viewed as base persons, of ambiguous and venal sexuality, whose words could not be trusted ... The theatre was an empty show of action without real consequences. Actors were dissemblers, people who pretended to be what they were not. They were praised precisely for their ability to deceive.[26]

Actors in Rome were expected only to provide entertainment, much of it displaying licentiousness and societal dysfunction. Further, actors were often labeled as "imposters" and "flatterers," not simply because they were imposters on stage but because they excelled at pretending to be someone else. Actors were also compared to prostitutes in Roman literature; just as prostitutes excel in faking love, actors are skilled in faking their true character. Neither prostitutes nor actors are sincere.[27] In fact, actors were often assumed to be prostitutes. Consequently, actors could not be trusted in society because of their skill in deception.

Actors were not admired the same way many entertainers are today. Rome was a military state—its soldiers and politicians were revered. Actors were primarily slaves and free foreigners and were denied many privileges of citizens. They were not permitted to be soldiers because they were viewed as the antithesis of warriors. In fact, if a soldier appeared on stage, he could

---

26. Edwards, *Politics of Immorality*, 99, 102.
27. Duncan, *Performers and Identity*, 91–159.

have been liable for capital punishment.[28] Actors, along with others of ill repute—criminals, prostitutes, and dishonorably discharged soldiers—were "legally branded as disgraceful."[29] Cicero identified several professions unbecoming of gentlemen, the worst of which were those involving "a great deal of downright lying . . . [and] misrepresentation" (i.e., acting).[30] He explained that because the Roman citizenry "considered the dramatic art and the theatre in general disgraceful, they desired that all persons connected with such things should be deprived of the privileges of other citizens."[31] Tertullian (d. 240 CE), the well-known Roman Christian author, wrote:

> We are bidden to put away from us all impurity. By this command we are cut off once for all from the theatre, the proper home of all impurity . . . Its supreme charm is above all things contrived by its filth—filth in the gestures of the actor of the farce—filth acted by the buffoon playing the woman, banishing all sense of sex and shame.[32]

The rabbis (the theological and legal heirs of the Pharisees) of the late first through the third centuries CE instituted a ban on Jewish attendance at the Roman theater because of its sexually immoral display and sleazy ambiance, although this ban may have been more rhetorical than practical.[33]

The authors of the Gospels, particularly of Matthew, chose the most unscrupulous profession in the Roman Empire to describe Pharisees. When readers of the Matthean Gospel encountered the word "hypocrites," they would have transferred all the baggage of play-actors onto the Pharisees. They would have understood that the author of Matthew accused Pharisees of not only being pretenders of piety but also the primary perpetuators of the dark, dysfunctional underbelly of society—liars, cheats, and prostitutes, undeserving of the privileges of ordinary citizens. Based on the previous chapter, such a characterization of Israel's moral leaders is fundamentally opposed to the scholarly, critical conclusions regarding Pharisees according to Josephus and certain episodes of the Gospels. The authors of Matthew and John were not presenting a picture of the real Pharisees and Jews, but instead sought to shape perceptions of them for their communities and for potential converts to the Jesus movement.

28. Edwards, *Politics of Immorality*, 102, 125.
29. Edwards, *Politics of Immorality*, 123.
30. Cicero, *De Officiis* 1.150, trans. Miller, 153.
31. Cicero, *De Republica* 4.10, trans. Keyes, 239.
32. Tertullian, *De Spectaculis*, 17, trans. Glover and Rendall, 275.
33. For a discussion of the early rabbinic sources on this issue, see Spielman, *Sitting with Scorners*, 159–244.

Moreover, the author of Matthew would call the Pharisees "hypocrites" through the words of Jesus precisely *because* they were following the law and living in accordance with God's precepts. Since Pharisees practiced what they preached, even to the extent that the populace perceived them as genuine, the author of Matthew could claim only that they were not sincere—that they simply *acted* to be seen of men. In order to contend with the popular Pharisees, the author of Matthew could attack only their hearts; however, it would have been impossible to judge their motives unless he had conclusive audio and video recordings of Pharisees doing and saying unethical and immoral things when they were not within public view. As mentioned in the Pharisee chapter (chapter 7), two frequently used words in relation to Pharisees in both Josephus and the Gospels are *díkaios* (righteousness toward men) and *eusébeia* (righteousness toward God). These two words recall to our minds the two great commandments, love God and love your neighbor (Matt 22:37–39; Mark 12:30–31)! Yet it was not these words that ended up in modern dictionaries under Pharisee; it was "hypocrite."

The accusation of covetousness and love of money is similar to hypocrisy. Philosophers in the Greco-Roman world criticized each other for being motivated by wealth and greed. Lucian, for example, claimed that his opponents "teach their doctrines for pay, and worship the rich, and are agog after money";[34] they "who recommended scorning money, clove to it tooth and nail, bickered about interest, taught for pay, and underwent everything for the sake of money."[35] A few authors of the Gospels use this same tactic and rhetoric to describe their late first-century opponents, the Pharisees. In the Gospel of Matthew, Pharisees seek "treasures on earth, where moth and rust consume" (Matt 6:19) and are "full of greed and self-indulgence" (Matt 23:25). In Luke, they are called "lovers of money" (Luke 16:14). This accusation was a stock attack among philosophers "from at least the time of Socrates."[36] It was a rhetorical tool employed to establish moral superiority over one's philosophical opponents. Philosophy (*philosophía*), literally "love of wisdom," was viewed by philosophers as morally superior to *philárgyros*, or "love of money." Several Hellenistic-era authors—including Plato, Philo, and Josephus—attempted to authenticate themselves and attack their opponents by claiming that they did not profit from their work and were not motivated by wealth, as were their opponents.[37] The accusation of Pharisees being consumed with monetary gain is strange considering that it is not

---

34. Lucian, *Dead Come to Life*, 34, trans. Harmon, 51.
35. Lucian, *Menippus*, 5, trans. Harmon, 83.
36. Mason, "Chief Priests, Sadducees, Pharisees," 141.
37. Brawley, *Luke–Acts and the Jews*, 60–61.

congruous with Josephus's portrayal of Pharisees: "The Pharisees simplify their standard of living, making no concession to luxury."[38] It was their simplistic lifestyle, according to Josephus, that endeared them to the populace. Such an accusation is better aimed at the priestly establishment. Again, attacking opponents' motives and calling them covetous and hypocritical is effective because it is difficult to disprove. The masses clearly recognize the righteous actions of the Pharisees; therefore, the heart is the only thing left to criticize.

Murder is another common accusation between rivals. In the hypocrisy chapter of Matthew 23, the author has Jesus condemning Pharisees "to hell" for being "descendants of those who murdered the prophets" (Matt 23:31–33, 35). He also condemns them for sins they have not yet committed: "I send you prophets, sages, and scribes, some of whom you will kill and crucify" (Matt 23:34). First, where is the evidence that Pharisees' ancestors murdered the prophets four hundred years prior during the last generations of the Israelite prophets? Who did they murder and when? Does it not seem strange that in this passage the author of Matthew, through the mouth of Jesus, does not condemn Pharisees for sins *they have recently committed* but for sins their faceless, nameless ancestors committed several hundred years in the past and also for the sins they "will" commit in the future? This is precisely the type of rhetorical warfare Aristotle and Cicero promoted: avoid identifying the actual deeds of your opponents and instead build a strawman with vague and emotional claims.

This Greco-Roman rhetorical convention of slandering philosophical opponents is found everywhere in early Jewish literature and in the New Testament. Apion, a Greek philosopher from Egypt in the early first century, accused Jews of being "seditious," "atheists," and "cowards" for worshiping an "ass's head" and for being "the only people who have contributed no useful invention to civilization." He called Moses the obligatory "charlatan" and "imposter."[39] In response, Josephus called Apion and his people "frivolous and utterly senseless specimens of humanity" who were so "blinded" by their "passions" that they contradicted themselves continually. He called Apion "seditious" and remarked that, unlike Apion's race, Josephus's "remained unadulterated."[40]

The first-century Jewish philosopher Philo also jousted with gentiles in his hometown of Alexandria in Egypt. He utilized much of the same

---

38. Josephus, *Ant.* 18.1.3, trans. Feldman.

39. Josephus, *Ag. Ap.* 2.6.68, 2.7.80, 2.8.92–96, 2.14.145, 2.14.148, 2.16.161, trans. Thackeray.

40. Josephus, *Ag. Ap.* 1.25.225–226, 2.6.69–70.

invective found in Greco-Roman literature and in the New Testament. He referred to the Alexandrian gentile population as "promiscuous," "arrogant," and "robbers." He accused them of behaving "with greater brutality and ferocity than even the most savage beasts, [destroying] every semblance of humanity about them." He criticized them for their inclination to "flattery," "trickery," and "hypocrisy." He called them "wicked, worthless men, who had imprinted the venom and evil disposition of their native asps and crocodiles on their own souls." Notice that these attacks are strikingly similar to those in the Gospel of Matthew against Pharisees, where they are called vipers, hypocrites, and evil souls.[41]

The Dead Sea sect at Qumran employed the same rhetorical techniques. They accused their opponents in Jerusalem of being "seekers of smooth things" (i.e., flatterers) who preferred "illusions" and "justified the wicked and condemned the just." They also called them "devilish" murderers.[42] It is also noteworthy that one of the major Pharisaic factions (the followers of Hillel) in the fourth century CE accused the first-century ancestors of the other faction (the followers of Shammai) of gaining popularity among the masses by murdering the Hillelite Pharisees. Prominent Jewish scholar Jacob Neusner has argued that this claim is clearly a product of fourth-century conflict that is imposed on first-century Pharisees.[43]

Multiple New Testament authors were no strangers to these rhetorical conventions. Paul warned the followers of Jesus in various regions to beware of those who preach a "different gospel" or "proclaim another Jesus" (Gal 1:6; 2 Cor 11:4). These alternate voices were Jewish teachers and probably followers of Jesus from Jerusalem who traveled to many of the same areas as Paul and preached about Jesus and Jewish law. Paul referred to his opponents as "dogs" and "evil workers" who "mutilate the flesh" (Phil 3:2). He labeled them "people pleasers" (Gal 1:10) and hoped they would, in their zeal of circumcision (because they were Jews), slip with the knife and "castrate themselves" (Gal 5:12). He also called his opponents "false apostles," "deceitful," and those who "disguise themselves as ministers of Christ" (2 Cor 11:5, 13). The author of 1 John, 2 John, and 3 John called his opponents—followers of Jesus who were once part of their community (1 John 2:19)—"anti-Christs" and "liars" (1 John 2:18, 22). He accused them

---

41. Philo, *On the Embassy to Gaius* 18.120, 122; 19.131; 25.162; 26.166, trans. Yonge, 768–72.

42. CD 1.14–2.1 and 1QH^a X, 31–38. See translation and discussion in Vanderkam, "Pharisees and the Dead Sea Scrolls," 226–27. For more examples and discussion, see Johnson, "New Testament's Anti-Jewish Slander," 434–41.

43. See Jerusalem Talmud Shabbat 1:4; Babylonian Talmud Shabbat 17a. See Neusner, *Rabbinic Traditions*, 3:266–68, 318.

of being "false prophets" who were "from the world," while they themselves were "greater [because] they were from God" (1 John 4:1–6). These types of accusations, especially those of "people pleasers" (i.e., "flatterers") and "disguisers" or "pretenders" (i.e., "hypocrites" or "play-actors"), are some of the most common pejoratives in the Greco-Roman world, as we have seen. These rhetorical strategies were perpetuated for several centuries and are found throughout early Christian literature.[44]

Takeaways

Based on the material in this chapter and the Pharisee chapter (chapter 7), it is extremely difficult to make the case that Pharisees were enemies of Jesus. Such a claim simply does not make sense after a critical exploration of all the available data from Josephus and the Gospels, an exploration that many scholars have undertaken. We have reviewed most of the episodes about Pharisees, or at least all of the types of episodes about Pharisees (because some are similar in their elements). Every hostile passage found in a particular Gospel is hard to reconcile with the other Gospels, as well as with Josephus. There are contradictions everywhere. Further, the hostile Pharisee passages smack of caricatures; they are congruous with the rhetorical standards of the Greco-Roman world. The fact that the authors of the Gospels of Matthew and John, for instance, are so vitriolic toward Pharisees suggests that Pharisaism and Christian Judaism shared the same space geographically, socially, and theologically. Perhaps Volkan, Freud, and Aristotle were right when they observed that kinship groups often display the greatest enmity toward each another. Consequently, kinship groups tend to save their harshest words for each other in order to illustrate to their constituents that they really are vastly different when in reality they are the same, save a few minor differences.

In short, the Pharisees as a group did not reject Jesus, at least from what we can tell about them from Josephus and the Gospels. If the author of Matthew was attempting to use extreme language in order to damage public perceptions of Pharisees, then he likely succeeded more than he had ever hoped because his slander resulted in an unprecedented and unwarranted character assassination that led to the demonization and murder of millions of Jews. In the next chapter we will discuss in more detail the context and reasons for hostility toward Pharisees and certain subgroups of Jews in the New Testament.

44. For many examples, see Harland, *Dynamics of Identity*, 161–81.

Chapter Ten

Why the Conflict and Hostile Rhetoric?

WHENEVER I PRESENT THE "name calling" material to my students and others, the first question they usually ask is something like, "If the Gospels were written by Jews or for Jews (or both), then why did they seem to demonize Jews? Wouldn't that be counterproductive if the goal is to demonstrate to Jews that Jesus is the messiah?" This is an important question. Two main factors exacerbated the use of invective against Pharisees and other Jews in the Gospels: the Jewish-Roman War of 66–70 CE and the evolving relationship between Christian Jews and non-Christian Jews.

Jewish-Roman Relations

The Jewish-Roman War started in 66 CE. The period between 6–66 CE was a relatively peaceful time for Jews and Romans. As Martin Goodman, professor of Jewish studies at Oxford University, informs us, "Roman comments about Jews were rarely hostile before the outbreak of the war in 66."[1] However, several skirmishes between Jews and Romans in the first century chipped away at this peaceful relationship setting the stage for war. In 19 CE, Jews were expelled from the city of Rome by Tiberius Caesar and in 49 CE they were thrown out again by Claudius Caesar, both for political reasons.[2] The relationship between Jews and Romans was periodically tense in Jerusalem as well. In the 30s, Pilate used funds from the temple treasury to pay for an aqueduct to Jerusalem. When a protest ensued, Pilate's soldiers

---

1. Goodman, *Rome and Jerusalem*, 366.
2. Goodman, *Rome and Jerusalem*, 369–70.

threatened to stab members of the crowd with daggers.[3] In the late 40s or early 50s during Passover, a Roman soldier exposed his genitals to the Jewish pilgrims and worshipers at the temple. The crowd erupted in protest, and, according to Josephus, Roman soldiers reacted by killing twenty thousand Jews.[4] In the 50s CE, Roman soldiers killed six hundred Jews for following a man who claimed to be a messianic prophet and who prophesied that Jerusalem's walls would tumble upon his command.[5] In 59–60 CE, Jewish and Greek inhabitants of Caesarea, a port city on the northern coast, began fighting over who "owned" the city. Violence steadily increased and Roman soldiers frequently arrested and punished the agitators on both sides. Although the violent conflict was suppressed, tension between Jews and gentiles (both Greeks and Romans) continued to simmer for several years.

In the spring of 66 CE, conflict in Caesarea exploded when Greek youths sacrificed an unclean bird (unclean according to Jewish law) near the entrance of the synagogue. Jews became even more incensed when the Roman governor Gessius Florus failed to punish the agitators. Shortly after, in Jerusalem, Florus was met with a hostile Jewish crowd. The rioters were enraged not only because of the incident in Caesarea but also because Florus had demanded higher taxes than his predecessors. He had plundered the temple treasury when the Jews would not pay them. Florus let his soldiers loose on the protestors, and, according to Josephus, 3,600 Jews including women and children were slaughtered.[6] The result was a province-wide revolt. Florus fled back to Caesarea leaving behind only a small Roman cohort in Jerusalem. An influential young priest named Eleazar suspended the daily sacrifices to Caesar and Jewish rebels seized control of both the Antonia fortress and Herod's palace.[7] At this point, a full-fledged war between Jews and Roman authorities in Judea and Galilee was inevitable.

The war lasted about four years, and by early autumn of 70 CE, the Romans had taken control of the Judean and Galilean countrysides, had razed Jerusalem, and burned the temple to the ground. Many thousands of people, both Jews and Romans, had been killed.[8] According to the Jews, Roman authorities were oppressive thugs; according to Roman authorities, Jews were uncivilized traitors. This Jewish-Roman tension in the latter half

---

3. Josephus, *Ant.* 18:60.
4. Josephus, *J.W.* 2.12.1; *Ant.* 20.5.3, trans. Feldman.
5. Josephus, *Ant.* 20.8.6.
6. Josephus, *J.W.* 2.13.7, 2.14.4–6.
7. Josephus, *J.W.* 2.17.2–6.
8. For more context on these conflicts, especially the war, see Goodman, *Rome and Jerusalem,* 7–25, 366–423; Schäfer, *History of the Jews,* 114–30.

of the first century CE greatly influenced how the authors of the Gospels wrote their narratives about Jesus, the reasons for which we will discuss shortly.

Intra-Jewish Conflict

The second factor that shaped the Gospels' portrayal of certain Jewish subgroups is conflict between the various Jewish groups. We have seen in previous chapters that rivalries within the Jewish community were common. Pharisees contended with Sadducees, the Qumran community near the Dead Sea contended with a subset of priests in Jerusalem, and followers of Jesus also contended with various Jewish groups. These rivalries gave rise to inflated and hostile rhetoric. The question for us is, if Jesus was largely friendly with the popular Pharisees, if he inspired far more people than he scandalized, and if the vast majority of Jews did not participate in the trial and crucifixion of Jesus, why, then, was the author of Matthew so angry at Pharisees and why was the author of John so derogatory toward Pharisees and Judean Jews? The answer is conflict—specifically conflict in the late first century between Jewish followers of Jesus and other subsets of Jews. Maarten Menken, the late New Testament scholar at Tilburg University (the Netherlands), saw the Gospel of John as a product, in part, of a traumatic schism between Jewish Christians and other Jews in the late first century. In other words, the entire narrative of this Gospel was highly influenced by this schism:

> If John's gospel is taken at face value, it easily becomes a stumbling block in Jewish-Christian dialogue: it seems that Jews are here completely rejected. If it is studied somewhat closer, it appears to be Jewish in its ways of thinking: John is very Jewish in his anti-Jewish arguments. The disputes that have to be presupposed behind this gospel appear to be to a large extent discussions between Jews and Jewish Christians who have experienced a traumatic split and are still in conflict.[9]

These ruptured relationships in the late first century seem to be written back into history during the ministry of Jesus. Academics call this an *anachronism*. An anachronism is some person, event, object, or idea in a story that does not belong in the time period of the story's setting but belongs in a later period. A classic example is from William Shakespeare, who used the word *clock* in *Julius Caesar*. The clock is an anachronism because clocks did not

---

9. Menken, "Scriptural Dispute," 460.

exist when Julius Caesar was alive. The conflict and harsh polemic between Jesus and his contemporary Jews found in the Gospels are also anachronistic. But what was the nature of this conflict in the late first century when the Gospels were being written?

This is a difficult question to answer. Numerous volumes have explored the issue of anti-Judaism in the Gospels and its causes. Yes, the Gospels were largely written for Jews or by Jews (or both), but the authors of the Gospels were clearly bitter toward other specific Jewish groups, though not toward Jews as a whole. One theory about the nature of this conflict, at least in relation to the Gospel of John, is that before the author of John wrote his Gospel, he and his Jewish-Christian community had a falling out with, or experienced hostility from, another group of Jewish believers in Jesus. Scholars have pointed to John 8 as possible evidence for this split. In that chapter, the author of John refers to Jews "who had believed in [Jesus]" (8:31) but who apparently later rejected him. We dealt with this section of John in the Pharisee chapter (chapter 7) and concluded that this episode makes little sense as coming from Jesus and that a later scribe probably inserted material into this episode. This section does, however, make more sense if the author of John is responding to the tense situation with his current opponents but is doing so through the lips of Jesus. The author of John might be criticizing a group of Jewish believers in Jesus that previously belonged to the author's community before the split occurred. After they became opponents, the author of John wrote his Gospel and consequently criticized certain Jews with his opponents in mind. This theory certainly fits with what we know about early Christian groups who formed factions and had rivalries with other Christians. It seems that Christianity in the late first century was not unified as a single body of believers but was significantly splintered, breaking off into rival factions. We see this very phenomenon in the writings of Paul.[10]

Another theory about the nature of this late first-century conflict, again in relation to the Gospel of John, is that the author of John is responding to conflict between his community—or even the larger Jewish-Christian population—and some other Jewish group that did not follow Jesus. Several elements in the Gospel of John might support this theory. First, we find encounters between "the disciples of Moses" and the "disciples of Jesus." For example, after Jesus heals a blind man, this blind man is reviled by some Jews for being Jesus' "disciple" and not a "disciple of Moses" like themselves (John 9:28). Elsewhere, Jesus reproves his Jewish opponents, saying "You do not have the love of God in you," and you have "set your hope on Moses," but

---

10. For more discussion and sources on this theory, see Bieringer et al., "Wrestling," 24–25.

you should "believe in me" (John 5:41–46). In the next episode, the author of John seems to downplay Moses again:

> Then Jesus said to them, "Very truly, I tell you, it was not Moses who gave you the *bread from heaven*, but it is my Father who gives you the true bread from heaven . . . for *I have come down from heaven*, not to do my own will, but the will of him who sent me" . . . Then the Jews began to complain about him because he said, "*I am the bread that came down from heaven*." (John 6:32–41; emphasis added)

There seems to be some identity contest in these passages that does not fit any early first-century setting in relation to Jesus' movement. In these passages we see Jesus and his disciples presented in contradistinction to Moses and his disciples (i.e., Jews) rather than Jesus and Moses portrayed as two important members of the same team. In the early first century, Jesus and his followers were likely not seen as outsiders to Judaism, so this material in the Gospel of John is somewhat confusing. This rhetoric does fit, however, within a late first-century setting when Jewish Christianity was becoming increasingly gentile in its population and in its proselytizing focus. James Dunn, emeritus professor of New Testament at the University of Durham, offers this useful explanation:

> The complexity of John's treatment of "the Jews" is best explained by the historical situation confronting the Fourth Evangelist. There is a large-scale consensus that John was writing at around the end of the first century, during the period [after the destruction of the temple in 70 CE] when the rabbinic council . . . began the lengthy process of rebuilding the nation around the Torah and of defining Judaism more carefully in the face of other claimants to the heritage of second Temple Judaism, including Christianity. In these circumstances it is very likely that John's use of "the Jews" (= the Jewish authorities) refers to a local Jewish leadership who identified with the objectives of the [new rabbinic council], or possibly even the [rabbinic council members] themselves. But it is also likely that John's usage reflects the claim beginning to be made at that time by the rabbinic authorities to be the only legitimate heirs to pre-70 Judaism, to be, in fact, "the Jews." At the same time, however, there were other (ethnic) Jews who must have been "caught in the middle," the heirs of the much more diverse forms of late second Temple Judaism caught between the competing claims

of [the rabbinic council] and others . . . including the Believers in Jesus Messiah.[11]

Perhaps because Jewish Christianity had veered from a core set of normative Jewish beliefs and practices in its worship of Jesus and was no longer an exclusively Jewish movement in the late first century CE, the opponents of the author of John and his community expelled Jewish Christians. We suspect this occurred because the author of John refers to "your law" as if he is an outsider to Judaism (8:17, 10:34). We do not know if this community by this point considered themselves outsiders to Judaism; however, it may be the case that they are made outsiders to their opponent's form of Judaism—not by choice but by expulsion.[12] Given this interpretation, the following passages come into focus, none of which fit an early first-century setting but probably provide evidence of this late first-century schism:

> The Jews had already agreed that anyone who confessed Jesus to be the Messiah *would be put out of the synagogue* (John 9:22; emphasis added)

> Nevertheless many, even of the authorities, believed in him. But because of the Pharisees they did not confess it, for fear that they would *be put out of the synagogue* (John 12:42; emphasis added)

> I have said these things to you to keep you from stumbling. *They will put you out of the synagogues.* Indeed, an hour is coming when those who kill you will think that by doing so they are offering worship to God (John 16:2; emphasis added)

The Gospel of Matthew is, along with the Gospel of John, one of the two most Jewish of the four Gospels, and it too seems to be responding to conflicts in the late first century between Jewish Christians and other groups of Jews. The situation to which the author of John seems to be responding is perhaps a similar situation (or even the same situation) to which the author of Matthew is responding.

As an (important) aside, at this point in the chapter some of my prepublication reviewers were becoming hyperfocused on the nuances of these theories about intra-Jewish conflict in relation to authors of Matthew and John. Some of them requested that I explain X and expound on Y. Again, this harks back to my comment in the introduction that we tend to seek certainty. We want all questions answered. Unfortunately, we lack the precise

---

11. Dunn, *Parting of the Ways,* 208.
12. For more on this theory, see Hakola and Reinhartz, "John's Pharisees," 138–40; Bieringer et al., "Wrestling," 25–28.

details needed to answer most specific questions about intra-Jewish conflict in the late first century. The purpose of the last few pages is to show that there was, indeed, conflict between early Christian communities and other Jewish groups. Regardless of which theory about the nature of this conflict is correct, the result is the same: conflict between these Jewish groups influenced how the Gospels were written. The bulk of this chapter is to explain what triggered this conflict in the first place.

In my interpretation of the data, the Pharisees probably played a key role in this overall intra-Jewish conflict involving the Jesus movement. As we have seen in the Pharisee chapter (chapter 7), the author of Matthew was ruthless in his portrayal of Pharisees and at times presented Jesus as an outsider to Pharisaic Judaism. We have argued that Jesus and his first followers probably functioned within a Pharisaic framework, and there seems to be no tension between Jesus' apostles and the various Pharisees that accompany Jesus around Galilee. Yet, about five decades later, the author of Matthew demonizes Pharisees in his Gospel. He makes them the *other* when, for example, he has Jesus contending with them in "their synagogues" (Matt 4:23, 9:35, 10:17, 12:9, 13:54). Our question: what happened, then, between Jesus' death and the destruction of the temple (ca. 30–70 CE) that turned the Jewish Christians and the Pharisees against each other, which in turn shaped how the author of Matthew (and the author of John to a lesser extent) wrote their gospels?

We have suspected that after the destruction of the temple, rabbinic/pharisaic authorities defined Judaism in new ways that necessarily alienated Jewish Christians. But perhaps this conflict started even before that redefinition of Judaism. Let us entertain one plausible explanation for the tension between Jewish Christians and other Jewish groups that originated before the destruction of the temple. This explanation may further help us understand why the Gospels are so hostile in their rhetoric toward Pharisees and other "Jews."

The Jerusalem Council

The chronology of events in Acts and in Paul's letters in the two decades after Jesus' death are presented differently, so we will stay approximate with our dates and not get bogged down with specifics. In the late 30s CE, Paul received a revelation from Jesus specifically to proselyte gentiles (Acts 9:4–6, 15, 22:15; Gal 1:1–2, 16). According to Acts, Peter also received a revelation around this time to take the Gospel to gentiles. Shortly after, Peter met Cornelius and ate with him at his house (Acts 10:11–46). When Peter went back to Jerusalem and recounted his recent experiences to his fellow Jewish Christian leaders, the "circumcised believers criticized him" for going among "uncircumcised men and eating with them" (Acts 11:1–18). These accusers were probably Jesus-believing Pharisees. We suspect this given Pharisees' sensitivity to mealtime customs of eating only with like-minded Jews and also given the information in Acts 15, which we will discuss shortly. This interaction between Peter and his accusers is perhaps the start of the long and tense conflict within the Jesus movement.

We must note that Peter's revelation is important for this discussion because it centered on food and Jewish mealtime culture. While Peter's *food* was being prepared, he "fell into a trance" (Acts 10:10) and saw animals descending from heaven. The Lord told him to kill and eat this unclean food. Peter responded, "By no means, Lord; for I have never eaten anything that is profane or unclean" (Acts 10:13). What does this tell us? It highlights that even though the broader issue was gentile inclusion into the Jesus movement without requiring them to convert to Judaism, the salient concern was over mealtime customs. the precise issue that Jesus repeatedly debated with Pharisees (according to the authors of the Gospels). This account in Acts 10 indicates that before his revelation in the late 30s, Peter was fully in agreement with Pharisaic positions on mealtime customs. We must remember this detail as we proceed.

Over the next decade or so after Peter's revelation, Paul traveled around the northeastern Mediterranean preaching to gentiles and converting many to the Jesus movement. In the late 40s or early 50s, Peter journeyed to Antioch in Syria (about three hundred miles, or four hundred kilometers north of Jerusalem) to meet with followers of Jesus in that region. What transpired while Peter was in Antioch suggests that tensions had worsened concerning this gentile issue since Peter's revelation about a decade earlier. Paul claims in his letter to the Galatians that he had an altercation with Peter in Antioch. Paul was upset because Pharisees, or "certain people" of the Jewish faction from Jerusalem, came to Antioch and preached that Jewish followers of Jesus must separate from gentile followers during meals (Gal 2:12). Apparently these Pharisaic Christians who "came from James [the brother of Jesus]" (Gal 2:12) were viewed as authoritative because Peter, Barnabas, and many other Jews heeded their instruction. Paul accused Peter of capitulating to these Jerusalem leaders only because he (Peter) "feared" these men (Gal 2:12–13). Paul even calls Peter and Barnabas "hypocrites," just as the authors of the Gospels later call Pharisees hypocrites (Gal 2:13).

These details are crucial to understanding this developing schism within the Jesus movement that started with questions over Jewish-gentile table-fellowship. It is here in the chronology of the early Jesus movement where we notice that the church comprised two major factions: the gentile faction led by Paul, and the Jewish faction led by Peter, James, and John (Gal 2:9). Paul acknowledges the existence of these two factions in his letter to the Galatians (Gal 2:7–9). This fact is also crucial in understanding the influences that shaped how the Gospels were written. As we just saw in Galatians 2, and will shortly see in Acts 15, Pharisees seemed to be influential within the Jewish faction of the Jesus movement.

The altercation between Paul and Peter in Antioch necessitated a meeting in Jerusalem. This broader problem had been festering for perhaps at least ten years, and it finally boiled over in Antioch when Paul confronted Peter. The subsequent meeting in Jerusalem has been termed the "Jerusalem Council." The issue of Jewish-gentile relations, specifically table-fellowship, raised broader questions over whether gentile followers of Jesus should be required to convert to Judaism and follow Jewish law. This widespread confusion about gentile converts is understandable. The Jesus movement initially started as a Jewish group, and Jewish law not only prohibited Jews from eating unclean food but also required that Jews make distinctions between the clean and the unclean, between the sacred and the profane (Lev 11). Many Jews, especially Pharisees, did not eat with non-Jews, the reasons for which we explained in the Pharisee chapter (chapter 7). However, now that gentiles were converting to the Jesus movement in larger numbers, questions arose concerning the social relations between Jewish and gentile followers of Jesus. Are gentiles impure? Can Jews and gentiles eat together? If gentiles are impure, should they be required to convert to Judaism and follow Jewish law? The confusion regarding these questions is apparent even in the leadership of the church, as Peter himself seemed unsure how to navigate these difficult waters. At the Jerusalem Council the two major factions of the Jesus movement deliberated over these very questions that were based on the Mosaic law.

The author of Acts explains that because "certain individuals" came from Judea to Antioch and taught, "Unless you are circumcised according to the custom of Moses, you cannot be saved," a great dissension arose (Acts 15:1–2). The word for "dissension" here is *stasis*, which can also mean "riot" or "revolt."[13] We learn a few verses later that these "certain individuals" who went to Antioch were Pharisees (15:5). The "believers who belonged to the sect of the Pharisees stood up [at the council] and said, 'It is necessary for

---

13. Arndt et al., *Greek-English Lexicon*, 764.

them to be circumcised and ordered to keep the law of Moses'" (15:5). The fact that Pharisees presented their case first possibly indicates that they were sizable and influential within the Jesus movement. We would find it strange that Pharisees were given a voice at the council if there were only a handful of them. Moreover, we infer their authoritative status because the only other people to stand and address the entire council were a few leaders of the Jesus movement: Peter, Paul (with Barnabas), and James.

This type of legal debate in Judaism over group identity, including requirements for gentile converts was common.[14] For example, the Tosefta, a second-century-CE rabbinic text, states that a gentile who observes every law in the Torah except even one is "like an apostate Israelite," and the Jewish community "does not accept him."[15] Two rabbis who led Israel during the generation of the Gospels supposedly debated this precise topic:

> With regard to a convert who was circumcised but did not immerse, Rabbi Eliezer says that this is a convert . . . With regard to one who immersed but was not circumcised, Rabbi Yehoshua says that this is a convert . . . And the Rabbis say: Whether he immersed but was not circumcised or whether he was circumcised but did not immerse, he is not a convert until he is circumcised and he immerses.[16]

The debate at the Jerusalem Council over conversion was expected given its Jewish context. The debate was not about whether gentiles should be allowed to join the Jesus movement; rather, the debate was about whether they must convert to Judaism in order to join the Jesus movement, as well as what the conversion procedures entailed. On one end of the spectrum Paul argued that gentile converts must only be required to immerse and that there should be no distinction between gentiles and Jewish followers of Jesus. In the middle of the spectrum James argued that gentile converts do not need circumcision but must be immersed *and* must follow certain key injunctions of Jewish law: abstain from food that has been sacrificed to idols, abstain from eating blood, abstain from eating the meat of strangled animals, and abstain from fornication (Acts 15:20, 29; cf. Lev 17, 18). On the other end of the spectrum Pharisees argued that gentile converts must be circumcised, must be immersed, and must observe the entire law (Acts 15:5; Gal 5:3). This spectrum of observance for gentile converts was not uncommon among early Jews, and so this legal debate in Antioch and Jerusalem is reasonable.

14. See Schiffman, *Who Was a Jew?*, esp. 19–40.
15. Tosefta Demai 2:4–5, in Neusner, *Tosefta*, 84.
16. Babylonian Talmud Yebamot 46a. Translation in *William Davidson Talmud*.

If the author of Acts is correct that a majority of the church officially sided with Paul on the gentile issue, then we can probably identify this very council as a major factor in the origins of a deep conflict between the gentile-inclusive faction (i.e., Pauline Christians) and the Jewish-centric faction (i.e., Pharisaic Christians) of the Jesus movement. Perhaps Peter and James were caught in the middle as Pharisaic-type Christians on the one hand and proponents of Paul's gentile conversion efforts on the other. From what we can gather from the New Testament and early rabbinic writings, the Pharisees were a table-fellowship group! As a reminder from the Pharisee chapter (chapter 7), Jewish scholar Jacob Neusner demonstrated that of the 341 passages in rabbinic literature on Pharisaism, 229 (67 percent) pertain to table-fellowship.[17] If the Pharisaic Christians were forced through this seismic change to welcome gentiles into their sacramental table-fellowship practice, and if the Jesus movement was rapidly morphing into a gentile-inclusive group without requiring gentiles to convert to Judaism, then Pharisaic followers of Jesus would have revolted.

What was once a highly Pharisaic group, and certainly an exclusively Jewish group in the days of Jesus, was now becoming a strange conglomeration of Jews who still follow the law and gentiles who do not follow the law because they are not subject to it (according to the ruling at the Jerusalem Council), with the only common ground between them being their loyalty to Jesus. That Pharisees would be enraged is expected. Their very lifestyle based on their ancient legal tradition was being undercut by Paul and others within the gentile faction of the Jesus movement. Circumcision was the sign of God's covenant with Israel. According to Genesis, God commanded all of Israel to be circumcised, and he also commanded that all male foreigners who wish to enter into the covenant be circumcised, otherwise they "shall be cut off from his people" (Gen 17:9–14; see also Lev 12:3). Even more relevant to the Pharisaic sensibilities of mealtime-fellowship is the injunction in the book of Exodus that any foreigner residing among covenant Israel who desires to participate in Passover and *eat with Israelites must be circumcised* (Exod 12:48). Therefore, gentiles who did not agree to be circumcised would not be included in God's covenant with Israel, according to the Pharisaic interpretation. So what would be the point of converting all these gentiles into the fellowship of Jesus and requiring those already within the covenant to eat with them? This was not a problem in the days of Jesus, because Jesus himself did not seek out gentile converts. However, twenty years later many of his followers were opening the floodgates to gentiles who, in the eyes of Jews, brought with them pagan impurities and a culture

---

17. Neusner, *From Politics to Piety*, 86.

of idol worship. Yes, Jesus charged his apostles to go into every nation and seek converts (Matt 28:19; Acts 10–11, 9:4–6, 15, 22:15; Gal 1:1–2, 16), but he was not clear about the procedure—about whether these converts must become Jews. Perhaps Pharisees interpreted Jesus' commission to mean that converts in every nation must be converted to Judaism, especially given the Jewish elements in the commission: (1) bring in disciples and (2) immerse them (Matt 28:19).

Given this context, we can now understand why this debate would have been frustrating for Jewish followers of Jesus. Moreover, regardless of how Jewish followers felt about the ruling at the Jerusalem Council, it seems that the ruling did not clear up confusion for everyone. In fact, the confusion seemed to get worse. About eight to ten years after the Jerusalem Council, when Paul was again in Jerusalem, James told him that many thousands of Jews who joined the Jesus movement thought that Paul was telling Jewish followers of Jesus "to forsake Moses, and . . . not to circumcise their children or observe the customs" (Acts 21:21). To solve this problem, Paul took the Nazarite vow temporarily, demonstrating to all Jews that he was still a Jew—in fact, he was among the most committed of Jews (Acts 21:22–26; Phil 3:5); thus, his message to not follow Jewish law was not directed at Jews but *only* at gentiles.

The Jerusalem Council was likely the beginning of the *parting of the ways* between Pharisees and the Jesus movement—two groups that had previously functioned within the same framework and enjoyed a somewhat cozy relationship during Jesus' ministry and probably for another ten years afterward. By the time the Gospels were being written, about 20–30 years after the Jerusalem Council, the rift between Pharisees and the church would have been deep and hostile.[18] Since Paul was a proud Pharisee, the Pharisaic followers of Jesus may have viewed Paul as a betrayer to Pharisaism and Judaism, making the rivalry between Pharisees and Pauline Christianity all the more hostile. We must remember that most of the New Testament, and certainly all of the Gospels, had been written *after* the Jerusalem Council, so they must be read and interpreted with that event in mind.

All Roads Lead to Rome

We have now identified and explained the two major factors that influenced how the Gospels were written: (1) Jewish-Roman relations, and (2) Intra-Jewish conflict (i.e., conflict *within* Jewish Christianity as well as conflict *between* Jewish Christians and other Jews). These two factors help explain

---

18. For a similar argument about this schism, see Chilton, "Paul and the Pharisees."

why the Gospel writers portrayed Romans, Pharisees, gentile peasants, and Judean authorities in certain ways. We now explore briefly how these two major factors are manifested in the Gospels.

Romans and Gentiles in the Gospels

Given the context of Jewish-Roman relations in the first century, we understand why the authors of the Gospels were reluctant to criticize Rome. Every good story needs a villain. As Volkan explained in an earlier quotation (chapter 9), every group necessarily identifies allies and enemies especially when the stakes are high. For the writers of the Gospels in the late first century, their allies were the Romans. Why? Well, if you were a Jew and you wanted to write a gospel about Jesus, would you make the Romans the villains of the story? No! Remember that Rome was at war with Jews about a decade before some of the Gospels were written. Thousands of Jews were slaughtered. This would make any Jewish writer—in this case, a Jewish-Christian writer—think twice about blaming Rome for the death of Jesus. Moreover, in 64 CE, Nero Caesar blamed Christians for a large fire that broke out in Rome. This was the first large-scale persecution of Christians by the Roman state. In the wake of the fire, Nero's popularity waned and so he began searching for a scapegoat. He set his sights on the Christians. This seemed like a logical choice since Christians were viewed by some as adherents of a strange and mischievous superstition, according to Tacitus, a member of the Roman senate. Nero ordered Christians to be crucified, torn apart by dogs, or used as torches at night to provide light to the city.[19] A fairly reliable tradition, based on both second-century Christian texts and archaeology, indicates that Paul died in Rome during the Nero persecution.[20] Moreover, Peter and James also died in the 60s, and a few years later the temple was destroyed and many Jews were killed or dragged into slavery.[21]

Not only were the authors of the Gospels and much of their audiences Jewish, but they were also Christian. Thus, in the wake of the war, and considering the absence of their primary first-generation leaders (i.e.,

---

19. Goodman, *Rome and Jerusalem*, 509–10; Lampe, *From Paul to Valentinus*, 82–84.

20. Barrett, "Pauline Controversies," 33–35.

21. The earliest tradition about James's death is in the writings of Josephus (see *Ant.* 20.200) and several early Christians believed that Peter died in the 60s CE in Rome shortly before the Jewish-Roman War. For brief explanation and sources see Powell, *Harpercollins Bible Dictionary*, 784.

Paul, Peter, and James), it follows that the authors of the Gospels would tread very lightly while composing their narratives about Jesus. The Roman authority is the last group of people they would have wanted to present as the villain and killer of their messiah. Had the authors of the Gospels gone scorched-earth on Rome (like the author of Matthew did on the Pharisees), they would have drawn a target on their own backs and threatened their own proselyting efforts.

We must also note that after 70 CE, Christians began distancing themselves from the larger Jewish community.[22] So we can see why Romans and Jews traded places in the Christian story. In the early first century, the Jews were the allies of the Jesus movement and Romans were enemies. By the late first century, Jews were increasingly becoming the enemies and the Romans were increasingly becoming the allies, even if fear was the motivator. Also noteworthy is that the Gospels were in part a type of missionary tract—a text that Christians used to teach both Jews and gentiles about Jesus. Even if the authors of the Gospels had not been fearful of Roman backlash, we would still expect them to soften the image of Rome for their potential gentile converts.

What we have, then, is a situation where the authors of the Gospels were caught between a rock and a hard place. On the one hand, they were trying to appeal to Jews; they accomplished this by culling quotes from the Hebrew Scriptures and by comparing Jesus to biblical figures by way of allusions and typologies. On the other hand, Roman citizens were now potential converts, and the Roman state could not be demonized; for these two reasons, it would not benefit the authors of the Gospels to make Roman authorities the enemy. For additional context, Josephus seemed to have experienced a similar dilemma: he was a Jew who was commissioned by Rome in the late first century *after* the Jewish-Roman War to write a history of the Jewish people. Consequently, Josephus found himself in his various works trying to (1) appeal to gentiles who were interested in the Judean system—law, history, and culture, and (2) defend surviving Jews against widespread postwar animosity. And he had to accomplish all this under the auspices of Rome. These at least are the general conclusions of prominent Josephus scholars Steve Mason and Tessa Rajak.[23] The parallel between Josephus and the authors of the Gospels are not exact, but we get the point. The Gospels were written to Jews (even though they were distancing themselves from the revamped post-war Jewish leadership) and also to gentiles who were

---

22. Goodman, *Rome and Jerusalem*, 366.

23. Mason, "Should Any Wish to Enquire Further," 64–103; Rajak, *Josephus*, esp. 185–222.

interested in the Jewish messiah, Jesus. And, like Josephus, they wrote these texts within a Roman context and had to be careful not to draw negative attention from Rome.

Given this context, we can understand now why Romans and gentiles in general are portrayed favorably in the Gospels despite the fact that the early Jesus movement in the late 20s was a strictly Jewish movement, was not interested in converting gentiles, and had their leader killed violently by Pontius Pilate. Thus, the ruthless monster Pilate (see chapter 8) becomes a nice guy and an ally in the Gospels. Indeed, all four Gospels soften Pilate's image (Matt 27:15–26; Mark 15:6–15; Luke 23:17–25; John 18:39–19:15). It is also intriguing that in the Gospel of John, "the Jews" cry out, "If you release this man, you are no friend of the [Roman] emperor" (John 19:13). The very people who were expected to be the spiritual leaders of the Jewish nation supposedly said, "We have no king but [Caesar]" (John 19:15). In Mark, it is a gentile woman who seeks out Jesus (Mark 7:26). In Matthew, it is the gentile magi who recognize Jesus the "king of the Jews" (Matt 2:11). Also in Matthew, Jesus tells a Roman centurion who believes in him, "Truly I tell you, in *no one in Israel* have I found such faith" (Matt 8:10; emphasis added). In Mark, after Pilate tries to save Jesus, it is a Roman centurion who recognizes that "truly this man was God's Son!" (Mark 15:39). In fact, it is often the case in the Gospel of Mark that demons and gentiles display stronger faith in Jesus' mission than do his own apostles (see, for example, Mark 3:11). We will discuss how the apostles are portrayed in the Gospels shortly.

Especially noteworthy is that in the Gospel of Luke, the Romans are forgiven for killing Jesus—"Father, forgive them; for they do not know what they are doing" (Luke 23:34)—while various subgroups of Jews in each Gospel (including Luke) are blamed for Jesus' death. The message is unmistakable: God will forgive the Romans but will punish Jews. We should mention that some ancient manuscripts of Luke lack Jesus' saying, "Father, forgive them; for they do not know what they are doing."[24] However, even if the author of Luke did not include this statement in his narrative, that a later Christian scribe living in the Roman Empire inserted it illustrates how the Roman context of early Christianity influenced Christian attitudes about Rome after the Jewish-Roman War. If we recall from the discussion in the previous chapter, all of this polemic was a rhetorical contest. Jesus probably did not really forgive the Romans while consigning Jews to hell.

It is intriguing that according to the author of Matthew, Jesus tells his disciples, "I am sending you out like sheep *into the midst of wolves* . . . Beware of them, for they will hand you over to councils and *flog you in their*

---

24. Omanson, *Textual Guide,* 152.

synagogues. And you will be dragged before governors and kings because of me, *as a testimony to them and the Gentiles*" (Matt 10:16–18; emphasis added). Is it any surprise that this episode is found *only* in Matthew? Again, the author of Matthew seems to be responding to the post–Jerusalem Council schism between Pharisees and Jewish-exclusive Christians on the one side and the gentile-inclusive Christians on the other. Jesus had just sent his original apostles to preach only throughout Israel. These Jewish "wolves" ("Pharisees" in Matthew's mind?) would flog them in the synagogues. They would be "dragged before governors and kings . . . as a testimony to the Gentiles." By the time the author of Matthew wrote this, these events had already occurred: the core of the church had distanced itself from Pharisees as well as the Jewish-exclusive faction of the Jesus movement; several leaders, including Paul, had been killed, but not by Pharisees; and the church had become increasingly focused on proselyting to gentiles. We would be quite confused had Jesus actually said this in the 20s; however, such language and details fit perfectly in the late 70s or early 80s when the author of Matthew was writing his Gospel.

Can we see now how the two major factors—(1) relations between Jews and Romans and (2) relations between Jewish Christians and other Jews—influenced the Gospels' portrayal of gentiles? Jewish-Roman relations that culminated in the destruction of the temple in 70 CE seem to be a major factor in the generous way Romans are treated in the Gospels. Likewise, the Jesus movement in the late first century had become increasingly interested in converting gentiles, especially given the debate at the Jerusalem Council, which is another reason why gentiles are treated kindly in the Gospels.

Pharisees in the Gospels

We have talked a great deal about Pharisees thus far, so we will not rehash here how they are portrayed in the Gospels. However, we do want to make sure we understand how the two major factors impacted the Gospels' portrayal of Pharisees. If our general assessment is correct that (1) the earliest followers of Jesus were Pharisaic-minded Jews and that many Pharisees followed Jesus, (2) that Pharisees were a table-fellowship group who wanted to preserve the purity and identity of covenant Israel, and (3) that the parting of the ways between Pharisees and the Jesus movement started in the 40s and 50s when the church ruled that gentile converts did not need to follow Jewish law and that there must be "no distinction between them and us" (Acts 15:9), then Matthew's hostile portrayal of Pharisees makes perfect sense.

Although the authors of the Synoptic Gospels were either Jews or writing to Jews (or both), they all seem to have supported the gentile mission of the church (see Matt 28:19; Mark 16:15; Luke 24:47). The hostile rhetoric toward Pharisees indicates that they were responding to the lingering issue that began in the late 40s and was debated at the Jerusalem Council. If the Pharisaic faction of the Jesus movement was arguing in the mid-to-late first century that Jews must not eat with gentiles because of impurities (Gal 2) while the gentile-inclusive faction was arguing for a unified church with no mealtime separation, then the mealtime episodes in the Gospels seem to be responding to this very debate. Remember from the Pharisee chapter (chapter 7) that every accusation from Pharisees of Jesus entertaining sinners and outsiders is in the context of table-fellowship.[25] Jesus and Pharisees in the Gospels discuss on several occasions whether outsiders should be included in the mealtime-fellowship. Pharisees always argue that outsiders should not eat with those within covenant Israel and Jesus always argues that they should be included to some extent. The nuances of these mealtime debates between Jesus and Pharisees may not be entirely historical because we see little to no evidence of a falling out between Jesus and Pharisees. It is likely that Jesus and Pharisees did discuss this general issue, but given that they seemed to have a strong relationship, it is hard to imagine that Jesus was as dogmatic on this issue as was Paul two decades later; it was not until that time that Pharisees start to become uneasy about the direction of the Jesus movement. The particulars of the debate and the mealtime settings in the Gospels were probably responses to the current, mid-to-late first-century disagreement between Pharisees and Pauline Christians.

The table-fellowship issue is addressed not only in the Pharisee mealtime episodes in the Gospels of Mark and Matthew but also in other non-Pharisee episodes. For instance, a gentile woman approaches Jesus and says, "Have mercy on me, Lord, Son of David." Jesus initially ignores her and then says, "I was sent only to the lost sheep of the house of Israel." The woman further begs for help and Jesus says, "It is not fair to take the children's food and throw it to the dogs." After she answers, "Yes, Lord, yet even the dogs eat the crumbs that fall from their masters' table," Jesus says, "Woman, great is your faith! Let it be done for you as you wish" (Matt 15:21–28; cf. Mark 7:24–30).

It is difficult to see this story as historical because of its literary structure and because of Jesus' repeated admonition throughout the Gospels to love and care for the downtrodden. Again, it is probably a late first-century response to the gentile debate within the church. Note the two key elements

---

25. See Matt 9:10–13, 11:19; Mark 2:15–17; Luke 5:30–32, 7:34, 15:1–2.

in the story that pertain to both the table-fellowship debate and the broader issue of gentile inclusion for those of great faith: (1) the interaction between Jesus and the believing gentile woman and (2) the food and mealtime motif of the interaction. The message of this episode is that Jesus compromised a bit and ministered to this gentile. We can almost hear the author of Matthew saying to the Pharisees through this story, "Look, even if the early church (as represented through Jesus in this story) was not sent to gentiles, Jesus ultimately showed mercy to those who recognized him as the Jewish messiah (i.e., 'Son of David') and welcomed them, at least in part, to the table."

We must remember that Pauline Christianity, or rather the gentile-inclusive faction of the Jesus movement, was victorious over the Jewish-exclusive faction of the Jesus movement. And as we know from human experience, history is written by the victors, or in this case, those who survived to tell the story. Thus, the authors of the Gospels, although writing to both Jews and gentiles were proponents of the gentile-inclusive mission of the church in the late first century. The conflicts between Peter and Paul in Antioch and the ruling of the Jerusalem Council in the 50s influenced how and why the Pharisees were demonized in the Gospels in the 70s and 80s. Many Pharisees were once part of the Jesus movement but later became disaffected, and the subsequent rivalry turned extremely bitter. Moreover, even the numerous Pharisees who never were followers of Jesus would have developed animosity toward the Jesus movement in the late first century because of the church's gentile-inclusive policy. I cannot help but wish that we had a Gospel written by the Pharisaic, Jewish-exclusive faction of the Jesus movement. How would their gospel about Jesus have treated the other side—the gentile-inclusive faction?

The other factor, Jewish-Roman relations, also influenced how the Pharisees are treated in the Gospels. Since Pharisees seem to have been the rivals of the Jesus movement in the late first century, and since the Gospels' authors were trying not to upset the Romans, especially after the Nero persecutions and the Jewish-Roman War, we understand why some of the Gospels (especially Matthew) portray Pharisees as hypocrites, or "play-actors." As explained previously, play-acting was viewed as perhaps the most unscrupulous and sleazy of any profession in the Roman Empire. The Roman author Cicero explained that because the Roman citizenry "considered the dramatic art and the theatre in general disgraceful, they desired that all persons connected with such things should not only be deprived of the privileges of other citizens, but should even be removed from their tribes by sentence of the censors."[26] Here Cicero refers to the earlier Roman precedent

---

26. Cicero, *De Republica* 4.10, trans. Keyes, 239.

of prohibiting actors from becoming Roman citizens. So not only is the author of Matthew buttering up the Romans by treating them generously in his Gospel, but he also seems to be consciously trying to sabotage Israel's post–70 leaders—Pharisees and rabbis—in the eyes of the Romans. The author of Matthew might even be suggesting through his rhetoric that Rome should persecute Pharisees and deny them privileges common to other non-citizens, or even revoke citizenship to those Pharisees who are Roman citizens.

Original Apostles in the Gospels

Since we have explained the Greco-Roman context of competition rhetoric and how this convention influenced the way in which authors of the Gospels portrayed their opponents (chapter 9), and since we have explained why the authors of the Gospels had opponents in the first place (current chapter), we should take a moment to discuss why the authors of Mark and Matthew criticize Jesus' original apostles, especially Peter. Many readers might catch on that the apostles are portrayed as a bit hard-headed, but the extent of hostility toward them seems to escape most nonacademic readers of the New Testament, but it is, indeed, present in the text. Why were the authors of Mark and Matthew so critical of Jesus' original apostles?

We might be able to identify a few reasons, given what we have already discussed in this chapter. We assume that the authors of Mark and Matthew were partial to the gentile-inclusive faction and the overall pro-gentile policy of the church. We assume this because gentiles are treated favorably in these Gospels, while both the apostles and the Pharisees are treated as faithless, bumbling idiots at best and murderous hypocrites at worst.

First, the original apostles seem to have been Pharisaic Jews. We assume this for all the reasons presented in the Pharisee chapter (chapter 7). Even if Peter, James, and the other original apostles were not technically "Pharisees," they seem to have been Pharisaic-type Jews according to their practices, beliefs, and interactions with Pharisees. If Pharisees—both Christian Pharisees and non–Christian Pharisees—had become bitter opponents of the gentile-inclusive Christian church after the Jerusalem Council, then we can see why many Christians in the late first century might have viewed the original Pharisaic apostles with contempt. This first reason is not a strong case by itself but must be considered alongside the reasons presented in the following paragraphs.

Second, the authors of Mark and Matthew were critical of the original apostles because these apostles were leaders of the Jewish faction of the Jesus movement and seemed to favor a Jewish-exclusive policy over a more robust gentile-inclusive policy, thus contributing to the animosity of later gentile-oriented Christians toward the original apostles. In fact, only in the Gospel of Matthew does Jesus instruct his disciples to, "Go nowhere among the Gentiles . . . but go rather to the lost sheep of the house of Israel" (Matt 10:5–6). In the few cases where Jesus does minister to gentiles, Jesus' apostles shun them. For example, when a gentile woman approaches Jesus—particularly a gentile *who recognized Jesus as a Jewish messiah*—the apostles say, "Send her away" (Matt 15:23). After Jesus' ministry, the original apostles (particularly Peter, James, and John) continued to preach only to the Jews.

After Jesus' death, this Jewish-exclusive agenda among the apostles, and especially Peter, continued. Yes, Peter received a revelation to take the gospel message to gentiles according to the author of Acts, but Paul makes him look weak and wishy-washy on this matter (Gal 2:11–14), suggesting that Peter was shunning gentiles because he "feared" other members of his Jewish-exclusive faction (Gal 2:12). Paul acknowledges that there were, indeed, two factions: "I had been entrusted with the gospel for the uncircumcised, just as Peter had been entrusted with the gospel for the circumcised" (Gal 2:7). Notice, however, that Paul suggests that the leaders of the Jewish faction—specifically Peter, James, and John—were reluctant to take the gospel to gentiles, but only "agreed" *after* "they recognized the grace that had been given to [Paul]" by God (Gal 2:9). Only then did Peter, James, and John "agree that we should go to the Gentiles" (Gal 2:9). The implication here, at least according to Paul, is that the leaders of the Jesus movement may never have agreed to proselyte gentiles had it not been for the manifestation of God's grace. Moreover, it was even *after* this agreement when Paul confronted Peter in Antioch and called him a hypocrite for refusing to eat with gentiles (Gal 2:13).

At this point, we might ask, "We have argued in the previous few paragraphs that the original apostles and leaders of the Jewish-exclusive faction were not in full support of the gentile policy. How can that be the case considering that Jesus tells the apostles to 'Go therefore and make disciples of all nations, baptizing them in the name of the Father and of the Son and of the Holy Spirit'" (Matt 28:19)? We have a few possibilities for interpretation:

(1) The Great Commission (Matt 28:19), as it is called, might not be historical to Jesus, but an insertion by the author of Matthew. The wording alone makes it suspect because the phrase, "Father and of the Son and of the Holy Spirit," is used widely in later Christianity, but not among Jews in the early first century. Such a phrase might have been confusing to the original apostles. Moreover, this commission is not found in Mark or John.

Mark 16:15 does say "Go into all the world and proclaim the good news to the whole creation," but it is commonly known that the last twelve verses of Mark (16:9–20) are not in the original manuscripts.[27] If Jesus really did change course and charge his apostles to take the Gospel message to all the world, meaning gentiles—which would have been a watershed event in the history of early Christianity—then why is this charge not contained in the Gospels of Mark or John? Further, if this Great Commission is historical, then it seems strange that we have little to no evidence in the New Testament that any of the original apostles undertook a proselyting journey in a gentile nation; the original apostles stayed primarily in Jerusalem and the immediate region even after Peter's revelation. Some might respond and say, "Well, maybe the apostles did not personally go on these gentile missions, but they sent Paul and others." Notice, however, that Paul claims to have received his proselyting charge from Jesus himself and that Peter, James, and John were not initially in agreement.

(2) Even if the Great Commission was a literal charge from Jesus, it might not have been clear to the apostles what he meant. When he said, "Make disciples of all nations," did they understand him to mean that they should go into all nations and bring Jews into the Jesus movement as they already had been doing in Judea and Galilee? Or, did they interpret him as saying that they should convert gentiles to the Jesus movement and that these gentiles must convert to Judaism in order to be members of the body of Christ? Confusion among the apostles is apparent given the debates and contention for the next two decades, culminating in the Jerusalem Council.

(3) The third reason why the authors of Mark and Matthew were so critical of Jesus' original apostles is because a rivalry had developed between the gentile-inclusive faction (led by Paul) and the Jewish-exclusive faction (led by Peter, James, and John) before the Jerusalem Council and was exacerbated after the Jerusalem Council. This rivalry was perpetuated for three or four decades, into the 70s and 80s when the Gospels were being written. So not only did the gentile-inclusive Christian faction have an intense rivalry with the Jewish-exclusive faction, but they also had a tense rivalry with the Pharisees, some of whom belonged to the Jesus movement (Acts 15:5). Michael Goulder, the late New Testament scholar at the University of Birmingham, explained this rivalry as follows:

> From as far back as we can trace it (to the 40s) there never was a single, united church. There were (in fact from the 30s) two missions: one run from Jerusalem, with Peter and the sons of Zebedee in charge, and later James, Jesus' brother, and other

---

27. Omanson, *Textual Guide,* 103–5.

members of his family; the other run by Paul, from various centers. The two missions were agreed about the supreme significance of Jesus, but they disagreed about almost everything else—the validity of the Bible, whether the kingdom of God had arrived or not, sex, money, work, tongues, visions, healings, Jesus' divinity, and the resurrection of the dead, for example. The New Testament gives the impression of a united, developing body of belief because it is a selection of writings; naturally it was selected by the winning mission, that is the Paulines, and that is why it consists of the Epistles of Paul (and his followers), and four Gospels, two of them ultra-Pauline and two building bridges to the Jerusalem [church].[28]

I tend to agree with Goulder that there were two major factions within the Jesus movement as we have discussed here; however, it is more likely, given our knowledge of competing groups in early Judaism and Christianity,[29] that there were numerous subfactions within each of these two major factions. Perhaps the best example is the Pharisaic Christian faction within the Jewish-exclusive mission led by Peter. In any case, the rivalry between these two Christian factions is apparent in the writings of Paul.[30]

Even before the Jerusalem Council, Paul seemed frustrated with the Jerusalem leaders. In his letter to the Galatians, Paul responds to Jewish-Christian leaders who came from Jerusalem and taught the believers in Galatia. Paul was upset about their teaching. He is adamant in his letter that he was not sent by humans, that his gospel is not of human origin, that he did not go up to Jerusalem (Gal 1:1–17), and that the leaders of the church in Jerusalem "contributed nothing to me" (Gal 2:6). When he finally did go to Jerusalem after three years, he stayed only for fifteen days and visited just a few apostles, and "did not see any other apostles" (Gal 1:18–22). He seems concerned that his gentile audience will disapprove of him mingling with the Jewish-exclusive faction in Jerusalem because he writes, "In what I am writing to you, before God, I do not lie!" (Gal 1:20). He then writes that fourteen years had passed since he went to Jerusalem a second time, and he traveled there only to represent the gentiles. Why is Paul so sensitive about his relationship with the Christian leaders in Jerusalem? It seems that Paul really wants his audience to know that he had very limited contact with them, perhaps because his gentile audience was already dissatisfied with the Jewish-exclusive party of the Jesus movement.

28. Goulder, *St. Paul versus St. Peter*, ix–x.

29. See Boyarin, *Border Lines*; Royalty, *Origin of Heresy*.

30. In addition to the examples presented in the next paragraph see several more in Goulder, *St. Paul versus St. Peter*, 24–98.

We know about Paul's rebuke of Peter at Antioch where he calls him a hypocrite, but in the same letter to the Galatians, Paul refers to some of the Jerusalem leaders as *so-called* leaders: those "who were supposed to be acknowledged leaders" (Gal 2:6). He labeled them "people pleasers" (Gal 1:10) and hoped they would, in their zeal of circumcision, accidently "castrate themselves" (Gal 5:12). Elsewhere, Paul calls his opponents "dogs" and "evil workers" who "mutilate the flesh" (Phil 3:2), an obvious reference to circumcision. He is angered that they have tried to "hinder us from speaking to the Gentiles so that they may be saved" (1 Thess 2:16). Paul may not have been referring to Peter, James, and John specifically with these pejoratives, but he certainly is referring to the Jewish-exclusive faction based in Jerusalem where James, the brother of Jesus, was the recognized leader.[31] Paul's letter to the Corinthians provides more evidence of these two competing parties within the Jesus movement. Paul addresses divisions within the church and mentions Peter's faction specifically: "For it has been reported to me . . . that there are quarrels among you, my brothers and sisters. What I mean is that each of you says, 'I belong to Paul' or 'I belong to Cephas [who is Peter]'" (1 Cor. 1:12–16).

It seems clear why gentile-inclusive Christians—including the authors of Mark and Matthew—would view the original apostles with some hostility. We should be careful not to overstate Peter's and James's opposition to the gentile mission. It seems clear that they did finally side with Paul but later gentile-inclusive Christians may not have been convinced that Peter and James were as authentic in their support of the gentile mission as the book of Acts seems to claim. The more time passed after Paul's conversion in the late 30s, the more hostility festered between these two factions. The result is that the Pauline Christians in the 70s and 80s took out their frustrations on the original apostles (the first leaders of the Jewish faction of the church), making them the boogeymen of the first-generation Christians.

This distaste toward the apostles, particularly Peter, is clearly manifested in the Gospels of Mark and Matthew. For example, the apostles show a lack of faith during a storm and Jesus says in Mark, "Have you still no faith?" (Mark 4:40) and in Matthew, "You of little faith" (Matt 8:26). Later, when Jesus walks on water, the apostles do not recognize him and their "hearts were hardened" (Mark 6:48–49, 52; cf. Matt 14:26). The apostles do not understand Jesus' parable and Jesus seems surprised and frustrated by their ignorance: "Are you still without understanding?" (Matt 15:16; cf. Mark 7:17–18). In the next chapter, the disciples again misunderstand Jesus and

---

31. For more on the identity of Paul's rivals, see DeSilva, *Letter to the Galatians*, 7–16.

he says, "You of little faith . . . Do you still not perceive? . . . How could you fail to perceive?" (Matt 16:8–11). In Mark, Jesus is even more pronounced in his disappointment: "Do you still not perceive or understand? Are your hearts hardened? Do you have eyes, and fail to see? Do you have ears, and fail to hear? And do you not remember? You of little faith . . . Do you still not perceive? . . . How could you fail to perceive? Do you not yet understand?" (Mark 8:17–21). In the next chapter a man approaches Jesus' disciples and ask them to heal his son, but they could not. Jesus then calls them "faithless" and asks "how much longer must I be among you?" (Mark 9:18–19). The author of Matthew ramps up the criticism when he adds to the episode in Mark: "You faithless and perverse generation, how much longer must I be with you? How much longer must I put up with you?" Jesus also scolds them for not having faith even as the size of a tiny mustard seed (Matt 17:16–20).

As we proceed through these two gospels, we notice that Jesus becomes increasingly frustrated with his disciples. In the next chapter, Jesus' criticisms of them are damning. When people brought "little children" to Jesus, his disciples "spoke sternly to them." Jesus became "indignant" and rebuked them (Mark 10:13–16). Matthew's account of this episode is much harsher. Jesus tells his disciples that children are the greatest in heaven. He then says, "Unless *you change* and become like children, you will never enter the kingdom of heaven . . . If any of you put a stumbling-block before one of these little ones who believe in me, it would be better for you if a great millstone were fastened around your neck and you were drowned in the depth of the sea" (Matt 18:3; emphasis added). But, alas, in the very next chapter when little children are brought to Jesus, his disciples chastise those who brought the children (Matt 19:13–14). The author of Matthew is subtly making the case to his gentile-inclusive readers that it would be better if these original disciples had never been born! Jesus warns them that "Unless you change . . . you will never enter the kingdom of heaven," but there is no hint in this Gospel that they did change. In fact, they get worse.

An intriguing phenomenon in the Gospels of Matthew and Mark is that the criticisms of Peter are significantly more hostile than the criticisms of the disciples in general. The portrayal of Peter in the Gospel of Matthew is so bloody that Robert Gundry, professor of New Testament for forty years at Westmont College, argued that Peter is a *false disciple* in the view of the author of Matthew.[32] Before Peter is put through the meat grinder in the latter half of this Gospel, the author of Matthew describes Peter in a parable:

> A sower went out to sow. And as he sowed, some seeds fell on the path, and the birds came and ate them up. Other seeds fell

---

32. Gundry, *Peter*.

on rocky ground, where they did not have much soil, and they sprang up quickly, since they had no depth of soil. But when the sun rose, they were scorched; and since they had no root, they withered away . . . Hear then the parable of the sower. When anyone hears the word of the kingdom and does not understand it, the evil one comes and snatches away what is sown in the heart; this is what was sown on the path. As for what was sown on rocky ground, this is the one who hears the word and immediately receives it with joy; yet such a person has no root, but endures only for a while, and when trouble or persecution arises on account of the word, that person immediately falls away. (Matt 13:3–6, 18–21; cf. Mark 4:3–19)

How do we know that this parable describes Peter? Because the seeds falling on rocky ground in this parable mirrors Peter's behavior precisely, just as Jesus' explanation makes clear. Peter often becomes enthusiastic at first ("sprang up quickly" in the parable), but because he has no roots he just as quickly withers away at the first sign of adversity. We will see this pattern with Peter as we explore what the Gospels say about him. Another clue that this parable describes Peter is the use of "rocky ground." Remember that Peter's name means "rock." Moreover, the verb *skandalizo* in the parable ("immediately falls away") is the same verb used later when Jesus tells the disciples that they would "become deserters" (*skandalizo*). Peter responded, "Even though all become deserters, I will not" (Mark 14:29; Matt 26:31–35), yet he does just that. Further, the noun form of this word is *skandalon* meaning "stumbling block," which is precisely what Jesus calls Peter later in the Gospel of Matthew: "But he turned and said to Peter . . . You are a stumbling-block [*skandalon*] to me" (Matt 16:23).

We all remember the story about Peter attempting to walk on water (Matt 14:22–33; Mark 6:45–52; John 6:16–21). In Mark, Peter has no role in this episode. However, in Matthew, Peter is made to look like a faithless fool. Note that *after* Jesus says, "it is I, do not be afraid," Peter responded, "*If* it is you . . . ," thus illustrating Peter's unbelief. Peter then exits the boat and walks on water for a moment but begins to fear right after Jesus tells him not to be afraid. This story harks back to the Parable of the Sower where the seed springs up quickly but withers just as fast. Jesus is forced to save Peter before saying, "You of little faith, why did you doubt?" Then to make it worse, the author of Matthew excludes Peter from those in the boat who exclaim, "Truly you are the Son of God" (Matt 14:22–33).

A few chapters later, Jesus asks his disciples, "Who do people say that the Son of Man is?" (Matt 16:13). Peter answers, "You are the Messiah, the Son of the living God" (Matt 16:16). This episode appears to save the image of Peter, especially since Jesus seems to subsequently state that Peter will be the foundation of the church; however, this "foundation" statement of Jesus is only contained in the Gospel of Matthew, so it is probably hostile to Peter. Instead of quoting Jesus as saying, "You are Peter, and on *you* I will build my church," the author of Matthew quotes Jesus as saying, "You are Peter, and on this rock I will build my church, and the gates of Hades will not prevail against it" (Matt 16:18). Here, Jesus shifts from "you" to "this rock." This is a crucial distinction because elsewhere in the Gospel of Matthew, Jesus identifies his own teachings (i.e., "these words") as the "rock" of his church, not Peter (7:24–26). If fact, the author of Matthew might be suggesting that if Peter were the rock, then the gates of hell would overpower the church, but since the "rock" is Jesus and his words, hell will not prevail against it.

We should also note that scholars are increasingly migrating to the conclusion that verses 18 and 19 are not original to Jesus. Even many Catholic scholars are convinced that this verse is an insertion by later Christians, which is significant since the Catholic Church has traditionally viewed Peter as the foundation of the church (i.e., the "first pope"). Ulrich Luz (professor emeritus at the University of Bern in Switzerland), has listed the reasons for this position. First, "my church" is not the language of Jesus, but has widespread usage in the late first century and second century. It appears just a few times *only* in the Gospel of Matthew (Matt 18:15–21). Second, "the gates of Hades" in verse 18 is a later Greek formulation, as opposed to an Aramaic formulation. Third, the designation of apostles as "rocks" of the tradition surfaces long after the death of the apostles.[33]

To make it worse for Peter, Jesus then tells his apostles that he must go to Jerusalem and suffer at the hands of the chief priests, and just as in the parable of the sower, Peter quickly turns from a person of faith to a person with no faith or understanding. He rebukes Jesus and tries to correct him. Jesus then calls Peter "Satan" and a *skandalon*, or "stumbling block" (Matt 16:22–23; Mark 8:31–33). Here, Jesus is consigning Peter to hell. How do we know this? Because every other occurrence of the word *skandalon* in the Gospel of Matthew refers to those who will be in hell (Matt 13:41–42; 18:7–9). Further, two chapters later, Jesus says, "Woe to the world because of stumbling-blocks" (*skandalon*) referring back to Peter in Matthew 16. Jesus continues, "It would be better for you if a great millstone were fastened around your neck and you were drowned in the depth of the sea" (Matt 18:6–7).

When Jesus prays in Gethsemane he tells Peter, James, and John (the future leaders of the Jewish-exclusive faction of the church) to stay awake,

---

33. Luz, *Matthew 8–20*, 356–60.

but they fall asleep three times. Jesus is grieved and says specifically to Peter, "So, could you not stay awake with me one hour?" (Matt 26:36–46; Mark 14:32–42). That same night Peter denies Jesus three times even though he said he would not. Again, the author of Matthew is relentless in his criticism of Peter. For example, Peter denies Jesus with an oath (Matt 26:72–74). Why is this denial by oath a problem? Because earlier in the Gospel of Matthew, Jesus prohibited his disciples from oath-taking, lest they "never enter the kingdom of heaven" (Matt 5:20, 33–37). Thus, by taking an oath while denying Jesus, Peter is ruling himself out of the kingdom of heaven. Moreover, while Peter is outside denying Jesus by oath, Jesus is inside refusing to take oath at the request of the high priest (Matt 26:63). These few subtle details heighten Peter's condemnation. In Matthew, Peter "went out and wept bitterly" after denying Jesus the third time (Matt 26:75). Each of the six occurrences of "weeping" earlier in the Gospel of Matthew refers to the weeping of the damned after the final judgment (Matt 8:12, 13:42, 13:50, 22:13, 24:51, 25:30), and three of these six occurrences associate weeping with being cast "outside" into darkness (Matt 8:12, 22:13, 25:30). The connection to Peter, then, is clear. Peter's weeping outside situates him among those who will be eternally damned.[34]

Again, can we see now how the two major factors—Jewish-Roman relations and intra-Jewish relations—influenced the Gospels' portrayal not only of gentiles and Pharisees but also of the original apostles? First, the authors of Mark and Matthew were partial to the gentile-inclusive faction of the church. Second, a hostile rivalry had developed within the church between the gentile-inclusive faction (led by Paul) and the Jewish-exclusive faction (led by Peter). Third, the original apostles—particularly Peter, James, and John—were thought to have been Pharisaic-type Jews who were antagonists to the early gentile mission. Given these three phenomena, it seems clear why the authors of Mark and Matthew would have disdain for the original apostles and why they would portray them so negatively. In fact, this anti-Peter sentiment was perpetuated in several early Christian communities in the second and third centuries, including those who wrote the Gospel of Thomas, Acts of Thomas, and Apocryphon of James. To be sure, some early Christian groups favored Peter and their texts have survived: Acts of Peter and the Twelve Apostles, Epistle of Peter to Philip, and Apocalypse of Peter.

At this point, some of us, particularly those of us who are Christians, might be jarred by the portrayal of the apostles and of Peter in Mark and Matthew. We might ask ourselves with some anxiousness, "Why should we

---

34. For these and many other examples, and for a larger discussion on Peter in the Gospel of Matthew, see Gundry, *Peter*; see also Goulder, *St. Paul versus St. Peter*, 18–23.

even venerate Peter if he was so bad? Does not this undermine the very authority of the early apostles? How can the early apostles be redeemed given their portrayal in Mark and Matthew?" We must note that the authors of Luke-Acts and John are not nearly as critical of Peter or the apostles. It seems that they attempt in their gospels to soften the image of the apostles where the other authors are hostile. As a reminder from the introduction of this volume, the author of Luke probably used Mark and Matthew when writing his Gospel.[35] Not only does he know Mark and Matthew, but he disapproves of some of their material. How do we know this? Because in Luke 1, the author of Luke tells Theophilus—the person most likely sponsoring the writing project—that while others have already attempted to write an orderly account of Jesus, he will write it again "so that you may know the truth" (Luke 1:1–4). The implication here is that the author of Luke believed that some of the material in these earlier gospels was false or perhaps greatly overstated.

In the Gospel of Matthew, Jesus rebukes the apostles during a storm and declares that they have no faith, but in Luke there is no rebuke (Matt 8:26; Luke 8:22–25). When Jesus walks on water in Mark the disciples' "hearts were hardened," but in John the disciples eagerly welcome him into the boat (John 6:21). In Matthew, Jesus saves Peter from drowning and says, "You of little faith" (Matt 14:31), but neither Luke nor John contains this story. In Mark and Matthew, Jesus is frustrated because of the disciples' lack of understanding (Matt 15:16, 16:8–11; Mark 7:17–18, 8:17–21), but the author of Luke omits these rebukes. Jesus calls Peter "Satan" in Mark and Matthew (Matt 16:21–23; Mark 8:31–33), but the author of Luke changes this episode by deleting Jesus' attack on Peter (Luke 9:22) and portraying him in a positive light. Unlike in Mark and Matthew, in Luke, Jesus does not say about the disciples, "It would be better for you if a great millstone were fastened around your neck and you were drowned in the depth of the sea" (Matt 18:6–7; Mark 9:42). All the apostles "forsook [Jesus] and fled" in Gethsemane in Mark and Matthew (Matt 26:56; Mark 14:50), but they do not in Luke and John (Luke 22:47–53; John 18:2–12). Luke removes all suggestions from Mark and Matthew that the apostles were not faithful to Jesus to the very end. In Mark and Matthew the apostles repeatedly fall asleep in Gethsemane, which causes Jesus to sorrow (Matt 26:36–46; Mark 14:32–42); while the apostles do fall asleep in Luke, the author of Luke adds that they fell asleep only "because of grief" (Luke 22:45).

---

35. For a discussion on this complex issue, see Goodacre, *Case Against Q*; Porter and Dyer, *Synoptic Problem*, 27–165.

So how can Christians venerate the apostles despite their actions and motives in the Gospels of Mark and Matthew? First, read the Gospel of Luke. Second, remember our discussion in the introduction about what the Gospels are? They do not claim to be detailed and accurate histories of Jesus' life. They do not attempt to engage in character development, which creates difficulty for us in identifying the motives of each character. The motives and actions of Jesus and the original apostles are subject to the prejudices and biases of the authors of the Gospels, all of whom probably never knew Jesus and the original apostles.

Takeaways

We started our exploration into Jesus' relationship with his Jewish peers in chapter 6. We have seen by now that there is significantly more to the story. The authors of the Gospels were not exempt from biases. They were not exempt from engaging in polemic against their opponents. They were apologists with a vengeance. As we examined the evidence we saw just how difficult it is to accept—hook, line, and sinker—that Judas betrayed Jesus, that Pharisees were Jesus' enemies, that "the Jews" rejected Jesus wholesale, that Pilate was a good-natured fella, that Peter is destined for hell, or that the original apostles were a bunch of faithless fools.

We can now understand not only *that* the authors of the Gospels used inflated rhetoric toward their opponents, a common element of Greco-Roman literature, but also plausible reasons why they did so. The Gospels must be understood within in the context of relations between Jews and Romans, relations between Jewish Christians and other Jews, and competition rhetoric in the Greco-Roman world. However, we should not overstate our conclusion and assume that the apostles are always portrayed negatively. The authors of the Gospels were constrained by the historical facts that Peter was Jesus' lead apostle; therefore, they had to acknowledge that fact in some of the traditions about Jesus, particularly the more well-known traditions.

As we have seen, the author of Matthew is relentless in his subtle (and sometime not so subtle) dismantling of Peter's character, faith, and legacy. The author of Luke on the other hand, does not demean the apostles and Peter. The author of John is also very reverential toward the apostles. Thus, Christians need not question the authority, character, and legacy of Peter and the apostles just because the authors of Mark and Matthew are turned off by them. We must also note that we cannot be completely confident that our conclusions in this chapter are exactly the way events played out in the first century in relation to Jewish-Roman and intra-Jewish relations. We cannot be so arrogant to think that we have figured out all the answers, but we must also be intellectually honest. We cannot shy away from this discussion of rhetoric to "save the Gospels" from being humanized. The texts say what they say and we are left to work it out. The best method for working out these difficult issues in the Gospels is to try to identify the authors' original intent based on the text instead of imposing our own biases onto the authors of the Gospels.

It is challenging for many Christians who hold the New Testament as Scripture to acknowledge that this collection of books contains some bias in its presentation of historical events and that its various authors often unfairly slandered their opponents. I have found that most people in my community, including my students, as well as most Christian students I have taught outside my own community, are completely unaware of the bias, the exaggerated rhetoric, and the anti-Judaism present in the Gospels. The well-known New Testament scholar James Charlesworth noticed a similar phenomenon at Princeton: "Two colleagues offered a course [on anti-Judaism in the Gospels] here at Princeton Theological Seminary in the fall of 1999. They were astounded by the ignorance and then the horror of the theological students when they confronted the anti-Jewish problems within the translations of the New Testament."[36] It seems shocking to most Christians that the human beings who wrote these texts are, indeed, human and had biases of their own. Charlesworth himself cautioned that while devotion to the New Testament is good, "it must not camouflage the fact that some passages in the New Testament are problematic and seem anti-Jewish." Many of us have privileged these texts to such a high degree that we tend to be incapable of recognizing the human elements contained within them.

---

36. Charlesworth, "Gospel of John," 479.

Chapter Eleven

Judaism and Jesus
Concluding Thoughts and Considerations

THE PRIMARY OBJECTIVES OF this book were at least fivefold: (1) to increase readers' knowledge-base about the context of the Gospels-Acts, (2) to help Christian readers more critically understand the nature of the Gospels-Acts, (3) to help foster appreciation and understanding for Jesus as a Jewish holy man according to many of his peers, (4) to help foster appreciation and understanding for Jesus as fully entrenched within a Jewish worldview (and not as one trying to denigrate and destroy Judaism), and (5) to help rescue the reputation of "the Jews" whom Christians have misrepresented, demonized, and murdered all based on atrocious scholarship and poor logic. As with objectives and desired outcomes of a university course, it is my hope that we have made significant progress toward these five primary objectives.

When I teach university courses, I periodically ask my students, "So what? What are the implications of this material? What do we learn about the nature of Scripture from the information in this book? What did we learn about the authors of the Gospels? What have you learned about yourself while engaging these issues?" In this book, we have had a series of lectures and discussions, so to speak. We have been introduced to many new ideas and have worked through many issues, some more complex than others. Here, we step back and discuss some of the broader implications and attempt to tie up loose ends where we are able. We will do this through a series of questions and answers, similar to how I engage with students at certain points throughout the semester. Some of the following questions are mine to the reader, some are questions that students have asked me in the past, and some are questions that I anticipate readers might ask after reading this book. As I do with my students, I encourage readers to not be so concerned with finding the right answer, but to wrestle with a range of plausible interpretations and to develop some level of comfort with ambiguity.

Throughout this book we have contextualized Jesus' Jewishness by drawing on literature from three major time periods: Hebrew Scriptures/Israelite literature (ca. 1000 BCE–300 BCE), Second Temple literature (ca. 300 BCE–200 CE), and rabbinic literature (ca. 200 CE–600 CE).

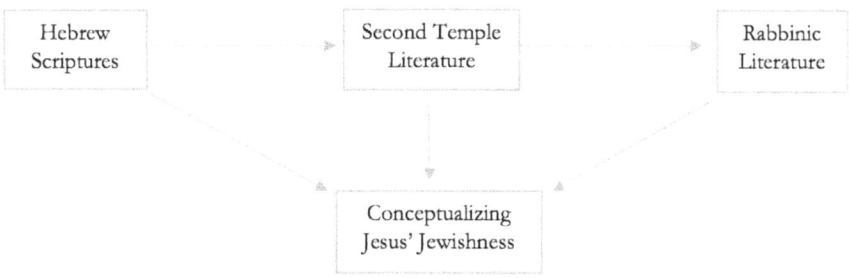

It seems fairly straightforward on how the first two bodies of literature can help us situate Jesus in his Jewish context. These texts were all written before or during the era of Jesus. But what do we learn about the relationship between the body of Jesus-traditions (preserved in the Gospels) and the body of rabbinic-traditions (preserved in rabbinic literature)?

The material in this book illustrates that many of the Jesus-traditions are strikingly similar to the traditions of other sages and Jewish holy men. How do we make sense of these similarities? Are they coincidences? Do they draw from the same well of Jewish cultural traditions? Did Jesus' stories influence the composition of later rabbinic stories, or did these rabbinic stories predate Jesus and then influence the authors of the Gospels?

One possibility is that the Jesus-traditions and the similar rabbinic traditions may have developed in relation to each other. For example, if Jesus and Rabbi Hanina ben Dosa really were close in function, time, and space—both were Galilean miracle workers in the first century CE as we explored in chapter 3—then the traditions about them may have bled into one another in subsequent generations. We saw many cases throughout this book where this is plausible; the following is a quick example not mentioned in an earlier chapter: while Rabbi Hanina's neighbor was building a house, he cut the beams too short to reach the walls. Hanina prayed and miraculously stretched the beams to the appropriate size.[1] Similarly, in the Infancy Gospel of Thomas (mid-second century CE), Jesus' father Joseph accidentally cuts a beam too short. Jesus then stretches the beam to the correct size.[2] Neither of these traditions date to the first century CE—they are later legends. The point, however, is that several of the same traditions are attributed to two different first-century Galilean Jewish holy men, which is not surprising. I should briefly mention that synagogues and churches were often built next to each other in antiquity. Indeed, Christians often attended synagogue services, even as late as the fourth and fifth centuries![3] This would pave the way for Christians being influenced by some rabbinic traditions and for Jews being influenced by certain Jesus-traditions; therefore, it is expected that the Jesus-traditions could easily become political and theological footballs among Jews and Christians as these two religions developed in direct relation to one another.

Another possible conclusion is that the Jesus-traditions preceded the rabbinic traditions, and that the rabbis appropriated and adapted the Jesus-traditions to counter Christian influences. During the fourth and fifth centuries, when the Christian population expanded significantly throughout the Roman Empire, the rabbis were producing their massive corpus, the Talmud (see Introduction). In the face of the proliferation of the Jesus-traditions the rabbis may have adopted these Jesus-traditions and attributed them to their own sages who lived in the Galilee. We can imagine the rabbis telling Christians through the Talmud, "No, it was not your Galilean miracle worker Jesus who did X or who said Y, but it was our Rabbi Hillel who did X and it was our Galilean miracle worker Rabbi Hanina ben Dosa who said Y." This conclusion is not a stretch because we know that the rabbis knew about Jesus; his name appears multiple times in the Talmud, and often in unsavory contexts.[4] In the Tosefta, a second-century rabbinic text (see Introduction), Rabbi Eleazar ben Dama was bitten by a snake. Another sage attempted to heal him in the name of Jesus of Nazareth. Rabbi Ishmael stepped in and said to Eleazar, "You are not permitted to accept healing from [Jesus]."[5] We learn from this, and numerous other examples in rabbinic literature, that (1) the rabbis knew about Jesus and (2) by the second century, some rabbis were already seeing Jesus (and Christianity) as an opponent.

1. Babylonian Talmud Taanit 25a.
2. Infancy Gospel of Thomas 13:1–3.
3. Charlesworth, "Christians and Jews," 321–22.
4. Schäfer, *Jesus in the Talmud*.
5. Tosefta Hullin 2:22–24, trans. Neusner, *Tosefta*, 1380–81.

A careful examination of rabbinic literature suggests that the rabbis attempted to do just that—to counter the Jesus-traditions by appropriating them or spinning off of them. Peter Schäfer (scholar of early Judaism who retired from Princeton University) demonstrated the reality of this very phenomenon. One of the best examples is a story of the birth of the messiah in the Jerusalem Talmud (see Introduction). In Jewish literature at the time of Jesus and before, there is little to no discussion about the messiah's mother or about the possibility that the messiah son of David will be slain. However, during the centuries after Jesus, when Christianity had become the most popular religion in the Roman Empire, the rabbis began circulating stories to counter the theological claims of Christianity, including a story about a baby messiah and his mother. This story seems to be parody against the Gospel tradition of Mary and her baby Jesus:[6]

> In my view of this [rabbinic] story is a complete and ironical inversion of the New Testament—the lowing cow versus the star; the Arab versus the angel of the Lord and/or the magi; the Jewish peddler versus the magi; diapers versus gold, frankincense, and myrrh; and the murderous mother versus the murderous king . . . It is a counternarrative, a parodistic inversion of the New Testament, of the Christian claim that this child Jesus, born in Bethlehem, the city of David, was indeed the Messiah. As such, it is of *great* theological significance. For it undermines the essence of the Christian message by arguing that no, this child Jesus is not the Messiah, at least not the Messiah who you Christians say lived among us on earth.[7]

Schäfer's explanation about this particular rabbinic story is relevant to the wider issue of the rabbis both knowing many of the Jesus-traditions and appropriating them to counter Christian claims. Another example of how this played out: in the first centuries of the Common Era, local traditions flourished throughout the Galilee about Jesus and his family. Curiously, during these centuries, a specific set of traditions also began to flourish among the rabbis and among local Jews in the Galilee about three biblical figures. Note that the rabbis were headquartered in the Galilee in Tiberias in these centuries. At first, the emphasis of these three figures seems random until we realize what is happening. These figures were Joseph the patriarch, Miriam (Moses's sister), and Joshua. They obviously share names with and

---

6. Schäfer, *Jewish Jesus*, 214–35.
7. Schäfer, *Jewish Jesus*, 231.

correspond to another set of revered figures: Joseph, Mary (Miriam in Hebrew), and Jesus (Joshua in Hebrew).[8]

Here is a brief explanation of this set of rabbinic traditions. According to the Hebrew Scriptures, Joshua was buried in the hill country of Ephraim (at Timnath Serah), but a later tradition (post-Jesus) placed his burial in the Arbel Valley, on the west side of the Sea of Galilee close to Jesus' headquarters at Capernaum. The folklore of Joshua's burial in this location contains similarities with the burial of the other Joshua (Jesus). Just after Joshua died, a quake shook the earth and an angel stood at his tomb. Likewise, according to the Gospel of Matthew, the earth shook when Jesus was in the tomb and an angel subsequently guarded it (28:2–3).[9] As with Joshua, Joseph the patriarch was buried in the territory of Ephraim as per the Hebrew Bible, but later tradition placed his tomb in lower Galilee between Sepphoris and Kana, where the other Joseph, Jesus' father, lived (Sepphoris was only three miles from Nazareth).[10] Finally, local tradition placed Miriam's well within the Sea of Galilee. The well magically accompanied the children of Israel into the land of Canaan and settled in the lake. Supposedly a leper was healed after spotting the well while bathing.[11]

It appears that these traditions of the biblical Joseph, Miriam, and Joshua were an outgrowth of attempts to counter the Christian traditions of the other Joseph, Miriam, and Joshua (Jesus). Elchanan Reiner (professor of Jewish history at Tel Aviv University) explains that these traditions flourished in late antiquity but faded in the Middle Ages as the powerful Christian empire tightened its grip on the region.[12] Given this context, it is not surprising to find numerous sayings and miracles in rabbinic literature of Galilean local heroes that are strikingly similar to Jesus. The Jesus-traditions were well-circulated among the rabbis in the second through sixth centuries and the rabbis seem to have repurposed some of these Jesus-traditions for their own local heroes, Rabbi Hanina ben Dosa being the most similar to Jesus (see chapter 3). This is how we might explain the many striking similarities between Jesus and some of the rabbis that are peppered throughout this book.

The more nuanced point is that Jesus is quintessentially Jewish in word and deed, as we have seen throughout this book. Thus, whether (1) the Jesus-traditions and the rabbinic traditions developed simultaneously and

8. Reiner, "From Joshua through Jesus," 94–105.
9. Reiner, "From Joshua through Jesus," 97–98.
10. Reiner, "From Joshua through Jesus," 95–96.
11. Reiner, "From Joshua through Jesus," 96.
12. Reiner, "From Joshua through Jesus," 98.

in relation to each other as Judaism and Christianity began to part ways, (2) the rabbinic traditions predated Jesus and influenced the Gospels' presentation of Jesus, or (3) the Jesus-traditions predate the rabbinic traditions and thus influenced how the rabbis presented some of their own traditions, the conclusion is the same: the Jesus-traditions were not so radical and hostile to Judaism. Jesus did not reject Judaism and the rabbis were accepting of most of Jesus' ideas; thus, Jesus cannot be divorced from his Jewish world. *The Jesus-traditions are Jewish traditions.*

In order to think through this issue a bit more, we circle back to the shamanic complex model, introduced in chapter 2. A few scholars have used this framework to study Jesus because it seems to be the best model for organizing the data regarding his nature as a multifunctional figure. Shamans function in multiple and disparate roles. A shaman is—at the same time—the community's healer, mystic, social worker, priest, seer, prophet, sage, historian, and teacher.[13] Pieter Craffert (chair of the Department of New Testament at the University of South Africa in Pretoria) identified three major biblical figures that best fit the shamanic model: Moses, Elisha, and Jesus, the very figures under exploration in chapter 2. Similarly, Lester Grabbe (professor emeritus of Hebrew Bible and Early Judaism at the University of Hull in England) found the shamanic model best to analyze several Israelite prophets, especially Elisha.[14] Jesus' shamanistic-style ministry led biblical scholar Scott D. Hill to view Jesus as a "local hero," just like Elijah and Elisha.[15] Local heroes are known for being extraordinary figures in a particular limited geographic region. Their deeds and teachings are perpetuated (both orally and in literature) for generations by the locals. Jesus himself invokes the names of local heroes in his teachings to maximize impact. For instance, Jesus mentions Jonah during the following exchange:

> When the crowds were increasing, he began to say, "This generation is an evil generation; it asks for a sign, but no sign will be given to it except the sign of Jonah. For just as Jonah became a sign to the people of Nineveh, so the Son of Man will be to this generation . . . The people of Nineveh will rise up at the judgment with this generation and condemn it, because they repented at the proclamation of Jonah, and see, something greater than Jonah is here!" (Luke 11:29–32)

Not only does Jesus mention Jonah but he compares himself to Jonah. Jesus invokes Jonah because he was a local hero—a prophet from Gath-Hepher, a

13. Craffert, "Shamanism and the Shamanic Complex," 152–53.
14. Grabbe, "Shaman, Preacher, or Spirit Medium," 117–32.
15. Hill, "Local Hero in Palestine," 37–74.

town only five miles from Nazareth (2 Kgs 14:25). If Jesus was in the region, he may have pointed toward Gath-Hepher while invoking Jonah's name.

Prominent figures in the region were often associated with local heroes who had lived long in the past. As Hill explained, "After death, heroes may in fact increase in ability to protect people and goods . . . and to bless their followers. Often living men are viewed as *incarnations or representatives of a known local hero.*"[16] This explanation is congruous with Jesus' experience. It is why some viewed him as a representative or incarnation of Elijah, Elisha, or John the Baptist, all of whom were local heroes in the Galilee:

> Who do people say that the Son of Man is?" And they said, "Some say John the Baptist, but others Elijah. (Matt 16:13–16)

> Now Herod the ruler heard about all that had taken place, and he was perplexed, because it was said by some that John had been raised from the dead, by some that Elijah had appeared. (Luke 9:7–8)

In the early rabbinic period (first through the fourth centuries CE), Galilean Jews would have added Jesus to the list of Galilean local heroes and preserved his traditions orally and in writing, as in the cases of the Gospels. Indeed, Jesus may have become a revered sage among the rabbis and his deeds and sayings might have been preserved in the Talmud had it not been for the growth of a new world religion, Christianity. Jesus eventually transcended the local hero status after the expansion of Christianity. Several of the rabbis mentioned in this book can also be considered local heroes. They are venerated in the areas in which they lived and ministered. Their tombs pepper the Galilee to this day, and many local residents and some pilgrims frequent them throughout the year for various reasons. We must keep this "local hero" model in mind when we read the Gospels because it helps explain the development of the body of Jesus-traditions that circulated for several decades until they were folded into the Gospel accounts in the late first century.

We have learned that the authors of the Gospels were highly informed about the Hebrew Scriptures and they reference them often in their Gospels. What role does Hebrew Scripture play in the Gospels?

The relationship between the Gospels and the Hebrew Scriptures is an important issue. Some early Christian writers in late antiquity did not like the Old Testament; they maintained that the New Testament was vastly superior to the Old Testament. Marcion (a mid-second-century Christian

---

16. Hill, "Local Hero in Palestine," 43; emphasis added.

in Rome), for example, hated the Old Testament and believed that the God of the Old Testament was evil. He posited that the God of the Old Testament was not the God of Jesus, and that the God of Jesus sent the Christ into the world to save humanity from the wrath of the evil Jewish God. Marcion was one of the first to form a "New Testament," or a Christian Bible. His Bible contained no Old Testament and his collection of books that we might view as a proto-"New Testament" contained only eleven books: ten of Paul's letters and the Gospel of Luke. Marcion not only left the Old Testament out of his Bible, but he edited out of his eleven books any conspicuous references to the Old Testament and favorable passages about Jewish law.[17]

The idea throughout Christendom (Middle Ages through the twentieth century) that the authors of the Gospels privileged the Hebrew Scriptures and drew heavily from it and that the Hebrew Bible was beloved Scripture to Jesus would have run counter to what Christians had been taught. The late Sean Freyne (professor of theology at Trinity College in Ireland), noticed that even Christian authors in the twentieth century who wrote about the Jewishness of Jesus were hesitant to see the salience of the Hebrew Scriptures for Jesus: "In most studies of Jesus' Jewish background there would appear to be a reluctance to envisage the idea that he himself . . . might have been influenced by the Jewish Scriptures."[18]

We saw numerous examples in almost every chapter of this book of just how much the authors of the Gospels relied on the Hebrew Scriptures to make their points. They quoted from it repeatedly, they compared Jesus to biblical figures, and they weaved motifs from the Hebrew Bible into their Gospels. The fantastic reference work, *Commentary on the New Testament Use of the Old Testament* (edited by two University of Cambridge alumni, Greg Beale and Donald Carson) is over 1,200 pages! The New Testament does not just contain a smattering of quotations, or even a few hundred references to the Hebrew Bible. No, there are thousands of references (both subtle and conspicuous) to the Jewish Scriptures in the New Testament. Thus, the Hebrew Scriptures play a massive role in the New Testament, and the more familiar one is with the Hebrew Scriptures, the better equipped one will be to understand the New Testament.

Material from the Hebrew Scriptures is manifested in the Gospels in various ways: allusions, quotations, paraphrases, and typologies. We have encountered all of these in this book. *Allusions* are indirect references to a person, place, or event. The themes of a particular episode in the Gospels, for example, might be intended to help the reader make a connection between

---

17. For more on Marcion and related context, see Ehrman, *Misquoting Jesus*, 17–44.
18. Freyne, *Jesus,* 19.

the story they just read and something contained in the Hebrew Bible without explicitly referring to it. A *quotation* is just that, a verbatim rendering of a passage from the Hebrew Bible. A *paraphrase* is a scriptural citation with minimal correspondence with the original quote. A paraphrase might have some additional words, for example, but a careful reader is expected to make the connection. *Typology*, from *typos*, literally means "impression" or "image." It essentially connotes a model or example. For instance, we learned that the Gospels, particularly Matthew, presents Moses and David as a type, or model, for Jesus—Jesus being the "antitype of," or one who is corresponded to, Moses and David. Typology should not be confused with allegory or symbolism.[19]

Aren't all these allusions and typologies in the Gospels really just fulfillments of Old Testament prophecies manifested in different ways?

Christians are often taught in Sunday school that the Hebrew Bible and the Mosaic law point to Jesus in totality; thus, any figure, idea, or passage in the Hebrew Bible that seems to speak of Jesus or that parallels Jesus' experience must have been a divinely orchestrated foreshadowing or foretelling of Jesus. It is not an exaggeration to say that certain fundamentalist Christians can find Jesus on every page of the Hebrew Scriptures. Many Christian readers look for "types and shadows" of Jesus in the Hebrew Bible. When they find some person or symbol that seems to resemble Jesus, according to their own theological beliefs, they attach divine design to that person or object. We have encountered many parallels and types in this book. Ahithophel conspired against David and then committed suicide; similarly, Judas conspired against Jesus and then committed suicide. Pharaoh became paranoid and ordered the murder of all Hebrew infants; similarly, Herod became paranoid and ordered the murder of all children under two years of age. Elisha raised a woman's son from the dead on the southern slope of Mount Moreh at Shunem; similarly, Jesus raised a woman's son from the dead on the northern slope of Mount Moreh at Nain. Joseph, David, and Jesus were all shepherds who started their ministries (so to speak) at age thirty. Joseph was sold into slavery by Judah; similarly, Jesus was sold to temple priests by Judah ("Judas" in Greek).

Are these examples "fulfillments of prophecy"? No. There is no prophecy being given in these examples, so Jesus could not have been their prophetic fulfillment. They are types. We must know the difference between those cases where the authors of the Gospels really do think that Jesus is

---

19. For discussion on these definitions in relation to how the New Testament authors utilized material from the Hebrew Bible, see Porter, "Further Comments," 98–110; Hays, *Echoes of Scripture*.

fulfilling an Old Testament prophecy and where the authors of the Gospels are simply infusing a particular Jesus-tradition with language from the Hebrew Scriptures to maximize impact for their readers. The reason why some stories in the Bible are emphasized repeatedly, generation after generation, while other stories are rarely discussed, is because some stories are better types for the human experience than other stories.

For example, why has the David and Bathsheba story gained much more traction for Jews and Christians than the Judah and Tamar story? Both are highly scandalous. It is because the Judah and Tamar story is not typical. How many experiences have you heard where a father's two sons are killed by God for not procreating with their deceased brother's wife, not to mention that the woman then pretends to be a prostitute to become impregnated by her deceased husband's father? Only on Jerry Springer would one hear such a story similar to Judah and Tamar. However, most of us can relate to David and Bathsheba because adultery and sexual crime cover-ups are common in our society. This helps us understand why the authors of the Gospels utilized some ideas and stories in the Hebrew Bible while ignoring others—because some are naturally better types for the human experience, and, therefore, are potentially more impactful for the reader. This does not mean that all these types in the Hebrew Bible were fulfillments of prophecy or were predetermined to point to Jesus, for example.

The problem with attributing all the parallels and types to divine design is that we might be inappropriately attributing actions and motives to God. Yes, there might be parallels, and yes, a particular person in the Hebrew Bible might be a type for Jesus—meaning that they had similar experiences, and therefore, might be presented in relation to each other—but that person or symbol might also resemble Saint Peter's life, George Washington's life, Martin Luther King Jr.'s life, your life, or my life, thus serving as a type. But this does not mean that you or I are literal divinely orchestrated fulfillments of these types. They might simply be parallels, and that is it. David Baker (Bible professor at the University of Sheffield) reiterates this issue as follows:

> Typology in Church history and today has frequently been taken to be a fanciful kind of biblical interpretation . . . Sometimes the word "typology" has been used for what is really symbolism or allegory but the most common failing is to find correspondences in trivial details. There is no historical or theological correspondence between Rahab's scarlet cord and the death of Christ, nor between the axe Elisha retrieved from the river and the cross. There is consistency in God's created order which makes it possible for there to be red and wooden objects in both Old and

New Testaments; but that does not mean that these things have any typical or exemplary importance for the Christian![20]

How do we interpret those cases where it seems that the authors of the Gospels were forcing the Hebrew Bible onto Jesus' story? In other words, are all these Jesus-Hebrew Bible parallels mentioned in this book historically reliable, or did the authors of the Gospels take liberties with some of the Jesus-traditions?

I have been asked this question by many students. Again, as human beings we want absolute clarity and truth. Are the Gospels photographs and tape recordings, so to speak, or are they Hollywood-type portrayals of the highlights of Jesus' ministry—conveying the author's understanding while taking liberties with the story to maximize effect?

We tend to get a little nervous at the possibility that the authors of the Gospels might have played with the texts a bit to maximize impact. On one end of the spectrum, some scholars have argued that the authors of the Gospels fabricated almost everything. They took the basic historical core of Jesus' ministry and wrote their Gospels with the Hebrew Scriptures sitting open in front of them, so to speak. They wrote their Gospels *so that* Jesus would be viewed as fulfilling prophecy, even if he really did not. This was termed by a prominent Christian scholar John Dominic Crossan (New Testament scholar and former Catholic priest) as *prophecy historicized*.[21] We might also call this *historicized drama*. In other words, the authors of the Gospels turned a fictitious drama into history; they took a collection of prophecies and types from the Hebrew Scriptures and created a story *around* those prophecies and types. Thus, the Jesus-traditions are not arrows that really did hit all the prophetic bullseyes, but rather they are bullseyes that were painted around the already-shot, prophetic arrows. That is one end of the spectrum.

At the other end of the spectrum is the view that God orchestrated everything. Nothing is a coincidence. Certain actions and sayings of Old Testament prophets were predetermined by God precisely to prefigure Jesus. The Bible is 100 percent historically accurate and theologically pure. All of Jesus' deeds and sayings are literal fulfillments of prophecies; they are indeed arrows that hit perfectly every single prophetic bullseye.

Any other position places the Gospels somewhere in the middle of this spectrum, and it is the responsibility of each Christian, based on careful study, to decide where on the spectrum they are most comfortable. Are the Gospels 90 percent fictitious and 10 percent historically accurate,

---

20. Baker, "Typology," 153–54.

21. For Crossan's position and other related positions see Goodacre, "Prophecy Historicized," 37–51.

or 10 percent fictitious and 90 percent historically accurate? This is precisely what scholars of the historical Jesus have been trying to determine for over 150 years. Mark Goodacre (prominent New Testament scholar at Duke University) replaces Crossan's term, *prophecy historicized,* with the term *tradition scripturalized.*[22] We might also call this "dramatized history." His argument is that much of the material in the Gospels really is largely based on historical facts but that the authors of the Gospels scripturalized the Jesus-traditions—hence the term, *tradition scripturalized.* The Gospels' authors presented Jesus' deeds and sayings through the language of the Old Testament. They took the historical events and dramatized them.

Here are some examples. We have already mentioned above the parallels between Jesus and David, between Jesus and Elisha, and between Judas and Ahithophel. Another example is Jesus' arrest in Gethsemane. Instead of just reporting that Jesus' disciples forsook him and fled (Mark 14:50; Matt 26:56), the authors of Mark and Matthew invoked a passage from the book of Zechariah: "Awake, O sword, against my shepherd . . . Strike the shepherd, that the sheep may be scattered" (13:7; cf. Mark 14:27; Matt 26:31). A proponent of *prophecy historicized* might conclude that the conflict in Gethsemane between Jesus and the soldiers is mostly fiction. The only reason why the authors of Mark and Matthew claimed that soldiers drew a sword on Jesus just before his disciples fled is because they wanted to invoke the passage in Zechariah 13:7. A proponent of *tradition scripturalized* might conclude that soldiers really did draw a sword on Jesus and that his disciples really did forsake him, and that the authors of Mark and Matthew saw an opportunity to maximize the impact of the story by invoking Zechariah 13:7.

Rather than simply explaining that Jesus was naked at his crucifixion like other criminals, the Gospels' authors conveyed the story through the language of Scripture: "They divided his clothes among themselves by casting lots" (Matt 27:35; Luke 23:34; John 19:24). These words are a direct quotation from Psalm 22:18: "They divide my clothes among themselves, and for my clothing they cast lots." Is this story *prophecy historicized* or *tradition scripturalized*?

We see the same phenomenon in the cross episode. It is unlikely that the authors of the Gospels knew exactly what Jesus said on the cross because (1) the Gospels were written 40–70 years after Jesus' death based on oral tradition, (2) the Gospels differ on what Jesus said, and (3) the original apostles were not present and the women who were present stood at a distance, according to all three Synoptic Gospels (Matt 27:55; Mark 15:40;

22. Goodacre, "Prophecy Historicized," 37–51.

Luke 23:49). Thus, rather than just reporting that Jesus cried out in agony (which is probably the only detail they knew), the author of Luke adds that Jesus, "crying with a loud voice, said, 'Father, into your hands I commend my spirit'" (Luke 23:46). The author of John writes that Jesus said, "It is finished" (John 19:30). They did not scripturalize the tradition, but they did put words into Jesus' mouth to fill out the story. Notice, however, that the authors of Mark and Matthew did scripturalize the tradition. Instead of stating that Jesus simply cried out in pain, they claimed that he specifically said, "'Eloi, Eloi, lama sabachthani?' which means, 'My God, my God, why have you forsaken me?'" (Mark 15:34; Matt 27:46). This is a direct quotation from Psalm 22:1: "My God, my God, why have you forsaken me? Why are you so far from helping me, from the words of my groaning?" We have seen countless other examples throughout this book of the authors of the Gospels filling out Jesus' story by utilizing the Hebrew Scriptures.

While reading the Gospels we must keep in mind that the authors of the Gospels knew the Hebrew Bible well and probably did, at times, compose some episodes with certain Hebrew Bible passages in mind so that these episodes would resonate more with the reader. In other words, there are Hebrew Bible-inspired embellishments in the Gospels. At other times, certain episodes that really are highly historical were presented in the Gospels with language that would help the reader recall beloved figures or passages from the Hebrew Scriptures. We gather from Paul's letters that Paul did not seem to care about the particulars of Jesus' life. He was not concerned with relating Jesus' parables and sermons. Why? Would not Paul have wanted to bolster his arguments and sermons with examples from Jesus' ministry? In fact, if we wrote down everything Paul said specifically about Jesus' deeds or sayings, all we would need is a 3 x 5 index card. Paul may have never heard most of Jesus' traditions. This seems plausible since Paul spent limited time with the original apostles. If he had heard about the Jesus-traditions, he might not have believed them to be genuine to Jesus, or he did not view them as important enough to repeat them. Instead, he seems to have viewed Jesus' atoning sacrifice as most central to Jesus' mission. Only later did Christians want a fuller story of Jesus the man. So they had to compile the oral traditions about him and then use elements from Hebrew Scripture to fill in the gaps. Thus, both *prophecy historicized and tradition scripturalized* are present in all four Gospels.

These three questions about the role of the Hebrew Bible in the Gospels bring us to a few important broader points. First, the Hebrew Scriptures was important to the writers of the Gospels; it was their Scripture. And since they added their own Jewish flavor to the Gospels based on elements in the Hebrew Scriptures, we can learn a lot about how the Jesus traditions can be situated in their early Jewish contexts by becoming more familiar with the Hebrew Bible. Second, the Hebrew Scriptures were important to the authors of the Gospels, and they were deeply important for Jesus as well. And if they were important for Jesus, should not they also be important to us? Most Christians tend to read Jesus back into Old Testament prophecies and stories and then conclude that "the Old Testament points to and testifies of Jesus." Yes, certainly this could be the case in some of those prophecies and stories, but could it not also be the case that the reverse is true: that Jesus and the authors of the Gospels pointed to and testified of the Old Testament? In other words, the fact that there are similarities between some of the Jesus stories and Old Testament stories does not necessarily suggest that the Old Testament points to Jesus but that perhaps Jesus and the authors of the Gospels point their readers to the Old Testament as a legitimate, helpful, authoritative, and sacred text.

If it is assumed that the Gospels are "ancient biography" and that they do contain elements of both "prophecy historicized" and "tradition scripturalized," then where does revelation come into play with these texts? At what point can they no longer be considered divine texts? Are these human texts or are they divinely revealed texts?

This is a great question and one that everyone must wrestle with. Some Christians believe that "the New Testament" as "a book" has been given to humanity by God himself in the precise wording of his desire. The problem, however, is that the individual authors never make this claim, at least not for the entirety of the New Testament. What might be the response of the author of the Gospel of Matthew, for example, if we traveled back in time and informed him that, "For 2,000 years since your death, billions of people have preserved your Gospel and have used it in their worship services. Some have viewed it as an infallible text. In fact, some have maintained that if God revealed himself to humanity in the form of a book, then that form would be in your Gospel (or the Bible as a whole). In other words, your text is God in book form!" And if we then asked him the following question, what might be his response? "In your view, is the book that you just finished writing akin to the books of Genesis, Psalms, or Jeremiah? Did you write down verbatim exactly what God told you to write, and is this book intended to be one of the greatest revealed texts ever dictated from God himself?" He might look at us strangely and say, "Uhhh . . . no. I just wrote the story of Jesus in a way that I felt would make the most impact for my community and to appeal to potential converts." If we asked Paul the same question, might not he say, "Well, thank you for the compliment, but I was really just writing letters [albeit, important letters] to groups of Jesus-followers in Galatia and

Corinth, among other places. Are you really telling me that these epistles were preserved for thousands of years and that people in numerous nations believed that every nuance in my epistles are absolute divine fact—as authoritative as Isaiah?! Wow, that's quite surprising!"

I mention this hypothetical discussion between us and some of the authors of the New Testament because it illustrates that we might be placing the Gospels on a higher authoritative pedestal than the authors of the Gospels themselves placed them. While most Christians from late antiquity to the present have viewed the New Testament as more authoritative than the Old Testament, the authors of the Gospels seem to have viewed the Old Testament as more authoritative than their own Gospels. This is why they appeal to the Old Testament as the ultimate authority. There is little evidence that the authors of the Synoptic Gospels, for example, viewed their own writings as texts that would replace the Old Testament, or even stand alongside the Old Testament texts. The authors of these three Gospels did not claim to have written a revelation from God (as did Isaiah or Amos), nor did they claim to have been prophets who received authority from God to write their texts (as did Ezekiel).

Maarten Menken, the late New Testament scholar at Tilburg University (the Netherlands) also wondered about the authoritative status of the original New Testament texts according to those who wrote them:

> Paul certainly claims authority for the gospel he preaches (see, e.g. Rom 1:16–17; Gal 1:6–12) and for himself as an apostle (see, e.g., Rom 1:1–7; 1 Cor 4:14–21), but he does not consider his letters as deserving the respect due to Holy Scripture, whereas in Christian tradition, they have achieved precisely the status of Holy Scripture. The late Dutch biblical scholar L. Grollenberg once suggested that if Paul had known the canonical status his letters would acquire, he would not have written them, or, more probably, he would have written them but he would have added at the end the order to destroy them after reading.[23]

Not only did the authors of the Gospels view the Old Testament as more authoritative than their own Gospels, the authors of some of the Gospels viewed the other Gospels as inferior to their own. How do we know this? Because, as we have seen in every chapter of this book, the author of Matthew changed some of the Jesus-traditions presented in the Gospel of Mark, which means that he did not believe the Gospel of Mark was equal to the books of the Hebrew Bible. Some scholars have argued that the author of

---

23. Menken, *Studies in John's Gospel and Epistles*, 73. For the Grollenberg quote, see Grollenberg, *Paul*, 8.

Luke used both Mark and Matthew to write his Gospel. If that is the case, then he too did not view these Gospels as authoritative Scripture because he himself claims that his Gospel is more accurate than these previously written Gospels (Luke 1:1–4).

If this is true, then how divine are the Gospels? What kind of revelation are they? We already discussed in the introduction that these texts are *ancient biography*, and that they do not claim to be 100 percent historical retellings of Jesus' life. The question of how authoritative the Gospels are in terms of their level of divinity is a question that we cannot answer with certainty. How could we? We do not even know who wrote these texts, let alone if God dictated the Gospels directly to them.

I do not broach this issue of the Gospels' sacred status to demean them. I mention all this to emphasize that "Scripture" means different things to different people. I am simply trying to make room for Christians who see the Gospels as simply retellings of key Jesus-traditions but who do not believe that they are divinity in book form or that they are infallible texts infused with the grand mystical hidden codes of heaven. Could it be that parts of the New Testament are not as divine or inspired as other parts? Could it be that not all Scripture is created equal and that we are dealing with a very human collection of books written by people who were attempting to explain, the best they knew how, their understanding of God's dealings with humanity? Is it possible that the Gospels are *human explanations* of revelatory and inspirational experiences, rather than *the* revelations and inspirations themselves? Is it not possible that the reason why the Gospels are considered "Scripture" today is (1) because of their influence on the history of Christianity and Western civilization, and (2) because they preserve traditions about Jesus, and that is it? In other words, could we still call these books "Scripture" even if God had no direct hand in their production?

Perhaps many divine truths in the Gospels have come from the divine to humanity through the human consciousness unscathed; however, alongside these truths come corrupted material, feeble articulations, and faulty explanations. This will always be the case when humans are involved. The portrayals of Pharisees in the New Testament, for example, are perhaps a result of the weakest and most vindictive of human proclivities. James Dunn, emeritus professor of the New Testament at the University of Durham, explains his position on the nature of Scripture as follows:

> If Jesus was a Jew living and working in the midst of Jews, then his actions and his teaching, the revelation which he brought and embodied, was tied in to the particularities of the history of that period. It could not be otherwise. The revelation was

first and foremost to Second Temple Jews and in terms adapted to their historical circumstances . . . If we do not hear the revelation through and in Jesus first and foremost in its historical particularity, *we are in serious danger of not hearing it at all.* For the revelation cannot be separated from its historically conditioned form; it is not a timeless kernel which can be somehow extricated from a time-conditional husk. *There is no such thing as a "pure" revelation . . .* Revelation *comes through dirty hands* and inadequate human language, and the all too vigorous altercations [between Jesus and Pharisees or between the Jewish-exclusive faction and the gentile-inclusive faction of the Jesus movement] in the first century *were an integral part of Christianity's emerging identity.*[24]

Some may not like this rationale, but if it ensures that fewer Christians will be scandalized by the humanness of the Gospels and keeps them "in the boat," so to speak, then perhaps it is worth considering.

Despite their humanness and their weaknesses, the Gospels are very special for a significant portion of the human population. Thus, these texts must be given careful attention. If we try to put ourselves in the shoes of the authors of Matthew, Mark, Luke–Acts, and John, we might see how they would be offended if they knew that many readers of their Gospels in the twenty-first century tend to reduce their texts to simple portrayals of Jesus meant to help people feel good, provide church-goers with cheesy and sappy Sunday school answers, or help people be good boys and girls. Did they really dedicate their lives to these highly complex and profound texts so that we can reduce them to simplistic emotional platitudes merely intended to foster fluffy, feel-good religion? In order to get the most out of these texts we must see them for what they are, or were originally meant to be, not for what we want them to be.

I have allocated space in various places throughout this book to discuss the nature of the Gospels because only until we understand what they are can we begin to situate Jesus within a Jewish context. Further, understanding the nature of these texts will prevent us from making grotesque and sensational claims, some of which have contributed to the persecution and death of millions of Jesus' own people, the Jews. Surveys of American adults reveal that only about 35 percent read the Bible at least once per week, and about 63 percent read it only once per month or less (30 percent of Mainline Protestants and 25 percent of Catholics read the Bible at least once per week). The few who do read the Bible tend to approach it superficially. Reading the Bible is different than *studying* the Bible. The percentages are

---

24. Dunn, "Embarrassment of History," 64–66; emphasis added.

probably significantly lower among those who explore the Bible with study aids. Fewer than 50 percent of American adults can name all four Gospels.[25] The Bible has simply lost power because the populace does not understand it. It is too archaic.

    If Christians continue to ignore both the Hebrew Scriptures and the Gospels, they will not understand Jesus and his ministry at a deeper, more impactful level. Falsehoods, overstatements, and anachronisms will continue to run amok. Christians will continue to perpetuate hateful and anti-Semitic interpretations that act as a stumbling block, not a stepping-stone. If Christians perpetuate old interpretations and poor logic, then we are in a way contributing retroactively to the persecution of the Jews and contributing to anti-Semitism in the future. It is our hope that we stop acting unchristian by contributing to the demonization of our brothers and sisters in humanity in our casual discussions, in our sermons, in our writings, in Sunday School, and in our lectures. We must not try to save the New Testament and its historicity at all costs, especially not at the expense of millions of Jewish lives and the reputation of Jews in general.

---

25. See Geiger, "Five Facts on How Americans View the Bible"; Barna Group, "Frequency of reading the Bible."

Bibliography

Aasgaard, Reidar. *"My Beloved Brothers and Sisters!" Christian Siblingship in Paul.* London: T. & T. Clark (2004) 45–49.

Abrahams, Israel, trans. *Hagigah.* The Soncino Babylonian Talmud 23. Teaneck, NJ: Talmudic, 2012.

Abramsky, Samuel, and Shimon Gibson. "Bar Kokhba." In *Encyclopaedia Judaica*, 2nd ed., edited by Michael Berenbaum and Fred Skolnik, 3:156–64. Detroit: Macmillan, 2007.

Abulafia, Anna Sapir. *Christian Jewish Relations 1000–1300.* New York: Pearson, 2011.

Alexander, Philip S. *The Targum of Canticles.* Collegeville, MN: Liturgical, 2003.

Allison, Dale C., Jr. *The New Moses: A Matthean Typology.* Minneapolis: Fortress, 1993.

Anderson, F. I., trans. "2 Enoch." In *The Old Testament Pseudepigrapha*, edited by James H. Charlesworth, 1:91–222. New York: Doubleday, 1983.

Aristotle. *Rhetoric.* In *The Basic Works of Aristotle*, edited by Richard McKeon, 1366b, 1354. New York: Modern Library, 2001.

Arndt, William F., et al. *A Greek-English Lexicon of the New Testament and Other Early Christian Literature: A Translation and Adaptation of the Fourth Revised and Augmented Edition of Walter Bauer's Griechisch-deutsches Wörterbuch zu den Schriften des Neuen Testaments und der übrigen urchristlichen Literatur.* Chicago: University of Chicago Press, 1979.

Aslan, Reza. *Zealot: The Life and Times of Jesus of Nazareth.* Sydney: Allen and Unwin, 2017.

Aune, David E., ed. *The Blackwell Companion to the New Testament.* Malden, MA: Wiley-Blackwell, 2010.

Aus, Roger David. *Caught in the Act, Walking on the Sea, and the Release of Barabbas Revisited.* Atlanta: Scholars, 1998.

Bagnall, Roger S., and Bruce W. Frier. *The Demography of Roman Egypt.* Cambridge, UK: Cambridge University Press, 1994.

Bailey, Kenneth. "The Manger and the Inn: The Cultural Background of Luke 2:7." *Bible and Spade* 20 (2007) 98–106.

Baker, David L. "Typology and the Christian use of the Old Testament." *Scottish Journal of Theology* 29 (1976) 137–57.

Baron, Salo W. "Population." In *Encyclopedia Judaica*, edited by Cecil Roth, 13:866–903. Jerusalem: Keter, 1971.

Barrett, C. K. "Pauline Controversies in the Post-Pauline Period." *New Testament Studies* 20 (1974) 229–45 .

Beale, Gregory K., and Donald A. Carson. *Commentary on the New Testament Use of the Old Testament*. Grand Rapids, MI: Baker Academic, 2007.

Beentjes, Pancratius C. "Prophets and Prophecy in the Book of Ben Sira." In *Prophets, Prophecy, and Prophetic Texts in Second Temple Judaism*, edited by Michael H. Floyd and Robert D. Haak, 135–50. New York: T. & T. Clark, 2006.

Berggren, N., et al. "The Looks of a Winner: Beauty and Electoral Success." *Journal of Public Economics* 94 (2010) 8–15.

Bertman, Stephen. "The Antisemitic Origin of Michelangelo's Horned Moses." *Shofar: An Interdisciplinary Journal of Jewish Studies* 4 (2009) 95–106.

Betlyon, John W. "Coinage." In *Anchor Bible Dictionary*, edited by David Noel Freedman, 1:1076–89. New York: Doubleday, 1992.

Bieringer, R., et al. "Wrestling with Johannine Anti-Judaism: A Hermeneutical Framework for the Analysis of the Current Debate." In *Anti-Judaism and the Fourth Gospel: Papers of the Leuven Colloquium 2000*, edited by R. Bieringer et al., 24–28. Assen, the Netherlands: Van Gorcum, 2001.

Blenkinsopp, Joseph. *Sage, Priest, Prophet: Religious and Intellectual Leadership in Ancient Israel*. Louisville, KY: Westminster John Knox, 1995.

Bond, Helen K. "Barabbas Remembered." In *Jesus and Paul: Global Perspectives in Honour of James D. G. Dunn for his 70th Birthday*, edited by B. J. Orapeza, C. K. Robertson, and Douglas C. Mohrmann, 59–61. New York: T. & T. Clark, 2009.

Boyarin, Daniel. *Border Lines: The Partition of Judaeo-Christianity*. Philadelphia: University of Pennsylvania Press, 2004.

———. *The Jewish Gospels: The Story of the Jewish Christ*. New York: New Press, 2012.

Brawley, Robert L. *Luke–Acts and the Jews: Conflict, Apology, and Conciliation*. Society of Biblical Literature 33. Atlanta: Scholars, 1987.

Brown, Francis, ed. *A Hebrew and English Lexicon of the Old Testament*. Version 4.3. Dania Beach, FL: Scribe.

Brown, Raymond. *The Birth of the Messiah: A Commentary on the Infancy Narratives in Matthew and Luke*. Garden City, NY: Doubleday, 1977.

Bryce, Trevor. *The Kingdom of the Hittites*. Oxford: Oxford University Press, 2005.

Burchard, C., trans. "Joseph and Asenath." In *The Old Testament Pseudepigrapha: Apocalyptic Literature and Testaments*, edited by James H. Charlesworth, 2:177–246. New York: Doubleday, 1985.

Burridge, Richard. *What Are the Gospels? A Comparison with Greco-Roman Biography*. Grand Rapids, MI: Eerdmans, 2004.

Cane, Anthony. *The Place of Judas Iscariot in Christology*. New York: Routledge, 2017.

Carlson, Stephen C. "The Accommodations of Joseph and Mary in Bethlehem: Κατάλυμα in Luke 2.7." *New Testament Studies* 56 (2010) 326–42.

Charlesworth, James H. "Christians and Jews in the First Six Centuries." In *Christianity and Rabbinic Judaism: A Parallel History of their Origins and Early Development*, edited by Hershel Shanks, 321–22. Washington, DC: Biblical Archaeology Society, 1992.

———. "The Gospel of John: Exclusivism Caused by a Social Setting Different from That of Jesus (John 11:54 and 14:6)." In *Anti-Judaism and the Fourth Gospel: Papers of the Leuven Colloquium 2000*, edited by R. Bieringer et al., 479–513. Assen, the Netherlands: Van Gorcum, 2001.

———. *The Old Testament Pseudepigrapha*. 2 vols. New York: Doubleday, 1985.

Chilton, Bruce. "Paul and the Pharisees." In *In Quest of the Historical Pharisees*, edited by Jacob Neusner and Bruce Chilton, 149-74. Waco, TX: Baylor University Press, 2007.

———. *Rabbi Jesus: An Intimate Biography*. New York: Doubleday, 2000.

Chrysostom, John. *Discourses against Judaizing Christians*. Translated by P. W. Harkins. Washington, DC: Catholic University of America Press, 1979.

———. "Patrologia Graeca 48.843-856." In *Jews and Christians in Antioch in the First Four Centuries of the Common Era*, edited by Wayne A. Meeks and Robert L. Wilken. Missoula, MT: Scholars' Press for the Society of Biblical Literature, 1978.

Cicero. *De Officiis*. Translated by Walter Miller. Loeb Classical Library 30. Cambridge, MA: Harvard University Press, 1913.

———. *De Oratore*. Translated by Edward W. Sutton and Harris Rackham. Loeb Classical Library 349. Cambridge, MA: Harvard University Press, 1942.

———. *De Republica*. Translated by Clinton W. Keyes. Loeb Classical Library 213. Cambridge, MA: Harvard University Press, 1928.

Cohen, Andrew C. *Death Rituals: Ideology and the Development of Early Mesopotamian Kingship*. Ancient Magic and Divination 7. Leiden: Brill, 2005.

Cohen, Jeremy. *Christ Killers: The Jews and the Passion, From the Bible to the Big Screen*. Oxford: Oxford University Press, 2007.

Cohen, Mark. *Under Crescent and Cross: The Jews in the Middle Ages*. Princeton, NJ: Princeton University Press, 1995.

Cohen, Shaye J. D. "Were Pharisees and Rabbis the Leaders of Communal Prayer and Torah Study in Antiquity?" In *Evolution of the Synagogue: Problems and Progress*, edited by Howard Clark Kee and Lynn H. Cohick, 89-105. Harrisburg, PA: Trinity International, 1999.

Collins, Adela Y. *Mark: A Commentary*. Hermeneia: A Critical and Historical Commentary on the Bible. Minneapolis: Fortress, 2007.

Collins, Adela Yarbro, and John J. Collins. *King and Messiah as Son of God: Divine, Human, and Angelic Messianic Figures in Biblical and Related Literature*. Grand Rapids, MI: Eerdmans, 2008.

Collins, John J. *Daniel: A Commentary on the Book of Daniel*. Hermeneia: A Critical and Historical Commentary on the Bible. Minneapolis: Fortress, 1993.

———. "Sibylline Oracles." In *The Old Testament Pseudepigrapha: Apocalyptic Literature and Testaments*, edited by James H. Charlesworth, 1:317-472. New York: Doubleday, 1983.

Collins, Nina L. *Jesus, the Sabbath and the Jewish Debate: Healing on the Sabbath in the 1st and 2nd Centuries CE*. London: Bloomsbury, 2014.

Corley, Kathleen E. *Private Women, Public Meals: Social Conflict in the Synoptic Tradition*. Peabody, MA: Hendrickson, 1993.

Craffert, Pieter F. "Shamanism and the Shamanic Complex." *Biblical Theological Bulletin* 41 (2011) 151-61.

———. *The Life of a Galilean Shaman: Jesus of Nazareth in Anthropological-Historical Perspective*. Eugene, OR: Cascade, 2008.

Crook, Zeba A. *Parallel Gospels: A Synopsis of Early Christian Writing*. New York: Oxford University Press, 2012.

Crossan, John Dominic. *Jesus: A Revolutionary Biography*. San Francisco: HarperSanFrancisco, 1994.

———. *The Historical Jesus: The Life of a Mediterranean Jewish Peasant.* San Francisco: HarperSanFrancisco, 1991.

Crossan, John Dominic, and Jonathan L. Reed. *Excavating Jesus: Beneath the Stones, Behind the Texts.* San Francisco: HarperSanFrancisco, 2001.

Daiches, Salis, trans. *Baba Mezia.* The Soncino Babylonian Talmud 32. Teaneck, NJ: Talmudic, 2012.

Dark, Ken. "Has Jesus' Nazareth House Been Found?" *Biblical Archaeology Review* 41 (2015) 54–63.

Davies, Stevan. "Who Is Called Bar Abbas?" *New Testament Studies* 27 (1981) 260–62.

Davies, William D. "The Jewish Sources of Matthew's Messianism." In *The Messiah: Developments in Earliest Judaism and Christianity*, edited by James Charlesworth, 494–511. Minneapolis: Fortress, 1992.

Davies, William D., and Dale C. Allison. *A Critical and Exegetical Commentary on the Gospel According to Saint Matthew.* Edinburgh: T. & T. Clark, 1991.

Deines, Roland. "God or Mammon: The Danger of Wealth in the Jesus Tradition and in the Epistle of James." In *Anthropologie und Ethik im Frühjudentum und im Neuen Testament: Wechselseitige Wahrnehmungen: Internationales Symposium in Verbindung mit dem Projekt Corpus Judaeo-Hellenisticum Novi Testamenti (CJHNT),* edited by Matthias Konradt and Esther Schläpfer, 327–86. Wissenschaftliche Untersuchungen zum Neuen Testament 322. Tübingen: Mohr Siebec, 2014.

———. *Jüdische Steingefässe und pharisäische Frömmigkeit: Eine archäologisch-historischer Beitrag zum Verständnis von Joh 2,6 und der jüdischen Reinheitshalacha zur Zeit Jesu.* Tübingen: Mohr Siebeck, 1993.

———. "The Pharisees between 'Judaism' and 'Common Judaism.'" In *Justification and Variegated Nomism: Volume I, The Complexities of Second Temple Judaism*, edited by Donald A. Carson et al., 443–504. Grand Rapids, MI: Baker Academic, 2001.

———. "Religious Practices and Religious Movements in Galilee: 100 BCE–200 CE." In *Galilee In the Late Second Temple and Mishnaic Periods: Life, Culture, and Society*, edited by David A Fiensy and James R. Strange, 1:93–96. Minneapolis: Fortress, 2014.

Derovan, David, et al. "Gematria." In *Encyclopaedia Judaica*, 2nd ed., edited by Michael Berenbaum and Fred Skolnik, 7:424–27. Detroit: Macmillan, 2007.

DeSilva, David A. *The Letter to the Galatians.* New International Commentary on the New Testament. Grand Rapids, MI: Eerdmans, 2018.

Dinnerstein, Leonard. *Antisemitism in America.* New York: Oxford University Press, 1994.

Donahue, J. R. "Tax Collector." In *Anchor Bible Dictionary*, edited by David Noel Freedman, 6:337–38. New York: Doubleday, 1992.

Duling, D. C., trans. "Testament of Solomon." In *The Old Testament Pseudepigrapha: Apocalyptic Literature and Testaments*, edited by James H. Charlesworth, 1:935–88. New York: Doubleday, 1983.

Duncan, Anne. *Performers and Identity in the Classical World.* Cambridge, UK: Cambridge University Press, 2006.

Dunn, James D. G. "The Embarrassment of History: Reflections on the Problem of 'Anti-Judaism in the Fourth Gospel.'" In *Anti-Judaism and the Fourth Gospel: Papers of the Leuven Colloquium 2000*, edited by R. Bieringer et al., 64–66. Assen, the Netherlands: Van Gorcum, 2001.

———. *Jesus, Paul, and the Law*. London: SPCK, 1990.

———. *The Parting of the Ways between Christianity and Judaism and Their Significance for the Character of Christianity*. London: SCM, 2006.

Edwards, Catharine. *The Politics of Immorality in Ancient Rome*. Cambridge, UK: Cambridge University Press, 1993.

Ehrman, Bart. *Jesus: Apocalyptic Prophet of the New Millennium*. Oxford: Oxford University Press, 1999.

———. *Misquoting Jesus: The Story Behind Who Changed the Bible and Why*. New York: HarperCollins, 2005.

Ericksen, Robert P. *Complicity in the Holocaust: Churches and Universities in Nazi Germany*. Cambridge, UK: Cambridge University Press, 2012.

Evans, Craig A. *Ancient Texts for New Testament Studies: A Guide to the Background Literature*. Peabody, MA: Hendrickson, 2005.

———. *Fabricating Jesus: How Modern Scholars Distort the Gospels*. Downers Grove, IL: InterVarsity, 2006.

———. *Jesus and His Contemporaries: Comparative Studies*. Leiden: Brill, 1995.

———. "Reconstructing Jesus' Teaching: Problems and Possibilities." In *Hillel and Jesus: Comparative Studies of Two Major Religious Leaders*, edited by James H. Charlesworth and Loren L. Johns, 397–426. Minneapolis: Fortress, 1997.

Eve, Eric. *The Healer from Nazareth: Jesus' Miracles in Historical Context*. London: SPCK, 2009.

———. *The Jewish Context of Jesus' Miracles*. New York: Sheffield Academic, 2002.

Falk, Harvey. *Jesus the Pharisee: A New Look at the Jewishness of Jesus*. New York: Paulist, 1985.

Feldman, Louis H. "Prophets and Prophecy in Josephus." In *Prophets, Prophecy, and Prophetic Texts in Second Temple Judaism*, edited by Michael H. Floyd and Robert D. Haak, 210–39. New York: T. & T. Clark, 2006.

Fiensy, David A. "The Galilean Village in the Late Second Temple and Mishnaic Periods." In *Galilee in the Late Second Temple and Mishnaic Periods: Life Culture and Society*, by David A. Fiensy and James Riley Strange, 177–207. Minneapolis: Fortress, 2014.

Fiensy, David A., and James Riley Strange. *Galilee in the Late Second Temple and Mishnaic Periods: Life Culture and Society, Volume 1*. Minneapolis: Fortress, 2014.

Finkelstein, Louis. *Mabo le-masekhtot Avot*. New York: Jewish Theological Seminary of America, 1950.

Fitzmyer, Joseph A. *The One Who Is to Come*. Grand Rapids, MI: Eerdmans, 2007.

Floyd, Michael H. "Introduction." In *Prophets, Prophecy, and Prophetic Texts in Second Temple Judaism*, edited by Michael H. Floyd and Robert D. Haak, 5. New York: T. & T. Clark, 2006.

Flusser, David, and R. Stephen Notley. *Jesus*. Jerusalem: Magnes, 1997.

Frankfort, Henri. *Kingship and the Gods, a Study of Ancient Near Eastern Religion as the Integration of Society and Nature*. Chicago: University of Chicago Press, 1948.

Freedman, Harry M., trans. *Baba Mezia*. The Soncino Babylonian Talmud 32. Teaneck, NJ: Talmudic, 2012.

———. *Kiddushin*. The Soncino Babylonian Talmud 30. Teaneck, NJ: Talmudic, 2012.

———. *Nedarim*. The Soncino Babylonian Talmud 26. Teaneck, NJ: Talmudic, 2012.

———. *Shabbat*. The Soncino Babylonian Talmud 12. Teaneck, NJ: Talmudic, 2012.

"Frequency of reading the Bible among adults in the United States as of January 2018." The Barna Group, American Bible Society, 2018. https://www.statista.com/statistics/299433/bible-readership-in-the-usa/.

Freyne, Sean. *Jesus, A Jewish Galilean: A New Reading of the Jesus-Story.* London: T. & T. Clark, 2004.

———. "Vilifying the Other and Defining the Self: Matthew's and John's Anti-Jewish Polemic in Focus." In *To See Ourselves as Others See Us: Christians, Jews, "Others" in Late Antiquity*, ed. Jacob Neusner and Ernst S. Frerichs, 117–43. Chico, CA: Scholars', 1985.

Geiger, Abigail. "Five Facts on How Americans View the Bible and Other Religious Texts." Pew Research Center, April 14, 2017. http://www.pewresearch.org/fact-tank/2017/04/14/5-facts-on-how-americans-view-the-bible-and-other-religious-texts/.

Gellar, Stephen A. "The Religion of the Bible." In *The Jewish Study Bible*, edited by Adele Berlin and Marc Zvi Brettler, 2021–40. Oxford: Oxford University Press, 2004.

Goodacre, Mark. *The Case Against Q: Studies in Markan Priority and the Synoptic Problem.* Salem, OR: Trinity, 2002.

———. "Jesus' Genealogy in Luke's Gospel." *NT Pod.* http://podacre.blogspot.com/2009/08/nt-pod-9-jesus-genealogy-in-lukes_19.html.

———. "Prophecy Historicized or Tradition Scripturalized?: Reflections on the Origin of the Passion Narratives." In *New Testament and the Church*, edited by John Barton and Peter Groves, 37–51. LNTS 532. London: T. & T. Clark, 2015.

Goodman, Martin. *Rome and Jerusalem: The Clash of Ancient Civilizations.* New York: Knopf, 2007.

Goulder, Michael. *St. Paul versus St. Peter: A Tale of Two Missions.* Louisville, KY: Westminster John Knox, 1995.

Gowler, David. *Host, Guest, Enemy, and Friend: Portraits of the Pharisees in Luke and Acts.* Eugene, OR: Wipf and Stock, 2008.

Grabbe, Lester L. "Shaman, Preacher, or Spirit Medium? The Israelite Prophet in the Light of Anthropological Models." In *Prophecy and Prophets in Ancient Israel*, edited by John Day, 117–32. London: T. & T. Clark, 2010.

———. "Thus Spake the Prophet Josephus . . . : The Jewish Historian on Prophets and Prophecy." In *Prophets, Prophecy, and Prophetic Texts in Second Temple Judaism*, edited by Michael H. Floyd and Robert D. Haak, 240–47. New York: T. & T. Clark, 2006.

Green, Joel B. *The Gospel of Luke.* Grand Rapids, MI: Eerdmans, 1997.

Green, Joel, et al., eds. *Dictionary of Jesus and the Gospels.* Downers Grove, IL: InterVarsity, 1992.

Grollenberg, L. *Paul.* Translated by J. Bowden. Philadelphia: Westminster, 1978.

Gundry, Robert H. *Peter: False Disciple and Apostate According to Saint Matthew.* Cambridge, UK: Eerdmans, 2015.

Hakola, Raimo, and Adele Reinhartz. "John's Pharisees." In *In Quest of the Historical Pharisees*, edited by Jacob Neusner and Bruce Chilton, 131–48. Waco, TX: Baylor University Press, 2007.

Ham, Clay Alan. "Reading Zechariah and Matthew's Olivet Discourse." In *Biblical Interpretation in Early Christian Gospels*, edited by Thomas R. Hatina, 2:85–97. London: T. & T. Clark, 2008.

Hare, D. R. A., trans. "Lives of the Prophets." In *The Old Testament Pseudepigrapha: Apocalyptic Literature and Testaments*, edited by James H. Charlesworth, 2:379–400. New York: Doubleday, 1985.

Harland, Philip A. *Dynamics of Identity in the World of the Early Christians.* New York: T. & T. Clark, 2009.

Hatch, Trevan. "Messianism and Jewish Messiahs in the New Testament Period." In *New Testament History, Culture, and Society: A Background to the Texts of the New Testament*, edited by Lincoln Blumell, 71–85. Provo, UT: BYU Religious Studies Center, 2019.

Havrelock, Rachel. *River Jordan: The Mythology of a Dividing Line.* Chicago: University of Chicago Press, 2011.

Hays, Richard B. *Echoes of Scripture in the Letters of Paul.* New Haven: Yale University Press, 1993.

Henze, Matthias. "Invoking the Prophets in Zechariah and Ben Sira." In *Prophets, Prophecy, and Prophetic Texts in Second Temple Judaism*, edited by Michael H. Floyd and Robert D. Haak, 120–21. New York: T. & T. Clark, 2006.

Herzog, William R., II. *Prophet and Teacher: An Introduction to the Historical Jesus.* Louisville, KY: Westminster John Knox, 2005.

Heschel, Susannah. *Abraham Geiger and the Jewish Jesus.* Chicago: University of Chicago Press, 1998.

———. *The Aryan Jesus: Christian Theologians and the Bible in Nazi Germany.* Princeton, NJ: Princeton University Press, 2008.

Hezser, Catherine. *Rabbinic Body Language: Non-Verbal Communication in Palestinian Rabbinic Literature of Late Antiquity.* Leiden: Brill, 2017.

Hill, Scott D. "The Local Hero in Palestine in Comparative Perspective." In *Elijah and Elisha in Socioliterary Perspective*, edited by Robert B. Coote, 37–74. Atlanta: Scholars, 1992.

Himmelfarb, Martha, trans. *Jewish Messiahs in a Christian Empire: A History of the Book of Zerubbabel.* Cambridge, MA: Harvard University Press, 2017.

Hirschfeld, Yizhar. *The Palestinian Dwelling in the Roman-Byzantine Period.* Jerusalem: Franciscan, 1995.

Horsley, Richard A. *Bandits, Prophets and Messiahs: Popular Movements in the Time of Jesus.* With John S. Hanson. Harrisburg, PA: Trinity, 1985.

———. *Galilee: History, Politics, People.* Valley Forge, PA: Trinity, 1995.

———. "'Like One of the Prophets of Old:' Two Types of Popular Prophets at the Time of Jesus." *Catholic Bible Quarterly* 47 (1985) 435–63.

———. "Synagogues in Galilee and the Gospels." In *Evolution of the Synagogue: Problems and Progress*, edited by Howard C. Kee and Lynn H. Cohick, 46–69. Harrisburg, PA: Trinity, 1999.

Huwiler, Elizabeth F. "Shunem." In *Anchor Bible Dictionary*, edited by David Noel Freedman, 5:1228–29. New York: Doubleday, 1992.

Ilan, Tal. *Jewish Women in Greco-Roman Palestine.* Peabody, MA: Hendrickson, 1996.

Isaac, Ephraim. "1 Enoch: A New Translation and Introduction." In *The Old Testament Pseudepigrapha Apocalyptic Literature and Testaments*, edited by James H. Charlesworth, 1:5–90. New York: Doubleday, 1983.

Jacobson, Howard. *The Exagoge of Ezekiel.* Cambridge, UK: Cambridge University Press, 1983.

James, M. R., trans. *The Apocryphal New Testament*. Oxford: Clarendon, 1924. http://www.earlychristianwritings.com/text/actsjohn.html.

Jastrow, Marcus. *Dictionary of the Targumim, the Talmud Babli and Yerushalmi, and the Midrashic Literature*. Peabody, MA: Hendrickson, 2006.

Jeffers, James S. *The Greco-Roman World of the New Testament Era: Exploring the Background of Early Christianity*. Downers Grove, IL: InterVarsity, 1999.

Jensen, Morten H. "The Political History in Galilee from the First Century BCE to the End of the Second Century CE." In *Galilee in the Late Second Temple and Mishnaic Periods: Life Culture and Society*, edited by David A. Fiensy and James Riley Strange, 51–77. Minneapolis: Fortress, 2014.

Jestice, Phyllis G. "A Great Jewish Conspiracy? Worsening Jewish-Christian Relations and the Destruction of the Holy Sepulcher." In *Christian Attitudes Toward Jews in the Middle Ages: A Casebook*, edited by Michael Frassetto, 25–42. New York: Routledge, 2013.

Johnson, Luke T. "The New Testament's Anti-Jewish Slander and the Conventions of Ancient Polemic." *Journal of Biblical Literature* 108 (1989) 419–41.

Johnson, Marshall D. *The Purpose of the Biblical Genealogies: With Special Reference to the Setting of the Genealogies of Jesus*. Cambridge, UK: Cambridge University Press, 1988.

Josephus. *Against Apion*. Translated by Henry St. J. Thackeray. Loeb Classical Library 186. Cambridge, MA: Harvard University Press, 1926.

———. *Against Apion*. Translated by John M. G. Barclay. In *Flavius Josephus Online*, edited by Steve Mason. Leiden: Brill, 2016.

———. *Jewish Antiquities*. Translated by H. St. J. Thackeray and Ralph Marcus. Loeb Classical Library 490. Cambridge, MA: Harvard University Press, 1930.

———. *Jewish Antiquities*. Translated by Louis H. Feldman. Loeb Classical Library 433. Cambridge, MA: Harvard University Press, 1965.

———. *Jewish Antiquities*. Translated by Louis H. Feldman. Loeb Classical Library 456. Cambridge, MA: Harvard University Press, 1967.

———. *Jewish Antiquities*. Translated by Ralph Marcus. Loeb Classical Library 365. Cambridge, MA: Harvard University Press, 1943.

———. *Jewish Antiquities*. Translated by Ralph Marcus and Allen Wikgren. Loeb Classical Library 410. Cambridge, MA: Harvard University Press, 1963.

———. *Jewish Antiquities*. Translated by Ralph Marcus and Allen Wikgren. Loeb Classical Library 489. Cambridge, MA: Harvard University Press, 1943.

———. *Jewish Antiquities*. "Judean Antiquities 3, Whiston 8.9, Niese 214–18." Translated by Louis H. Feldman. In *Flavius Josephus Online*, edited by Steve Mason. Leiden: Brill, 2016.

———. *Jewish Antiquities*. "Judean Antiquities 8, Whiston 2.5, Niese 42–49." Translated by Christopher T. Begg and Paul Spilsbury. In *Flavius Josephus Online*, edited by Steve Mason. Leiden: Brill, 2016.

———. *Jewish War*. Translated by H. St. J. Thackeray. Loeb Classical Library 203. Cambridge, MA: Harvard University Press, 1927.

———. *Jewish War*. Translated by H. St. J. Thackeray. Loeb Classical Library 210. Cambridge, MA: Harvard University Press, 1928.

———. *Jewish War*. Translated by Louis Feldman. Loeb Classical Library 456. Cambridge, MA: Harvard University Press, 1965.

———. "Judean War 2, Whiston 13.4, Niese 258–260." Translated by Steve Mason. In *Flavius Josephus Online*, edited by Steve Mason. Leiden: Brill, 2016.

———. "Life of Josephus." Translated by Steve Mason. In *Flavius Josephus Online*, edited by Steve Mason. Leiden: Brill, 2016.

Kasser, Rodolphe, et al., trans. *The Gospel of Judas: From Codex Tchacos*. Washington, DC: National Geographic, 2006.

Kaufmann, Thomas. *Luther's Jews: A Journey into Anti-Semitism*. Oxford: Oxford University Press, 2017.

Kee, Howard C. "Testaments of the Twelve Patriarchs." In *The Old Testament Pseudepigrapha: Apocalyptic Literature and Testaments*, edited by James H. Charlesworth, 1:794–95. New York: Doubleday, 1983.

———. "The Terminology of Mark's Exorcism Stories." *New Testament Studies* 14 (1968) 232–46.

Kensky, Allan. "Moses and Jesus: The Birth of a Savior." *Judaism* 42 (1993) 43–49.

King, Amy, and Andrew Leigh. "Beautiful Politicians." *Kyklos* 62 (2009) 579–93.

Kinman, Brent. *Jesus' Entry into Jerusalem: In the Context of Lukan Theology and the Politics of his Day*. Leiden: Brill, 1995.

Klassen, William. *Judas: Betrayer or Friend of Jesus?* Minneapolis: Fortress, 1996.

Klijn, Albertus F. J. "2 Baruch." In *The Old Testament Pseudepigrapha: Apocalyptic Literature and Testaments*, edited by James H. Charlesworth, 1:615–52. New York: Doubleday, 1983.

Kloner, Amos, and Nissu Boaz. *The Necropolis of Jerusalem in the Second Temple Period*. Leuven, Belgium: Peeters, 2007.

Koenig, John. *New Testament Hospitality*. Philadelphia: Fortress, 1985.

Koepke, Nikola, and Joerg Baten. "The Biological Standard of Living in Europe during the Last Two Millennia." *European Review of Economic History* 9 (2005) 61–95.

Koester, Craig R. *Revelation, The Anchor Yale Bible*. New Haven, CT: Yale University Press, 2014.

Koskenniemi, Erkki. *The Old Testament Miracle-Workers in Early Judaism*. Tübingen, Germany: Mohr Siebeck, 2005.

Lachs, Samuel. *A Rabbinic Commentary on the New Testament*. Hoboken, NJ: KTAV, 1987.

LaCocque, André. *Jesus the Central Jew: His Times and His People*. Atlanta: Society of Biblical Literature, 2015.

Lampe, Peter. *From Paul to Valentinus: Christians at Rome in the First Two Centuries*. Minneapolis: Fortress, 2003.

Lawrence, Jonathan David. *Washing in Water: Trajectories of Ritual Bathing in the Hebrew Bible and Second Temple Literature*. Atlanta: Society of Biblical Literature, 2006.

Leuchter, Mark. *Samuel and the Shaping of Tradition*. New York: Oxford University Press, 2013.

Levinson, John R. "Philo's Personal Experience and the Persistence of Prophecy." In *Prophets, Prophecy, and Prophetic Texts in Second Temple Judaism*, edited by Michael H. Floyd and Robert D. Haak, 194–209. New York: T. & T. Clark, 2006.

Lewittes, Mendell. *Jewish Marriage: Rabbinic Law, Legend, and Custom*. Northvale, NJ: Jason Aronson, 1994.

Lucass, Shirley. *The Concept of the Messiah in the Scriptures of Judaism and Christianity*. London: Bloomsbury, 2011.

Lucian. *The Carousal.* Translated by Austin M. Harmon. Loeb Classical Library 14. Cambridge, MA: Harvard University Press, 1913.
———. *The Dead Come to Life.* Translated by Austin M. Harmon. Loeb Classical Library 130. Cambridge, MA: Harvard University Press, 1921.
———. *Icaromenippus.* Translated by Austin M. Harmon. Loeb Classical Library 54. Cambridge, MA: Harvard University Press, 1915.
———. *Menippus.* Translated by Austin M. Harmon. Loeb Classical Library 162. Cambridge, MA: Harvard University Press, 1925.
———. *Timon.* Translated by Austin M. Harmon. Loeb Classical Library 54. Cambridge, MA: Harvard University Press, 1915.
———. *True Story.* Translated by Austin M. Harmon. Loeb Classical Library 14. Cambridge, MA: Harvard University Press, 1913.
Luz, Ulrich. *Matthew 8–20.* Hermeneia: A Critical and Historical Commentary on the Bible. Minneapolis: Fortress, 2001.
Luz, Ulrich, et al. *Matthew 21–28: A Commentary.* Minneapolis: Fortress, 2005.
Maccoby, Hyam. "Jesus and Barabbas." *New Testament Studies* 16 (1970) 55–60.
———. *Jesus the Pharisee.* London: SCM, 2003.
———. *Judas Iscariot and the Myth of Jewish Evil.* New York: Free Press, 1992.
———. *Revolution in Judea: Jesus and the Jewish Resistance.* New York: Taplinger, 1980.
MacDonald, Dennis R. *Mythologizing Jesus: From Jewish Teacher to Epic Hero.* Lanham, MD: Rowman and Littlefield, 2015.
Magen, Izchak, and Levana Tsfania. *The Stone Vessel Industry in the Second Temple Period: Excavations at Ḥizma and the Jerusalem Temple Mount.* Jerusalem: Israel Exploration Society, 2002.
Marcus, Joel. *Mark 1–8: A New Translation with Introduction and Commentary.* New York: Doubleday, 2000.
Martin, Laura. "The Jew in the Thorn Bush: German Fairy Tales and Anti-Semitism in the Late Eighteenth and Early Nineteenth Centuries: Musäus, Naubert and the Grimms." In *Violence, Culture and Identity: Essays on German and Austrian Literature, Politics, and Society*, edited by Helen Chambers, 123–41. New York: Peter Lang, 2006.
Martin, Raymond. *Capistrum Iudaeorum.* 2 vols. Edited by Adolfo Robles Sierra. Würzburg, Germany: Echter Verlag, 1990–1993.
Mason, Steve. "Chief Priests, Sadducees, Pharisees and Sanhedrin in Acts." In *The Book of Acts in Its Palestinian Setting*, edited by Richard Bauckham, 115–77. Grand Rapids, MI: Eerdmans, 1995.
———. *Flavius Josephus on the Pharisees: A Composition-Critical Study.* Leiden: Brill, 2001.
———. *Josephus and the New Testament.* Peabody, MA: Hendrickson, 1992.
———. "Josephus's Pharisees: The Narratives." In *In Quest of the Historical Pharisees*, edited by Jacob Neusner and Bruce D. Chilton, 3–40. Waco, TX: Baylor University Press, 2007.
———. "Should Any Wish to Enquire Further (*Ant.* 1.25): The Aim and Audience of Josephus's *Judean Antiquities, Life.*" In *Understanding Josephus: Seven Perspectives*, edited by Steve Mason, 64–103. Sheffield, UK: Sheffield Academic, 1998.
———. "Was Josephus a Pharisee? A Re-Examination of Life 10–12." *Journal of Jewish Studies* 40 (1989) 31–45.

McKnight, Scot. "Jewish Missionary Activity: The Evidence of Demographics and Synagogues." In *Jewish Proselytism*, edited by Amy J. Levine and Richard I. Pervo, 1–33. Lanham, MD: University Press of America, 1997.

Meier, John P. *A Marginal Jew: Rethinking the Historical Jesus*. 5 vols. New Haven: CT: Yale University Press, 1991–2016.

Melito. On the Pascha. In *Christ Killers: The Jews and the Passion from the Bible to the Big Screen*, edited by Jeremy Cohen, 56–70. Oxford: Oxford University Press, 2007.

Menken, Maarten J. J. "Scriptural Dispute between Jews and Christians in John: Literary Fiction or Historical Reality? John 9:13–17, 24–34 as a Test Case." In *Anti-Judaism and the Fourth Gospel: Papers of the Leuven Colloquium 2000*, edited by R. Bieringer et al., 445–60. Assen, the Netherlands: Van Gorcum, 2001.

———. *Studies in John's Gospel and Epistles*. Leuven: Peeters, 2015.

Merritt, Robert L. "Jesus Barabbas and the Paschal Pardon." *Journal of Biblical Literature* 104 (1985) 57–68.

Mitchell, David. "A Dying and Rising Messiah in 4Q372." *Journal for the Study of the Pseudepigrapha* 18 (2009) 181–205.

———. "The Fourth Deliverer: A Josephite Messiah in 4QTestimonia." *Biblica* 86 (2005) 545–53.

———. "Messiah bar Ephraim in the Targums." *Aramaic Studies* 4 (2006) 221–41.

Miura, Yuzuru. *David in Luke–Acts: His Portrayal in Light of Early Judaism*. Tübingen, Germany: Mohr Siebeck, 2007.

Mullen, E. Theodore, Jr., "Hosts, Hosts of Heaven." In *Anchor Bible Dictionary*, edited by David N. Freedman, 3:301–4. New York: Doubleday, 1992.

Nagar, Yossi, and Hagit Torgee. "Biological Characteristics of Jewish Burial in the Hellenistic and Early Roman Period." *Israel Exploration Journal* 53 (2003) 164–71.

Netzer, Ehud. *The Architecture of Herod the Great Builder*. Grand Rapids, MI: Baker Academic, 2006.

Neusner, Jacob. *From Politics to Piety: The Emergence of Pharisaic Judaism*. Eugene, OR: Wipf and Stock, 2003.

———. *Judaism and Scripture: The Evidence of Leviticus Rabbah*. Chicago: University of Chicago Press, 1986.

———. *The Mishnah: A New Translation*. New Haven, CT: Yale University Press, 1988.

———. *The Rabbinic Traditions about the Pharisees before 70*. Atlanta: Scholars, 1971.

———. *The Tosefta: Translated from the Hebrew with a New Introduction*. Peabody, MA: Hendrickson, 2002.

Neyrey, Jerome H. "Ceremonies in Luke–Acts: The Case of Meals and Table Fellowship." In *The Social World of Luke–Acts: Models for Interpretation*, edited by Jerome H. Neyrey, 361–87. Peabody, MA: Hendrickson, 1991.

Niehaus, Jeffery Jay. *Ancient Near Eastern Themes in Biblical Theology*. Grand Rapids, MI: Kregel, 2008.

Niehoff, Maren. *The Figure of Joseph in Post-Biblical Jewish Literature*. Leiden: Brill, 1992.

Novikoff, Alex. "The Middle Ages." In *Anti-Semitism: A History*, edited by Albert S. Lindemann and Richard S. Levy, 63–78. New York: Oxford University Press, 2010.

Oakman, Douglas E. *Jesus and the Economic Questions of His Day*. Lewiston, NY: E. Mellen, 1986.

Omanson, Roger L. *A Textual Guide to the Greek New Testament*. Stuttgart, Germany: Deutsche Bibelgesellschaft, 2006.

Origen. *Contra Celsum*. Translated by Henry Chadwick. Cambridge, UK: Cambridge University Press, 1965.

Paffenroth, Kim. *Judas: Images of the Lost Disciple*. Louisville, KY: Westminster John Knox, 2001.

Papias. "Frag. 3." Translated by Alexander Roberts and James Donaldson. Logos Virtual Library. http://www.logoslibrary.org/papias/fragments/03.html.

Pardes, Ilana. *The Biography of Ancient Israel: National Narratives in the Bible*. Berkeley: University of California Press, 2000.

Parry, Donald W., et al. *The Prophetic Voice at Qumran: The Leonardo Museum Conference on the Dead Sea Scrolls, 11–12 April 2014*. Leiden: Brill, 2017.

Peterson, William L. "ΟΥΔΕ ΕΓΩ ΣΕ [ΚΑΤΑ]ΚΡΙΝΩ. John 8:11, the *Protevangelium Iacobi*, and the History of the *Pericope Adulterae*." In *Sayings of Jesus: Canonical and Non-Canonical: Essays in Honour of Tjitze Baarda*, edited by William Lawrence Petersen et al., 191–221. Leiden: Brill, 1997.

Philo. *On the Embassy to Gaius*. In *The Works of Philo*, translated by Charles D. Yonge, 757–90. Peabody, MA: Hendrickson, 1993.

———. *On the Embassy to Gaius*. Translated by F. H. Colson. Loeb Classical Library 379. Cambridge, MA: Harvard University Press, 1962.

———. *The Works of Philo: Complete and Unabridged*. Translated by Charles D. Yonge. Peabody, MA.: Hendrickson, 1993.

Pickup, Martin. "Matthew's and Mark's Pharisees." In *In Quest of the Historical Pharisees*, edited by Jacob Neusner and Bruce D. Chilton, 67–112. Waco, TX: Baylor University Press, 2007.

Pilch, John J. *Healing in the New Testament: Insights from Medical and Mediterranean Anthropology*. Minneapolis: Fortress, 2000.

———. "Sickness and Healing in Luke-Acts." In *The Social World of Luke-Acts: Models for Interpretation*, edited by Jerome H. Neyrey, 181–209. Peabody, MA: Hendrickson, 1991.

Pope Francis, "Address of His Holiness Pope Francis to the Pontifical Biblical Institute." Libreria Editrice Vaticana, May 9, 2019. http://w2.vatican.va/content/francesco/en/speeches/2019/may/documents/papa-francesco_20190509_pont-istitutobiblico.html

Porter, Stanley E. "Further Comments on the Use of the Old Testament in the New Testament." In *The Intertextuality of the Epistles: Explorations of Theory and Practice*, edited by Thomas L. Brodie et al., 98–110. Sheffield, UK: Sheffield Phoenix, 2006.

Porter, Stanley, and Bryan Dyer, eds. *The Synoptic Problem: Four Views*. Grand Rapids, MI: Baker Academic, 2016.

Porusch, Israel, trans. *Meilah*. The Soncino Babylonian Talmud 48. Teaneck, NJ: Talmudic, 2012.

Powell, Mark A. "Do and Keep What Moses Says (Matthew 23:2–7)." *Journal of Biblical Literature* 114 (1995) 419–35.

———. *The Harpercollins Bible Dictionary*. New York: HarperOne, 2011.

———. *Introducing the New Testament: A Historical, Literary, and Theological Survey*. Grand Rapids, MI: Baker Academic, 2009.

———. "The Religious Leaders in Luke: A Literary-Critical Study." *Journal of Biblical Literature* 109 (1990) 93–110.

Priest, J. "Testament of Moses, A New Translation and Introduction." In *The Old Testament Pseudepigrapha: Apocalyptic Literature and Testaments*, edited by James H. Charlesworth, 1:919–34. New York: Doubleday, 1983.
Rabbinowitz, Joseph, trans. *Midrash Rabbah Deuteronomy, Volume 7*. London: Soncino, 1983.
———. *Taanith*. The Soncino Babylonian Talmud 19. Teaneck, NJ: Talmudic, 2012.
Rainey, Anson F., and R. Steven Notley. *The Sacred Bridge*. Jerusalem: Carta, 2006.
Rajak, Tessa. *Josephus: The Historian and His Society*, 2nd ed. London: Duckworth, 2004.
Rapp, Christof. "Aristotle's Rhetoric." In *Stanford Encyclopedia of Philosophy*, edited by Edward N. Zalta. https://plato.stanford.edu/archives/spr2010/entries/aristotle-rhetoric/.
Rawson, B. *Children and Childhood in Roman Italy*. Oxford: Oxford University Press, 2003.
Reed, Jonathan L. *The HarperCollins Visual Guide to the New Testament: What Archaeology Reveals about the First Christians*. New York: HarperCollins, 2007.
———. "Mortality, Morbidity, and Economics in Jesus' Galilee." In *Galilee in the Late Second Temple and Mishnaic Periods: Life, Culture, and Society, vol. 1*, edited by David A. Fiensy and James R. Strange, 242–52. Minneapolis: Fortress, 2014.
Reiner, Elchanan. "From Joshua through Jesus to Simeon bar Yohai: Toward a Typology of Galilean Heroes." In *Jesus among the Jews: Representation and Thought*, edited by Neta Stahl, 94–105. New York: Routledge, 2012.
Reinhardt, Wolfgang. "The Population Size of Jerusalem and the Numerical Growth of the Jerusalem Church." In *The Book of Acts in Its Palestinian Setting*, edited by Richard Bauckham, 237–65. Grand Rapids, MI: Eerdmans, 1995.
Renn, Stephen D. *Expository Dictionary of Bible Words*. Peabody, MA: Hendrickson, 2005.
Riesner, Rainer. "Bethany Beyond the Jordan." In *Anchor Bible Dictionary*, edited by David N. Freedman. 1:703–5. New York: Doubleday, 1992.
Robbins, Austin. "Tomb and Teeth: A Dentist's View of Ancient Israelites." *Bible and Spade* 8 (1995).
Römer, Thomas, and Jan Ruckel. "Jesus, Son of Joseph and Son of David, in the Gospels." In *The Torah in the New Testament*, edited by Michael Tait and Peter Oaks, 65–81. New York: T. & T. Clark, 2009.
Royalty, Robert M. *The Origin of Heresy: A History of Discourse in Second Temple Judaism and Early Christianity*. New York: Routledge, 2013.
Rubinstein, William D. "Anti-Semitism in the English-speaking World." In *Anti-Semitism: A History*, edited by Albert S. Lindemann and Richard S. Levy, 150–65. New York: Oxford University Press, 2010.
Runesson, Anders. *The Origins of the Synagogue: A Socio-Historical Study*. Stockholm: Almqvist and Wiksell, 2001.
Runesson, Anders, et al. *The Ancient Synagogue from Its Origins to 200 C. E.: A Source Book*. Leiden: Brill, 2008.
Saldarini, Anthony. *Pharisees, Scribes, and Sadducees in Palestinian Society: A Sociological Approach*. Grand Rapids, MI: Eerdmans, 1988.
Saller, Richard P. *Patriarchy, Property and Death in the Roman Family*. Cambridge, MA: Cambridge University Press, 1994.
Sanders, E. P. *The Historical Figure of Jesus*. London: Penguin, 1995.

Schäfer, Peter. *The History of the Jews in the Greco-Roman World*. London: Routledge, 2003.

———. *Jesus in the Talmud*. Princeton: Princeton University Press, 2007.

———. *The Jewish Jesus: How Judaism and Christianity Shaped Each Other*. Princeton: Princeton University Press, 2012.

Schiffman, Lawrence H. *Qumran and Jerusalem: Studies in the Dead Sea Scrolls and the History of Judaism*. Grand Rapids, MI: Eerdmans, 2010.

———. *Reclaiming the Dead Sea Scrolls: Their True Meaning for Judaism and Christianity*. New York: Doubleday, 1994.

———. *Who Was a Jew?: Rabbinic and Halakhic Perspectives on the Jewish Christian Schism*. Hoboken, NJ: KTAV, 1985.

Scholem, Gershom, ed. *The Messianic Idea in Judaism: And Other Essays on Jewish Spirituality*. New York: Schocken, 1971.

Sennacherib Prism, column 1, line 3. See translation at http://www.kchanson.com/ANCDOCS/meso/sennprism1.html.

Seow, Choon-Leong. "Hosts, Lord of." In *Anchor Bible Dictionary*, edited by David N. Freedman, 3:304–7. New York: Doubleday, 1992.

Shachter, Jacob, trans. *Sanhedrin*. The Soncino Babylonian Talmud 34. Teaneck, NJ: Talmudic, 2012.

Sigal, Phillip. *The Halakah of Jesus of Nazareth According to the Gospel of Matthew*. Lanham, MD: University Press of America, 1986.

Silver, Abba Hillel. *The History of Messianic Speculation in Israel*. Whitefish, MT: Kessinger, 2003.

Simon, Maurice, trans. *Berakhot*. The Soncino Babylonian Talmud 1. Teaneck, NJ: Talmudic, 2012.

Skarsaune, Oskar, and Reidar Hvalvik, eds. *Jewish Believers in Jesus: The Early Centuries*. Peabody, MA: Hendrickson, 2007.

Slotki, Israel W., trans. *Erubin*. The Soncino Babylonian Talmud 13. Teaneck, NJ: Talmudic, 2012.

———. *Niddah*. The Soncino Babylonian Talmud 52. Teaneck, NJ: Talmudic, 2012.

———. *Sukkah*. The Soncino Babylonian Talmud 16. Teaneck, NJ: Talmudic, 2012.

———. *Yebamoth*. The Soncino Babylonian Talmud 24. Teaneck, NJ: Talmudic, 2012.

Smith, Dennis E. "Greco-Roman Meal Customs." In *Anchor Bible Dictionary*, edited by David Noel Freedman, 4:651–53. New York: Doubleday, 1992.

———. "The Historical Jesus at Table." In *Society of Biblical Literature 1989 Seminar Papers*, edited by D. J. Lull, 466–89. Atlanta: Scholars, 1989.

———. "Table Fellowship as a Literary Motif in the Gospel of Luke." *JBL* 106 (1987) 613–38.

Smith, Jonathan Z. "What a Difference a Difference Makes." In *To See Ourselves as Others See Us: Christians, Jews, "Others" in Late Antiquity*, edited by Jacob Neusner and Ernest S. Frerichs, 3–48. Chico, CA: Scholars, 1985.

Smith, Patricia, et al. "The Skeletal Remains." In *Excavations at Ancient Meiron, Upper Galilee, Israel, 1971–72, 1974–75, 1977*, edited by Eric M. Meyers et al., 110–20. Cambridge, MA: American Schools of Oriental Research, 1981.

Smith-Christopher, Daniel. "Daniel (Book and Person, Hebrew Bible/Old Testament)." In *Encyclopedia of the Bible and Its Reception*, 6:86–94. Berlin: De Gruyter, 2013.

Spielman, Loren. *Sitting with Scorners: Jewish Attitudes toward Roman Spectacle Entertainment from the Herodian Period through the Muslim Conquest.* New York: Jewish Theological Seminary of America, ProQuest Dissertations, 2010.

Strack, Hermann Leberecht, and Günter Stemberger, eds. *Introduction to the Talmud and Midrash,* translated by Markus N. A. Bockmuehl. Minneapolis: Fortress, 1996.

Strange, James F. "Nain." In *Anchor Bible Dictionary,* edited by David Noel Freedman, 4:1001. New York: Doubleday, 1992.

Strickland, Debra Higgs. *Saracens, Demons, and Jews: Making Monsters in Medieval Art.* Princeton, NJ: Princeton University Press, 2003.

Sussman, Abigail B., et al. "Competence Ratings in US Predict Presidential Election Outcomes in Bulgaria." *Journal of Experimental Social Psychology* 49 (2013) 771–75.

Telford, William. *The Barren Temple and the Withered Tree: A Redaction-Critical Analysis of the Cursing of the Fig-Tree Pericope in Mark's Gospel and Its Relation to the Cleansing of the Temple Tradition.* Sheffield, UK: JSOT, 1980.

Tertullian. *De Spectaculis.* Translated by Terrot R. Glover and Gerald H. Rendall. Loeb Classical Library 250. Cambridge, MA: Harvard University Press, 1931.

Theissen, Gerd, and Annette Merz. *The Historical Jesus: A Comprehensive Guide.* Minneapolis: Fortress, 1998.

Thompson, Thomas L. "If David Had Not Climbed the Mount of Olives." *Biblical Interpretations* 8 (2000) 42–58.

Throup, Marcus. "Mark's Jesus, Divine?: A Study of Aspects of Mark's Christology with Special Reference to Hebrew Divine Warrior Traditions in Mark, and in Relation to Contemporary Debates on Primitive Christology." PhD diss., University of Nottingham, 2014.

Tobin, Gary A., and Sid Groeneman. *Anti-Semitic Beliefs in the United States.* San Francisco: Institute for Jewish & Community Research, 2003.

Todorov, Alexander, et al. "Inferences of Competence from Faces Predict Election Outcomes." *Science* 308 (2005) 1623–26.

Tov, Emanuel, ed. *The Dead Sea Scrolls Electronic Library.* Leiden: Brill, 2006.

Trachtenberg, Joshua. *The Devil and the Jews: The Medieval Conception of the Jews and Its Relation to Modern Anti-Semitism.* Philadelphia: Jewish Publication Society, 1983.

Tropper, Amram. "Children and Childhood in Light of the Demographics of the Jewish Family in Late Antiquity." *Journal for the Study of Judaism* 37 (2006) 299–343.

———. "The Economics of Jewish Childhood in Late Antiquity." *Hebrew Union College Annual* 76 (2005) 189–233.

Turkewitz, Julie, and Kevin Roose. "Who Is Robert Bowers, the Suspect in the Pittsburgh Synagogue Shooting?" *New York Times,* October 27, 2018. https://www.nytimes.com/2018/10/27/us/robert-bowers-pittsburgh-synagogue-shooter.html.

Turner, David L. *Matthew.* Grand Rapids, MI: Baker Academic, 2008.

van Aarde, Andries. "Jesus as Fatherless Child." In *The Social Setting of Jesus and the Gospels,* edited by Stegemann Wolfgang et al., 65–83. Minneapolis: Fortress, 2002.

van der Horst, Pieter Willem. *Ancient Jewish Epitaphs: An Introductory Survey of a Millennium of Jewish Funerary Epigraphy (300 BCE–700 CE).* Kampen, the Netherlands: Kok Pharos, 1991.

Vanderkam, James. "The Pharisees and the Dead Sea Scrolls." In *In Quest of the Historical Pharisees*, edited by Jacob Neusner and Bruce D. Chilton, 225–36. Waco, TX: Baylor University Press, 2007.

Vermes, Geza. *The Complete Dead Sea Scrolls in English*. New York: Penguin, 1998.

———. *Jesus the Jew: A Historian's Reading of the Gospels*. Philadelphia: Fortress, 1981.

Volkan, Vamik D. "The Need to Have Enemies and Allies: A Developmental Approach." *Political Psychology* 6 (1985) 219–47.

Von Wahlde, Urban C. "The Relationships between Pharisees and Chief Priests: Some Observations on the Texts in Matthew, John and Josephus." *New Testament Studies* 42 (1996) 506–22.

Walzer, Michael. *In God's Shadow: Politics in the Hebrew Bible*. New Haven, CT: Yale University Press, 2012.

Webb, Robert L. *John the Baptizer and Prophet: A Socio-Historical Study*. Sheffield, UK: Sheffield Academic, 1991.

Welch, John W. "Miracles, *Maleficium*, and *Maiestas* in the Trial of Jesus." In *Jesus and Archaeology*, edited by James H. Charlesworth, 349–83. Grand Rapids, MI: Eerdmans, 2006.

Wilkins, Michael J. "Barabbas." In *Anchor Bible Dictionary*, edited by David N. Freedman, 1:607. New York: Doubleday, 1992.

The William Davidson Talmud. The Sefaria Library. https://www.sefaria.org/Berakhot.61b?lang=bi.

Wise, Michael O., et al. *The Dead Sea Scrolls: A New Translation*. New York: HarperSanFrancisco, 2005.

Wrede, William. *Das Messiasgeheimnis in den Evangelien: zugleich ein Beitrag zum Verständnis des Markusevangeliums*. Göttingen: Vandenhoeck und Ruprecht, 1901.

———. *The Messianic Secret*. Translated by James C. G. Grieg. Cambridge, UK: James Clarke, 1971.

Wright, N. T. *Jesus and the Victory of God*. Minneapolis: Fortress, 1996.

Yadin, Yigael. *The Temple Scroll: The Hidden Law of the Dead Sea Sect*. New York: Random, 1985.

Zacharias, H. Daniel. *Matthew's Presentation of the Son of David*. London: Bloomsbury T. & T. Clark, 2017.

Zwiep, Arie W., et al. "Judas Iscariot." In *Encyclopedia of the Bible and Its Reception*, 14:938–58. Berlin: De Gruyter, 2017.

Index of Subjects

Anti-Semitism (based on New Testament Interpretation), 135–143, 151
Apostles (original twelve) in the Gospels, 233–243
Baptism, 37–50
    Bat Qol (Voice from Heaven), 48–50
    Dead Sea Sect at Qumran, 41–42
    Jesus, 42–50
    John the Baptist, 37–40
    opening of heaven, 44–47
    location of Jesus' Baptism, 37–38
    Spirit descending, 47–48
Barabbas (see *"Crucify Him" Episode*)
Birth Narratives
    Bethlehem, 126–127
    house and cave, 24–25
    magi, 59, 125–127
    similarities with Moses, 57–60
    star, 126–128
Calming the Storm, 91–94
"Crucify Him" Episode, 193–200
David, Jesus as type of, 116–117, 121–132, 150–151
Dead Sea Scrolls (and Qumran)
    exorcisms, 87
    immersion practices, 39–42
    invective and polemic, 213
    messianic expectations, 103–104, 117
    prophetic activity, 76
    texts of, 8
Elijah, 31, 46, 53, 58, 62, 65–69, 84, 85, 89–90
Elisha,
    starts ministry at the Jordan River, 46–47
    Jesus as Elisha, type of, 31, 65–72, 79, 81, 89–90, 91, 94, 250
    miracle worker, 81, 89–90, 91, 94
Family Dynamics, 25–34
Food Miracles, 94–95
Genealogy of Jesus, 121–125
Gospels
    what are the Gospels, 14–19
    when were the Gospels written, 10–12
    who wrote the Gospels, 12–14
Healings, 81–89
    sickness and disease, 28, 81–82, 88
    exorcisms, 85–88
Hebrew Scriptures, role of in Gospels, 252–258
Immersion Rituals (see Baptism)
Jewish Followers of Jesus, 200–201
Jewish-Roman Relations, 215–217
John the Baptist
    birth of, 58
    Elijah, type of, 65–69
    immersion rituals of, 37–40
    location of Jesus' Baptism, 37–38
    relation to Jesus, 15, 56–57, 186, 251
    voice of crying in the wilderness, 45
Jordan River, 37–38, 46, 61, 66, 69, 108
Joseph the Patriarch
    Jesus as Joseph, type of, 116–121
    monument in Galilee, 248–249
Josephus
    attacks against Apion, 212
    John the Baptist, 37–40

Josephus (*continued*)
   learned youth, 33
   messianic activity in first century, 107–112
   Pharisees, 154–169
   writings of, 5–6, 228
Joshua
   Jesus' name, 2, 46, 57
   Jesus as type of, 44, 46, 57
   Jordan River, 46
   monument to Joshua in Galilee, 248–249
Judas, 143–152
Mary (mother of Jesus)
   alleged adultery, 123–124
   birth of Jesus, 24–25, 117
   relation to Elizabeth, 57, 64
   Miriam (Hebrew Bible), in relation to, 57, 58, 64, 248–249
Messiahs in the First Century, 107–109
Messianic Expectations, 103–107, 143–152
Messianism in Early Judaism, 97–107, 110–112
Miracle Workers in Early Judaism, 80–95
Moses
   Jesus as a new Moses, 45–47, 56–65
   Moses types in Jewish tradition, 54–56
Name Calling in Greco-Roman Literature, 202–214
Paul
   a Pharisee, 168, 170
   rivalry with Peter and Jewish leadership, 221–241
Peter in the Gospels (see also *Apostles [original twelve] in the Gospels*), 238–243

Pharisees, 154–184, 207–212, 221–226, 230–233
   "hypocrites" in Matthew, 207–211
   friends of Jesus, 168–172
   Jerusalem Council, 221–226
   Johannine passages, 178–183
   leniency of, 166–168
   "lovers of wealth" in Luke, 211–212
   "murders" in Matthew, 212
   origins of, 154–157
   Pope Francis on, 184
   popularity of, 157–159
   portrayal of in Gospels, 230–233
   religious devotion of, 159–165
   Sabbath healing episode, 174–178
   table-fellowship, 170–172
   "testing" Jesus, 173–174
   theological positions of, 165–166
Physical Characteristics of Jewish men, 34–36
Prophets in Early Judaism, 73–80
Rabbis (prominent)
   Akiva, 41, 49, 55, 56, 128, 191
   Hanina ben Dosa, 49, 83–84, 88, 95, 133, 246, 249
   Hillel, 48, 49, 55–56, 123
   writings of, 6–8, 246–251
   Yohanan ben Zakkai, 55
Romans and Gentiles in the Gospels, 227–230
Shaman 52–53
Son of David, 100, 103, 112, 116, 121–122, 125, 128–132, 169,
Son of God, 15, 98–99, 104, 115–116
   Son of Man, 98, 101–104, 116, 141, 193, 239, 251
Temple Cleansing, 189–191
Water Walking Episode, 91

Index of Ancient Texts

OLD TESTAMENT/ HEBREW BIBLE

Genesis

1	92
1:2	47, 92
1:3	47
1:28	27
2:18	27
2:24	27
9:6-7	28
17:9-14	225
18:10	58
18:11	58
18:19	34
22:1	174
25:21	58
25:23	58
29:31	58
30:22-24	117
35:16-19	126
35:16-20	117, 120
37:2	117, 120
37:3	117
37:4-8	118, 120
37:11	118, 120
37:23	118, 121
37:26-27	118, 149
37:26-28	118, 120
37:28	117, 120
38	124
40:1-3	118, 121
40:19	118, 121
40:22	118, 121
41:29	118, 120
41:40	118, 121
41:46	120
41:46-49	118, 120
48:7	126
49	103
49:10	103
49:10-11	128
49:24	99 n10

Exodus

1:22	59, 64
2:15	59, 64
3:14	131, 132
4:19	60, 64
4:22	60, 61
6:23	57, 64
12:37	62
12:48	225
13:2	60
13:3	60
14:21	91 n69
15:20-21	57
15:24-25	60
16:1-4	60
16:4	61
18:21	62
18:25	62
19:3	63, 65
21:32	118, 149
23:7-8	168

Exodus (continued)

24:1	63
24:12	63
24:15-18	63
24:16	64
26:59	57
28:41	98 n2
30:30	98 n2
31:1-5	31
31:6-11	32
31:14-15	175
32:15	63
34	140
34:5	63, 102
34:28	62, 64
34:29	63
34:29-30	63-64
34:35	63-64, 140
35:1-3	175
35:31	31
35:35	31, 32
36:59	64
38:23	31, 32
40:13	98 n2

Leviticus

7:35	98 n2
10:10	160
11	223
12:3	225
13-17	40
16:32	98 n2
17	224
18	224
19:27	36
21:18-23	130
23:30	175 n64
23:42-43	64
26:6	92

Numbers

1:5-16	61
3:3	98 n2
11:12	60
12:6	74
15:31-33	175
16	200
19	40
21:7	43 n66
22:5-6	126
22:8-9	74
24	126, 127, 128
24:2	126
24:17-19	126
32:13	61
35:25	98 n2

Deuteronomy

1:15	62
4:19	128
6:7	34
7:10	175 n64
7:20	175 n64
7:24	175 n64
8:2-3	62, 65
8:10	62
9:9	63, 65
10:5	63
11:13-21	43
11:19	34
12:2	175 n64
12:3	175 n64
13:1-2	80
14:1	36
16:13	64
18:15	54, 77
18:18	54
18:22	10
24:16	198
31:12	34
33:2	128
34:1-4	63, 65
34:7	55

Joshua

3	61
3:7	46
3:16-17	46
4	61
7:7	175 n64
24:32	121

INDEX OF ANCIENT TEXTS 283

Judges

5:20	127 n34
10:15-16	43 n66
13:2-5	58

Ruth

3:1-9	124
4:18-22	124
4:21-22	124

1 Samuel

1:1-20	58
3:1-21	75
3:3-9	74
7:3-4	43 n66
9	35
9:2	36
9:9	75, 98 n3
9:16	98 n3
10:1	98 n3
15:1	98 n3
15:17	98 n3
16	36
16:1-3	98 n3, 126, 131
16:6	98 n4
16:7	36
16:11	128, 131
16:12-13	98 n3
17:4	34
24:6	98 n4
24:10	98 n4
26:9	98 n4
26:11	98 n4
26:16	98 n4
26:23	98 n4
28	74

2 Samuel

1:14	98 n4
1:16	98 n4
3:39	43 n64
5	130
5:2	99 n11
5:4	128, 131
5:6	130
5:8	130

7	100, 103
7:1-17	75
7:7-8	99 n11
7:14	100, 103
7:16	100, 103
11	124
11-12	75
12:7	98 n3
14:25	36
15:12	132, 150
15:14	131, 132
15:30	128, 132
15:31	132, 150
16:1-2	128, 132
17:1	131, 132
17:23	132, 150
18:9	129
18:9-17	129
19:21	98 n4
20:4-10	132, 150-151
22:51	98 n3
23:1	98 n3
24:1-25	75
24:10	43 n64

1 Kings

1:32-37	129
1:32-39	132
1:34	98 n3
1:39	98 n3, 129
1:45	98 n3
10:10	125
13:18-22	75
17-18	89
17-22	75
17:8-16	66, 67
17:17-24	66, 67
18:41-45	89
18:42	84, 133
19:8	62, 64
19:15-16	98 n2, 98 n3
19:17-21	65
19:19	31
21:27-29	43 n64
22:14	74
22:17	99 n11
22:19	128
23:1-7	43 n66

2 Kings

2	65
2:8	66, 67
2:8-14	66, 67, 69, 71, 91
2:12	66, 67
2:13-14	46
2:14	69, 71
4:1-7	66, 67, 70
4:8-37	71
4:18-37	66, 67, 70
4:38-41	70
4:42-44	70, 71, 95
5:1-19	70, 71
5:19	70
6	71
6:1-7	69
6:6	91
9:1-3	98 n2, 98 n3
9:1-13	75
9:6	98 n2, 98 n3
9:12	98 n2, 98 n3
10:19	175 n64
13:14	66, 67
14:25	251
19:18	175 n64
22:6	31
23:4-14	190
23:21-24	190
25:4-6	98 n3

1 Chronicles

22:15	31
29:5	31

2 Chronicles

4:2-4	31
15:8-15	43 n66
24:12	31
29:3-19	190
30:1-14	190
30:6-9	43 n66
34:11	31

Ezra

3:7	31
10:1	43 n66

10:10-12	43 n66

Nehemiah

8:14-17	64

Job

3:8	92
5:24	26
9:8	91
11:18	92
17:13	92 n70
22:11	92 n70
26:12	91, 92
38:7	127 n34
41:31	91 n69
42:6	43 n64

Psalms

2	50
2:2	98 n4
2:7	46, 50, 99, 128, 131
3	92
3:5	92
4	92
4:8	92
8	130
8:1	130
18:50	98 n4
20:6	98 n4
22:1	257
22:18	256
23:1-4	99 n10
27	131, 132
27:1-2	131, 132
28:8	98 n4
28:9	99 n10
33:7	91 n69
34:18	41
35	131, 132
35:1-6	131, 132
41	150
41:9	132, 150
45	125
45:8	125
51:2	40
51:7	40
51:17	41

57	136	11:1	103
57:4	136	11:8	39
64	136	13:10	193 n14
64:2-8	136	15:2	36
72	125	19:1	102
72:10-11	125	25:6-8	94
72:15	125	27:1	92
74:13-14	92	29:18	92 n70
77:19	91 n69	30:6	39
78:70	128, 131	34:4	193 n14
78:70-71	99 n11	40	45, 46
80:1	99 n10	40:3	45
88:12	92 n70	40:9-11	45
89:9	99	42	50
89:10	99	42:1	50
89:22-23	99	43:16	91 n69
89:25	99	45	104
89:26-27	99	45:1	98, 104
89:39	98 n4	50:1	43 n65
89:51	98 n4	51:9-10	91, 92
95:7	99 n10	51:15	91 n69
100:3	99 n10	53	105
102:26	45	55:3	100
104:3	102	53:3-7	106
104:6-7	91	54:5-8	43 n65
106	91	56:7	190
106:8-9	91	57:15	41
107:10	92 n70	59:1-5	39
107:14	92 n70	60:2	92 n70
107:28-29	91	60:2-6	125
110:1	99	63	46
118:26	129	63:11	47, 60, 61
132:10	98 n4	63:11-13	45
		64:1	45

Proverbs

3:23-24	92

Isaiah

1:1	75
1:9	43 n64
1:16	40
3:24	36
5	191
5:20	92 n70
9:6-7	100
11	103

Jeremiah

2:2	43 n65
2:32	43 n65
3:6-14	43 n65
3:20	43 n65
7	109, 190
7:6-24	43
7:11	109, 190
8:2	128
8:13	192
18:7-8	43 n66
19	149

Jeremiah (continued)

19:1-13	149
19:11	149
19:31	128
23:5	100
23:5-6	44
31:6-8	130
31:32	43 n65
32:1-15	149
33:15-16	44
46:22	39
47:5	36

Ezekiel

1:1	45
3:14	75
16:8-14	43 n65
16:32-34	43 n65
16:43	43 n65
16:59-62	43 n65
18:20	199
32:7	193 n14
34	99
34:1-10	99 n11
34:11-31	99 n10
34:23-24	100
36:25-27	40, 41
37:22-25	100
43:1-5	189

Daniel

7:2-3	92
7:13-14	102
8:10	127 n34
9	106
9:26	106
9:27	10

Hosea

1:2	43 n65
2-4	43 n64
2:2	43 n65
2:7	43 n65
2:14-20	43 n65
3:1-3	43 n65
3:4-5	100

9:1	43 n65

Joel

1:8	43 n65
2:2	92 n70
2:10	192
2:31	192
3	188, 192, 193
3:12	193
3:15	192
3:18	94

Amos

4:6-13	43
9:11	100
9:13-14	94

Jonah

1-2	91 n69

Micah

5:2	126, 131
7:1-6	192
7:8	92 n70

Zephaniah

1:15	92 n70

Haggai

1:12	43 n64
1:14	43 n64
2:6	45

Zechariah

8:6-12	43 n64
9-14	117
9:4-7	117
9:9	128
11:12-13	149
11:13	149
12:10	116, 117, 129
13:7	256
14	109, 188, 189, 190, 193

INDEX OF ANCIENT TEXTS   287

14:1-20	117
14:4	129, 190, 192
14:6-20	190
14:21	189, 190

ANCIENT NEAR EASTERN TEXTS

Sennacherib Prism
column 1, line 3 — 99 n9

DEUTEROCANONICAL BOOKS

Tobit
2:1	171 n58
7:9	171 n58

Sirach
9:15-16	172 n60
24:33	76 n11
32:31	172 n60
39:1	76 n11
48:12-14	68 n38

1 Maccabees
4:46	54 n6, 75 n9, 155 n2
14:41	54 n6, 155 n2

2 Maccabees
3:6	148

1 Esdras
4:10	171 n58

3 Maccabees
5:16	171 n58

PSEUDEPIGRAPHA

2 Baruch
29:3-4	93 n74
29:3-8	94 n78

1 Enoch
10:19	94 n80
46:1-4	102
48:2-10	103
69:29	103

2 Enoch
71:1-11	58 n21

4 Ezra
7:28-30	105 n30

Lives of the Prophets
21:1-15	58 n22, 69 n40
22:1-17	69 n41

Psalms of Solomon
17:21	103 n23
17:26-36	104 n27
17:32	103 n23

Sibylline Oracles
3:652-654	104 n28
3:741-750	94 n79

Testament of Gad
2:3-4	118 n10

Testament of Judah
24:2	47 n69

Testament of Levi
18:3	127 n36

Testament of Moses
7:1-7	191 n10
11:16	55 n11
12:1-2	63 n34

Testament of Solomon
16:1-5	93 n73

INDEX OF ANCIENT TEXTS

DEAD SEA SCROLLS

1Q20 (1QapGen)
20:28-29	87 n50

1QH-a (Thanksgiving Hymn)
14:22-24	93 n72

1QHa X
31-38	213 n42

1QpHab
1:49	n52

1QS
3:1-9	41 n61
5:13-14	39 n52

1QSa
2:11-12	171 n57
2:14-15	104 n25

4Q175
1:1-8	54 n7

4Q242 (4QPrNab)
Frags. 1,
2a, 2b, 3	87 n51

4Q252
5:1-4	103 n22

4Q521
Frags. 2+4 ii 1	104 n24
Frags. 2+4 ii 1-12	104 n29

CD
1.14-2.1	213 n42
19:10-11	104 n26

Damascus Document
10.16-19	176 n65
12.4-6	176 n66

ANCIENT JEWISH WRITERS

Josephus

The Life
1.2.9-12	33 n32
1.2.11-12	40 n57
1.5	158 n17
2.12	157 n13
21	167
45.235	23 n1, 185 n2

Against Apion
1.15	206 n18
1.25.225-226	212 n40
1.37	76 n15
1.40	75 n6
2.6.68	212 n39
2.6.69-70	212 n40
2.7.80	212 n39
2.8.92-96	212 n39
2.14.145	212 n39
2.14.148	212 n39
2.16.161	212 n39
2.17	159 n21

Jewish Antiquities
2.9.2	59 n25, 64
2.9.3	58 n18, 64
3.218	75 n7
4.8.49	54 n9
8.2.5	86 n48
13.10.5	158 n16, 159 n22
13.10.5-6	166 n43
13.10.6	166 n42, 176 n68
13.10.7	76 n12, 158 n17
13.13.5	159 n21
13.15.5	158 n19
13.15.5-13.16.6	158 n18
13.299-300	77 n22
13.372-373	112 n51
14.2.1	90 n61
14.4-5	110 n46
14.7.110	148 n50

INDEX OF ANCIENT TEXTS 289

14.9.3-4	166 n45	2.4.2	107 n35
14.163-176	157 n12	2.4.3	108 n36
14.172-174	156 n8	2.5.1-2	111 n47
15.1-4	157 n12	2.8.14	165 n34, 165 n35, 165 n36, 166 n39
15.3	156 n8, 166 n45		
15:50-56	101 n16	2.12	159 n21
15:222-236	101 n16	2.12.1	112 n52, 216 n4
15:247-251	101 n16	2.13.7	216 n6
15:365-372	101 n16	2.14.4-6	216 n6
16:392-394	101 n16	2.17.2-6	216 n7
17.2.4	76 n12, 156 n10, 156 n11	2.17.8-10	109 n43
		2.20.6	109 n44
17.10.5	107 n34	2.21.1	109 n44
17.10.6	107 n35	2.119-161	40 n58
17.10.7	108 n36	2.243	167
17.10.8	107 n33	2.301	167
17.10.9-10	111 n47	2.316	167
18.1.1	108 n40	2.336	167
18.1.2	207 n19	2.409-417	167 n47
18.1.3	165 n35, 165 n37, 166 n38, 166 n40, 166 n41, 208 n23, 212 n38	2.411	167
		2.422	167
		2.428	167
18.1.4	157 n15	2.648	167
18.3.1-2	101 n17, 101 n18, 159 n21, 196 n25, 216 n3	3.8.9	76 n13
		3.351-354	77 n22
18.4.1	76 n12, 108 n38, 196 n25	3.400-402	77 n22
		4.6.1	109 n44
18.5.2	41 n60, 108 n37, 187 n4	4.7.1	109 n44
		4.9.4-5	109 n44
18.12-17	165 n34	4.457	89 n60
18.18-22	40 n58	6.5.2	76 n12
18.116-119	37 n44, 38 n47	6.5.2 §285	127 n31
20.5.1	108 n39, 133 n41	6.5.3	109 n42, 190 n8
20.5.3	112 n52, 216 n4	6.5.3 §289	127 n32
20.8.6	108 n41, 133 n42, 216 n5	6.5.4 §312-313	127 n33
		6.9.4	109 n44
20.8.181	148 n51	7.1.2	109 n44
20.9.1	166 n44	7.2.2	109 n44
20.105	159 n21	7.5.3-6	109 n44
20.200	227 n21	13.4	78 n24
117-118	40 n53		

PHILO

Jewish War

1.2.8	76 n12	*On the Contemplative Life*
1.68-69	77 n22	
1.110	159 n23, 208 n22	57	172 n59
2.4.1	107 n34	64	172 n59
		67-68	171 n57

INDEX OF ANCIENT TEXTS

That God Is Unchangeable

7-8	42 n62

Hypothetica

7:13	182 n79

On the Life of Joseph

2	119 n13

On the Embassy to Gaius

18.120	213 n41
18.122	213 n41
19.131	213 n41
25.162	213 n41
26.166	213 n41
300-303	199 n32

On the Life of Moses 1

60	119 n14
264	126 n29, 126 n30

On the Life of Moses 2

2-3	54 n8

On the Special Laws

1.269	42 n62
2:29	34 n33
2:236	34 n33

NEW TESTAMENT

Matthew

1	64
1:1	121, 122
1:1-17	14, 121
1:17	122
1:18-23	117, 120
1:18-25	124
1:19	57
1:20-21	57
1:21	46, 58
1:21-26	16
2	64
2:1	125
2:1-6	69
2:1-7	59
2:2	117, 120
2:11	24, 229
2:13	117, 120
2:13-14	59, 64
2:16	59, 64
2:19-20	60, 64
3:1-2	39
3:2	67, 68
3:3	45
3:3-6	39
3:7	38, 67, 68, 179 n76
3:7-9	39
3:7-10	38, 41
3:10	67, 68
3:10-14	39
3:11	37
3:15	42, 43
3:15-17	39
3:16	45, 47, 61
3:17	15, 48, 49, 50, 61, 83, 117, 120, 128, 131
3:18	39
3:19-20	39
4:1-11	46
4:2	62, 64
4:3	61
4:4	62, 65
4:8	63, 65
4:10	63, 65
4:17	67, 68
4:23	177 n73, 221
5-7	63, 65
5:1	63
5:20	241
5:33-37	241
6:2	177 n73
6:5	177 n73
6:16	208
6:19	211
7:10	67, 68
7:24-26	240
8:1	63
8:1-4	85
8:5-13	83
8:10	229

8:12	241	14:1	187
8:14-15	85	14:5	67, 68, 186
8:23-27	91	14:6-11	67
8:26	237, 242	14:10	68
8:28-33	87 n52	14:13-21	70, 95 n81
9:9	160	14:20	62
9:9-13	13	14:21	62
9:9-17	170 n52	14:22-33	69, 91, 239
9:10-13	161 n28, 231 n25	14:26	237
9:13	160	14:31	242
9:18-25	188	15:1-20	170 n52
9:20-22	91	15:14-22	131
9:27	121, 130	15:16	237, 242
9:27-31	85	15:21-28	87 n52, 88, 231
9:32	87 n52	15:22	121
9:35	177 n73, 221	15:23	234
10:1	86	15:32-33	118, 120
10:1-6	61	15:32-39	70, 95 n81
10:5-6	234	15:37	118, 120
10:16-18	230	15:38	62
10:17	221	16	19, 240
10:17-18	177 n73	16:1	179 n76
11:9	67, 68	16:1-4	174
11:14	65	16:6	179 n76
11:16-19	67	16:8-11	238, 242
11:19	161 n28, 171, 231 n25	16:11-12	179 n76
12	174, 198	16:13	239
12:9	147, 177, 182, 221	16:13-16	251
12:9-14	177 n73, 182	16:13-20	53, 115, 145
12:10	175	16:16	239
12:22	87 n52	16:18	240
12:22-23	130	16:18-19	240
12:24	82, 87	16:21-23	242
12:34	67, 68, 147	16:22	145
12:39	147	16:22-23	240
12:42	87	16:23	239
13	177	17:1	63
13:3-6	239	17:2-6	64
13:18-21	239	17:4	64
13:41-42	240	17:5	49, 63, 83, 117, 120, 128, 131
13:42	241		
13:50	241	17:10-13	65
13:53-58	177 n73	17:14-18	87 n52
13:54	31, 177, 221	17:14-20	88
13:55	30, 31, 32	17:16-20	238
13:56	31	18:3	238
13:57	31, 73	18:6-7	240, 242
14	71	18:7-9	240

Matthew (*continued*)

Reference	Page(s)
18:12-14	162
18:15-21	240
19:3-12	173
19:13-14	238
19:14	91
20:30-31	121, 130
21:2-9	129, 132, 189
21:5	128
21:9-15	130
21:10-11	56
21:10-17	129
21:11	67, 68, 73
21:12	189, 190
21:13	148
21:14	130
21:15	130
21:16	130
21:17	191
21:23	164
21:26	67, 68
21:45	168 n49, 179 n77
21:46	67, 68, 73, 164, 195
22:13	241
22:15	164
22:16	164
22:23	166
22:34-45	173
22:37-39	211
23	198, 207
23:1-7	177 n73
23:2	207
23:2-3	207
23:3	170, 207
23:5	208
23:7-8	147
23:13-15	207
23:15	147
23:23-29	207
23:25	148, 211
23:27	147
23:27-28	208
23:31	147
23:31-33	212
23:33	147
23:34	177 n73, 182, 212
23:35	212
24-25	79 n26, 192
24:2	11
24:29	193
24:30	193
24:51	241
25:30	241
26:14	118, 120
26:14-16	143, 148
26:15	118, 148, 149
26:25	144, 147
26:31	256
26:31-35	239
26:36-46	241, 242
26:46	131, 132
26:49	147
26:51	159 n21
26:53	131, 132
26:56	118, 120, 150, 242, 256
26:63	241
26:64	115
26:72-74	241
26:75	241
27	149
27:3	118, 148, 149
27:3-10	132, 146, 149
27:4	146
27:5	150
27:7-10	149
27:8	11, 149
27:9	118, 149
27:11-26	67
27:15-26	194, 229
27:16-17	194, 195
27:18	118, 120
27:19	198
27:22	198
27:23	199
27:24	198
27:25	198
27:28	118, 121
27:35	256
27:46	257
27:54	18
27:55	256
27:57-60	79
27:62	168 n49, 179 n77
28:2-3	249

28:15	11	6:3	30
28:16-20	143	6:4	73
28:19	42, 226, 231, 234	6:14	187
		6:15	73
Mark		6:20	186
1:2-3	45	6:30-44	70, 95 n81
1:5	38	6:34	37
1:10	45, 47, 61	6:40	62
1:11	15, 46, 48, 49, 50, 61, 83, 128, 131	6:45-52	69, 91, 239
		6:48-49	237
1:12-13	46	6:52	237
1:13	62	6:56	91
1:25	93	7:1-23	170 n52
1:29-31	85	7:2-5	12
1:32-34	87 n52	7:3-4	12
1:40-45	85	7:8	12
1:43-45	115 n4	7:11	12
2:13-17	13	7:17-18	237, 242
2:13-22	170 n52	7:24-30	87 n52, 88, 231
2:14	160	7:26	229
2:15-17	161 n28, 231 n25	7:31-35	85
2:17	160	7:34	12
3	174	7:36	115, 115 n4
3:5	175	8	19
3:6	175	8:1-10	70
3:7	12	8:1-13	95 n81
3:11	86, 229	8:4	118, 120
3:15	86	8:5-8	118, 120
3:17	195	8:11-12	173
3:19	144 n41	8:17-21	238, 242
3:22	82, 87	8:22-26	84
4:3-19	239	8:28-30	53, 115, 145
4:11	115 n4	8:29	12
4:35-41	91	8:29-30	115 n4
4:39	91	8:31-33	240, 242
4:40	237	9	19
5	88	9:2	63
5:1-13	88	9:5	64
5:1-20	87 n52	9:7	49, 63, 83, 128, 131
5:9	12	9:9-13	65
5:15	12	9:11	65
5:22-23	188	9:14-29	88
5:25-34	91	9:18-19	238
5:35-42	188	9:20	86
5:41	12	9:25	86, 93
5:43	115 n4	9:42	242
6	68, 71	10	12
		10:2-12	173

Mark (continued)

10:13-16	238
10:46	12
10:47-48	121
11:1-10	129, 132, 189
11:11	191
11:12-14	192
11:12-18	79 n26
11:15	189, 190
11:15-17	129
11:15-18	191
11:17	148, 190
11:20-25	79 n26, 192
11:23	192
11:27	164
12:1-8	191
12:1-12	79 n26, 191
12:12	195
12:13	79 n26, 164
12:15	12
12:18	12, 166
12:30-31	211
12:34	173
12:38-40	190
12:41-44	190
13	192
13:2	10
13:3	192, 193
13:7	10
13:24-25	192-193
13:26	193
14:2	12
14:3-4	171
14:5	149
14:10-11	144, 144 n41
14:18	144
14:27	256
14:29	239
14:32-42	241, 242
14:36	12
14:42	131, 132
14:45	132
14:47	159 n21
14:50	242, 256
14:56-57	198
14:56-59	79 n26, 191
14:61-62	115
15:6-15	194, 229
15:11	198
15:14	199
15:16	12
15:22	12
15:26	193
15:34	12, 257
15:39	12, 18, 229
15:40	256
15:42	12
15:43-46	79
16:9-20	235
16:15	231, 235

Luke

1	64, 67, 68
1:1-4	242, 260
1:5	57, 64, 66, 69
1:7	58
1:13	58, 69
1:15	58
1:17	65
1:26-31	57
1:27	121
1:30	58
1:31	46
1:32	121
1:34	58
1:36	56
2:3	24
2:4-5	117, 120
2:6	24
2:7	24
2:8-14	59, 127
2:8-20	126
2:9-11	16
2:11	126
2:25-32	69
2:41-47	33, 34
3:4	45
3:7	38
3:7-9	38, 41
3:8-9	39
3:12	38
3:21	45
3:22	15, 47, 48, 49, 50, 61, 83, 128, 131

INDEX OF ANCIENT TEXTS 295

3:23	118, 120, 131	10:19	84
3:23-38	14, 121, 125	10:25-37	173
4:1-13	46	10:34	24
4:2	62	11:1-36	158
4:24	73	11:14-20	82, 87
4:27	54	11:16	174
4:35	93	11:29-32	250
4:35-40	87 n52	11:31	87
4:38-39	85	11:37-41	170 n52
4:38-41	86	11:37-44	158
4:40	87	11:39-44	158-159
5:12-14	85	13:10-13	87
5:17-26	183	13:10-17	176
5:27	160	13:13	85
5:27-39	170 n52	13:14	176
5:30-32	161 n28, 231 n25	13:15-16	176
5:32	160	13:17	176
6	174	13:31	79, 169
6:11	177	14:1-6	170 n52
7:1-10	83	14:1-24	170 n52, 172
7:11-17	70, 71	14:7-11	171 n57
7:12-15	188	14:12-13	171
7:20	195	15:1	162
7:28	195	15:1-2	161 n28, 231 n25
7:33	195	15:4-8	162
7:34	161 n28, 171, 231 n25	15:7	162
7:36-46	171	15:8-10	162
7:36-50	170 n52	15:11-32	162, 169 n51
7:39	73	15:31	163, 169
8:22-25	91, 242	15:31-32	163
8:25	91	16:14	148, 211
8:26-39	87 n52	17:11-19	70, 71
8:40-42	188	17:19	70
8:42-48	91	17:21	163, 169
8:49-55	188	17:22-37	163
9	19	18:1-8	163
9:1-10	37	18:9	164
9:7-8	187, 251	18:9-14	163
9:8	73	18:11	164
9:10-17	70, 95 n81	18:35-39	169
9:14	62	18:38-39	121
9:19-21	53, 115, 145	19:29-44	129, 132, 189
9:22	242	19:39	169, 189
9:35	49, 83	19:40	189
9:35-36	49	19:41	129, 132
9:37-42	87 n52	19:42-44	79
9:37-43	88	19:44	11
9:49-50	84	19:45	189

Luke (continued)

19:45-46	129
19:46	148
20:19	195
20:20	164
20:27	166
20:39	32
21:5-37	79 n26, 192
21:6	11
22:3	86, 143, 147
22:3-6	148
22:11	25
22:45	242
22:47-53	242
22:49-50	159 n21
22:67-68	115
23:4	18
23:14	18, 187, 199
23:17-25	194, 229
23:22	18
23:32-33	118, 121
23:34	229, 256
23:41	18
23:46	257
23:47	18
23:49	257
23:50-56	79
24:13-21	143
24:18	1
24:19	1, 73, 79
24:28-33	1
24:47	231

John

1:1-4	16
1:23	45
1:28	37
1:31-33	56
1:32	47
1:35-44	37
1:42	195
1:45	56
1:49-50	115
2:1-10	94
2:1-11	70
2:13-22	11
2:15	190
2:19	79, 191
3:1-2	32
3:1-21	79, 170
4:5	118, 121
4:19	73
4:25-26	118
4:26	115
4:46-53	83, 84
5:14	82
5:41-46	219
6	19, 71
6:1-15	70, 95 n81
6:14	56, 73
6:15	116
6:16-21	69, 91, 239
6:21	242
6:32-41	219
6:35	118, 121
6:51	118, 121
6:70-71	143, 146, 147
7:5	118, 120
7:32	179, 179 n77
7:32-53	180
7:40	56
7:45	168 n49, 179 n77
7:46	179
7:47-49	179
7:48	179
7:51	168
8	218
8:1-11	174, 180
8:6	174
8:7	180
8:12	47
8:12-59	180
8:13	180
8:14-21	180
8:17	220
8:22	180
8:31	147, 181, 218
8:37	181
8:41	124
8:44	142, 147, 181
8:59	181
9:2	82
9:3	82
9:5	47
9:5-7	85

INDEX OF ANCIENT TEXTS 297

9:17	73
9:22	220
9:28	218
10	19
10:11-14	117, 120, 131
10:34	220
11:2	181
11:6	188
11:17	188
11:19-44	188
11:47	168 n49, 179 n77
11:47-53	189
11:47-57	181
11:48	11
11:57	168 n49, 179 n77
12	181
12:3	149
12:6	148
12:12-19	129, 132, 189
12:15	128
12:19	181
12:36	47
12:42	79, 180, 181, 220
12:42-43	182
13:1-10	171
13:2	143, 147
13:10	42
13:18	132, 150
13:23	171
13:25	171
13:27	143, 144, 147
13:29-30	145
14	181
14:31	181
16:2	220
18:1-3	181
18:2-12	242
18:3	168 n49, 179 n77
18:6	131, 132
18:10	159 n21
18:31-33	10
18:37-38	10
18:38	199
18:39-19:15	194, 229
19:13	229
19:15	229
19:23	118, 121
19:24	256
19:30	257
19:34	129
19:38-40	79
20	14
20:20-24	14
20:30-31	18
21:10	171 n58

Acts

1:6	143
1:13	195
1:18	132, 150
1:18-19	146
1:23	195
2:32-34	118, 121
3	200
3:22	56
5:17	168
5:30	118
5:34-40	168
5:36	108 n39
5:37	108
6	177
6:7	79
6:14	177
8:9-11	126
9:4-6	221, 226
9:15	221, 226
10	200, 222
10-11	226
10:10	222
10:11-46	221
10:13	222
11:1-18	222
12	177
13	200
13:30-33	15
13:32-33	50
15	222, 223
15:1-2	223
15:5	79, 170, 200, 223, 224, 235
15:9	230
15:20	224
15:29	224
16	200
16:10-17	13

Acts (continued)

18	200
19:3-4	41
20	200
20:5-15	13
21	200
21:1-18	13
21:20	201
21:21	226
21:22-26	226
21:38	109
22:3	83, 170
22:15	221, 226
23:6-8	166
23:9	168
26:4-6	170

Romans

1:1-7	259
1:3-4	15
1:16-17	259

1 Corinthians

1:12-16	237
1:23	143
4:14-21	259
11:14	36
11:23	146
15:5	146

2 Corinthians

11:4	213
11:5	213
11:13	213

Galatians

1:1-2	221, 226
1:1-17	236
1:6	213
1:6-12	259
1:10	213, 237
1:16	221, 226
1:18-22	236
1:20	236
2	223, 231
2:6	236, 237
2:7	234
2:7-9	223
2:9	223, 234
2:11-13	160
2:11-14	234
2:12	222, 234
2:12-13	222
2:13	222, 234
5:3	224
5:12	213, 237
5:22-23	205

Philippians

3:2	213, 237
3:5	226

Colossians

4:11-14	13
4:14	13

1 Thessalonians

2:16	237

2 Peter

2:15-16	126

1 John

2:18	213
2:19	213
2:22	213
4:1-6	214

Jude

1:11	126

Revelation

1:3	76
2:14	126
9:1	127 n34
12:4	127 n34
13:1	92, 122
13:18	122
21:1	92

RABBINIC WORKS

Mishnah

m. Avot
1:1	155 n3
1:1-12	123 n22
1:2-18	155 n3
5:21	26 n9

m. Berakhot
5.1	84 n42
5:5	83 n40

m. Hagigah
1:8	6
2:5	171 n56

m. Eduyyot
8:7	65 n35

m. Parah
8:10	38 n46

m. Sheqalim
4:3	191 n9

m. Sotah
9.12	75 n8

m. Sukkah
4:9	159 n21

m. Ta'anit
3:8	90 n63

m. Yevamot
16.3	188 n6

22:7	76
22:10	76
22:18	76
22:19	76

m. Yoma
8.9	41 n60

Tosefta

t. Berakhot
3.2	84 n42
4:8	171 n56, 171 n58

t. Demai
2:4-5	224 n15

t. Hullin
2:22-24	247 n5

t. Pesah
2:15	76 n16

t. Qiddushin
1:11	30 n26

t. Sotah
13.3	48 n73

BABYLONIAN TALMUD

b. Bava Batra
74b	92 n71
126b	84 n44

b. Bava Metzi'a
59b	49 n76, 94 n77

b. Berakhot
3a	48 n72
5b	85 n46
33a	84 n42, 84 n43
34b	82 n36, 83 n38, 83 n41
61b	49 n77

b. Eruvin

13b	49 n75
43a-b	65 n36
100b	124 n26

b. Hagigah

15a	48 n70

b. Qiddushin

29b-30a	26 n11
81a	88 n55

b. Megillah

14a	58 n20, 59 n23, 74 n2
21a	63 n34

b. Me'ilah

17b	88 n53

b. Nedarim

41a	82 n33

b. Niddah

31a	27 n14

b. Pesahim

112b	88 n54

b. Sanhedrin

11a	48 n73, 49 n74, 56 n15
67a	124 n26

b. Shabbat

17a	213 n43
55a	82 n34, 199 n31
89a	63 n32
104b	124 n26
108b	84 n44
151b	188 n6

b. Sotah

12b	58 n19, 59 n24, 59 n26
13a	58 n20, 59 n23
48b	49 n74

b. Sukkah

28a	56 n16
52a	117 n7

b. Ta'anit

23a	90 n65
23b	90 n67
23b-25b	90 n68
24b	49 n78, 83 n39
24b-25a	95 n82
25a	247 n1

b. Yevamot

46a	224 n16
62b	26 n10
63b	28 n15

JERUSALEM TALMUD

y. Berakhot

4:1, 7c	83 n37

y. Ketubbot

12.3	85 n45

y. Shabbat

1:4	213 n43
14:4	84 n44

y. Sotah

1:4	84 n44
13:2	49 n74
24b	48 n73

TARGUMS

Targum Pseudo-Jonathan
Deut 30:4	65 n36
Exod 40:9-11	116-117 n6

Targum to Song of Songs
2:12	48 n71
4:5	116 n6
7:4	116 n6

Targum Tosefta to Zechariah
12:10	116 n5, 116 n6

MIDRASH AND RELATED LITERATURE

Mekilta Exodus
14:13	47 n68

Midrash Betzah
5:2	176 n69

Midrash Shabbat
7:2	176 n69

Rabbah Exodus
1, 22	58 n20
1, 26	59 n27
15.22	92 n71

Rabbah Deuteronomy
11:10	63 n33

Rabbah Genesis
2:4	48 n70
13:7	90 n62

Rabbah Numbers
13.2	57 n17

18.22	92 n71

Sifre Deuteronomy
357	56 n14

EARLY CHRISTIAN WRITINGS

1 Clement
13:2	10
48:4	10

2 Clement
13:4	10

Acts of John
vv. 89-90	35 n38

Chrysostom
Discourses against Judaizing Christians
11, 25-26	151 n61

Infancy Gospel of Thomas
13:1-3	247 n2

Origen
Contra Celsum
27-32	124 n27
31	124 n27
198-199	135 n2

Papias
"Frag. 3"	146 n45

Tertullian
De Spectaculis
17	210 n32

INDEX OF ANCIENT TEXTS

GRECO-ROMAN LITERATURE

Aristotle
Rhetoric
bk. 1, ch.9,

1366b, p.1354	205 n7
1367a-1367b, p. 1356	205 n8
1367b, p. 1357	205 n9

Athenaeus
Deipnosophistae

14.641D	171 n56

Cicero
De Officiis

1.150	210 n30

De Oratore

2.43.182-183	205 n10

De Republica

4.10	210 n31, 232 n26

Plato
Laws

2.671C-672A	170 n54

Symposium

175A	171 n56, 171 n58
176E	172 n59
177D-177E	171 n57

Plutarch
Table Talk

612D	170 n54
612D-612E	172 n59
614E-615A	170 n54
616C	170 n54
616E	170 n54
616F-617E	171 n57
660B	170 n54

Tacitus
Annals

15.44.3	193 n16

www.ingramcontent.com/pod-product-compliance
Lightning Source LLC
Chambersburg PA
CBHW071232230426
43668CB00011B/1408